REAL LIFE HEROES

Real Life Heroes: Toolkit for Treating Traumatic Stress in Children and Families (second edition) is an organized and easy-to-use reference for practitioners providing therapy to children with traumatic stress. This step-by-step guide is an accompanying text to the workbook *Real Life Heroes Life Storybook* (third edition) and provides professionals with structured tools for helping children and caregivers to reintegrate painful memories and to foster healing from traumatic experiences and disrupted attachments. The book is a go-to resource for practitioners in child and family service agencies and treatment centers to implement trauma-informed, resiliency-centered and evidence-supported services for children with traumatic stress.

Richard Kagan, Ph.D., is the author and co-author of 10 books on treatment and services for children and families with traumatic stress, and has published over 30 articles, chapters, and papers on practice and research issues in trauma therapy, child welfare, foster care, adoption, professional development, program evaluation, and quality improvement in family service and behavioral health-care programs.

REAL LIFE HEROES

*Toolkit for Treating Traumatic Stress
in Children and Families*

SECOND EDITION

Richard Kagan

Routledge
Taylor & Francis Group

NEW YORK AND LONDON

Second edition published 2017
by Routledge
711 Third Avenue, New York, NY 10017

and by Routledge
2 Park Square, Milton Park, Abingdon, Oxon, OX14 4RN

Routledge is an imprint of the Taylor & Francis Group, an informa business

First edition published by Routledge 2007

Library of Congress Cataloging in Publication Data
A catalog record for this book has been requested

ISBN: 978-1-138-96347-4 (hbk)
ISBN: 978-0-415-51807-9 (pbk)
ISBN: 978-0-203-12353-9 (ebk)

Typeset in Times New Roman
by Florence Production Ltd, Stoodleigh, Devon, UK

"Life is not a problem to be solved but a mystery to be lived."
—Joseph Campbell

To my children and their families,
Michael, Joshua, Michelle, Cindy, Avni, Andrew, Maya, Gia, Tesi, Amit, and Reena

and

To my parents for teaching me to love the adventure of science
and that there was nothing more important than raising children

Contents

Introduction

Real Life Heroes® (RLH) is a practitioner-developed treatment program for traumatic stress that has been successfully implemented in a wide range of child and family mental health and family service programs since 1998. RLH provides practitioners with easy-to-use tools, including a life storybook, manual, multisensory creative arts activities, and psycho-education resources to engage children and caregivers in evidence-supported trauma treatment. RLH helps practitioners reframe referrals based on pathologies and blame into a shared 'journey,' a 'pathway' to healing and recovery focused on restoring (or building) emotionally supportive and enduring relationships and promoting development of affect regulation skills for children and caregivers. Creative arts, movement activities, and shared life story work provide a means for children and caregivers to develop the safety and attunement needed for reintegration of traumatic memories coupled with development of increased security and affect regulation.

What Makes RLH Different?

> - **Engages Hard-to-reach Children**
> - **Builds Safety & Stability Needed for Trauma Reintegration**

Real Life Heroes® focuses on the developmental needs of children ages 6–12 and has been successful with adolescents with Complex Trauma who have delays in their social, emotional, or cognitive development. RLH is a relationship-focused treatment that counters the effects of interpersonal traumas and works to increase children's attachments with caregivers and pride in their abilities, family, and cultural heritage as an "antidote to shame" (Herman, 2011). The model also includes activities that help children and caregivers develop self- and co-regulation skills and create the security needed for Life Story Integration following experiences of chronic interpersonal traumas. The RLH format includes a workbook and session rituals that provide an easy-to-learn and transferable structure that allows children

and caregivers to continue trauma treatment if they move between programs or practitioners, and includes primary roles for residential counselors, parents, resource parents, mentors, and other caring adults. The *RLH Toolkit* integrates core components of evidence-supported treatment for Complex Trauma (Relationships, Emotional Self- and Co-Regulation, Interactional Behaviors, and Life Story Integration) from referral and assessment through service planning, treatment sessions, treatment reviews, outcome evaluations, and termination of services with fidelity tools to support supervisors. The model guides flexible adaptation of tools to engage a wide range of families and adjust for changes in a child and caregiver's stability to maintain safety and progress in treatment.

Unlike trauma-focused treatments, RLH does not require graduated exposure to identified traumas from the beginning of treatment. RLH can be used with children often excluded from trauma-centered treatments, including children with suspected traumas that have not been acknowledged or validated, with children who have had frequent hospitalizations, and with children whose caregivers are not able or willing to work in trauma-focused treatment. Similar to other treatment models for Complex Trauma, work on trauma reintegration is not recommended when children are currently demonstrating severe anxiety, severe depression, acute psychosis, moderate or high-risk suicide attempts, overwhelming guilt and shame, impaired affect regulation abilities, substance dependence, or intoxication.

Why Use *Real Life Heroes*®?

- Research-tested for efficacy with children and families in child welfare and behavioral health programs.
- Integrated framework keeps treatment focused on 'best practice' components of treatment for Complex Trauma (Cook et al., 2003; Ford & Cloitre, 2009).
- Easily adaptable to match the needs and strengths of diverse children, families, and programs.
- Enables new practitioners to readily implement trauma and attachment-centered treatment and offers advanced skill-building and tools for experienced staff.

- 'Ready to go' toolkit promotes expedited training and implementation by practitioners with little time for workshops, or session preparation.
- Flexible Session Structure and use of the *RLH Life Storybook* promotes fidelity and sustains implementation after initial training.
- Works well with other trauma treatments to build safety and stability for desensitization.
- Ideal for use with children at risk of placement or living in foster or kinship care or adoptive families.
- It's fun!

How Can *Real Life Heroes*® Help Programs Overcome Challenges to Implementation of Trauma-Informed Child and Family Services?

RLH was developed to meet the challenges of implementing trauma treatment in child and family services with children and families who were not amenable to trauma-focused treatment or were not improving with cognitive behavioral therapies or other trauma-informed interventions that focused primarily on children's development of self-regulation skills and desensitization of traumatic memories. RLH was developed and tested with children who did not meet the criteria for other treatment models, including children who had not yet disclosed primary traumatic experiences or where suspected traumas had not been acknowledged or validated, and children living in placement programs (or at high risk of placement) who lacked safe, non-offending caregivers who were able and willing to participate in trauma-focused therapy. RLH training and consultation programs have successfully engaged and trained practitioners in child and family service programs with limited time for training programs and have been successfully implemented with all practitioners in program-wide training that was not limited to the most motivated or skilled clinicians.

What Do Children, Parents, and Supervisors Say About *Real Life Heroes*®?

"I have so many more people in my life that can help me now. I am not alone anymore."
— 12-year-old boy in Parsons Foster Family Care

"Heroes has inspired me to be something I did not think I could be 10 months ago. I thought I was going to give up, fall into a hole, have kids (young) and be like my mother. . . . I am my own hero . . . And now I will be someone and I hope to inspire others!"
— 15-year-old girl in Parsons Home-Based Prevention of Placement Program who was helped to return to family living after living with a family friend and placement in two group care programs

"I really like the centering activities . . . I have used them in my own recovery, and I have noticed a big difference they have made in my son's anger."
— Parent at Parsons Child and Family Guidance Clinic

"I gave her (the foster care clinician) a hard time about doing it (*Real Life Heroes*®) in the beginning, but once I did it, I really liked it!"
— Birth parent in Parsons Foster Family Care program

"It's not one more thing. It's the thing."
— Home-based Intensive Case Coordination Program Director

Research Support

> - **Practitioner-Developed • Research-Tested • Supervisor-Endorsed •**

Real Life Heroes® is listed in the U.S. National Registry of Evidence-Based Programs and Practices by the Substance Abuse Mental Health Services Administration (SAMHSA), the SAMHSA National Center for Trauma-Informed Care "Models for Developing Trauma-Informed Behavioral Health Systems and Trauma-Specific Services," and as one of the National Child Traumatic Stress Network's (NCTSN) Empirically Supported Treatments and Promising Practices. The 2007 *RLH Practitioner's Manual* was rated as addressing eight of nine core domains identified for Intervention Objectives and Practice Elements developed by the NCTSN Core Curriculum on Childhood Trauma Task Force (Strand, Hansen, & Layne, 2012). The only domain missing, Therapist Self-Care, has been included in RLH training programs and the *RLH Toolkit* since 2007.

RLH treatment has been successfully pilot tested in home-based and placement child welfare services (Kagan, Douglas, Hornik, & Kratz, 2008), and utilized in a wide range of child and family service agencies in the United States and Canada. In the pilot study, results from data collected after a four-month interval indicated significant reduction in child self-reports of trauma symptoms and reduced problem behaviors on caregiver checklists. Results from data collected after a 12-month interval included a reduction in parent reports of trauma symptoms for children who received more of the RLH intervention and increased security/attachment to caregivers over time. The HEROES Project, a SAMHSA-funded community practice site of the NCTSN, evaluated use of *Real Life Heroes*® in seven child and family service and behavioral health treatment programs and found statistically significant reductions in traumatic stress and behavioral problems on standardized measures. Children receiving RLH in this study did not have placements or psychiatric hospitalizations (Kagan, Henry,

Richardson, Trinkle, & Lafrenier, 2014a). These studies lacked randomized control groups; however, the HEROES Project included all practitioners in a wide range of child and family service programs working with high-risk and multiproblem families in state or Medicaid-funded programs and was not limited to selected practitioners or doctoral candidates, as in many other research studies. RLH is listed as 'High' in Child Welfare System Relevance by the California Evidence-Based Clearinghouse for Child Welfare and cited as a recognized mental health treatment for children in foster care (Baker, Brown, Schneiderman, Sharma-Patel, & Berrill, in press).

What's in the *RLH Toolkit*?

The second edition of the *Real Life Heroes Toolkit* provides practitioners with an easy-to-use guide for conducting treatment for children and families with Complex Trauma from initial assessments to service planning, and chapter-by-chapter guidelines for use of *Real Life Heroes Life Storybook* third edition. The format serves as a 'grab and go' resource for tools that can augment clinical practice by advanced practitioners or serve as a detailed step-by-step protocol for new practitioners. Practitioners can turn to the section of the *RLH Toolkit* that matches where they are in the *Real Life Heroes Life Storybook*. Using the chapter-by-chapter format ensures that core components of Complex Trauma treatment are addressed. Model fidelity is promoted by practitioner and supervisor review of *Chapter Checkpoints* (key components of each chapter) and the *Progress Note* or the abbreviated *Fidelity Progress Note*, which highlight completion of RLH core components (REAL). At the same time, Session Structure and use of the workbook can be readily adapted for children at different levels of development, for diverse families, and for a wide range of treatment programs.

Part I of the *RLH Toolkit* provides a chapter-by-chapter guide, including: Objectives, Overview (a brief rationale based on core principles and research for implementing key components that can be shared with caregivers, team members, and collaterals), Step by Step interventions, *Chapter Checkpoints* (essential elements of each chapter), Tips (strategies to increase effectiveness and overcome common challenges), Pitfalls to Avoid, and Toolkit Resources included in the *RLH Toolkit*, as well as references and links to other books, manuals, and online resources.

Part II provides strategies found effective in adapting the model for use with adolescents, younger children, adoptive families, children's psychotherapeutic groups, and as part of integrated trauma-informed services.

Part III provides recommended books and URL links to resources for children, caregivers, and practitioners.

Part IV lists common issues that can pose challenges (obstacles) to trauma and attachment treatment, with recommended strategies for overcoming these challenges. Challenges are organized by phase of treatment (e.g., assessment, skill-building, trauma experience reintegration).

Part V provides practitioners with handouts that can be reproduced by practitioners who have purchased this *RLH Toolkit* for use in RLH treatment with their clients from assessment to discharge. Part V also includes a guide to accessing recommended materials and supplies and fidelity tools. Key components of the model are listed in *Chapter Checkpoints*, which serves as a practitioner 'cheat sheet' for core model components and can also be used as a structured tool for consultation and supervision. The *RLH Progress Note* provides an easy-to-complete check-off format for RLH fidelity components and at the same time encourages practitioners to write in critical issues, safety plans, trauma triggers, and constructive vs. dysfunctional beliefs. A *Bookmark* is provided to highlight key components and sequence for sessions. The *Bookmark* also serves as a reminder to children of the Session Structure.

Preface

Foundations for Complex Trauma Treatment

Real Life Heroes® (RLH) is based on research and practice in treatment of children who have experienced multiple types of traumas and impaired relationships with primary caregivers[1] and other family members. A condensed review of research and the framework for RLH treatment is provided below. A detailed foundation for RLH treatment is available in *Rebuilding Attachments with Traumatized Children: Healing from Losses, Violence, Abuse and Neglect* (Kagan, 2004).

Relational Trauma, Developmental Delays, and Dysregulation

Children referred to child and family mental health and family service programs have often experienced multiple types of co-occurring traumas, including neglect, emotional, physical and/or sexual abuse, along with losses, changes, or disruptions in their relationships with caregivers (Cohen, Mannarino, Murray, & Igelman, 2006). The National Survey of Child and Adolescent Well-Being (Stambaugh et al., 2013) found that 51% of children reported to have experienced maltreatment had experienced four or more adverse childhood experiences (ACEs) compared to 13% in the ACE study (Felitti et al., 1998). The ACE study demonstrated the impact of childhood abuse and hardships on development of high-risk behaviors, addictions, and early deaths in adults, and found that adults who had experienced four or more ACEs as children had up to 12 times the risk of severe health problems. Greeson et al. (2011) found that children and adoles-cents in foster care programs had experienced a mean of five types of traumas, including one caregiver-related trauma (e.g., abuse or neglect), and that children with Complex Trauma had experienced an average of six types of traumas.

Children who have experienced multiple traumas often present with a wide spectrum of developmental delays that appears associated with cumulative risk factors (Shonkoff, 2010). Richardson, Henry, Black-Pond, and Sloane (2008) found that 71–88% of children in child welfare programs had moderate to major delays in receptive and expressive language, fine motor skills, sequential abilities, visual processing, and memory functions. Nearly 90% of the children had significant problems with inattention, as well as high levels of aggression, rule-breaking, social difficulties, and total behavior problems. Greater developmental delays were significantly associated with the number of types of maltreatment events experienced by children.

Multiple exposures to trauma and breakdowns of attachment have been associated with symptoms of Complex Trauma, including impairment of affect and impulse regulation, cognitive functioning, dissociation, somatization, relationships, and sense of self (Cook et al., 2003). Children with Complex Trauma may respond to reminders of past traumas with physiological dysregulation and re-enactments of previous behaviors and relationships, including re-victimization. Experiences and symptoms of children with Complex Trauma extend beyond the definition of PTSD in the DSM V (American Psychiatric Association, 2013) and have led to a call for a new diagnostic category, 'Developmental Trauma Disorder' (van der Kolk, 2005), and application of treatment interventions matched to these children (Cook et al., 2005).

Guidelines for Complex Trauma Treatment

For children with Complex Trauma, 'best practice' guidelines (Cook et al., 2003; Ford & Cloitre, 2009) recommend use of evidence-supported interventions that build both the self-regulation skills and the attuned relationships between children and caregivers necessary for children to have the safety and security needed for traumatic memory processing. Cloitre et al. (2011) found that treatment for PTSD related to childhood abuse was more effective when treatment was provided sequentially and addressed problems with affect dysregulation and interpersonal relationships followed by trauma-focused exposure, rather than providing these components separately. Recommended components for treatment of Complex Trauma in

TABLE 0.1
Recommended 'Best Practice' Guidelines for Treatment of Complex Trauma

Components	RLH
Developing safety and stability for the child and family	✓
Relational engagement linking the child, primary caregiver, and therapist	✓
Relational and strengths-based diagnosis, treatment planning, and outcome monitoring	✓
Increasing self-regulation of emotion, attention, memory, decision-making, information processing, consciousness and motivation, body movements, and relational interaction	✓
Trauma experience integration matched to the child and caregiver's capacity	✓
Increasing positive emotions and a positive self-identity	✓
Preventing and managing relational discontinuities and psychosocial crises	✓

Source: Adapted from Cook et al. (2003) and Ford and Cloitre (2009)

children (Cook et al., 2003; Ford & Cloitre, 2009) are listed in Table 0.1.

Latency: A Window of Opportunity

Behavioral and mental health problems have been reported to markedly increase for school-age children in child and family service programs (Griffin et al., 2011). Latency provides a window of opportunity to prevent the increasing incidence of high-risk behaviors (aggression to others, self-abuse, and suicide attempts) commonly reported as children in child welfare programs move into adolescence. In addition, latency provides a critical time to put into place protection and guidance to prevent increased traumatic experiences for latency-age children. The National Survey of Child and Adolescent Well-Being (Stambaugh et al., 2013) found that the percentage of children following reports of maltreatment who had experienced four or more adverse childhood experiences jumped from 43% to 68% from ages 6–10 to 11–17.

Challenges for Treatment of Complex Trauma

Despite research demonstrating that adversity in childhood leads to a range of behavioral and health problems (Felitti et al., 1998), trauma-impacted children are rarely referred to child and family services, mental health, or juvenile justice programs because of their experiences of trauma. Children are typically referred for treatment of severe and often high-risk behavior problems that have become disruptive to families, schools, and communities. Often, children and caregivers have not been able to share the worst traumas they have experienced and may lack safety and protection from repeated traumas. Children may also lack safe caregivers who are able or willing to participate in trauma treatment.

Child welfare and mental health services seek to help these children; however, services have often been fragmented and hampered by the lack of availability of mental health practitioners who have had the training, supervision, and support needed to provide evidence-supported treatment for children who have experienced multiple traumas and disrupted attachments to primary caregivers. Treatment programs have often focused on behavioral problems and mental health diagnoses, without addressing youth's exposure to traumas, trauma reactions, and how trauma is linked to youth's problems (Kisiel, Fehrenbach, Small, & Lyons, 2009).

Implementing recommended treatment components for Complex Trauma (see Table 0.1) is challenged by common expectations of children, caregivers, and systems of care that service providers will focus on specific behaviors rather than what happened to children. Children often feel they are diagnosed as sick, bad, or delayed, that problems lie within themselves, and that they need to somehow change their behaviors. Caregivers may experience themselves labeled as bad or ineffective parents and come to believe that children are out of their control. Therapists may feel unable to utilize many evidence-based trauma treatments because traumas have not been acknowledged or validated or because caregivers are unable or unwilling to participate in trauma treatment. Practitioners have also struggled to implement exposure-based trauma treatments with children with high-risk behavior problems, with children who have moved in and out of foster, kinship, or adoptive placements and psychiatric hospitalizations, and with children and caregivers who have not acknowledged traumatic experiences or been willing to participate in trauma-focused treatment. Therapists may also feel pressured to change or control children who have bounced from program to program, accumulating increasing distrust of service providers with each new counselor, hospitalization, or placement.

Resiliency-Focused Treatment

Real Life Heroes® (RLH) was developed to help practitioners implement evidence-supported treatment components and overcome the myriad of challenges in child and family services, mental health, school-based, and juvenile justice programs. Unlike trauma-focused treatments, RLH does not require acknowledgment or validation of traumas or graduated exposure to traumas from the onset of treatment. RLH is a resiliency-focused treatment that has proven successful in engaging children and caregivers to help each other after multiple traumas, including losses, neglect, physical, emotional, and sexual abuse, domestic violence, and impaired parenting. RLH activities and the *RLH Life Storybook* help children and caregivers develop the safety and trust needed to share, or acknowledge, what happened in families where the worst traumas have remained untold.

RLH follows the sequential process recommended by Cloitre et al. (2011). Development of emotionally supportive relationships, child-caregiver attunement, and both self- and co-regulation skills helps create the security for practitioners to implement strategies for trauma-experience integration strategies and interventions. Rather than focusing on behavior problems or known traumas, resiliency-focused treatment works to build relationships and skills that, in turn, can allow development of a life narrative centered on children and caregivers breaking free of constricted and negative beliefs and developing broader perspectives and skills. The focus of this work is on repairing the breakdowns of relationships along with the impact of traumas on the minds and bodies of family members (van der Kolk, 2014). Resiliency-focused treatment helps children and families to move from a preoccupation with surviving cycles of crises to overcoming hardships and learning to use what they have learned to pevent or better manage stressors. Healing relationships and development of self and co-regulation with multisensory mind and body skill-building provides the foundation for trauma experience reintegration.

Relational Healing for Relational Traumas

The *Real Life Heroes* Toolkit

RLH (Kagan, 2004, 2007a, 2007b) is a manualized therapy centered on use of a life story workbook and structured session activities matched to the phase-based components recommended by the NCTSN Complex Trauma Workgroup and 'best practice' guidelines for treatment of Complex Trauma in children (Cook et al., 2003; Ford & Cloitre, 2009). RLH also includes core components of evidence-based treatment for trauma in child welfare programs (see Table 0.2) listed in the NCTSN Child Welfare Toolkit (Chadwick Trauma-Informed Systems Project,

TABLE 0.2
Core Components in Evidence-Based Trauma Treatment

Components	RLH
Parent support, conjoint therapy, or parent training	✓
Building a strong therapeutic relationship	✓
Providing psycho-education	✓
Emotional expression and regulation skills	✓
Anxiety management and relaxation skills	✓
Cognitive processing or reframing	✓
Strategies that allow exposure to traumatic memories and feelings in tolerable doses so that they can be mastered and integrated into the child's experience	✓
Personal safety training and other important empowerment activities	✓
Resilience and closure	✓

Source: NCTSN Child Welfare Toolkit (Chadwick Trauma-Informed Systems Project, 2013)

2013). Tools and activities were designed for use with children ages 6–12 and have been used successfully with adolescents with Complex Trauma functioning at a latency level of social, emotional, or cognitive development.

Real Life Heroes® helps practitioners reframe referrals based on pathologies and blame into a shared 'journey,' a 'pathway' to healing and recovery focused on restoring (or building) emotionally supportive and enduring relationships and promoting development of affect regulation skills for children and caregivers. To do this, the model utilizes the metaphor of the heroic journey (Campbell, 1968) and highlights the importance of engaging caregivers and a collaborative team of caring adults working together with an integrated trauma and resiliency-centered framework to help children with Complex Trauma. Learning about heroes includes sharing stories of how family members and people with the child's ethnic heritage have overcome hard times. RLH encourages children to develop their own strengths, resources, and coping skills, building on strengths in their families and cultural heritage. Creative arts and shared life story work help children and caregivers develop safety, attunement, and affect modulation skills, which, in turn, promotes disclosure or acknowledgement of traumatic experiences and the stability needed for reintegration of traumatic memories as parts of a child's life. *Real Life Heroes*® helps children and caregivers overcome shame and transform children and caregivers from feeling overwhelmed, alone, damaged, no good, or unlovable into heroes who work together to help themselves, their families, and their communities become stronger than the nightmares of the past.

RLH provides practitioners with easy-to-use tools, including the *Life Storybook*, manual, assessment protocols, creative arts activities, and psycho-education resources designed to engage hard-to-reach children and caregivers in trauma- and resiliency-focused services. For adolescents, activities incorporate higher-level interests, skills, and media (e.g., use of keyboards instead of xylophones, greater use of video instead of drawings, and activities matching workbook pages without necessarily using the *Life Storybook*). Tools and procedures were developed and tested in a wide range of child and family service and behavioral health programs, including children with symptoms of Complex PTSD who lacked stable relationships with caregivers they could count on to provide a safe home and work with them in therapy, and children referred for high-risk behaviors that threatened the safety of children, families, organizations, and communities.

RLH also provides a step-by-step Session Structure and promotes creative flexibility to support requisite skills and relationships for the treatment of Complex Trauma. Interventions and activities are prioritized in service plans and sessions to help children and caregivers progress sequentially along two complementary dimensions: children's level of self-regulation and the strength and availability of emotionally supportive relationships (adapted from Saxe, Ellis, & Kaplow, 2007). In each session, children learn to recognize clues in their own bodies and how to share these safely while staying modulated.

Sessions begin with children and caregivers sharing feelings nonverbally on thermometers for stress, self-control, and feeling mad, sad, glad, and safe. Centering activities at the beginning of sessions utilize movement, focusing, and mindfulness activities to engage children and caregivers to learn and practice skills and to reduce stress. Practitioners may also include magic or another activity to make sessions special and promote hope. Children and caregivers then complete pages from the *Life Storybook*.

The *Life Storybook* helps children share experiences and develop affect modulation skills with art, rhythm, music, movement, and theater arts. Practitioners help children (and caregivers) transform their drawings into stories (or movies) with a beginning, middle, and an end so children learn they can 'move through' both good times and 'tough times,' and make things better in their lives instead of feeling hopeless, shamed, or overwhelmed. Chapters in the *Life Storybook* match recommendations (Cook et al., 2003; Ford & Cloitre, 2009) for phase-based development of safety, self-regulation, emotionally supportive relationships, desensitization of trauma reminders, and reintegration of painful memories to foster healing.

Core Components

RLH focuses on four primary components for strengthening resiliency skills and resources: Relationships, Emotional Self- and Co-Regulation, Action Cycles, and Life Story Integration. These components frame an integrated protocol that begins with developmentally based assessments and guides service planning, prioritization of treatment objectives, selection of session activities, fidelity, review of progress, overcoming challenges (obstacles) to change, and use of evaluation measures. Practitioner application of the RLH core components (REAL) helps distressed children to answer critical questions (see Figure 0.1) and restore trust and self-confidence after experiences

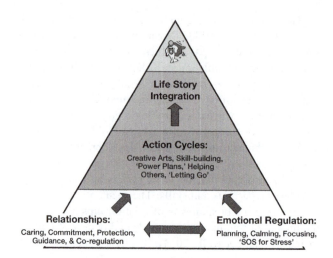

Figure 0.2 RLH Component-Based Toolkit

of relational trauma that have eroded the foundation of their emotional support and stability.

Primary components guide practitioner application and adaptation of RLH treatment to a wide range of children and families. Components are supplemented by practical tools and activities (see Figure 0.2) matched to the strengths and needs of children, families, and communities in a client-driven process that progressively builds strengths.

Relationships and **Emotional Regulation** provide the foundation for all RLH work. RLH activities promote attunement, self- and co-regulation, and rebuilding a 'protective shield' for children. Activities focus on strengthening (or building) safe, emotionally supportive relationships with caregivers, mentors, and other caring adults and fostering the courage to broaden perspectives and try out new behaviors. Work on Emotional Regulation includes helping children and caregivers to develop affect recognition, expression and modulation skills, change beliefs and scripts guiding reactions, and develop increased executive functions (planning, considering consequences, adapting responses, problem-solving), social skills, and arousal modulation (affective and somatic regulation). All work is focused on helping children and caregivers achieve their goals, which, in turn, increases and sustains engagement.

RLH builds on family therapy models (e.g., structural family therapy) (Minuchin & Fishman, 1981) and use of activities in sessions as 'enactments' to help children and caregivers understand and change patterns of interaction, **Action Cycles**. Homework activities are used to reinforce changes in patterns and grow the strength of new patterns of interactions. From a developmental perspective, children functioning at a latency level have a great need for consistency to thrive. Structured session activities help caregivers and children move beyond long-standing behavior patterns that may have helped at one time (e.g., limiting emotional expression in the midst of crises), but

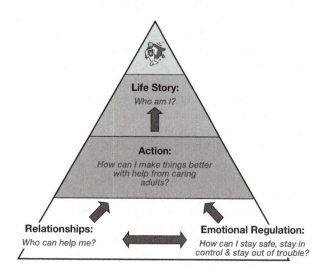

Figure 0.1 Restoring Stability after Traumatic Experiences

have limited attunement, connection to other family members, trust, and support, leaving family members feeling detached and isolated or desperately clinging in an overly dependent manner. Activities are used to promote consistency and predictability and counter the effects of chaotic, disorganized, anxious, or avoidant attachments.

RLH activities promote playful interactions that are fun and geared to moving children and families developmentally. Creative arts activities include drawing, rhythm, music, movement, photography, and moviemaking. Mindfulness and centering activities are incorporated from yoga techniques for children (Flynn, 2013; Guber & Kalish, 2005; Harper, 2013). RLH Action Cycle activities also include development of Power Plans that engage children and caregivers to develop, test, adapt, and reinforce use of safety plans with practical reminders (e.g., 3 × 5 cards that can be carried in a pocket or backpack or mounted on a refrigerator or kitchen wall). Action Cycle activities highlight helping others as part of the RLH emphasis on learning from heroes. Activities also include interactions to promote 'letting go,' to help children and caregivers grieve losses and rebuild relationships.

Chapter by chapter, practitioners help empower children and families by strengthening skills and resources, and reducing the power of multiple and serial traumas that have afflicted their past and shaped high-risk behaviors. Shared activities help children and caregivers grow stronger than their fears and change old ways of coping (Action Cycles) that got them into trouble. The *Life Storybook* helps children change how they see themselves from feeling hurt, unwanted, damaged, or hopeless, to feeling and understanding that they can 'move through' the traumas of the past to experiences of security with emotionally supportive adults committed to guiding and caring for children.

Life Story Integration in *Real Life Heroes*® is a sequential process designed to help children and caregivers become stronger than traumatic memories. Using the developmental perspective of latency-age children, this can be visualized as the trauma memory being larger and more powerful than the child. Through work on RLH materials, children grow in strength with caregiver support to become larger and larger (Rojano, 1998) than the traumatic memory, with caregivers helping them overpower the threat of old memories and current fears.

RLH tools can be used to engage and empower caregivers to develop courage, resources, and skills, to become caring and protective heroes for their children and to model how children can become heroes in their own lives. RLH promotes using family experiences rather than avoiding remembering what happened in the past and reliance on hyper-vigilance, hyper-arousal, impulsive reactions, dissociation or depression, and high-risk behaviors. Children and caregivers learn to utilize increased sensitivities, awareness, understanding, skills, and relationships to change family interactions from a daily struggle to get by, to 'survive,' to learning, practicing, and reinforcing new responses that help them to succeed and 'thrive.'

As children experience renewed attunement and support, they become able to develop interests and talents. These can become special attributes, hero qualities, that can help the child and caregivers in the future to prevent or minimize future traumas, to succeed in accomplishing goals, and to help others by sharing what was learned. In this process, the child and caregivers reshape the meaning of past events and develop stronger identities together.

Life Story Integration promotes shared experiences of working together to overcome fears and develop shared pride. Chapter activities include opportunities for trauma memory reintegration with an emphasis on how children and caring adults have developed resources to prevent future traumas and how children and caregivers are making their lives different than the past. Storytelling and moviemaking are used to help children stay modulated, express sensory, emotional, and cognitive memories, and to desensitize fears that have been overpowering. Life Story Integration works to counter the isolation and stress associated with shame following multiple traumas. And, reintegration of life stories promotes linkages of children and caregivers with their families, cultural heritage, and communities.

Integrated Treatment

Core components (REAL) frame the RLH integrated toolkit (see Figure 0.3), which includes developmentally based assessments, service planning, session structure, fidelity, and evaluation measures for use by practitioners, consultants, supervisors, and program directors to ensure fidelity and maximize effectiveness. The *RLH Toolkit* includes tools for practitioners and programs to utilize from referral to discharge to keep services focused on recommended components for treatment of Complex Trauma.

RLH treatment was designed to be used by child and family service systems along with the NCTSN Child Welfare Toolkit (Chadwick Trauma-Informed Systems Project, 2013) and the NCTSN Resource Parent Curriculum

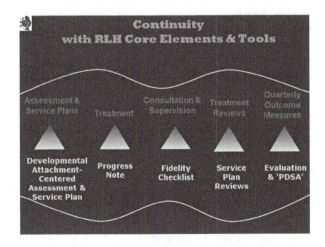

Figure 0.3 RLH Integrated Treatment

(Grillo, Lott, & Foster Care Subcommittee of the Child Welfare Committee, 2010) to implement the 'Essential Elements of a Trauma-Informed Child Welfare System' (Chadwick Trauma-Informed Systems Project, 2013). Guidelines are included in Part II of the *RLH Toolkit* for integration of RLH with home-based intensive care programs and children's psychotherapeutic groups. The RLH integrated toolkit can enable a wide range of mental health and child welfare programs to implement evidence-supported trauma and resiliency-focused treatment within an integrated trauma-informed framework that incorporates curricula and tools developed by the NCTSN for therapists, case managers, residential counselors, educators, foster and adoptive parents, home-based counselors, mentors, and other caring adults.

Developmental Research and 'REAL'

Research on the impact of abuse and neglect on children's development provides a foundation for the RLH focus on **R**elationships, **E**motional Self- and Co-Regulation, **A**ction Cycles, and **L**ife Story Integration. Increased rates of psychopathology have also been long recognized as an outcome of maltreatment and disrupted attachments to caregivers (Egeland & Sroufe, 1981). Resilience following exposure to trauma has been found to be related to the strength of children's relationships with caregivers and their sense of social support, while lack of social support has been linked to increased rates of psychopathology (Bal, De Bourdeaudhuij, Crombez, & Van Oost, 2005; Nooner et al., 2012).

Experiences of early childhood of abuse and neglect lead children's nervous systems to be over-reactive to stress and prone to dysregulation (Gunnar & Donzella, 2002). And, repeated experiences of traumatic stress have been linked to neurobiological changes in children that impact their ability to regulate emotions (DeBellis et al., 1999). Maltreated children have been found to have significantly reduced capacity to regulate emotions, to recognize and identify feelings, and to be able to use words to describe interpersonal factors linked to feelings (Shipman, Edwards, Brown, Swisher, & Jennings, 2005). Development of Emotional Regulation has been recognized as an essential component in efforts to prevent maladaptive behavior, to increase adaptive behavior, and to reduce psychopathology (Cicchetti, Ackerman, & Izard, 1995; Kim & Cicchetti, 2010).

Abuse and neglect have also been linked to children having negative images of themselves, a poor sense of their ability to make things better, and feelings of helplessness. Experiences of trauma decrease an individual's sense of being able to control what happens to them (Schiraldi, 1999). Children who were neglected and sexually abused have been found to have a higher external locus of control compared to other children (Bolger & Patterson, 2003), and low internal locus of control has been found to be related to maladaptive coping behavior and higher rates of psychopathology (Haine, Ayers, Sandler, Wolchik, & Weyer, 2003; Scott et al., 2010). Development of an internal locus of control has been associated with resilience in individuals who experienced trauma (Cook et al., 2005; Kushner, Riggs, Foa, & Miller, 1993).

The emphasis on Life Story Integration in *Real Life Heroes®* was developed to help children overcome the shame and self-denigration that often follows emotional abuse and placements in child welfare programs or psychiatric hospitals. Latency-age children are especially susceptible to shame, especially following emotional abuse. Studies have found that: maltreated children ages 5–7 showed increased feelings of shame with age (Bennett, Sullivan, & Lewis, 2010); guilt reactions to events increased between ages 5 and 9 (Zahn-Waxler & Van Hulle, 2012); children ages 8–13 were more likely to blame themselves for their abuse (Hazzard, Celano, Gould, Lawry, & Webb, 1995); and children ages 6–11 expressed more guilt over uncontrollable or accidental events than other age groups (Graham, Doubleday, & Guarino, 1984).

Resiliency-Focused Treatment

Real Life Heroes® is a resiliency-focused treatment for increasing emotionally supportive relationships, emotional self- and co-regulation, a child and caregiver's sense of self-efficacy, and stronger identities for children and caregivers who have experienced traumatic stress. RLH was designed to promote children's development of self-regulation skills following traumas that stymied developmental growth and led to dysfunctional and often high-risk behavior patterns. Changing negative family interaction patterns is promoted by practicing new patterns of interaction (Action Cycles), which, in turn, increase the child and caregiver's capacity to make things better (competence) and feelings of self-control. Reinforcing success, emotional support, and self-efficacy provides a foundation for reintegration of traumatic experiences into a stronger identity (Life Story Integration) for both children and caregivers.

Co-regulation activities are provided in each session and matched to children's developmental level. Co-regulation is promoted with patterned, repetitive, multisensory, rhythmic, and fun activities that are respectful of the child, family, and their cultural heritage (adapted from Perry, 2014). Examples include children and caregivers balancing peacock feathers (Macy, Barry, & Gil, 2003), blowing bubbles, playing with Play-Doh, or playing a musical instrument. The emphasis on co-regulation in RLH is based on neurobiological research that has demonstrated that attachments are critical for social and emotional development. "The early social environment, mediated by the primary caregiver, directly influences the final wiring of the circuits in the infant's brain that are responsible for the future social-emotional development of the individual" (Schore, 2003b, p. 73). Similarly, self-regulation and co-regulation go together from the time a child is born.

Self-regulation is based on "affective exchanges throughout early infancy. This includes the repeated experiences of arousal escalation and de-escalation that occur in dyadic interactions. It also includes the frequent occurrences of distress-relief cycles with which the caregiver is associated" (Sroufe, 1995, p. 152). Caregivers use looks, tones of voice, gestures, language, and bodily movement to co-regulate their children.

Traumatized children can learn to thrive in a safe environment with nurturing caregivers, and neurological systems can regenerate lost functions (Doidge, 2007). Disrupted co-regulation can be renewed by helping caregivers to attune to their children through creative arts and sensorimotor activities.

Rebuilding Trust and Attachments after Traumas

Families may be challenged by external traumatic events (tornados, terrorism, community violence) or internal traumas (severe illness, death, job losses, domestic violence). It's not just traumatic events themselves, but the impact of those events on children's primary relationships, that shapes the severity of their traumatic stress. For children, the difference between surviving adversity and getting PTSD often centers on how their primary caregivers are able to cope and maintain the safety and security of relationships to their children. That's why relational traumas (e.g., emotional abuse, impaired parenting, or family violence) are so difficult for children. These traumas crack the foundation of their lives. For these families, Complex Trauma therapy has to tackle rebuilding these foundations (after Ghosh-Ippen, 2006) to create the capacity for development of higher-level social and problem-solving skills and reintegration of traumatic events.

Trust and attachment provide the foundation for children's development. RLH provides a structured format for promoting re-attunement and was designed to help children with traumatic stress build the interpersonal resources needed to reintegrate painful memories and begin healing from experiences of abuse, neglect, family violence, severe illness, death, or major losses in their lives. Activities are designed to rebuild or build attachments with caring committed adults and provide opportunities for caring adults to help children build skills, create safety, and overcome traumas that have impaired their development. Ideally, activities involve caring, safe parents, but the workbook can be used to search for or foster trust with other caring adults committed to protecting, guiding, and nurturing children into adulthood.

The intent of this approach is to make it safe enough for children and caregivers to develop the skills and confidence needed to integrate physiological reactions, emotions, and beliefs tied to stressful experiences. The RLH workbook can be used by therapists as a framework to show children that caring adults can make their world safe enough so that children can reduce their hyper-vigilance and threat avoidance behaviors sufficiently to allow them to learn vital skills and gain a better understanding of how trauma shapes behavior. With each chapter, children are challenged to grow and develop skills, understanding, and beliefs that will help them cope more effectively.

RLH fosters the attachments children need in order to develop socially, emotionally, and cognitively into successful adults and to become good parents for their own children. The central challenge in this work is to find and help committed caring adults become the heroes children need in order to re-establish safety so that children can learn and develop critical skills. Workbook activities help children and caregivers to remember past events, the good and the bad times, and to create a shared story built on child, family, and cultural strengths and the courage to overcome past traumas. Caregivers become the 'wise and trusted guides' that children need to become heroes in their own lives and make it possible for children to manage intense affective responses and to prevent traumatic reactions from continuing into future generations.

A dual-track approach is provided to foster the understanding, courage, and skills of both caregivers and children. Activities in the workbook provide opportunities for children and parents to bridge gaps that have developed, to communicate nonverbally and verbally, building a new or renewed sense of communication that includes self-reflection and meaning. For caregivers, activities provide opportunities to 'witness' (after Herman, 1992a), to demonstrate acceptance of children's experiences, and to pass along what adults have learned, including strengths from children's extended family and cultural heritage that helped family members manage and overcome adversity.

Just as traumatic stress often involves breakdowns in relationships, healing is promoted by reconnecting caring adults and children: face to face, "brain to brain" (Siegel and Hartzell, 2003). Facial looks, tone of voice, and touch are critical to demonstrate adults' attunement and acceptance of children (Schore, 2003a). Shared activities can be used by caring adults to demonstrate their commitment to help disempower children's fears and foster children's strength and courage within a nurturing, committed relationship.

With each page of the RLH workbook, therapists coach adults to attune to children and restore trust that caregivers will protect, nurture, and guide their children. Repairing trust means acknowledging what adults have done wrong, taking responsibility for what they did, and showing children that adults will protect them in the future. To rebuild trust, adults can share what led up to their actions and what they are going to do instead in the future. Each activity provides an opportunity for caring adults to work on reconnecting or building stronger relationships with children and overcoming the distrust, and often the shame, fostered by events when adults acted out of control, misunderstood children, or hurt children by neglecting them or lashing out. The *RLH Toolkit* also includes a *Power Plan* for caregivers that can be used to increase understanding of how traumatic stress has affected children and to develop a trauma-informed plan to prevent and respond to children's reactions to reminders of previous traumas.

Charting a Pathway to Healing

Psychological assessment of children's attachments and social, emotional, and cognitive functioning guides effective therapeutic interventions. Attachment-centered treatment is most effective when based on a careful assessment of the caring and strengths of family and extended family members, as well as conflicts, traumas, and safety risks. This requires a careful evaluation of children's perspectives and the triggers leading to repetitive trauma behaviors using multiple sources and tools. Asking children, as well as caregivers, about trauma exposure and symptoms is a critical part of assessment and needs to include separate evaluations with parents and children, given the high frequency of abuse, neglect, and domestic violence reported in families referred to children's mental health and child welfare programs.

Effective work with parents and other caregivers requires a careful assessment of their commitment and ability to help children heal, adults' capacity for managing intense affective reactions, and their willingness to work on rebuilding safety, re-attunement, managing their own trauma reactions, and guiding children to maturity. Interventions work best when matched with the strengths, interests, and special talents of children and families, including their ethnic and family heritage, spirituality, and ties to community resources. The *RLH Toolkit* includes simple tools that practitioners can utilize (see: *The Pledge*) to identify strengths and needs, enhance safety, and uncover openings to engage children and caregivers into client-centered treatment.

The intent of assessment in RLH is to open up pathways to healing and growth. Assessment begins from the first contact with children and caregivers and continues as an ongoing process throughout treatment. Repeated administration of session and three-month follow-up evaluation measures helps practitioners keep treatment focused on what is real for children and families. Evaluation results identify issues of concern and reinforce progress.

When children have been placed away from their biological parents, or have been threatened with placement, it is important to work with children and family members to identify both a primary and a back-up caregiver who would be willing to work with children on the tasks outlined below. Working on both reuniting and a back-up, 'concurrent' plan restores hope and focuses services on essential work to move children quickly out of temporary placements. However, for many children, this is a challenging task and they do not have to have a primary or backup caregiver to start. The *RLH Life Storybook* can be used to help identify children's wishes for building or rebuilding attachments and this can guide service planning,

including: visits for children in foster care or in-patient mental health programs, searching for caring adults, and building or rebuilding attachments with caregivers for the future.

Developmentally Targeted Interventions

Assessment of how children function emotionally and socially provides clues that can guide a therapist to points in children's development when their 'protective shield' of caring and protection may have broken down and they experienced relational traumas. Rebuilding trust in caregivers and self- and co-regulation skills is targeted to the developmental level when children experienced relational traumas. When traumas have impacted children's attachments, healing means rebuilding trust that caring adults will maintain their commitment, rather than move in and out of children's lives. Even for older adolescents, it is important to connect each youth with someone who will actively and consistently check on them, follow up, monitor, exercise authority, and 'hassle' them enough to show they care, and will continue to care over time. Before children are asked to work on overcoming past traumas, it is also important to establish the safety, acceptance, and emotional support needed at the developmental level during which the children were traumatized. By focusing on both strengthening youths and rebuilding, or building, long-term caring relationships, therapists can help children and adolescents grow beyond the developmental phase where they became traumatized.

Workbook chapters engage children and caring adults to explore critical moments in children's development. Activities provide a structure to identify and repair gaps in relationships and skills around specific events or time periods in children's development. RLH uses multimodal activities to promote relationship and skill development targeted to the developmental age when children's core trust in relationships broke down. Re-attunement and rebuilding trust is promoted through 'doing with' activities involving a therapist and, whenever possible, safe caregivers, working together with art, music, and movement to learn new ways of coping and to reintegrate memories of traumatic events.

A 10-year-old child who was never able to master the basic trust required for a secure attachment as a toddler will usually need to work with a therapist and a caring parent-figure with repeated interactions that foster basic trust in a parent or substitute parent to care for his or her basic needs over an extended time. Similarly, a 12-year-old youth who was traumatized as a preschool child and functions developmentally like a 3–4-year-old will typically require activities and skill-building at a 3–4-year-old level. And, a 15-year-old youth who was traumatized as an 8–12-year-old, but received nurture and caring in his or her first seven years, can be helped to develop skills and relationships from an 8–12-year-old level when his or her social and emotional development was stymied. In each case, a therapist can help children develop more age-appropriate skills and perspectives within the newfound safety of therapeutic and family or substitute family relationships.

Guiding Principles

Real Life Heroes® addresses three primary issues (Kagan, 1996) to promote developmental growth and healing for children who have experienced Complex Trauma:

- Children need caring and committed adults who will care for them through good times and bad, protect and guide them now and into adulthood, and help them to integrate a life story based on mastery and hope, a life story that includes what they saw, felt, heard, thought, and did over time.
- Trauma processing takes place within safe relationships with caregivers and therapists who prove they are strong enough and committed enough to experience children's pain and guide children to reintegrate the fragmented experiences of their lives, to grieve losses, and to learn new behaviors. Caregivers play a critical role in trauma therapy by showing children that their experience has been heard and believed by people who care enough about them to protect them, set limits, implement safety plans, and keep the 'monsters' of the past away.
- Children and caregivers who have experienced traumas can develop skills they can utilize to calm themselves, to gain control over their fears and nightmares, and to replace high-risk behaviors, isolation, and shame with positive relationships and achievements that help themselves, their families, and their communities.

Building Strengths, Chapter by Chapter

RLH incorporates recommended components for treatment of Complex Trauma in children (Cook et al., 2003; Ford & Cloitre, 2009) into phase-based treatment, beginning with resiliency-focused assessment and service planning, introduction to the *Life Storybook*, and engagement of caregivers to commit themselves to protecting children's safety to share with *The Pledge*. The *Life Storybook* provides a structured curriculum that fosters the safety needed to engage children and caring adults to work progressively to build children's self-regulation skills, trust in relationships, and to reduce the impact of traumatic stress. The workbook is organized into 12 chapters that address core components of treatment for Complex Trauma.

The *Life Storybook* includes an *Introduction for Parents and Caring Adults*, which summarizes guidelines to promote effective use of this book including safety guidelines, promoting creativity, the making of heroes, how to facilitate storytelling, when to bring in a therapist, and a note for therapists. The importance of validation is stressed, and the *Life Storybook* book begins with *The Pledge* in which helping adults promise to respect children's perceptions, thoughts, and feelings. *The Pledge* marks the beginning of the adventure and a contract to strengthen or find caring, committed adults who will validate and protect children.

Chapter 1 provides an introduction to how stress from 'tough times' and traumatic events can lead to traumatic stress, and conversely how building skills for modulation and strengthening emotionally supportive relationships can help children stay in control, prevent, or heal from traumatic stress, and achieve their goals. Children and caregivers are also introduced to the structured format of RLH sessions that begins with safety messages, use of *My Thermometers* to gauge the children and caregivers' current emotional functioning, centering activities to promote self- and co-regulation, work on pages of the workbook, 'homework' to continue skill and relationship development, and scheduling the next session. Chapter 1 activities focus on building a shared understanding of how trauma works, and developing initial safety plans, *Pocket Power Cards*, that can help remind children and caregivers how they can reduce stress and traumatic stress reactions. The chapter ends with the Hero's Challenge, an invitation to children and caregivers to start a new 'journey' in which they build skills, strengthen relationships, develop safety, and learn how to become stronger than fears and nightmares from the past.

Chapter 2 introduces children to the structured format of the *Life Storybook* and use of creative arts. The heading at the top of the page directs children to visualize a memory

---

PHASE I

Core Components: Relationships, Emotional Self- and Co-Regulation, and Action Cycles (Interaction Patterns)

The Pledge

1. The Hero's Challenge
2. A Little about Me
3. Heroes and Heroines
4. Power Plans
5. My Family
6. Important People
7. Mind Power
8. Changing the Story: The ABCs of Trauma

PHASE II

Core Components: Life Story Integration (Trauma Desensitization and Identity)

9. Timelines and Moves
10. Through the Tough Times
11. Into the Future
12. My Story

or a fantasy and then to picture it below with a drawing or a photograph, to imagine how it would sound as a song, or to show how it would look through movement as a dance or a movie. Therapists can use the format outlined in the *RLH Toolkit* to engage children in creative arts activities that foster integration of experiences and enhancement of strengths. A question at the bottom of the page directs children to write a brief note about something special in their picture. Questions were designed to build up children's sense of being valued and their sense of competence in different situations. The completed page will typically contain both children's visual memories and a short narrative to add additional details and children's understanding of what was most important.

Chapter 2 provides opportunities for children to learn to recognize and express a range of feelings in a safe way. Some children find this easy and others require a great deal of practice in developing affect management skills. The *RLH Toolkit* includes guidelines for helping children utilize drawing, rhythm, tonality, and movement as part of each session's structure and keep themselves within their "window of tolerance" for stress (Siegel, 1999). In the first few pages, children are invited to draw a little about themselves and later to share this with safe, caring adults who are helping them write this book. This process provides a means for children to test and confirm that caring adults accept that it is normal to have a wide range of feelings. This is especially important for children who have experienced separations and traumas, leading them to become constricted in their feelings, beliefs, and sense of hope. Caring adults can use this chapter to show children how they see they are special and that they are committed to listening to children and respecting their perspectives. Chapter 2 gives adults an opportunity to validate how children have been successful and to show acceptance of children's wide ranges of feelings. Children who feel they can trust the adults who are helping them will be much more willing to move ahead in the book.

Chapter 3 invites children to draw, act out, or write brief stories of people in their lives who acted like a hero. By making this a shared activity with a parent, relative, or another caring adult, children learn that they are not alone and that important people in their lives value and commit themselves to caring for one another. At the same time, adults can learn from children what they look for in a hero. Chapter 3 also provides a place for children to remember how they have helped others and to envision what they could do in the future to help make things better for their families and communities. The heroes theme promotes hope that children and the adults who care about children can make things better and encourages children to learn skills modeled by the people and fictional characters they admire. Chapter 3 builds on the conception of heroes as people who help others and contribute to their families and communities. Helping others is an integral part of building self-esteem and shaping tomorrow's citizens and leaders. Chapter 3 emphasizes the courage to help others and the making of a hero, including the power of self-awareness, self-soothing, and focusing skills as attributes of heroes.

Chapter 3 helps children identify people from their families, ethnic group, community, and broader culture who have acted as heroes as a means of rekindling hope and modeling mastery over traumas. Heroes in this workbook refer to women and men; boys and girls. Children are invited to draw, act out, or write a brief story of someone in their lives who has acted like a hero.

Workbook pages focus children on how real people, including popular icons and fictional heroes, struggled to build strengths and overcome adversity. The importance of building strengths is accentuated and then utilized to reinforce understanding of trauma and healing from Chapter 1 that can help children reduce feelings of shame about trauma reactions and to focus instead on skill development in recognizing and managing how they cope with trauma reminders. Skill development and proactive mastery of trauma reminders is promoted with the framework of the "hero's journey" (Campbell, 1968). The *RLH Toolkit* provides specific guidelines to help children develop affect modulation skills calm themselves with slow 'belly' breathing, 'progressive muscle relaxation,' 'Safe Place' imagery, 'thought-shifting,' and other affect regulation skills.

This chapter also provides a place for children to remember how they have helped others and to envision what they could do in the future. In this way, *Real Life Heroes®* helps children see how they are special within their families and communities. Helping others is an integral part of building self-esteem and shaping tomorrow's citizens and leaders. Chapter 3 emphasizes the courage to help others as an integral part of becoming a hero, including the power of self-awareness, self-soothing, and focusing skills as common attributes of heroes.

Chapter 4 builds on the image of heroes to help children develop their own self-awareness of strengths, stressors, typical reactions, and ways they can make things better with help from caring adults. These are skills that children can develop with practice, including exercises in therapy sessions and 'homework' assignments. Chapter 4 helps children develop a resilience-focused safety plan, a *Youth Power Plan*, that can be condensed into a *Pocket Power Card* for children to carry with them to remind them of effective coping skills and resources. Caregivers can complete their own *Caregiver Power Plan*, which is provided in the *RLH Toolkit*.

Chapter 5 helps children to remember people who cared for them day by day, through sickness and health. Memories of being valued and of positive people are often lost or minimized when children have experienced difficult times in their lives. This chapter provides an opportunity to expand children's awareness of people who have helped, even in small ways, and to highlight resources in their lives, including their own talents. Children can also bring in images of heroes and heroines from stories, music, movies, fantasy, and real life. Chapter 5 also provides a framework to help children to diagram the roots of their family tree, highlighting ties to family members, friends, caring adults, pets, mentors, and other sources of support.

Chapter 6 helps children to remember a wide range of people who have helped them and to build upon the strengths, skills, beliefs, and supportive relationships that helped them to enjoy 'good times.' Children are invited to imagine creating their own special holidays (after Evans, 1986), free from the constraints with which they lived. This exercise often yields important clues to children's inner wishes and unspoken needs. Therapists can use the desires for relationships with important people identified by children in Chapter 6 to guide work on building or rebuilding supports for children. The intent is to help children learn from what works in 'good times' to help them later to master the 'tough times.'

Chapter 7 encourages children to develop skills to make things better in their lives with mindfulness and increased modulation. This chapter includes opportunities for children to strengthen calming and self-soothing skills and develop positive beliefs in their own capacity. Safe Place imagery is reinforced with drawing, rhythm, music, and movement, and children develop a symbolic 'protective shield' to remind them of resources in their families, their cultural heritage, and themselves.

In Chapter 8, children explore how they can use an understanding of how trauma experiences can lead to repeated cycles of trauma reactions. Psycho-education on the "The ABCs of Trauma" is coupled with a guide to how children change cycles of trauma reactions, "Changing the Story," just as a director of a movie can change how a story unfolds. CBT (cognitive behavioral therapy) exercises help children replace dysfunctional beliefs with positive self-statements. Exercises in Chapter 8 prepare children for the difficult work ahead, transforming legacies of victimization and shaming into a self-image of surviving, coping, and growing in strength, bringing out the 'hero inside' troubled children.

Chapter 9 provides a chronicle to record children's moves between different locations or homes. Moves, especially for children in placement, often mean losses of relationships and lead to children feeling blamed or blaming themselves for what happened. By asking children to share what they think happened, therapists and caring adults can address dysfunctional beliefs and attributions. Learning children's perspectives on moves can also be used to guide services to help children to find out what really happened and to provide opportunities, when necessary, for children to make up for mistakes they made that hurt other people. In this way, information gathered in Chapter 9 can be used by therapists to help with the trauma-processing and reintegration activities outlined in Chapter 10.

Children can also use Chapter 9 to develop a timeline of good and bad events. Ratings of events from 'worst' to 'best' can help children to see how forces outside their control have affected their lives, and at the same time to develop a sense of time, including a past, a present, and a future. This helps children develop the understanding that they don't have to remain stuck in uncomfortable positions.

After children complete the timeline, it is helpful to emphasize how we can learn from the tough times and that it is just as important to learn from the good times. Therapists can ask children to draw a line connecting each circled number on the right side, then turn the page horizontally so the page number is on the right side. This highlights every year in children's lives when the line went up and can be used as a guide to learn more from children about what helped make things better in those years. Who helped in those special times and how did children help themselves?

The timeline helps to identify positive events in children's lives. By looking more closely at these important and often neglected times, caring adults can help children learn lessons about who helped them succeed, how they helped themselves, and how they and important people in their lives overcame problems. In this way, successes from the past can expand children's sense of hope to deal with problems in the present or the future.

Before moving ahead and dealing with tough times in Chapter 10, therapists and caring adults ensure that safety plans and emotional supports are in place for children and also for caring adults. Therapists and caring adults check whether children are ready to move on to more difficult issues by assessing their ability to reduce their *Knots* sufficiently to manage stress without dangerous behaviors.

In Chapter 10, children are encouraged to remember and enlist the skills and resources that helped them in the past in order to learn from difficult times in their lives and desensitize a series of progressively more difficult tough times. A 'Five-Chapter' storytelling format is provided to make storytelling easier and encourage use of nonverbal creative arts modalities, drawing, rhythm, music, and movement. 'Five-Chapter' Stories emphasize 'moving through' traumas to safe times and staying within children's 'window of tolerance.' The format includes: What happened (Chapter 2); What helped children and people they loved get through (survive) the 'tough time' (Chapter 3); A safe time and place after the traumatic event when children felt cared for and protected (Chapter 4); What led up to the traumatic event (Chapter 1); and How children could prevent or reduce 'tough times' now that they are older, smarter, and stronger with help from caring adults (Chapter 5). Stories can be shortened to three chapters if children are unable to handle the 'Five-Chapter' format. 'Three-Chapter' Stories include: What happened (Chapter 2); A safe time and place after the event when children felt cared for and protected (Chapter 3); and What led up to the event (Chapter 1). Structured questions utilized in trauma desensitization, (e.g., Trauma-Focused Cognitive Behavioral Therapy) (Cohen, Deblinger, & Mannarino, 2006) help elicit details of traumatic memories and reinforce children's resilience. 'Five-Chapter' and 'Three-Chapter' Stories highlight how children and adults can learn from the past and increase children's sense of security by visualizing, enacting, and describing how they and their families can use the resources they now have to prevent or minimize the impact of 'tough times' in the future. The emphasis on relationships and the roles of adults can be used to reinforce how caring adults would help children to master what was impossible to face in the past and to ensure that children are not left feeling alone and vulnerable to repeated traumatic events.

Chapter 10 also includes three activities designed to help children share times when they did something that hurt other people, accidentally or deliberately, and to develop ways they could apologize and help make up for what their behavior did to other people. These exercises provide opportunities to work on the shame that many traumatized children carry, and which can drive cycles of trauma reactions, including self-abusive or high-risk behaviors. Developing forms of apology and restitution works best when it's possible to link this to the child and family's cultural heritage, and how their family or religion has provided a means to learn from mistakes and promote healing for everyone involved.

Chapter 11 provides a chance for children to develop images of themselves becoming successful in the future, highlighting positive, enduring relationships and contributions children could make when they are older. Workbook pages invite children to identify important people who they see as important in their lives and the kind of relationships they would like to have. Chapter activities can be used to guide service planning and linkage of children to educational and vocational programs to help them achieve their goals.

Chapter 12 strengthens children's sense of how they have moved through 'tough times' and become stronger and smarter. Children are invited to share what they have learned in a letter to other children who experienced similar 'tough times', building their sense of themselves as a hero, using the skills and resources they have gained to help others, a core component of the hero's journey (Campbell, 1968).

The workbook ends by encouraging children to put their memories together into a short narrative story of their life. Children can write their life stories as traditional autobiographies, using pages at the end of the book, or separately with a word processor, to allow flexibility, easy revisions, and more pages. The completed narrative can then be inserted into the end of the workbook. Children are also encouraged to insert important photos of themselves and important people in their lives.

Children are invited to create their own title page as the final step in this book, a title that reflects how they have mastered 'good times and bad.' Examples of titles include: "My Book about Good Times and Bad," "All about Me," "My Family and Me," "My Life from A to Z," and "How I Learned to Enjoy My Life." They can use the title page provided and remove the *Real Life Heroes*® cover or paste a new cover over the publisher's cover. This makes the book their own, from the book's cover to the last page.

Individualized Treatment

Success with the workbook is fostered by:

*   developing safety for children and their families;
*   building self-soothing skills;
*   engaging and strengthening emotionally supportive relationships; and
*   adapting use of the workbook to each child's special needs and the strengths and resources in their family and their cultural heritage.

Children develop resources and enhanced security and skills by working with safe, caring adults to complete chapters of the workbook. The length of time needed to complete all of the workbook chapters varies with the level of emotional support and safety children have at the beginning of treatment and how long it takes to find, engage, and rebuild (or build) trust with safe, emotioally supportive caregivers committed to helping them overcome traumas. The workbook was designed to be completed in 25–30 sessions, approximately six months of weekly appointments; however, treatment can be extended when it takes longer to find and engage caregivers, and the workbook can also be continued in subsequent treatment.

It is not necessary to complete all the chapters in order to see positive changes. The workbook can be used in programs that do not allow the time, or number of sessions, needed to make it through the entire workbook. The more chapters children and caregivers complete, the better the outcomes (Kagan et al., 2008). Significant changes have been found in pilot studies (Kagan et al., 2014a) at three- and six-month follow-up evaluations using standardized measures of behavior and change in trauma symptoms. The length of time and number of sessions needed appears to vary directly with children's level of security and strength of emotionally supportive relationships at the beginning of treatment. Children who have a safe, non-offending, and validating caregiver who is able and willing to participate in treatment can typically 'move through' the workbook very quickly. Children who have experienced interpersonal traumas and multiple types of traumas typically need much more time to rebuild trusting relationships and the safety to desensitize reactions to reminders of past traumas. For children with Complex PTSD, a minimum of 24 sessions is recommended. The *Real Life Heroes Life Storybook* and toolkit provide structured opportunities to help these children for the extended time needed to search for and engage caring adults and to develop the child's and caregiver's understanding, skills, and resources to reintegrate their lives.

Page by page, working on the *Life Storybook* helps children reconnect to caring adults and express memories, including thoughts, feelings, and actions. This helps traumatized children with the often difficult task of creating an integrated and strength-enhancing life story, to share their past, and to see if caregivers will accept them, including past experiences, what they did that helped, what they did that hurt others, and how they have grown and changed. Completing the workbook helps children desensitize reminders of painful events that in the past blocked them from being able to express a coherent and integrated narrative. 'Telling the story' and reintegrating painful events becomes possible as children grow stronger and with repeated testing and demonstration of safety plans.

Therapists and mentors working individually with children can integrate work on developing self-esteem with development of writing and communication skills. Writing a summary of children's life stories in Chapter 12 is facilitated by utilizing the structure of children's timelines from Chapter 9. Children can put together a summary of the most important experiences in their lives, beginning with how their parents came to be together, their birth, and how family members have coped with good times and bad, leading to children's achievements. This may require 'detective' work, including finding safe ways to contact and interview relatives, former therapists, foster parents, and practitioners in governmental agencies who worked with them. The narrative can emphasize how children mastered difficult situations and developed skills with help from important people.

By the end of the workbook, children should be able to identify people who cared about them in the past *and* the present, and who they would like to have in their lives in the future. Children should also be able to verbalize, picture, or dramatize strengths and lessons they have learned about themselves and their families. Finally, children should be able to express in words, art, music, and movement how they could manage tough times with the help of caring adults in the present and future.

Developing Safety for Reintegration of Traumatic Memories

Children need to become secure enough within their primary relationships to caring adults and therapists, and also within their own bodies, in order to safely re-experience and reintegrate difficult memories and feelings. It is important to develop basic safety and affect regulation capacity *before* trauma processing (van der Kolk, 2003). Re-exposing children to memories of victimization without developing necessary safety and affect management skills can lead to restimulation of overwhelming pain, perceptions of helplessness, and dissociative reactions (Pitman et al., 1991). Too much arousal sensitizes children and associates therapy with pain, confirming the power of the trauma. Similarly, exposing children to repeated reminders of past traumas can strengthen trauma reactions.

Real Life Heroes® utilizes a structured series of non-verbal creative arts modalities to help children feel safe enough to process past traumas and reduce trauma reactions. Activities promote self-control, creativity, substitu-

tion of fun for threat avoidance, and development of positive beliefs to counter dysfunctional thoughts that reinforce traumas. Children learn that previously unbearable memories can be managed and that thoughts and feelings can be modulated without returning to the overwhelming distress of traumatic events.

Safety and reduction of children's threat avoidance behaviors depends on developing and maintaining relationships with caring and committed adults. Techniques and protocols cannot replace the support children receive from caring adults and skilled therapists working step by step, and day by day, to help them modulate anxiety, develop skills, and develop solutions to crises that have often left children, their parents, and grandparents feeling trapped for generations. Therapy sessions can reinforce confidence through shared activities that emphasize how children's lives are different now and how caring adults will protect them, even when they re-experience the smells, sounds, images, and feelings associated with past traumas.

Safety plans are a critical part of this work, and need to include specific and viable plans to assure children how caring adults will protect them and people they love from repetitions of past violence, abuse, neglect, and loss. This begins with a careful assessment of past traumas, current dangers, emotional support, and protection from repeated traumas from children's perspectives. Treatment promotes validation by significant adults of children's experiences, acceptance by caring adults of the responsibility to develop and implement step-by-step action plans for protection of children and family members, and demonstration that adults will maintain this commitment over time.

Caring adults often need to build skills for self-soothing, affect management, safe relationships, parenting, and conflict management. Parents and other adults lead the way to healing by demonstrating to children that they can handle reminders of traumatic events without losing control of their own affective responses in a way that threatens children.

Affect management skills can be fostered through combinations of support groups, classes on parenting, anger management, and prevention of domestic violence, *and* work in *individualized* therapy to develop, practice, and implement *self-control* safety plans. Completing a class helps provide vital information, but is rarely sufficient to effect change. Children, parents, and authorities need to share, understand, and experience over time that safety and relapse prevention plans have been implemented.

Children cannot simply begin trusting a mother or father who was not able, or was unwilling, to stop neglect or violence. Trust is impossible when parents remain locked into denial of how their children were harmed, or worse, continue to threaten children to not talk, or even to recant disclosures, in order to regain their parents' love. If children were hurt by emotional, physical or sexual abuse and threatened to keep secrets, they very likely will never be able to fully trust that parent again and may also never be able to completely rely on a nonabusive parent who failed to keep them safe. Non-family protectors, orders of protection, alarm systems, and guard dogs may be necessary for these children to feel safe enough to sleep at night and learn critical skills.

A parent or caring adult will typically need to prove that children are safe for at least the same amount of time that the abuse and neglect was allowed to continue. So, if parents were too overwhelmed to protect children for a year, it will usually take another year of validation and testing to rebuild the trust that was lost. Families can celebrate passing the anniversary dates of past traumas as a way to demonstrate how much they have changed and how children no longer have to be afraid.

In the interim, other caring adults need to be involved in children's lives and show children that they will watch for signs of the violence or neglect cycle starting again and take action if this happens. Bringing in strong caring adults becomes a key part of safety plans for children to reunite safely with parents and families when neglect or violence took place.

In addition to relational security, children and caregivers often need to learn to utilize self-soothing skills in order to replace the hyper-arousal, irritability, and inability to relax that is often part of Complex Trauma reactions. For children with high levels of anxiety, it is important to find ways to reassure children, to help them to relax, and to strengthen their sense of security before completing Chapter 10. The objective is to help children feel calm enough to be able to think and try out different ways to manage previously stressful situations.

Developing 'Safe Place' imagery is very helpful, and the *Life Storybook* provides a series of activities to promote and strengthen children's (and caregivers') abilities to bring up imagery and feelings associated with feeling safe in relationships. Safe Place imagery can be reinforced with tapping, eye movements, alternating sounds (Shapiro, 2001), repeated soft chords, or other simple repetitive and soothing aids. Patterned repetitive stimulation may 'trick' a trauma-activated brainstem into allowing children to learn new ways to perceive and cope with traumatic events (for information on the use of EMDR, see, e.g., Shapiro, 2001; Tinker & Wilson, 1999). Healing rituals, such as prayer alongside a comforting adult, drumming, chanting, dance, or singing hymns and reassuring tunes, may also be very helpful.

Children can also be guided in developing self-soothing skills with exercises in deep muscle relaxation, visual imagery, and meditation (see, e.g., Cohen et al., 2006; Munson & Riskin, 1995). For children who have difficulty managing frustrations and anger, exercises in anger management may be very useful (see, e.g., Eggert, 1994; Whitehouse & Pudney, 1996). Similarly, children with difficulties focusing attention may benefit from workbooks that provide guidance around slowing down and sustaining attention (see, e.g., Nadeau & Dixon, 1997).

Research and Evaluation Studies

Therapists have consistently reported positive results implementing RLH during 16 years of case studies with children with Complex PTSD involved in home-based or clinic-based family counseling and with children who have been living in foster families and residential treatment centers due to dangerous behaviors and often repeated experiences of physical or sexual abuse, and neglect. A pilot research study (Kagan et al., 2008) was conducted to evaluate the effectiveness of this model with 41 children and adolescents at Parsons Child and Family Center, a community practice site of the National Child Traumatic Stress Network. Data from the Parsons study were utilized to assess changes from enrollment and at four, eight, and 12 months of treatment in child and family service programs. Therapists reported that the model helped them to engage children who had experienced neglect, abandonment, physical and sexual abuse, domestic violence, multiple losses, and separations, including histories of placements away from families of origin, and that the curriculum helped therapists persevere with application of cognitive behavioral therapy components over time, as noted on chapter checklists and in informal feedback sessions. At four months, children demonstrated statistically significant reductions in trauma symptoms on child self-reports evaluated with the Trauma Symptom Checklist for Children, (TSCC) (Briere, 1996) and problem behaviors reported by primary caregivers on the Conners Behavior Rating Scale—Parent-Long Version (Conners, 1997). At the end of the 12-month study period, results included:

- Reduced trauma symptoms reported by the adult caregiver on the PROPS (Greenwald & Rubin, 1999a, 1999b) in relation to the number of *Real Life Heroes®* chapters completed ($p < .001$).
- Increased security/attachment over time reported by children ($p < .05$) on the security scale (Kerns, Klepac, & Cole, 1996).

The HEROES Project (Kagan et al., 2014a) evaluated the effectiveness of *Real Life Heroes®* (RLH) with 119 children in seven child and family service and behavioral health programs, ranging from home-based family counseling to residential treatment. The study included a comparison of outcomes with children provided systematic RLH treatment compared to children provided trauma-informed 'treatment as usual' services on two critical measures for child welfare programs: avoiding out-of-home placements for children in home-based care and preventing psychiatric hospitalizations of all children served. The study also evaluated the impact on measured outcomes of the number and types of interpersonal traumas experienced and the importance of implementing RLH core components with fidelity. Results included statistically significant decreases from baseline to six months in child behavior problems on the Child Behavior Checklist (CBCL) internalizing and total behavior scales (Achenbach & Rescoria, 2000b), the anger subscale of the Trauma Symptom Checklist for Children (TSCC) (Briere, 1996), the UCLA PTSD Reaction Index-Parent Version re-experiencing, avoidance, hyper-arousal, and total symptoms scales (Rodriguez, Steinberg, Saltzman, & Pynoos, 2001), and the UCLA PTSD Index-Child Version avoidance and total symptoms scales. Significant reductions were also found with repeated measures at three-month assessments from baseline to nine months on the CBCL, the UCLA Parent and Child Versions, and the PTSD subscale of the TSCC. None of the children receiving RLH had placements or psychiatric hospitalizations, a positive, but not significant, trend, compared to some of the children receiving trauma-informed 'treatment as usual' provided by practitioners in the same programs trained in RLH and other trauma treatments (e.g., TF-CBT) who were placed or hospitalized. Outcome analyses focused on changes on standardized measures for children who had experienced one or more of the following types of trauma exposure: an 'impaired caregiver,' grief/loss, physical abuse, and emotional abuse. Results supported hypotheses that children receiving RLH's relationship-focused treatment would demonstrate statistically significant reductions in behavior problems reported on the CBCL. The HEROES Project also demonstrated significant improvements with an all-practitioner training program which was not limited to selected practitioners or doctoral candidates as in many other research studies on trauma treatments.[2] Overall, the study supported the effectiveness of implementing trauma and resiliency-focused treatment in a wide range of child welfare programs and the importance of providing sequential attachment-centered treatment for children with symptoms of Complex PTSD.

Links to Other Treatment Models

RLH is one of several treatment models identified by the National Child Traumatic Stress Network (NCTSN) as an evidence-supported and promising practice for treatment of children with Complex PTSD (Ford & Courtois, 2013). Practitioners will find similar components in each of these models and can utilize RLH in combination with other Complex Trauma treatments, such as ARC (Blaustein & Kinneburgh, 2010), Integrative Treatment of Complex Trauma (Briere & Lanktree, 2013), and Trauma Systems Therapy (Saxe et al., 2007), to identify formulation-driven priorities for treatment. RLH tools, including the workbook chapters and session activities, can then be implemented to address these needs and goals. RLH also works well in conjunction with group-centered treatment models for Complex Trauma, including SPARCS (DeRosa et al., 2008) and TARGET (Ford & Russo, 2006).

RLH and ARC (Blaustein & Kinneburgh, 2010) share the same focus on relational engagement and developing the capacity of children and caregivers to use self- and co-regulation skills to be able to participate in trauma experience integration-focused interventions, including development of a shared understanding of trauma experiences. RLH can be used to build the safety, supportive relationships, and self- and co-regulation skills needed for exposure-based and trauma-focused treatments such as EMDR (Shapiro, 2001), Progressive Counting (Greenwald, 2013), and adaptations of TF-CBT (Cohen et al., 2006) for Complex Trauma. Primary components of TF-CBT (PRACTICE) are addressed in *Real Life Heroes*® chapters and the RLH Session Structure (see Table 0.3). Trauma processing components of TF-CBT, EMDR, and Progressive Counting can also be incorporated into the RLH Session Structure and facilitated by use of Chapter 10 of the *RLH Life Storybook* (see Chapter 10 in the *Toolkit* for guidelines).

TABLE 0.3
TF-CBT and Corresponding RLH Components

TF-CBT	RLH		
	Life Storybook **Chapters**	**Session Structure**	**Supplementary Tools**
Psycho-education	1		NCTSN resource parent curriculum, Complex Trauma, grief, and parent handouts
Parenting skills	1, 3, 5	✓	*RLH Caregiver Power Plan*; NCTSN resource parent curriculum and parenting guides
Relaxation skills	1, 4, 7	✓	*RLH Youth Power Plan, Pocket Power Cards*
Affect expression and modulation skills	2, 4, 7	✓	
Cognitive coping skills	7, 8, 10, 11		
Trauma narration and cognitive processing of traumas	10, 11	✓	
In vivo mastery of trauma reminders	10	✓	
Conjoint child-parent sessions	1–12	✓	
Enhancing safety and future developmental trajectory	1, 4, 7, 10, 11, 12	✓	

How Is *Real Life Heroes*® Different than Other Treatment Models?

Real Life Heroes® was developed to engage children and families who did not respond to existing CBT and trauma exposure-based treatments and was designed to work in hard-pressed children's mental health and social services programs. RLH targets the developmental needs of children and adolescents who are functioning developmentally at a latency level, a critical age group for Complex Trauma treatment. In addition, RLH:

- focuses on developing resiliency for children and caregivers;
- promotes the courage for children and caregivers to share traumatic experiences as part of their life stories, within the context of their family and cultural heritage, rather than on desensitizing specific trauma events;
- focuses on children's primary relationships with caregivers and targets rebuilding (or building) emotional support, attunement, safety, and trust to counter shame and isolation;
- makes it easier to engage children and families who lack trust in service providers or adults in general;
- can be used with children and families where traumas are suspected but not acknowledged or validated by family members or authorities;
- can be used without graduated exposure to trauma experiences from the beginning of treatment, a requirement in trauma-focused treatments, such as TF-CBT (Mannarino, Griffen, Cohen, & Kliethermes, 2014);
- continues assessment and service planning as an ongoing process and engages children and caregivers to share through workbook chapter activities and with multiple modalities (art, rhythm, music, and movement);
- makes it possible to work on reintegration of trauma events that are hidden; as safety and stability increases, children and caregivers typically disclose or validate suspected traumas, which can be addressed in later chapters of the *Life Storybook*;
- promotes continued progress in trauma treatment when children move from program to program or therapist to therapist through use of RLH tools and session structure;
- provides 'ready-to-go' materials for hard-pressed practitioners, including step-by-step guides for developing self- and co-regulation, with slow breathing, yoga, movement, and storytelling activities that promote child-caregiver attunement and trust;
- assures implementation of evidence-supported components of treatment for Complex Trauma with fidelity tools that can be utilized in supervision and consultation;
- can be used with diverse families in a wide range of programs with different mandates and length of treatment and with families with a range of safety and stability; and

- provides an integrated framework for resiliency-focused treatment of children with traumatic stress that can be utilized by teams of service providers in home- and clinic-based services, foster, kinship or group care, special education schools, and a wide range of child and family services.

The Therapeutic 'Journey'[3]

Children present a paradox with time. On the one hand, children are blessed with the rest of their lives to make things better. On the other hand, children have no time to wait for the parenting and safety they need. Every child who has been placed away from home knows that you can lose your parents and family. 'Permanency' defies the reality of change, and yet fostering children's trust in caregivers is necessary for children to develop the skills and modulation they need to succeed. Each day of living with the threat of renewed neglect, abuse, or family violence leaves children more and more convinced that adults cannot be trusted and reinforces coping patterns based on hyper-vigilance, reactivity to perceived threats, defiance, and high-risk behaviors.

The experience of serial traumas does not dissipate into the air or fade away with time. Instead, for many children, it's as if time stops. Children showing symptoms of traumatic stress often act as though their social and emotional growth, their personal movement through time, has stopped. Behaviors seem to repeat children's yearning to cling to lost parents or to cycles of loss and rejection. It's not so much a purposeful re-enactment, but rather a repetition in keeping with traumatic constriction of children's beliefs and children's ongoing struggle to both master and yet avoid the pain of what has happened. Repetitions keep children focused on resolving broken attachments, and yet, without any resolution, children remain trapped in time.

Violence and rejection wound children, physically, psychologically, and spiritually. Traumatized children act as if they are entranced "by a wicked cursor," as one youth told me. They become lost in time, trapped by curses of neglect, abuse, and abandonment. Traumatized children often act as though there is no past and no future, just the present. And, the present becomes a repetition of what children could not change, often the script traumatized children came to believe about themselves. "I am unlovable, undeserving, and deep down, bad, damaged, or crazy." Traumatized children often appear to repeat disruptive behaviors that punctuated past rejections or losses. This puts them temporarily in control of time, but in a risky manner.

For a youth in crisis, it's as if they have climbed aboard the highest and fastest roller coaster. The gate has shut and they're off. Entreaties, warnings, or commands from adults become irrelevant. The action and excitement of risky behaviors becomes children's way of life fostered by neural patterns and repeated re-enactments with family members, at school, and the community. Unchecked, crises and danger can dominate children's lives.

Committed adults can change this cycle and help free children from this curse. Practitioners and family members can reopen children's experiences of time and join with children to become stronger than the traumatic 'monsters' of the past. Resilience can be built upon the commitment and support of children by adults who validate their experience (Farber & Egeland, 1987); someone who cares enough to listen to children and to see all sides of children in distress.

Children, however, often resist caring adults' efforts to change their lives. It often appears safer for complexly traumatized children to remain immersed in repeated crises than to risk changes and the pain of re-experiencing another breakdown of trust or attachment. Caring adults may face fiercely resistant children guarding the door to healing, reunification, or adoption.

Underneath the defiance and resistance inherent in traumatic stress reactions, caring adults can find hurt children. Therapists can help caring adults persevere with the understanding that children's 'problem behaviors' often mark their unspoken terror and can light a path to both children's pain and solutions (Kagan, 2003). Children's behaviors can guide therapists and caring adults to children's core dilemmas, often the traumas that led to the breakdowns of children's trust and attachments. Therapists can help caring adults utilize an understanding of how traumas have led to children's behaviors and have been reinforced as survival mechanisms. Rather than focusing on demands for children to stop problem behaviors, caring adults can demonstrate to children that their old behaviors are not needed anymore, that caring adults will not respond with the abuse, neglect, rejections, or abandonment that traumatized children have often come to expect, and that, together, caring adults and children can learn new ways of coping with reminders of past traumas.

Real Life Heroes® challenges children and caregivers to cross the 'threshold into a different world,' a life in which parents (biological, kinship, or adoptive) and other caring adults dare to face children's worst nightmares. This may begin with promises or legal papers, but these mean little to traumatized children. Trust requires confronting and passing the tests of fire from children's past.

The secrets of success for caring adults, just as in mythic stories, revolve around learning from each challenge (after Campbell, 1968). Hurt and hurting children provide clues to solutions. Behaviors light a path to unresolved and painful conflicts and children's deepest terrors. Claiming and guiding children helps them succeed. Blaming, labeling, and rejection foster obstacles and turmoil.

Therapists can serve as mentors to help caring adults and children learn from provocative behaviors and to remain focused on helping caring adults become heroes for their children. Therapists can help parents to understand and then detach themselves from children's behaviors, building on the caring side of family members, and empowering parents with skills, support, and a little magic in the eyes of their children. Therapists help caring adults to understand how traumas affect children and then use this understanding to add power to committed parents. Symbolically, work on *Real Life Heroes*® can help to demystify children and re-mystify and empower caring adults.

Therapists can guide caring adults to calm themselves, to step back, to listen with their hearts, to watch for patterns of behavior, and to welcome children's challenges as clues to discover their past. Troubling children often re-enact interactions stemming from past traumas. This gives returning or adoptive parents the opportunity to enter their children's 'real' world, and become 'real' parents by overcoming their worst nightmares. For caring adults and therapists, this means strengthening themselves with understanding, skills, and support so that they can feel children's pain and develop an understanding of the perceptions, beliefs, and feelings of children's worlds, no matter how frightening or how close children's terrors may be to adults' own experiences in their lives.

By accepting the challenge behind each behavior, therapists and caring adults open up solutions to children's fears, fears that typically revolve around critical traumas in their past, and often very real experiences of abandonment and violence. Therapists can use behavioral messages as keys to the doors that act as barriers, separating hurting children from the wounded children within. Crises can be utilized as the "calls to adventure" (Campbell, 1968) by which children test the reality of parents' commitment and the promises of a better life in their new world.

The Hero's Quest

The image of a hero matches the enormity of this challenge. Joseph Campbell (1968) wrote of mythic heroes' call to adventure and the hero's courage to enter unknown territory. Heroes from legends, biblical tales, and mythology have always represented mankind's effort to move forward, the creative advance (Campbell, 1968), versus the darkness of fears and the powerful forces that maintain oppression. Neglect, emotional, physical, and sexual abuse, and exposure to family and community violence continue to be the curse for children around the world, regardless of their nation's relative wealth or power. Caring adults can utilize an understanding of trauma and resilience, their experience, and courage to overcome children's nightmares. In therapy, these become real stories of struggle, risk, and transformation. And, as in all hero stories (Campbell, 1968), these heroes, children and caregivers, bring back lessons. We can learn from their stories about how to vanquish our fears and make all of our lives better.

Caregivers working to reclaim traumatized children experience "unimaginable torments, superhuman deeds, and impossible delights," like the heroes of myths and legends (Cousineau, 1990, p. 1). They must weather children's storms and overcome their nightmares with cunning, conviction, and strength. Caring adults can help children move beyond trauma and its aftermath, the terror and rage, the desecration of children's bodies, the demonization of the self, and children's adaptation to crises with hyper-vigilance, impulsivity, and distrust. And, by so doing, caregivers become true heroes for troubled (and troubling) children and their communities.

The quest requires caregivers, children, and their allies to muster the courage and their combined strength to cope with a "succession of trials" (Cousineau, 1990, p. 18). With each trial, parents, practitioners, and children challenge the power of trauma and work to learn from the past. With each success, the power of children's nightmares is reduced. 'Monsters' become real again, with weaknesses and vulnerabilities.

'Crisis,' from the Greek, referred to separation (Vogler, 1998), and in most stories and legends of heroes, crises marked both a time of loss or death of past relationships and an ordeal through which the hero of the story becomes transformed and, in essence, reborn (Campbell, 1968; Vogler, 1998). The challenge for parents and therapists is to help children overcome crises of separations, losses, and often psychological or physical violence through a series of ordeals.

Facing 'trials' means, in effect, changing children's 'present,' from repetitions of beliefs, feelings, and behaviors that leave children mired in the past. Children can be guided to experiment with new ways to cope. The adventure reopens possibilities and children's futures. Parents, practitioners, and children can rewrite the meaning of traumas and, over time, transform children's life stories from living within a state of trauma to living with trauma in the past. And, children and caregivers can learn to incorporate the strengths they have learned into reintegrated identities as heroes who care for others in their families and communities.

Courage to Tell the Story

PTSD has been defined as "unspeakable terror" (van der Kolk, 2003). Serial traumas and the breakdown of attachments often leave children (and caregivers) feeling vulnerable and ashamed for what they did or failed to do. "Shame derives its power from being unspeakable" (Brown, 2012). Shame in this sense works like a curse in ancient myths, entrapping children and caregivers in cycles of traumas. Shame is also a significant factor in Complex Trauma (Herman, 2014). Healing from serial traumas and shame means developing the courage to share the 'unspeakable,' the vulnerability and shame that keep children and caregivers feeling trapped and isolated from emotionally supportive relationships.

Courage comes from the root word 'cor,' the Latin word for 'heart'; and courage, in its original form, meant "To speak one's mind by telling all one's heart" (Brown, 2010). In its original form, courage addressed the challenge of what one felt, thought, and did over time. Courage required an integration of mind and body similar to current conceptions of trauma and healing from trauma (van der Kolk, 2014) through mindfulness, movement, neurofeedback, and attention to messages stored and expressed through the body. The original meaning of 'courage' is also similar to the pioneering concept of the "healing theory" (Figley, 1989) for family traumas that required each family members to share their experiences of what they saw, heard, smelled, touched, felt, and did, and then to use this multisensory understanding to develop a plan to prevent similar traumatic experiences from recurring, and by so doing to restore the security children need to thrive.

The *RLH Life Storybook* helps children and caregivers develop the capacity to use their minds and bodies to share what had been 'unspeakable,' to tell the story of who they are with their whole hearts. In *Real Life Heroes®*, courage means telling the story of one's life, including strengths and vulnerabilities, good times and tough times, successes and failures, proud moments, and feelings of guilt for hurting others. Telling the story reduces the power of shame and frees children (and caregivers) to develop their potential, transforming traumatized children into tomorrow's heroes who give back to others.

Stronger and Stronger

Chapter by chapter, children build stronger identities. The *RLH Toolkit* includes a chart, Stronger and Stronger, that can be copied and used to help reinforce children's progress in completing the workbook. At the end of Chapter 12 of the workbook, children can compare their drawing of themselves as a hero with their image of themselves from a 'tough time' in the past in Chapter 10. Therapists can help children visualize how they have grown while their problems stayed the same size (Rojano, 1998) or shrank in power.

Therapists can adapt the workbook to individual children by selecting the most relevant pages. The most important activities are highlighted in italics; these pages have also been found to be especially useful in assessments of critical factors for work on rebuilding attachments, grieving losses, and healing. By combining the structured approach of the *Life Storybook* with more open-ended art, music, dance, or other modalities, therapists can help children to recover important connections and skills that may have been lost after traumas and to develop solutions beyond the constraints of verbal expression.

The workbook can be used very much like a guide or map for the journey ahead. Through activities and collaborative work, children can build on strengths and resources to rewrite their life story. In this way, RLH life story work can be used not just to tell children's stories, but to rebuild stories of people who cared and will care for children through their lifetimes. The heroes in children's life stories are the real people who define what it means for children to belong to a family and a community, people with the courage to help transform hurt and hurting children into heroes for the future.

Resources

Rebuilding Attachments with Traumatized Children: Healing from Losses, Violence, Abuse and Neglect (Kagan, 2004) provides a comprehensive discussion of trauma and attachment theory, research, and detailed guidelines for therapeutic interventions, including tools for assessment and service planning, engaging parents and guardians, permanency work, and activities to promote secure attachments. *Rebuilding Attachments* includes practical tools for helping children and caring adults overcome adversity and transform themselves from victims to heroes in their own lives. Recommended resources on attachment-centered treatment include: *Attachment-Focused Family Therapy* (Hughes, 2007); *Attachment-Focused Family Therapy: Workbook* (Hughes, 2011); *The Attachment Therapy Companion: Key Practices for Treating Children and Families* (Becker-Weidman, Ehrmann, & LeBow, 2012); and *Reciprocal Influences of Attachment and Trauma: Using a Dual Lens in the Assessment and Treatment of Infants, Toddlers, and Preschoolers* (Lieberman & Amaya-Jackson, 2005).

Recommended guides to treatment of Complex Trauma include: *Treating Complex Traumatic Stress Disorders in Children and Adolescents* (Ford & Courtois, 2013) and *Treating Traumatized Children: Risk, Resilience, and Recovery* (Brom, Horenczyk, & Ford, 2009). Please also see *Principles of Trauma Therapy* (Briere & Scott, 2014) and *The Body Keeps the Score: Brain, Mind and Body in the Healing of Trauma* (van der Kolk, 2014). For treatment of young children, see *Psychotherapy with Infants and Young Children: Repairing the Effects of Stress and Trauma on Early Attachment* (Lieberman & van Horn, 2011).

The NCTSN website (www.nctsn.org) includes valuable resources for practitioners developed by the Complex Trauma Workgroup, including the Complex Trauma White Paper.

For an aid to advocacy, recruitment, and trauma training in foster care, adoption, and child and family services, see *Wounded Angels: Inspiration from Children in Crisis*, second edition (Kagan, 2017b). *Wounded Angels* includes stories of how traumatized children challenge therapists, parents, teachers, and policymakers to work together to overcome the power of terror and how practitioners can utilize children's behaviors to engage caring adults, develop effective services to overcome core dilemmas of families in crisis, and renew hope for healing after chronic and severe traumas.

Notes

1. 'Caregivers' refers to birth, kinship, and adoptive parents, grandparents, relatives, guardians, and other adults who children look to for nurture, protection, and guidance.
2. Meta-analysis research (Curtis, Ronan, & Bourdin, 2004) found a tendency toward greater treatment effects when evidence-based treatment was provided by doctoral candidates in comparison to therapists working in community programs.
3. Sections below excerpted from Kagan (2004).

Part I
RLH Life Storybook

The Pledge

Engaging Children and Caregivers with Resiliency-Focused Assessments, Service Planning, and Trauma-Informed Systems of Care

---

OBJECTIVES

- Trauma and resiliency-focused assessments are used to identify strengths, needs, and openings for engaging children, families, and service providers to work together to increase strengths and reduce the power of trauma reactions.
- Caregivers are engaged to sign *The Pledge*, committing themselves to help children develop the courage to share their experiences (thoughts, feelings, and reactions) and to work together to help children grow stronger than traumatic experiences, to learn from caregivers how to cope with 'tough times,' and to develop new skills with safety and protection by caregivers.

OVERVIEW

'Passing the Tests': Practical Strategies to Uncover Openings to Engagement and Skill-Building

Assessment in *Real Life Heroes*® is designed to open up pathways to healing. Resiliency-focused tools are utilized to identify strengths and resources, as well as needs, risks, and reasons for referral. Trauma and resiliency tools provide the 'map' and 'compass' for the therapeutic journey. In RLH, the map is a strength-based attachment and trauma-centered assessment of children and families. The compass is a service planning tool that keeps therapists and caring adults focused on core factors in RLH: Relationships, Emotional Self- and Co-Regulation, Action Cycles, and Life Story Integration. These coordinates point the way forward to help children and families move out of cycles of crises that often lead to referrals for services.

The first step in this process is engagement. Children and caregivers referred to child and family services, mental health, or juvenile justice programs have often learned to distrust therapists and case managers and to expect shaming, rejection, or abandonments from service providers. They may present as mired in cycles of high-risk crises (Kagan & Schlosberg, 1989). Engagement requires uncovering often-hidden child, family, and cultural strengths, wishes,

and dilemmas underlying behavioral problems and restoring hope that things can get better by working together by building on child, family, and cultural strengths and changing how families cope with traumatic stress.

Children and families who have experienced relational traumas and the breakdown of emotionally supportive and protective relationships often test therapists and service providers:[1]

> "I'm not tellin' you nothing."
>
> "I'm not talkin' about [dad, mom, what I did]."
>
> "I don't draw."
>
> "I don't do tests."
>
> "I can't control my anger."
>
> "Do I have to do this?"
>
> "I'm bipolar, borderline, chemically imbalanced . . ."

These tests help children find out if therapists, caregivers, and other adults will repeat patterns of interaction children have experienced, and represent tried and proven ways that children and caregivers have learned to cope with adversities that are often unknown to practitioners at the time of referral. Practitioners can welcome child and caregiver 'tests' or fight them, label them, and use them to defend treatment failures.

Engaging caregivers is facilitated by developing a partnership between professional team members and caregivers, joining together to make things better, and to accomplish child and family goals. Respect for caregivers is essential, as is getting away from blaming children, parents, or other professionals.

Therapists demonstrate respect by introducing themselves as a partner in a quest to find solutions to challenges and problems that have distressed families, rather than as an expert who will diagnose problems and prescribe what children and caregivers need to do. Therapists engage caregivers by demonstrating genuine caring and respect for caregivers' positive goals and efforts to make things better. Trauma psycho-education helps reframe problems from blaming children or parents to stress reactions that anyone could experience. This can reduce children and parents' expectations that therapists see them as bad, damaged, or unworthy. Many parents worry that something is wrong with their children or themselves. Validating parents' experiences and efforts to make things better can help establish a partnership in which parents join with therapists to overcome problems.

In RLH, the detective is the symbol of assessment as a discovery process. Using a trauma and resiliency 'lens,' practitioners can appreciate how each message provides clues to how children and families have coped. For many children, 'avoidance' works and is reinforced since anxiety goes down (Wehrenberg, 2008). The resiliency-focused clinician creates sufficient safety and incentives for children and caregivers to explore other, more effective ways to manage distress and risk. From a resiliency-focused perspective, assessment is a privilege. Practitioners honor this privilege by respecting what children and caregivers are dealing with and demonstrating how sessions can be safe and can build on the wishes and goals of children and caregivers to make things better.

Why is it that children disclose to some practitioners and not others? I have been very moved by the hundreds of children (and caregivers) who have disclosed physical, emotional, and sexual abuse to me, as well as often hidden interest and talents in a first psychological evaluation, when they haven't shared these experiences in multiple previous treatment programs and psychiatric hospitalizations. The chart below summarizes principles and strategies I've learned to uncover openings for engagement as part of a resiliency-focused assessment for traumatic stress.

Safety First

Safety messages (see *Step by Step* below) are critical in the treatment of Complex Trauma. RLH builds on standard practitioner and program safety messages about confidentiality and state and federally mandated guidelines by addressing sensitive issues following child and family experiences of traumas. The goal is to make each RLH session a special time and place, a sanctuary, where children and caregivers can feel safer to explore new possibilities.

RLH is not for everyone. Assessments are used to determine the best treatment program for each child and family and to differentiate Complex Trauma from other conditions. RLH was developed and tested for children who had experienced multiple traumas and the breakdown of emotionally supportive relationships with caregivers. RLH was also developed for children and adolescents whose cognitive, emotional, or social development is at a latency (6–12-year-old) level. Other treatment models (e.g., TF-CBT or EMDR) may be more efficient in helping children with acute traumas or children with PTSD who have a stable, emotionally supportive relationship with a nonoffending caregiver who validates children's traumatic experiences, is able and willing to participate in trauma treatment, and is committed to raising children to maturity. Contraindications for use are listed in Table P.1. Some children may require preliminary therapeutic work to develop sufficient safety for RLH treatment. However, for many children, RLH, like other trauma treatments, can be utilized with children who 'move through' predictable cycles of stability and distress and may appear "stably unstable" (Mannarino et al., 2014). Therapists can utilize the RLH format to focus on resiliency, creative arts activities, Emotional Regulation skill-building, and safety steps to expand the range of eligible children for trauma treatment.

Safety also means meeting with children and caregivers separately to determine how safe they feel with different people, including other family members or service providers. Before children are asked to share workbook materials with caring adults in or out of sessions, caring adults demonstrate that they have met the safety criteria listed in Table P.2. RLH can be provided to children and safe, supportive caregivers together. When that is not possible, separate sessions can be provided with opportunities for children to share their work in limited safe ways, a special drawing, or later in treatment. Therapists can work with caregivers to become safe by demonstrating criteria in Table P.2 and validating children's experiences, including traumas involving the caregiver. Ideally, caregivers demonstrate commitment to "protect, provide, and guide" (James, 1989, 1994) and model for children the courage to grow and change. Caregivers can do this by completing their own *Real Life Heroes Life Storybook*, or a substitute life story that includes experiences, thoughts and feelings and addresses key points in each RLH chapter.

Practitioner and Systems Development

Writing the *Life Storybook* and use of the *RLH Toolkit* should be directed by a skilled trauma therapist (psychologist, social worker, or psychiatrist) who has completed training in understanding trauma and implementing trauma treatment. The NCTSN Core Curriculum in Child

ASSESSMENT PRINCIPLES AND STRATEGIES

Assessment has multiple goals:

- To develop a picture of children's primary relationships and their level of emotional support and Emotional Regulation within each relationship.
- To track children's emotional connections and their experiences of caring, concern, and safety.
- To identify emotional conflicts in relationships.
- To develop hypotheses about what has interfered with development and what can promote growth.
- To create an integrated perspective of arousal patterns, regulation, and relationships.
- To shape a meaningful plan for the child and family within their cultural heritage.
- To work together with children, caregivers, team members, and collaterals to generate 'next steps' to learn more and test the accuracy of clinical hypotheses and formulations.
- To get the funding needed for the most effective services.
- To build service plans centered on child and caregiver goals, so children and caregivers become partners in the RLH 'journey'.
- Use of ongoing assessments of progress to reshape services to increase efficacy.

Assessment begins with each practitioner and recognition that we need to earn a child and caregiver's trust, rather than simply expect or demand it. Before starting an assessment, we can use the same self- and co-regulation steps to center and calm ourselves that we recommend for clients, and check:

- How we feel inside.
- How we see ourselves.
- How we see each child and family.
- Our goals for assessment.
- Who can help us carry out a trauma and resiliency-informed assessment.

Assessment gives us an opportunity to define ourselves or be defined by children or caregivers' expectations of what treatment means. We can use assessment to:

- Change the paradigm many children and caregivers expect from service providers.
- Demonstrate respect versus shaming.
- Demonstrate in practice how RLH involves children and family members as partners versus subjects for treatment or adversaries in a battle of wills.
- Demonstrate that 'client-driven treatment' is more than an expression by focusing on what is important to children and family members, as well as mandates from funding sources.
- Focus on uncovering pathways to healing rather than continuing old patterns and interventions that have not been successful in accomplishing child and family goals.

Assessment starts the engagement process:

- To treat 'relational trauma,' the therapist-child-caregiver relationship is critical.
- Assessment starts to define child-caregiver-therapist-team relationships.
- By including trauma and resiliency interview activities and surveys into assessment, children and caregivers see that the therapist and team are able to help them with sensitive issues they may been afraid to bring up before or felt that previous treatment providers were not able or willing to address.

Assessment is developmental:

- Children's verbal and nonverbal behaviors provide clues to their development levels for cognitive, Emotional Regulation, and social and bodily functioning. For instance, Adrianna, a 14-year-old, may have cognitive reasoning skills at an 8-year-old level, social skills more like a 5-year-old, and may react to stressors like a 2-year-old with temper tantrums (hitting, kicking, stomping).
- Using clues to the child's developmental level, we can focus on what happened at that time in Adrianna and her family's life to understand the context of how trauma reactions may have developed. For Adrianna, this included her experiencing her mother and father's fights from age 1–3, including several violent beatings. Now, at age 14, she is referred for aggressive behaviors and going '0–100' in bodily arousal. By understanding this girl's sensitivity to signals for fighting, Adrianna and her caregivers, teachers, and other caring adults can learn what triggers her reactions and help prevent trauma reactions with both preventive steps and Emotional Regulation skill-building.

ASSESSMENT PRINCIPLES AND STRATEGIES—*continued*

- Understanding the child's developmental level also helps us learn how children experience messages. This can guide how we can help caregivers, teachers, and others communicate more effectively.

Assessment is multisensory, multimodal, culturally informed and metaphorical:

- Since trauma often represents 'unspeakable terror,' therapists can use body language, nonverbal behaviors, and behavior patterns as clues to what can't be said in words.
- Tracking nonverbal expression and movement provides clues to shifting emotions in relationships.
- To guide services, practitioners also need to learn from family members the meaning of behavior patterns within the family's experiences, cultural heritage, and spiritual values.
- Practitioners can help caregivers to decode trauma reactions by looking at the coping functions of behavior patterns.

Assessment provides tools for children (and caregivers) to share important feelings and relationships:

- Assessments can use tools to open conversations about topics that children or caregivers have not been able to share.
- Use of a child and caregiver self-report trauma exposure and trauma symptom scale shows children (and caregivers) that the therapist is able to work with a range of distressing events.
- To promote nonverbal expression, therapists can bring nonverbal tools (e.g., a drum, a xylophone, markers) to offer alternative means of expression that can convey otherwise hidden feelings.

Assessment is strengths-oriented and uncovers hidden caring, talents, and interests:

- What and who do children like?
- What and who gets a smile?
- How have family members overcome adversity?
- What strengths and values have been passed down to children from their family and cultural heritage or spiritual orientation?

Assessment is multi-informed, accesses multiple sources, and is ongoing:

- Trauma- and resiliency-informed assessments include trauma exposure and symptom surveys, as well as evaluations of emotional support, protection, guidance, and skills.
- The *RLH Life Storybook* and Session Structure guides development of a shared understanding of child and family traumas and resiliency.
- Service and treatment reviews provide opportunities to expand this shared understanding and incorporate new sources of information, and point out 'next steps' for further assessment to help guide services and increase the effectiveness of treatment.

Assessment is pragmatic:

- Practitioners work in the context of time limits, required assessments, funding source mandates, and high-risk behaviors.
- Practitioners can use diagnoses (e.g., the DSM-5) to get services needed and, at the same time, use psycho-education about trauma to help families see beyond the limitations of diagnostic categories

Assessment focuses on what is most important for children and caregivers:

- What moves children and caregivers to do something to make things better?
- What are their primary concerns, fears, and goals?
- What parts of their lives make them feel good about themselves?
- What brings out their caring?
- What rekindles hope?

Assessment can be fun!

TABLE P.1

Indications and Contraindications for Use of RLH

- RLH can be used with children ages 6–12 who have experienced single or multiple types of traumas and have mild to severe symptoms of traumatic stress. RLH has also been successful with adolescents who function emotionally, socially, or cognitively in the latency range of development.

- RLH was especially developed to help practitioners working in child and family services programs with hard-to-engage children and caregivers who have experienced relational traumas and show symptoms of Complex Trauma.

- Comprehensive assessments are needed to differentiate traumatic stress from other disorders and to assess safety in children's families and homes.

- Formal inventories of dissociation may be necessary to assess children's stability and differentiate dissociation from drug-induced behaviors. Symptoms of dissociation that warrant caution and safety measures include:

  - mumbled, garbled verbalizations;

  - repetitive movements;

  - lack of awareness of time or place;

  - lack of awareness of the therapist's identity or of self;

  - trance-like movements or visual fixations;

  - sudden changes in movement that don't fit with children's stories;

  - inability to remember if they really did something or just imagined doing it;

  - not being able to remember actions observed by others;

  - finding themselves in a place and not knowing how they got there;

  - inability to feel parts of their body; and

  - hearing voices or seeing things that weren't really there.

- **RLH is not recommended for children who are actively suicidal, violent, or psychotic, or children at imminent risk of being harmed or becoming self-abusive, suicidal, violent, or engaging in life-threatening behaviors.**

TABLE P.2

Criteria for Involving Caregivers in Conjoint RLH Sessions

Caregivers demonstrate that they will keep children safe by:

- Giving children support and permission to share what they experienced.

- Validating children's experiences, including traumas involving the caring adult.

- Owning responsibility for what has happened, including failure to protect children.

- Committing themselves to protecting children from anyone, even other family members.

- Identifying how the caregiver sees children as special and part of his or her life.

- Showing they are able to manage exposure to reminders of past traumas and their own reactions without re-traumatizing children so that they can keep themselves and children safe when children share memories.

Children indicate in private to the therapist that:

- They feel safe to share with the caring adult present; and

- They are able and willing to signal to the therapist and other protective adults if they, at any time, feel unsafe with the caregiver present.

Trauma (NCTSN, 2012a) provides new practitioners with a foundation for mastering specific treatment models. Training in RLH and other Complex Trauma treatment interventions is available from the author and other model developers. When children are in foster or adoptive families, it is important that therapists are also knowledgeable about the experience of placement, permanency laws, and critical issues in foster care and adoption. See the NCTSN Guide to Empirically-Supported and Promised Practices (NCTSN, 2012b), the National Register of Evidence-Based Programs (SAMHSA), or the California Clearinghouse for Evidence-Based Child Welfare (CEBC, 2014) for details on accessing information on training programs for trauma treatments, and the Spaulding Center for Children (2014) and ATTACh (2014) for curricula to develop competence in adoption.

The therapist serves as a "witness" (Herman, 1992a) and a guide for the journey ahead, someone who is able to experience and also to contain the chaotic dysregulation of a child and family with traumatic stress. To do this, therapists need training, supervision, and support for attachment and trauma therapy. This is especially important whenever children have experienced events in which they feared someone would be seriously harmed or die from family violence, and when children appear agitated, lose awareness of what is happening around them, or act in ways that put themselves or others at risk of being hurt.

Before working with children, therapists are urged to complete the *Real Life Heroes Life Storybook* for themselves, utilizing the flexibility and creativity suggested for work with children and adults and monitoring themselves for 'triggers' and any needed work on self-protection. Therapists need to be able to keep themselves as well as children safe from secondary traumatic stress with support from supervisors, program directors, and organizational leaders. In the HEROES Project (Kagan, Henry, Richardson, Trinkle, & LaFrenier, 2014b), therapists were asked to develop and implement their own safety plan, including awareness of their own triggers, ongoing consultation, and assistance from supervisors.

For children in placement, foster or kinship parents and residential counselors play critical roles in providing support and guidance as team members implementing common 'Essential Elements of Trauma-Informed Child Welfare' (Child Welfare Collaborative Group & National Child Traumatic Stress Network, 2008). The NCTSN Resource Parent Curriculum (Grillo et al., 2010) or START (Benamati, 2004) provide curricula for trauma and resiliency-focused training for resource parents and residential counselors.

Trauma-informed treatment is very difficult to sustain in mental health and social services agencies without organizational support for implementation of trauma-informed principles and practices. Implementation of Sanctuary® (Bloom & Farragher, 2013) has been effective in promoting ongoing organizational systems change that fosters trauma-informed practices at every level of complex systems. Components of NCTSN trauma-informed systems are listed in Table P.3. RLH components for preventing, reducing, and ameliorating traumatic stress are intended for service providers as well as for children and caregivers.

TABLE P.3
NCTSN Trauma-Informed Child and Family Service System: Definition and Components

- A trauma-informed child- and family-service system is one in which all parties involved recognize and respond to the impact of traumatic stress on those who have contact with the system, including children, caregivers, and service providers. Programs and agencies within such a system infuse and sustain trauma awareness, knowledge, and skills into their organizational cultures, practices, and policies. They act in collaboration with all those who are involved with children, using the best available science, to facilitate and support the recovery and resiliency of children and families.

- A service system with a trauma-informed perspective is one in which programs, agencies, and service providers:

    1. Routinely screen for trauma exposure and related symptoms;

    2. Use culturally appropriate evidence-based assessment and treatment for traumatic stress and associated mental health symptoms;

    3. Make resources available to children, families, and providers on trauma exposure, its impact, and treatment;

    4. Engage in efforts to strengthen the resilience and protective factors of children and families impacted by and vulnerable to trauma;

    5. Address parent and caregiver trauma and its impact on the family system;

    6. Emphasize continuity of care and collaboration across child-service systems; and

    7. Maintain an environment of care for staff that addresses, minimizes, and treats secondary traumatic stress, and that increases staff resilience.

Source: NCTSN (2012a)

RLH Trauma and Resiliency-Focused Assessment and Service Planning: 'Opening the Conversation'

The key to engagement in trauma and resiliency-focused treatment is to start use of trauma assessments in the first sessions, rather than waiting until some later point when children might seem more comfortable or engaged. The problem with waiting is that children and caregivers develop an expectation of what sessions include and don't include. To start asking about experiences of domestic violence or sex abuse in later sessions may be experienced as a disruption of what may feel like an implicit contract about what sessions will address and not address.

Use of trauma exposure and symptom surveys shows children and caregivers that practitioners and team members can talk about everything from experiences of hurricanes to sex abuse. Surveys provide tools to 'open the conversation' about trauma and create openings for engagement. Children and caregivers see that therapists and therapeutic team members go beyond overt behaviors and are able and willing to help families deal with what is most important.

Typically, trauma assessment tools are initiated in the first or second sessions. In a traditional 45–60-minute session format (Clarkson-Hendrix, 2011), the first session would focus on what children and caregivers are looking for (goals), assessment of who's important to children and their relationships to key people in their lives (an ecomap), and gathering information about children's developmental level, attachments, special interests, talents, strengths, family and cultural values, and behavioral problems leading to referral. The second session would include trauma exposure and symptom surveys completed by caregivers and children, behavioral surveys, attachment measures, and any required surveys for funding sources. The third session would include introducing RLH if appropriate, with the *RLH Life Storybook*, contracting with caregivers and children on an initial service plan using the *RLH Trauma and Resiliency-Focused Assessment and Service Plan* (see Part V), and laying out a plan for regular *RLH Service Plan Reviews* typically every 6–12 weeks to help keep treatment focused on achieving child and caregiver goals. This structure can be easily adapted to 'open access' assessment and service programs, home-based, clinic-based, foster care, or residential treatment programs with varying lengths of time for initial assessments. 'Collaborative documentation' is encouraged wherever possible to promote child and caregiver ownership of service plans and to fit assessment and service planning within practitioner time limitations.

Use of the *RLH Trauma and Resiliency-Focused Assessment and Service Plan* ensures that assessments address core components of assessment identified in evidence-supported treatment for Complex Trauma (Cook et al., 2003; Ford & Cloitre, 2009), including: child and caregiver goals, developmental level, relationships, Emotional Regulation, Action Cycles (child and family interaction patterns), and level of Life Story Integration of significant experiences. Each of these components guides the practitioner to shape interventions that can engage children and caregivers to work in trauma treatment.

Client-owned treatment begins with practitioners and other team members demonstrating that they will listen and heed the goals of children and caregivers. Service plans are shaped to achieve these goals. The challenge in child and family services is to frame services that are mandated by funding sources with the reality and heartfelt goals of children and caregivers when a large percentage of children and families are mandated or feel pressured by authorities to work in treatment programs. Safety is always essential, and messages from children that homes, siblings, caregivers, neighborhoods, or schools are unsafe must always be heeded. In addition, messages from caregivers that they are unwilling or unable to stop dangerous behaviors, or that they cannot or do not plan to nurture, guide, or protect their children, should also be respected and used to shape realistic service plans. In mental health services, DSM-5 diagnoses and ICD codes can be used to justify funding for Complex Trauma treatment with diagnoses for: anxiety disorders, trauma and stress-related disorders, depressive disorders, disruptive, impulse-control and conduct disorders, and bipolar and related disorders when traumatic experiences and reactions play a central role. V codes in the DSM-5 can be used to frame the context for traumatic experiences (e.g., physical abuse). A diagnosis of PTSD is not necessary to justify Complex Trauma treatment given the limitations of the current diagnostic standards and lack of a diagnosis for Complex Trauma or Developmental Trauma Disorder (van der Kolk, 2005).

Understanding children's developmental level is critical for focusing treatment on the point in children's development when social and emotional development was stymied and using behavioral management interventions geared to child's developmental level of cognitive reasoning and self-regulation.

Focusing on a broad network of relationships with family members, potential mentors, and peers expands the possibilities for building (or rebuilding) supportive connections for children (or caregivers) who feel unsupported and alone. Service plans can target renewing or strengthening relationships, or learning about and grieving important relationships that have been lost. Targeting relationships within the first few minutes of assessments helps convey to children that this treatment will focus on who is most important in their lives, who is 'there for them,' and opens up possibilities for children who feel isolated and hopeless.

Emotional regulation is assessed in the context of primary relationships identified by asking children to complete the *Circles of Caring* (included in Part V). Children are then asked to rate their feelings when they are with the most important people in their lives using *My Thermometers* (included in Part V) to gauge the children's subjective feelings of stress, self-control, anger, sadness, happiness, and safety, along with attachment-focused interview questions outlined below (see Step by Step). This gives practitioners a quick attachment-centered ecomap of children's comfort and emotional self- and co-regulation with important people in their family and community.

Assessing attachment patterns increases the probability of effectively connecting with children and caregivers and utilizing effective treatment interventions. Relational traumas can break down trust and security in primary relationships, the child's 'protective shield,' and also shape arousal patterns. Complex trauma typically follows childhood exposure to unpredictable and uncontrollable dangers and when children's attachments with caregivers who nurture and protect them have been disrupted or never were formed (Cicchetti & Lynch, 1995). RLH interventions are shaped to match the type of attachment and arousal patterns frequently demonstrated by children and caregivers. This is outlined for three types of insecure attachments in Table P.4.

Strategies for children with anxious and chaotic disorganized attachments include helping children and caregivers learn to recognize signs of stress, to welcome these signs as signals from their bodies, and then implement *Power Plans* developed in Chapter 4. Caregivers can minimize stress reminders, where possible, preparing children to deal with predictable stress reminders, by watching children for signs of distress, and then by reassuring children of the caregivers' presence to counter the children's fears. Children can practice *Power Plans* that work for them and include mind-body activities that help them focus and stay modulated. This can include SOS for Stress (in Chapter 1), with slow breathing, imagery of safe places where children felt cared for, and emotional support from caregivers. Children can be encouraged to use the energy in anxiety to do something productive that reinforces feeling good and to use exercises in Chapter 8 to change beliefs from "I'm bad, unworthy, damaged, sick, hateful, unwanted," to "I can help others. I can do these good things: ___ , ___ ."

Strategies for children who present with avoidant attachments include helping caregivers learn to recognize signs of stress and consistently guiding children to focus on goals and increasing their motivation to implement *Power Plans* to achieve goals. Experiential activities can also build greater attunement and empathy for others.

Attachment and arousal patterns are also linked to children and caregivers' typical interaction patterns (Action Cycles) and the developmental level of the family. Session and 'homework' activities are promoted to build on caring and goals of family members and to increase the use of interaction patterns that counter trauma reaction patterns identified in the assessment. Activities and interventions build the security for children to safely share traumatic experiences while working together with caring adults to create a healing strategy (Figley, 1989) to prevent or minimize repetition of traumatic reaction patterns. To make this work, new interaction patterns need to be practiced in sessions, at home, and in other parts of children's worlds (e.g., school classrooms).

TABLE P.4
Insecure Attachment Patterns, Arousal Levels, and Intervention Strategies[2]

Attachment Pattern	Ambivalent/Preoccupied	Dismissive/Avoidant	Chaotic Disorganized
Arousal Patterns	Hyper	Hypo	Hypo to hyper cycles often in response to subtle relational cues
Relationship Behaviors	Clingy, dependent; worries about caregiver or caregiver behaviors; fearful of rejections or abandonments	Flat affect; superficial or detached responses to others; little or no eye contact, looking away or down; shares little of substance about self; detached, avoids close relationships; lacks trust; does not expect caring, believes must take care of themselves on their own	Rapid impulsive shifts from dependent to avoidant, from regulated 'in control' to dysregulated 'out of control' and from clingy to detached; appears unpredictable without understanding children's experiences of caregivers; may move toward people or challenges and then pull away abruptly; dissociation used when children can't physically escape stressors
Problem Behaviors	Reactive; agitated; fear-driven	Planned; goal-driven; lack of sensitivity to others; does not accept responsibility	Reactive; dysregulated; impulsive; limited awareness, understanding, or reasoning; poor problem-solving
Intervention Strategy Examples	Provide safety and reassurance of primary relationships; prepare for transitions; use soft voices, calm and caring facial demeanors; avoid loud demands that could increase arousal level; provide multisensory self- and co-regulation activities that begin at child's arousal level and are not overwhelming	Engage children and caregivers to work on goals; outline and enforce clear limits and consequences; increase motivation to achieve children's goals by complying with home, school, and community standards; stay calm when children provoke; utilize understanding that children may be repeating behaviors linked to past traumas or testing limits; increase and maintain commitment for supervision (24/7) by caregivers with community and family support	Provide intervention strategies for both anxious and avoidant attachments; engage and empower caregivers to provide consistency, 24/7, across service systems; when caregivers or therapists make a mistake (e.g., do not keep a promise), acknowledge the mistake, apologize, and re-commit to keeping commitments and overcoming challenges that serve as trauma reminders leading to dysregulation

Prioritization of Treatment

RLH focuses treatment and session plans on two primary factors of Complex Trauma: the breakdown of emotionally supportive and protective relationships with caregivers and the dysregulation of children's (and often caregivers') affect, cognitions, social relationships, and bodily functioning. Assessments of the strength (Low to High) of emotionally supportive enduring relationships and the level of the child's self-regulation are used to guide the focus for service and session plans. This is illustrated in Table P.5. below, which is included in the RLH Trauma & Resiliency-Focused Assessment and Service Plan for each child.

Children and families with Complex Trauma typically cycle up and down in levels of self- and co-regulation in response to stressors (e.g., poverty, violence, financial insecurity, environmental threats) that may not be known to practitioners. As described above, RLH provides two easy-to-use tools, the *Circles of Caring* and *My Thermometers* (included in Part V) to help practitioners quickly assess a child's level of emotional support and emotional regulation. Use of these two tools from the beginning of treatment helps practitioners guide use of time for activities in each session to maximize the child and caregiver's staying within their capacity for self- and co-regulation. At the same time, prioritization helps direct the practitioner to activities that can optimally help the child and family move to greater levels of security and stability.

Focusing on the child and caregiver's levels of self-regulation and emotionally supportive relationships increases engagement in initial sessions and helps maintain engagement by demonstrating that practitioners will adapt sessions and service plans to best meet changing situations and needs. RLH is a flexible system that promotes continued work, step by step, on components of Complex Trauma treatment while helping children, caregivers and practitioners stay safe, within everyone's "window of tolerance" (Siegel, 1999).

Prioritization of treatment also reflects the child's developmental level in respect to the RLH core components (REAL): **R**elationships, **E**motional Regulation, **A**ction Cycles, and **L**ife Story Integration. It is helpful to estimate children's developmental levels for each component in terms of their highest levels of current functioning with support and also their levels of functioning during stress reactions. For example, a 15-year-old youth may demonstrate social relationships and emotional regulation at a level typical of 12-year-olds much of the time but, when triggered by reminders of past traumas, the youth may revert to social relationships and emotional regulation more typical of 4-year-olds. The developmental age shown in trauma reactions often reflects when traumatic events disrupted children's trust and basic attachments. Accordingly, estimating the developmental age during trauma reactions can help focus assessments of trauma exposure.

TABLE P.5
Treatment Priorities[3] for Sessions and Service Plans

	STRENGTH OF EMOTIONALLY SUPPORTIVE ENDURING RELATIONSHIPS		
	High	**Medium**	**Low**
High	**Transforming** Trauma Integration with Caregivers Self-Image, Identity, Future Goals Promoting Enduring Relationships **Chapters 1–12**	**Integrating** Attachments, Caregiver Regulation, and Life Story Integration Strengthen Relationships and Caregiver's Capacity to Manage Stress and Triggers; *Caregiver Power Plan* Accepting What Happened **Chapters 1–12**	**Strengthening** Attachments and Support Search for and Strengthen Supportive Relationships; Recover Memories of Caring; Caregiver Skills, Resources, and Modulation; Child Self-Care *With or without* Caregiver **Chapters 1–7**
Medium	**Integrating** Regulation with Caregiver Guidance and Life Story Integration Stress Management Skills for Triggers, Co-Regulation, Self-Image and Future Goals Accepting What Happened **Chapters 1–12**	**Integrating** Attachments, Regulation for Child and Caregiver, Life Story Integration Strengthen Supportive Relationships, Memories of Caring; *Power Plans* to Manage Stress and Triggers; Regulation and Co-Regulation Accepting What Happened **Chapters 1–12**	**Coping** Attachments, Regulation and Support Supportive Relationships, Recover Memories of Caring; Affect Regulation Skill-Building; Child Self-Care *With or without* Caregiver **Chapters 1–7**
Low	**Strengthening** Affect Regulation and Co-Regulation, *Power Plans*, Memories of Caring **Chapters 1–7**	**Coping** Affect Regulation and Co-Regulation, Memories of Caring, *Power Plans* **Chapters 1–7**	**Restoring Safety** Safety 'SOS' Skill-Building, Protective Relationships, Community Support and Hope, Affect Regulation, Child Self-Care *With or without* Caregiver **Chapters 1–4**

Left axis label: CHILD SELF-REGULATION

For some youths, the developmental levels for current functioning and during trauma reactions may be similar for **R**elationships, **E**motional Regulation, **A**ction Cycles, and **L**ife Story Integration. Other youths may have different levels for each of the REAL components. Assessment of these levels can help guide service planning. Table P.6 illustrates how this framework can guide prioritization of core components at different stages of treatment.

The *Circles of Caring* and *My Thermometers* can be repeated at service reviews (e.g., every 6–12 weeks), along with other standardized assessment tools, to help teams assess progress, identify challenges, and work together to develop more appropriate service plans. The team process for maintaining focus on RLH core components is provided in the *RLH Service Plan Review* (included in Part V).

Introducing the *Life Storybook*

As noted above, in a typical behavioral health or home-based program, the first two to three sessions would address elements of the *RLH Trauma and Resiliency-Focused Assessment and Service Plan*, along with required surveys or interviews for the program. The next session

TABLE P.6
Developmental Assessment-Driven Treatment Planning

Treatment Component	Developmental Age Highest level (with support) to lowest level (trauma reaction)	Priority
Relationships: Emotional Support Commitment Guidance		
Emotional Regulation: Self-Regulation Co-Regulation		
Action Cycles: (Interactive Patterns) Learning Caring Helping Others Having Fun		
Life Story Integration: Positive Memories Trauma Experiences		

would be used for contracting. If children and caregivers have experienced significant traumatic stressors, show mild to severe levels of trauma symptoms, and are sufficiently stable for psychotherapy (see Table P.1), then practitioners can introduce the *RLH Life Storybook* to caregivers and children.

In contracting sessions, it is important to demonstrate how caregivers are needed to help children change behavior patterns and reduce traumatic stress. This can be facilitated by using the Introduction to Traumatic Stress and *Real Life Heroes®* for Caregivers (included in Part V) or by pulling out a copy of the *RLH Life Storybook* and referring to the Introduction for Parents and Caring Adults. Both include a brief description of traumatic stress, core components of RLH treatment, how RLH works in sessions, and skill and relationship goals. Therapists can share the workbook to illustrate what will be covered. The workbook provides structure and enhanced safety for working with the therapist. Children and caregivers can see visually how treatment focuses on strengths and skill development, that treatment is similar to workbooks that children and adolescents commonly complete, and that RLH treatment has boundaries and limits, rather than requiring an open-ended commitment to what may seem like a 'forever' process of examining child and family pathology.

The emphasis on heroes can be introduced as a way to help children build on their interests and skills, and to learn from the strengths in people they admire in their families, communities, and cultural networks. Focusing on heroes moves children and caregivers away from typical emphasis on pathologies and diagnoses, and provides a means to engage children in a shared quest, using creative arts activities to work, step by step, with a therapist to build skills and confidence. In this context, life story work can be introduced as an adventure. The therapist serves as a guide, committed to helping children and caregivers overcome whatever obstacles lie ahead. And, the *Life Storybook* provides the structure for keeping the quest safe and moving forward, utilizing activities and the Session Structure to foster skill development and to reshape beliefs and behaviors that have hindered children's development.

Therapists can encourage children and caring adults to utilize the workbook to uncover or strengthen special 'qualities' in themselves, in their families, and in the people who care (or cared) about them, the special qualities that have helped them through good times and bad. In this way, life story work becomes an invitation to regain power in their lives. For traumatized children and adults, this means moving from a history of victimization to an understanding of oneself as a hero in one's own story and to enlarge this story with a past, a present, and a future. In RLH, the goal is to help children and caregivers change a life story focused on a stress-filled struggle to survive to a shared 'journey' in which children and caregivers revive caring, connections, and commitment to help each other learn to thrive.

Mentors for the Therapeutic 'Journey'

> **Transforming a stress-filled struggle to survive into a shared quest to revive and thrive**

As in all quests, it helps to work with a mentor, someone who models for children how it is possible to overcome problems and who recognizes special qualities in children. The therapist servers as a mentor but also as a guide to the larger quest. When children are living apart from biological parents, foster parents or extended family members can often become especially important mentors. It is very valuable to engage children to develop their special talents with a mentor who can function outside of the family and therapy sessions. It is not necessary that a mentor know exactly how children can succeed, but rather a mentor shows children that there is a way out of difficult situations, and what may seem to be hopeless quandaries can be solved. Mentors can be paid or volunteers recruited by therapists or already part of children's lives. Relatives or older siblings can often provide mentoring for children. Clergy, coaches, drama teachers, local musicians, and skilled craftspeople may also provide mentoring. Caring adults can also serve as mentors.

Ideally, mentors are people who have experienced some of the adversity affecting children and have found ways to utilize their experiences to foster special skills. The mentor can then pass along these special skills, enabling children to succeed. In keeping with the theme of heroes, mentors can be asked to facilitate children's sharing what they learned in the future with others.

A temporary mentor and a therapist, however, are insufficient when children lack a safe home and a nurturing adult committed to raising children to maturity. For children in placement or children who lack a safe home with a non-offending caring and committed guardian, the first step in the therapeutic journey needs to involve rebuilding children's sense of hope that they can rebuild (or build) secure and supportive relationships. Service plans and therapeutic goals often need to explicitly target searching for, finding, and strengthening relationships between children and safe, caring, committed adults.

The Pledge

Caregivers, therapists, and other caring adults involved in children's treatment are asked to sign a statement at the beginning of the *RLH Life Storybook* that explicitly gives children permission to share their feelings, thoughts, and perceptions. Adults commit themselves to validate children's experiences and to work to help children increase their skills and reduce traumatic stress reactions. Signing *The Pledge* represents a contract between the therapist, caregivers, mentors, and other team members and caring adults committed to helping children.

Children who have experienced relational traumas have learned they cannot trust adults saying something or signing a piece of paper. With this in mind, therapists can help shape use of the *Life Storybook* activities and Session Structure to help children develop the courage to find out whether they can truly share what they think, feel, and remember, and whether the adults in their lives will really work to make children's worlds safe enough for them to 'tell the story' of what they experienced. RLH tools and sessions can help caregivers demonstrate that they can be trusted.

Service Plans and Reviews

Signing *The Pledge* can become part of a formal service plan to achieve child and caregiver goals and address identified needs. The RLH Trauma and Resiliency-Focused Assessment and Service Plan can be used to guide development of interventions that target identified needs and to engage service providers to focus on key elements of trauma-informed, resiliency-focused treatment, including: validation of the child and caregiver's goals, developmentally targeted interventions, phase-based interventions, ongoing assessment, and developing strategies to overcome challenges.

The *RLH Service Plan Review* (included in Part IV) keeps team members working together to provide integrated resiliency-focused treatment. *Service Plan Reviews* engage caregivers, children, and team members to review how services are working and update goals, services, and treatment strategies. Consistency and fidelity is provided by focusing progress on developing core components (REAL): Relationships (nurture, guidance, protection), Emotional Self- and Co-Regulation, Action Cycles (what helps children modulate and what increases trauma reactions), and Life Story Integration (traumatic events, beliefs, strengths, identity). *Service Plan Reviews* also identify obstacles and challenges, strategies to overcome challenges (including additional or revised assessments or services), action plans (who will do what, by when), and comments by children and caregivers. The *Service Plan Review* includes a prioritization chart (see Table P.7) to help focus team members

TABLE P.7
Service Review Prioritization

Core Components	Priority: 1, 2, 3, 4
Relationships and Permanency[4]	
Emotional Self- and Co-Regulation:[5] Child	
Emotional Self- and Co-Regulation:[6] Caregivers	
Emotional Self- and Co-Regulation; Preventing Sec. PTSD	
Action: 'Safety First'; Replace Trauma Reaction Cycle with Power Plans	
Action: Replace Trauma Reaction Cycle with Power Plans	
Action: Activities, Skills, Talents, Interests	
Life Story Integration	

on core components with the option to write in additional high-priority objectives. Priority levels are rated from 1 to 4 based on team consensus, which, in turn, drives prioritization of action plans:

1. Not a significant problem at this time (1–2 times a year, little risk, or can be deferred).
2. Occasionally a significant problem (1–2 times a month, low risk, or can be deferred).
3. Frequently a significant problem (1–2 times a week, moderate risk, needs attention soon).
4. Critical problem (almost every day, high risk, or needs immediate attention).

STEP BY STEP

Team and Program Development	Engage program and agency leaders and conduct an initial evaluation of organizational readiness with the Trauma-Informed System Change instrument (Richardson, Coryn, Henry, Black-Pond, & Unrau, 2012) and the Professional Quality of Life: Compassion Satisfaction and Fatigue Version 5 (Stamm, 2009) to assess program implementation of trauma-informed practices and secondary traumatic stress (or similar measures).
	Develop an integrated training program that provides a common foundation in trauma and resiliency-informed treatment for all program staff and caregivers involved in services. Use of the NCTSN 'Essential Elements for Child Welfare' (Chadwick Trauma-Informed Systems Project, 2013) is recommended for child and family service organizations along with NCTSN curricula, including:
	• The Resource Parent Curriculum, *Caring for Children Who Have Experienced Traumatic Stress* (Grillo, Lott, & Foster Care Subcommittee, 2010) is recommended for foster, kinship, and

adoptive parents, as well as adaptations for residential counselors and in-home family support workers.

- *The Child Welfare Trauma Training Toolkit* (2nd edition) (Child Welfare Collaborative Group, National Child Traumatic Stress Network, & The California Social Work Education Center, 2013) for social services administrators, supervisors, and workers.
- *Juvenile Justice Curriculum* (NCTSN, 2012d).
- *Educators Curriculum* (NCTSN, 2008)

Provide an introduction to RLH and the roles of team members in RLH in implementation including use of the *RLH Service Plan Review*.

Develop teams to learn, adapt, and evaluate use of RLH to achieve program and agency mission and goals with 'plan-do-study-act' organizational development practices linked to QI, program development, and program evaluation.

Develop agency and program policies and procedures to implement and sustain trauma and resiliency-focused services.

Assessment Framework	Utilize the Trauma and Resiliency-Focused Assessment and Service Plan to guide assessments in treatment programs for traumatic stress. Trauma assessments typically follow trauma screening and are ideally conducted by therapists who will continue to work with children and caregivers in treatment so children do not have to repeat information. Focus assessments on uncovering openings to engage children and youths by searching for what is most important, strengths, primary needs, and obstacles to resolving traumatic stress reactions. Demonstrate that the therapist is able to talk about and help children and caregivers deal with traumatic events and will not shame children or caregivers. See children and caregivers separately unless this is unsafe or not possible. Avoid asking sensitive questions of children with caregivers present until children have demonstrated they feel safe sharing with caregivers and that caregivers have demonstrated they are committed to caring for, protecting, and validating children's experiences. Bring multimodal tools (e.g., a drum or xylophone, squish balls or fidget toys) to show that the therapist uses multisensory tools and respects multiple means of expression. Use standardized trauma measures of trauma exposure and trauma symptoms to open up conversations about traumatic experiences.
Welcome Children and Caregivers	Thank children and/or caregivers for meeting with practitioner. Outline use of first 1–3 sessions to learn about child and caregiver goals, strengths, and needs, followed by a planning session or review conference to discuss assessments and develop a treatment or service plan that addresses child and caregiver goals and meets program or funding source requirements. The following sample protocol can be adapted as an introduction to this three-session format for many programs: *First Session with Therapist:* Therapist introduces self. "I work with children and parents on dealing with the good things that happened, and the very hard things. Girls, boys, moms, dads, grandmas, and grandpas have told me about all kinds of things they have gone through: good times where they felt cared for, vacations, holidays, and hard times like hurricanes, car accidents, moms hurting dads, dads hurting moms, children being hurt by grown-ups, children being touched sexually. And, I've heard how boys, girls, moms, dads . . . make things better." "In the _____ program, we take the first three sessions to get to know what you are looking for, what's working well, and what you'd like to change. In our first session, I want to hear what you and [caregivers] are looking for. In the second session, I usually ask some questions and do

	some surveys to help us put together a plan to help you reach your goals. Then, in our third session [in some programs this may be called a medical review, or a contracting review meeting], I'll share some ideas and see what you think. Anything we do has to work for you and your mom, dad, [cite only safe caregivers with legal guardianship]. We will also have to fill out some forms along the way for _____ [funding source]."
	After this introduction, I would go on with safety messages and then introduce the *Circles of Caring* and *My Thermometers* (see below).
	Second Session with Therapist: One of the ways we learn about children is to find out if they have experienced anything that they felt was scary, dangerous, or violent [show UCLA PTSD Scale, Trauma History Checklist, or another trauma exposure scale]. This is a very short list of questions. For example, were you in a hurricane?
	Similarly, introduce other surveys utilized, such as the Trauma Symptom Checklist for Children (TSCC).
	Third Session with Therapist: "Now, I'd like to get your thoughts and share some impressions from our first two sessions, the goals you listed, and the surveys you filled out, so we can put together a plan." This can be adjusted to meet program requirements. See *RLH Service Plan Review* in Part V for an outline.
Safety Messages; Safety Signal	In addition to required confidentiality and safety messages, acknowledge expectations, promote sharing, and identify a signal that the child or caregiver can use to signal if they are becoming too distressed. Children must feel free to be able to signal or say, "Stop, I need to take a break," and then be able to utilize some form of distraction, imagery, tension release, physical exercise, prayer, or meditation that works to soothe themselves. This should be a nonverbal signal (after Shapiro, 2001) as children with traumatic stress often lose the capacity for verbal communication. For example:[7]
	"I'm a psychologist [social worker, psychiatrist, nurse] and I ask 'nosy' questions. I talk to children coming into [program name] about what happened in their lives that were good, things that they like to do, and things they didn't like, including things that were scary, dangerous, or violent. There's nothing you have to tell me. I'm going to count on you to stop me if I ask things that are too hard to talk about. How do you let people know people when they are asking about things that are making you too stressed?"
	After identifying a signal, it is helpful to add, "I may need to ask your help if I miss the signal . . . " These messages help to reduce the pressure on therapists and keep the responsibility for informing regulation on the child or caregiver.
Circles of Caring	Utilize *Circles of Caring*[8] in the first 15 minutes of individual assessment with children to focus on their perception of who is important in their lives.
	Use directions listed and ask children to write in names.
	If children have trouble doing this, they can draw in pictures of people or ask the therapist to write in names.
	Ask children to circle the names of those people who they trust enough that they could tell those people what happened during the best and worst times in their life: what they saw, heard, thought, and felt.
	Note missing people from children's families, including people who children do not want to put in their circles. For instance, if children put 'dad' outside the circles, it will be important to learn about their fathers.
My Thermometers and **Attachment Ecogram**	Introduce *My Thermometers* (in Part V) after children complete *Circles of Caring*.
	Assess how children feel with important people listed in the inner circle, and other important people identified by the therapist, to develop a social emotional ecomap. Ask children:

	"If _____ [e.g., your mother] were here with us today in this room, where would she be sitting?
	"Show me how you would be feeling on the thermometers if she [e.g., your mother] was here with us."
	"If I asked _____ [e.g., your mother], what were some of the things she liked the best about you, what would she say?"
	"If I asked _____ [e.g., your mother] what were some of her biggest concerns about at _____ [age of child],what would she say?"
	"If I asked _____ [e.g., your mother] what would be her greatest wish for you at this age, what would she say?"
	Use information gathered in the RLH Trauma and Resiliency-Focused Assessment and Service Plan (Part V) to chart an initial social, emotional ecomap of children's primary relationships.
Attachment-Focused Screening Survey and Important People Questionnaire	Use the Attachment-Focused Screening Survey (in Part V), or similar tools, to help children share feelings, perceptions of themselves and relationships with significant others, and to identify depression, dissociation, and substance abuse issues as part of a comprehensive assessment. The Attachment-Focused Screening Survey is intended to complement trauma exposure and symptom assessments, and includes projective sentence completion questions, depression/dissociation/substance abuse screening, and drawings.
	Use interview questions, including the Important People Questionnaire (in Part V), to identify caregivers who helped children in the past and who could be resources in the present. This survey can be used as a verbal interview or a self-report measure.
Standardized Assessment Measures	Comprehensive assessments are recommended, including standardized tests in the following categories:
	• Trauma exposure and trauma symptom scales completed by children and caregivers. These scales help therapists start a conversation about traumatic events and show children (and caregivers) that the therapist is able to talk about a range of distressing events:
	– The UCLA PTSD Reaction Index for DSM-IV, Child, Adolescent, and Parent versions (Pynoos, Rodriquez, Steinberg, Stuber, & Frederick, 1998) provides combined trauma exposure and symptom scales for children and caregivers.
	– The Trauma History Checklist and Interview (Habib & Labruna, 2006) provides a trauma exposure interview for adolescents that can be modified for children (available free of charge).
	– The Child PTSD Symptom Scale-CPSS (Foa, Johnson, Feeny, & Treadwell, 2001) provides a trauma symptom scale (available free of charge).
	– The CROPS and PROPS (Greenwald & Rubin, 1999b) provide low-cost child and caregiver symptom scales.
	• A broad symptom survey completed by children and caregivers. Recommended surveys include:
	– The Trauma Symptom Checklist for Children-TSCC (Briere, 1996) provides a highly validated self-report measure with validity scales.
	– The CANS-Trauma version provides a broad practitioner-administered survey that includes interviews with caregivers about a wide range of symptoms, including trauma symptoms. Specialized training is required for this test.
	• Behavior rating scales are useful for differentiating anxiety reactions from ADHD and disruptive behavior problems and for outcome assessments. Recommended surveys include:
	– Ohio Mental Health Consumer Outcomes System Ohio Youth Problem, Functioning, and Satisfaction Scales: Parent Rating—Short Form and Youth Rating—Short Form.
	– The Conners Parent Rating Scale, Long Version (Conners, 1997).
	– Child Behavior Checklist (Achenbach & Rescoria, 2000b).

	• Measures of relationships and attachments. Recommended surveys include:
	  – The Security Scale (Kerns et al., 1996).
	  – Resiliency Scales (Pearson Clinical & Embury, 2007) includes self-report scales for mastery, relationships, and reactivity.
	
	• Caregiver and practitioner well-being and secondary traumatic stress scales are recommended as part of trauma-informed systems interventions (e.g., the ProQOL for practitioner and caregiver compassion satisfaction, secondary PTSD, compassion fatigue).
	
	Projective tests can help engage children to share expectations about relationships and their perceptions of who they can trust or not trust. Use of the Roberts Apperception Test (Roberts, 1986) and Projective Storytelling Cards (Casebeer Art Productions, 1989) can also open up conversations about difficult issues.

Introduction to RLH	For children who meet the criteria for use of RLH (Table P.1), invite caregivers and children to look over the *RLH Life Storybook* and introduce its use to help children and caregivers build on child, family, and cultural strengths to build skills, improve relationships, and reduce stress reactions that have been leading to problems at home, school, or other situations. Introduce workbook activities, including drawing, tapping rhythms, making up music, acting out stories, and other creative arts. Show how RLH can be different than more traditional counseling. Stress emphasis on unleashing creativity and encouraging expression of feelings, passions, and development of connections through empathy and helping others. Share RLH Introduction to Traumatic Stress and *Real Life Heroes®* for Caregivers or Introduction for Caregivers in the *RLH Life Storybook* to provide brief overview of traumatic stress, how RLH works, and description of chapters. Address caregiver and child goals and values and share how RLH can help them address needs and build on strengths shared in initial sessions. Emphasize how RLH is resiliency-focused and has been successful in pilot studies with children and families (e.g., "*Real Life Heroes®* is a strength-based treatment program for managing stress and improving relationships with parents, family members, and other caregivers. *Real Life Heroes®* helps children, parents, and families to decrease problem behaviors related to traumatic stress following difficult or traumatic experiences such as severe illness or injury, deaths, neglect, emotional, physical, or sexual abuse, family violence, community or school violence."). Show how RLH builds skills and strengths as building blocks to achieve child and family goals using the pyramid in the Introductions for Caregivers in Part V and the *RLH Life Storybook*. Stress the critical role of caregivers in RLH work and how use of RLH can help caregivers gain or rebuild respect as they help their children to develop the skills, courage, and confidence to learn new ways to solve problems and succeed at home, school, and in the community.
The Pledge	Ask children to write in their names on *The Pledge*. Invite caregivers and other service providers who will be involved in RLH sessions to sign *The Pledge*. Stress how caregivers are committing themselves to help children and that this book is for children to use to share whatever they think, remember, or feel.
Service Plans	Use the RLH Trauma and Resiliency-Focused Assessment and Service Plan (in Part V) to guide initial service plans. Reinforce safety messages and the child and caregiver's safety signals. Focus interventions and treatment to achieve children's and caregiver's goals. Adapt interventions to match children's emotional, social, and cognitive level of development.

	Develop intervention strategies based on children's attachment and arousal patterns (Table P.4).

Use criteria for involving caregivers in sessions (Table P.2).

Arrange for mentors to help develop creative arts or other special skills in areas of interest whenever possible (e.g., music, theater arts, or sports) to promote expressive skills, confidence, and self-esteem. Mentoring is especially important for children who have fewer than three safe, caring adults committed to helping children into adulthood. Mentors need to commit to minimally a six-month relationship, but it works best when children can continue to work with a mentor for several years, and ideally to maturity. Mentors should have training in understanding trauma and trauma behaviors, as well as preparation and ongoing consultation at least once a month with children's therapists on how to deal with predictable trauma-related behaviors.

Prioritize services and sessions based on children's self-regulation and level of emotionally supportive relationships (Table P.5).

Use RLH Strategy and Activity Guide in Part V for recommended activities matched to Service Plan Priorities (e.g., safety).

For children in placement or at high risk of placement, service plans need to include efforts to find or strengthen children's relationships with both a primary and a back-up caregiver who could raise children to maturity. |
| **Initial Safety Plans** | Plan with caregivers and team members to utilize separate individual sessions to begin work with potential caring adults and children with the understanding that children's work will be shared when safe, with children's consent, and with protection established for each disclosure. Confidentiality, as in all therapeutic work, is limited by requirements to report neglect and abuse or dangers to children and adults to appropriate authorities. Separate sessions for children are essential until parents/guardians validate children's experiences of trauma and implement viable safety plans.

Develop, implement, and practice safety plans with caregivers and team members to address known threats to children and caring adults and 'triggers' leading to trauma reactions.

Safety plans need to include:

- Identification of triggers and indicators leading to past crises.
- Strategies prepared in advance to help caring adults and children stay in control.
- A list of names and phone numbers of safe caring adults children can contact in every part of their day: at school, after-school programs, at home, etc.
- What each adult identified in the safety plan and children can do to prevent another cycle of violence.
- A plan to practice implementation of safety plans on a frequent enough basis to make them feel natural and expected when triggers are identified.

Therapists need to be able to keep themselves as well as children safe. Therapists should develop and implement their own safety plans, including awareness of their own triggers, ongoing consultation, and assistance from supervisors.

At the beginning of work, it is helpful to normalize how intense feelings are a normal part of healing. Remembering past events can rekindle both happy and painful feelings, including sadness, loneliness, or anger. It is also natural for children (and adults) to sometimes remember other events after sessions. This can be presented as a natural process in developing strength as a person and mastering old problems.

For children in placement because of abuse or neglect, essential safety steps need to include messages to the children from the first days of placement and repeated at review conferences (see Kagan, 2004), including:

- what needs to happen to restore safety and caring in their families;
- what will be done to help their parents or guardians;
- what their parents are doing to work on reuniting; |

	• a back-up (concurrent) plan if parents are unable or unwilling to work on reuniting; • who will keep the children safe during placement; and • what children can do while parents work to reunite (e.g., go to school, learn skills, continue sports, hobbies, music, etc., and learn how to succeed, become responsible, and help others).
Service Plan Reviews	Encourage children and adolescents to indicate caring adults they would like to have present at review conferences. Caring adults can be involved, as necessary, by teleconference, videoconferencing, or with follow-up telephone calls if they cannot be present. Schedule review conferences to occur at least every eight weeks. When children are in placement, review conferences are needed every four to six weeks to keep work moving forward on rebuilding attachments, to establish and maintain safety, to meet federal and state requirements (e.g., the Adoption and Safe Families Act), and to maintain hope for children.[9] Update assessments of core components and progress on achieving children's and caregiver's goals. Identify challenges to achieving goals and develop strategies for overcoming challenges. Prioritize work on core components: Relationships, Emotional Self- and Co-Regulation, Action Cycles, Life Story Integration, and other important goals (Table P.7). Document plans for what will be done by when and by whom with review dates.
Adaptations and Fidelity	Promote adaptations of RLH for diverse families, communities, and programs by working with child, family, and cultural strengths and norms while, at the same time, addressing RLH core components. Utilize *RLH Chapter Checkpoints* and *Progress Notes* (in Part V) as part of ongoing program supervision and consultation to assure fidelity. Repeat Trauma-Informed Systems Survey (Richardson et al., 2012) and the Professional Quality of Life: Compassion Satisfaction and Fatigue Version 5 (Stamm, 2009) to assess program implementation of trauma-informed practices and assess protection of team members from secondary traumatic stress as part of annual program evaluations.

>>> TIPS

➤ Use assessment tools and interviews to identify what is most important to children and caregivers, including:

 – what makes children and caregivers smile;
 – what can't be talked about;
 – what leads to trauma reactions; and
 – current or potential caring adults who can validate, protect, and guide children.

➤ Ensure that children and caregivers are able to signal when feeling unsafe (e.g., raising their left hand, looking at the door) and understand the therapist will stop talking about things that are too distressing in that session.

➤ Demonstrate the courage to address 'tough times' that children and their families have experienced by using trauma exposure and symptom surveys and validating known experiences of past traumas, 'saying the words' (Schlosberg, 1989) to show the therapist has heard or read what was already disclosed or validated in previous assessments or services.

➤ If children can identify fewer than two caring adults, or lack a viable permanency plan, help them understand that *Real Life Heroes*® and other team services will be used to search for and find caring adults willing to help them.

PITFALLS TO AVOID ➤➤➤

➤ Initial sessions focus on behavior problems. Children or parents experience assessment and service planning as a process to identify how bad, sick, or damaged they are.

➤ Children believe that treatment is focused on their changing their behaviors in order to complete a treatment program (e.g., to return home from residential treatment) without recognition of caregivers taking responsibility for rebuilding (or building) safety, nurture, and guidance for children, and helping children overcome the impact of traumatic stress in their family or community.

➤ Children perceive primary caregivers or family members mandating denial or minimization of traumas and that this is accepted or supported by therapists and other caring adults.

➤ Omitting an individual evaluation with children that addresses safety concerns, triggers for trauma reactions, and attachments, including what children need to feel safe with significant adults in their lives.

➤ Children are living in unsafe homes, risks are not validated, and safety plans are not developed. Similarly, children in placement have heard messages from parents, extended family members, and authorities that children must return to an unsafe home.

➤ Parents or guardians break pledges to create safety from repetitions of past traumas and children perceive that the therapist and other significant adults accept this without addressing this overtly, developing safety plans, and helping everyone involved grieve lost days and setbacks in permanency work.

➤ Parents or guardians are unable physically or psychologically to raise children as primary caregivers, but this is not addressed in permanency work.

➤ Parents or guardians use rejection, threats of placement, and 'time-outs' away from the family as discipline, triggering children's traumatic stress reactions to reminders of past losses, rejections, or abandonments.

CHAPTER CHECKPOINTS

Trauma-Informed Systems: Preparing for the Therapeutic Journey

☐ 1. Develop trauma- and resiliency-informed service systems in which programs and practitioners:

 __ routinely screen for trauma exposure and related symptoms;
 __ assess child and caregiver goals, strengths, resources, and cultural heritage;
 __ use culturally sensitive, evidence-based assessment and treatment for traumatic stress and associated mental health symptoms;
 __ make resources available to children, families, and providers on trauma exposure, its impact, and treatment;
 __ engage in efforts to strengthen the resilience and protective factors of children and families;
 __ address parent and caregiver trauma and its impact on the family system;
 __ emphasize continuity of care and collaboration across child-service systems; and
 __ maintain an environment of care for staff that addresses, minimizes, and treats secondary traumatic stress, and that increases staff resilience.

☐ 2. Arrange support, training, and ongoing consultation for practitioners, supervisors, and agency leaders to sustain trauma-informed services.

Trauma and Resilience-Focused Assessment: 'A Map and a Compass'

☐ 1. Complete the *Trauma and Resiliency-Focused Assessment and Service Plan*, including:

 __ assessment of the child and caregiver's primary goals;
 __ children's developmental level;
 __ primary relationships and potential caregivers and mentors using *Circles of Caring*;
 __ child, family, and cultural resources;

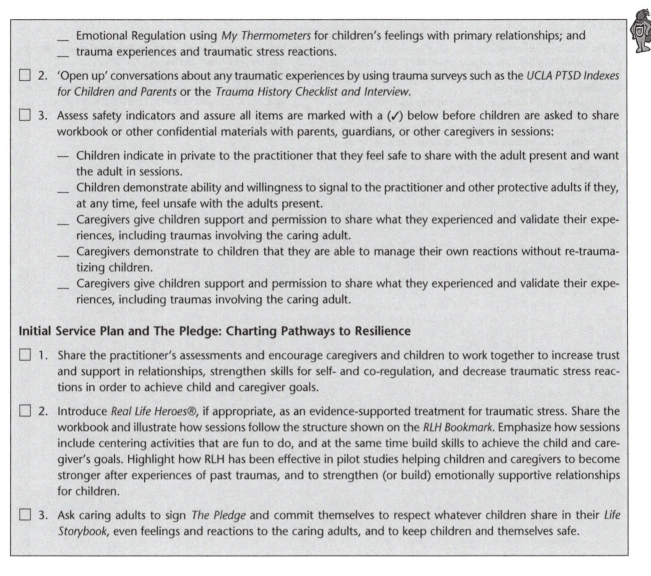

___ Emotional Regulation using *My Thermometers* for children's feelings with primary relationships; and

___ trauma experiences and traumatic stress reactions.

☐ 2. 'Open up' conversations about any traumatic experiences by using trauma surveys such as the *UCLA PTSD Indexes for Children and Parents* or the *Trauma History Checklist and Interview*.

☐ 3. Assess safety indicators and assure all items are marked with a (✓) below before children are asked to share workbook or other confidential materials with parents, guardians, or other caregivers in sessions:

— Children indicate in private to the practitioner that they feel safe to share with the adult present and want the adult in sessions.

___ Children demonstrate ability and willingness to signal to the practitioner and other protective adults if they, at any time, feel unsafe with the adults present.

___ Caregivers give children support and permission to share what they experienced and validate their experiences, including traumas involving the caring adult.

___ Caregivers demonstrate to children that they are able to manage their own reactions without re-traumatizing children.

___ Caregivers give children support and permission to share what they experienced and validate their experiences, including traumas involving the caring adult.

Initial Service Plan and The Pledge: Charting Pathways to Resilience

☐ 1. Share the practitioner's assessments and encourage caregivers and children to work together to increase trust and support in relationships, strengthen skills for self- and co-regulation, and decrease traumatic stress reactions in order to achieve child and caregiver goals.

☐ 2. Introduce *Real Life Heroes®*, if appropriate, as an evidence-supported treatment for traumatic stress. Share the workbook and illustrate how sessions follow the structure shown on the *RLH Bookmark*. Emphasize how sessions include centering activities that are fun to do, and at the same time build skills to achieve the child and caregiver's goals. Highlight how RLH has been effective in pilot studies helping children and caregivers to become stronger after experiences of past traumas, and to strengthen (or build) emotionally supportive relationships for children.

☐ 3. Ask caring adults to sign *The Pledge* and commit themselves to respect whatever children share in their *Life Storybook*, even feelings and reactions to the caring adults, and to keep children and themselves safe.

RESOURCES

Strategies to overcome challenges (obstacles, problems) are provided in Part IV of the *RLH Toolkit*.

For additional information and guidelines on trauma and attachment-centered assessments, engagement strategies, and service planning tools, see:

- *Rebuilding Attachments with Traumatized Children: Healing from Losses, Violence, Abuse and Neglect* (Kagan, 2004) for detailed guidelines for trauma- and attachment-centered assessments (see Chapter 5).
- *Families in Perpetual Crisis* (Kagan & Schlosberg, 1989) for guidelines on engaging families, especially families mandated or referred with pressure from external sources to participate in treatment (see especially Chapters 2, 3, and 4).
- *Wounded Angels: Inspiration from Children in Crisis* (Kagan, 2016b) for stories of children in crisis mental

health and foster care placements that can help caregivers learn how they can follow clues from children's behaviors to develop opportunities to help children to regain safety and develop social and emotional skills after traumatic experiences.

For additional information on development of trauma-informed treatment programs, see *Restoring Sanctuary* (Bloom & Farragher, 2013) and *Creating Trauma-Informed Child Welfare Systems: A Guide for Administrators* (Chadwick Trauma-Informed Systems Project, 2013).

For additional information on preventing compassion fatigue and increasing practitioner resilience, see www.pro qol.org, and resources from the NCTSN Secondary Trauma Workgroup at www.nctsn.org (e.g., *Organizational Impact and Intervention of STS*) (Ross, Streider, & Vrabel, 2012).

NOTES

1. For detailed guidelines on using a resiliency-focused approach to engage children and families who present with serial crises, see Kagan and Schlosberg (1989, Chapters 3 and 4).
2. Adapted from Strauss (2013).
3. Grid adapted from Saxe et al. (2007). Capacity refers to "window of tolerance" (Siegel, 1999).
4. Permanency goal criteria: primary and back-up plan (or work to develop primary or back-up plan) and identification of significant caring adults or families committed to youth.
5. Includes trauma, resilience, and developmental psycho-education.
6. Includes trauma, resilience, and developmental psycho-education.
7. Adapted from Kagan and Schlosberg (1989).
8. Adapted from Antonucci (1986).
9. For detailed guidelines for permanency work for children in placement, see Kagan and Schlosberg (1989) and Kagan (2004).

1

The Hero's Challenge

Trauma and Resilience, Psycho-Education, and Initial Safety Plans

---

OBJECTIVES

- Caregivers and children begin the 'therapeutic journey' with an introduction to traumatic stress that reinforces child, family, and cultural strengths within a resiliency framework for understanding and reducing traumatic stress.
- Caregivers and children experience RLH sessions as a special time, a sanctuary in their week, when they can feel safe enough to try out new behaviors and test out attunement, support, and safety.
- Children and caregivers learn and practice multisensory 'SOS' skills for self- and co-regulation and develop SOS Picture Power Cards.
- Children and caregivers develop initial safety plans, including Safety First cards.

Chapter 1 of the *Life Storybook* is designed to engage caregivers and children by normalizing traumatic stress reactions and emphasizing how children, caregivers, and other caring adults can make their lives better by using an understanding of how traumatic stress works. Understanding how our brains work can help children and caregivers to self- and co-regulate their feelings. Chapter 1 provides a brief introduction to brain and body responses to stress and use of multi-sensory activities and initial safety plans to help prevent trauma reactions and to calm down when children and caregivers are stressed. Chapter 1 is also used to introduce the RLH Session Structure and to demonstrate how therapists will maintain safety during sessions.

Trauma and Resilience Psycho-Education

The alarm bell metaphor (Ford & Russo, 2006) is utilized in Chapter 1 to highlight how our bodies react to stress and how natural responses can become problematic. The introduction to traumatic stress was written at an 8–12-year-old reading level and has been very successful in engaging caregivers. It was moved to the beginning of the *Life Storybook* because of the importance of helping caregivers step back and use an understanding of traumatic stress to more effectively care for, protect, and guide their children.

Engagement and effective trauma-informed discipline is enhanced by encouraging caregivers to use their adult capacity to understand how misbehaviors may represent how children are stuck in trauma reaction cycles and how they can help children learn to change misbehavior into successful behavior and thus achieve caregiver and child goals.

The chapter includes a supplementary handout for caregivers (in Part V), Trauma Symptoms and the Brain, which therapists can use to link components of RLH interventions to a brief overview of neurobiology that can be adapted to diverse caregivers. Brain functioning can be illustrated by how children's (or adults') brains function in three states of stress (Perry & Szalavitz, 2006): (1) secure: whole brain; (2) alarm mode: limbic; and (3) reacting: limbic-brain stem. Key concepts to share include the roles of four brain structures: the amygdala, hippocampus, orbito-frontal (left and right) cortex, and the corpus callosum in helping children function, how children's capacity for self-regulation develops 'brain to brain' (Schore, 2003a), the power of caregivers in developing children's self- and co-regulation, and how traumatic stress reactions serve as a coping mechanism with common survival responses: flee, fight, and freeze.

This handout frames children's development in simple terms, 'bottom-up, inside-out.' This is linked to how care givers, therapists, and educators can help children develop self-regulation skills following normal child development patterns from infancy through childhood: (1) caregiver regulates; (2) child co-regulates with caregiver; and (3) child self-regulates. This progressive model of skill development can then be used to frame progressive steps for helping children whose development was stymied at an earlier age due to traumatic stress. For instance, a 13-year-old who functions socially and emotionally at more of a 2–3-year-old level, when he or she experienced repeated incidents of domestic violence, emotional abuse, and physical abuse, can be helped to progressively move from 'co-regulation' with a safe caregiver to 'self-regulation' as an adolescent who gets help from safe caregivers, teachers, and friends. Using an understanding of normal development helps caregivers and educators to set realistic expectations and provide the support, supervision, and guidance children need at their developmental level to succeed and move forward to develop more advanced skills.

Caregivers can also be given NCTSN guides (NCTSN, 2012c) explaining how traumatic stress works or encouraged to read handouts from *Caring for Children Who Have Experienced Traumatic Stress*, also available at no charge from www.nctsn.org. However, in child and family services, it has proved most effective to include trauma psycho-education in sessions as a foundation for later RLH components. Providing information on specific types of traumatic experiences that children and caregivers have experienced (e.g., tornados, domestic violence) is also recommended, and guides are available from www.nctsn.org and other sites.

Introducing how trauma works is intended to be both fun and informative. The emphasis of this chapter is on what children, caregivers, and other caring adults can do to use neuroscience to help prevent trauma reactions and modulate feelings. Understanding a few processes can help. For instance, Siegel (2014) describes how he has intrigued adolescents with discussions of how the brain works and how mindfulness exercises activate the release of chemicals that can soothe anxious feelings. The prefrontal region of the brain, for instance, can secrete gamma-aminobutyric acid, which one of his teenage patients called "gaba goo," which works like a 'soothing salve' to calm the amygdala. Discussions of brain science engage children and caregivers and empower them to use brain science to help them manage stress and achieve their goals with increased self- and co-regulation. For caregivers who will read books, *The Whole-Brain Child* (Siegel & Bryson, 2012), *No-Drama Discipline* (Siegel & Bryson, 2014), and *Brain-Based Parenting* (Hughes & Baylin, 2012) are recommended.

Empowering Caregivers, Creating Initial Safety Plans

Chapter 1 was designed to engage caregivers to utilize a trauma and attachment perspective to understand their children. While the psycho-education on stress and trauma is written at a fourth- to fifth-grade level, adults often respond with an 'aha,' recognizing how events in children's lives and their own have led to reactions. Chapter 1 normalizes reactions and takes the mystery, and thus the power, away from reactive behaviors.

Chapter 1 also begins co-development of child-caregiver safety plans. In keeping with the resiliency framework, these are called *Power Plans*. *Power Plans*, beginning with the SOS Picture Power Card (in Chapter 1 and also Part V of the *RLH Toolkit*) introduce the use of multisensory self- and co-regulation. These cards can be cut out of the *Life Storybook* and pasted or taped on to 3.5 × 5 cards to create pocket reminders for children to take to school or for caregivers to mount on refrigerators or other important places in their homes.

The SOS Picture Power Card is provided first and combines visual imagery of a safe place and relationships for children with guided practice in self- and co-regulation using the acronym SOS.[1] The first 'S' in SOS provides a structured activity for children and caregivers to help each other learn and practice slow breathing exercises to slow down and modulate agitation. The 'O' represents increased awareness of resources (e.g., a caring aunt who can be called at any hour any day, a kind, caring principal at school, safe adults in the neighborhood, dogs or cats that can guard children during the night, alarm systems). The final 'S' highlights a key principle in *Real Life Heroes®*, that heroes 'Seek Help and Help Others.' The heroes image involves working together with family, friends, teachers, and other caring adults to make the world safer and better.

Children are then invited to draw a picture of themselves doing something that helps them calm down. As noted above, RLH stresses looking for clues to how children self-modulate (after Warner, Cook, Wescott, & Koomar, 2014). The Safety First Card engages children and caregivers to use commonly recognized senses (sight, smell, hearing, touch, taste) along with Movement-Balance, which includes children's proprioceptive and vestibular senses.

Expanding the 'Window of Tolerance'

Trauma therapy may be experienced as risky for families struggling to get by. Keeping secrets and not saying out loud 'what happened' can become accepted over time as implicit rules that must never be violated and critical for survival of a family. From a trauma perspective, this is part of a child and family's (or community's) avoidance of trauma, the "unspeakable terror" (van der Kolk, 1996). The *RLH Life Storybook* and Session Structure progressively expand a child and caregiver's "window of tolerance" (Siegel, 1999) for stress and promote safety to try out new behaviors and broaden the use of more complex problem-solving skills. As children feel more regulated and safer, they often share undisclosed or previously 'unspeakable' traumatic events, enabling trauma processing, a new future, and Life Story Integration.

Life Storybook chapters promote development of skills, emotionally supportive relationships, enhanced safety, and modulation in a progressive, phase-based approach promoting Life Story Integration:

- Chapter 1: Multisensory Initial Safety Plans
- Chapter 2: Affect Regulation, Expression, Modulation
- Chapter 3: Learning Skills Inspired by Heroes
- Chapter 4: *Power Plans* for Self- and Co-Regulation
- Chapters 5–6: Building and Strengthening Relationships
- Chapters 7–8: Mindfulness, Imagery, CBT Worksheet
- Chapter 9: Creating an Organized Framework for the Child's Life Story
- Chapter 10: Reintegration of Traumas
- Chapter 11: Developing a Positive Identity for the Future
- Chapter 12: Reintegrating the Child's Life Story with Enhanced Skills and Resources

Session rituals work to increase RLH core components: Relationships with protective caregivers and Emotional Self- and Co-regulation. Rituals serve to foster attunement and strength-based child-caregiver interactions (Action Cycles) that can replace cycles of crises.

To promote trust, therapists are encouraged to develop a routine for each session that highlights how these are special times. Life story work can become a magical time for children and a chance for caregivers to pass along lessons and values from their family and cultural heritage. Therapists and parents can set the mood by working with children in a comfortable and quiet setting, minimizing distractions, and offering limited choices to give children a sense of control while reinforcing the safety children need from adult-led structure, something they may have lacked in their homes or communities. Multimodal and multisensory activities help children focus and reduce excessively high arousal levels. Guided activities make sessions special times where children can feel good about themselves. For instance, serving a sweet, herbal tea or hot cocoa and a special kind of cookie creates an aroma and taste that conveys comfort and support. Allowing children to select their favorite herbal tea or juice each day, reading the label, and choosing the taste, smell, and attributes they want (e.g., 'calming' or 'invigorating') helps empower and soothe children from the inside out. Pointing out something special in the day or introducing a brief magic trick, a Magical Moment, can increase hope that something good could happen.

The room utilized should be become a 'sanctuary' from children's stress, protected by the therapist and any caring adults who are invited to participate. Predictability, respect for safety, and routines help children develop confidence that caring adults will keep them safe, and in turn renew confidence that energy spent on 'threat detection' and avoidance can be at least temporarily reduced within this special time.

The therapist's role is also critical in creating safety for children and caregivers to risk addressing traumas. In group care and foster family care programs, it works best to separate the roles of case planners/managers from therapists and caring adults. Children and caring adults will naturally bring the day's or week's most pressing issues to the case manager, and extra effort and time will be needed by the case manager to separate therapy time from management of case planning, permanency, milieu, foster parent supervision, and other day-to-day management issues. It is also important to maintain the 'sanctuary' of the special times set aside for children's appointments, even when other children are acting out their distress. When one therapist must bear responsibility for both case management and therapy sessions, it has worked well to bring in interns or family support workers who can take on the clinical work for children and families under supervision of a trained clinician. Making therapy sessions predictable and safe in group care, foster family care, and school-based programs requires endorsement and implementation by administrators, supervisors, staff, and clients of core principles of trauma therapy, including protection, maintaining therapy sessions, respect for staff, children, and families, and incorporation of democratic values to make the organization a Sanctuary® that fosters healing and recovery.

The RLH Session Structure was designed to promote enjoyable activities and to foster children's creativity through use of music, art, and movement. This process accentuates nonverbal meaning and exposure time for nonverbal processing before working on reintegration with words. The workbook pages in each chapter begin with relatively innocuous items and build to somewhat more challenging questions. Therapists are encouraged to be creative in how they utilize written questions, listed on each page. Therapists can adapt the workbook to best facilitate each child's interests and talents and to utilize the therapist's own talents and enjoyment of art and music. Therapists can also build on what children do to calm down (Ayres, 1979; Warner, Koomar, Lary, & Cook, 2013). So, for example, with children who like to dance to express themselves and reduce stress, the movement part of the Session Structure could be emphasized for both storytelling and self- and co-regulation.

Session Structure

The RLH Session Structure is layered like a sandwich. The top (beginning) includes openings to promote safety and hope and to assess children's current level of modulation. The middle (meat/cheese) involves centering activities to increase self- and co-regulation and workbook pages to promote skill development and Life Story Integration. The bottom (end of the session) includes closing rituals to promote carry-over to the home, homework to reinforce

TABLE 1.1
Matching Session Components to Children's and Caregiver's 'Window of Tolerance'

Session Component	Include Every Session	Time Range (Minutes)
Openings		3–8
Welcome		
Safety Messages (first sessions and as needed)	✓	
Thermometers (to assess self-regulation)		
Magical Moment (to make session special and increase hope)		
Centering Activity		5–30
Breathing, yoga, mindfulness, or movement to increase self- and co-regulation	✓	
Connection activity (e.g., 'Improv,' conjoint music, or child-caregiver yoga to promote attunement, trust, and storytelling)		
Life Storybook **(1–5 pages per session)**		10–40
Drawing or art substitute (collage, photographs, video . . .)	✓	
Rhythm alone (drum, tambourine . . .)	✓	
Rhythm and tonality (xylophone, keyboard . . .)	✓	
Movement for important drawings (dance, gesture, enactment with puppets or action figures . . .)	✓	
Mirroring with caregiver (when safe caregiver is available)	✓	
Three- (or five-) chapter stories (for important stories and Chapter 10)		
Closings		5
Thermometers and Safety Steps (as needed)		
Normalize Feelings of Stress after Sessions (first few sessions)	✓	
Homework (matched to *Life Storybook* pages and needs)	✓	
Progress Note ('collaborative documentation,' fidelity)		

what was started in sessions, and engagement to come back to the next scheduled session.

RLH sessions are designed to be flexible. Session components are adjusted to match children's level of regulation and level of emotionally supportive relationships. Choice of activities is also shaped by children's cognitive, social, and emotional development and the type of sensorimotor activities (e.g., drawing, movement, mindfulness) that children use to self- and co-regulate. In addition, the

> **Session components are matched to the child and caregivers' level of self and co-regulation, and emotionally supportive relationships.**

extent of caregiver involvement in sessions is adjusted to match children's safety, the caregiver's ability to stay regulated, and children's benefits from time alone with the therapist. Table 1.1 outlines session components, which components are recommended to be implemented in every session, and a recommended time range for implementation of each component.

Selection of Centering Activities

Centering activities are included in each session to develop self- and co-regulation skills, including greater skills for calming, focusing attention, and attunement of children with safe caregivers. Traumatized children need to feel they can control bodily experiences and develop trust in touch activities with safe caregivers who are attuned to their needs and strengths. By starting sessions with a centering activity, children learn to feel in the first few minutes of sessions that they, and safe caregivers, can do something to calm their bodies down.[2] Conjoint multisensory breathing, yoga, and movement exercises help to develop this trust in sessions with carry-over to homework assignments for practice. Mindfulness, yoga, and movement activities give children permission to experiment with different ways to modulate arousal and to promote play with caregivers and children who have been caught up in conflicts or stress.

Recommended centering activities are provided in Part V with step-by-step guidelines. Centering activities are matched to chapter content to progressively increase skill development and trust in relationships through RLH phase-based treatment. However, suggested activities can be can be used by therapists with any chapter to engage children and caregivers and to promote mindfulness and modulation. Yoga and movement exercises were adapted from multiple sources, including Ayres (2004), Flynn (2013), Guber

---

SAFETY FIRST

Yoga poses and movement exercises require a safe space free from dangerous objects or hard surfaces that a child or caregiver could fall on. Some children or caregivers may find certain exercises to be difficult and some positions may remind children, or caregivers, of previous traumas. Suggested activities are not meant to replace the guidance of certified yoga teachers, sensory-integration or movement therapists or medical treatment for specific disorders. Centering activities should be guided by a therapist trained in trauma treatment and should not be required. Please consult a physician, or ask your clients to consult their physicians, if you or your clients have any concerns about their capacity to do an activity safely.

TABLE 1.2

Centering Activities for Caregivers and Children: Suggested Movement Level for Self- and Co-Regulation Activities

		Strength of Emotionally Supportive Enduring Relationships		
		High	Medium	Low
Child Self-Regulation	High	Low Movement	Low Movement	Low to Moderate Movement
	Medium	Low to Moderate Movement	Low to Moderate Movement	Moderate Movement
	Low	Moderate Movement	High Movement	High Movement

and Kalish (2005), Harper (2013), MacLean (2009), Marra (2004), Siegel (2010), Snel (2013), Stanchfield (2007), and Warner et al. (2014). Activities include breathing skills matched to 'SOS for Stress', introduced in Chapter 1, balancing (e.g., with peacock feathers) (after Macy et al., 2003), balancing with yoga positions, and two-person yoga balancing and trust exercises. See referenced books for pictures of yoga positions and more detailed instructions by experts in yoga, movement, and sensorimotor integration therapies.

To select activities for sessions, therapists are encouraged to look for children's own 'pathways' to regulation. Watch for what types of activities help children to self-regulate (Ayres 1979; Warner et al., 2013) and for what helps children and caregivers to co-regulate, then build on what works. Some children (and caregivers) need more gross motor movement-based activities to calm down (e.g., walking, bouncing up and down on a Disc 'o' Sit). And, children who are more dysregulated often benefit from more movement-based activities. As children become more secure within themselves and within their primary relationships, they are typically better able to utilize more imagery and meditation-based forms of mindfulness.

Table 1.2 provides a framework for matching selection of centering activities with children's level of self-regulation and the strength of children's emotionally supportive relationships based on the level of movement in activities. Table 1.3 shows how a sample of activities can be matched to levels of movement.

Activities can be adapted to each child's level of arousal and also to his or her developmental level. Experimentation can be promoted by being respectful, attuned, playful, and

TABLE 1.3

Movement-Based Centering Activities for Self- and Co-Regulation

Movement	Sample Activities
High ↑ ... ↓ Low	Fitness ball
	Disc 'o' Sit
	Mindful motion: walking, swimming . . .
	Juggling
	Peacock feather balancing
	Countdowns
	Yoga self-balance
	Yoga two-person balance
	Coffee can pass
	Drumming
	Blowing bubbles
	Mindful breathing
	Mindful eating
	Mindful meditations
	Mindful imagery

curious (after Hughes, 2009). It helps to invite children to try out activities (e.g., "Would you like to try . . . rolling on the physioball?"). It is also important to ask children to direct how they want any pressure or movement in two-person activities with caregivers (e.g., a caregiver rolling a physioball on children's backs). Therapists should check in with children to remind them of their control (e.g., "How does this feel?", "Do you want caregivers to use more or less pressure?", "Should the caregiver 'smoosh' down softer or harder?") (after Flynn, 2013).

Certain positions or body experiences can remind children of traumatic experiences that may be unknown to the therapist or caregivers. If children become more reactive, it is important to respect their need to regain control when triggered. Safety steps and 'SOS for Stress' can be utilized, building on what helps children to modulate when stressed.

Adapted Use of the *Real Life Heroes Life Storybook*

Therapists can also adjust use of the *Life Storybook*. The workbook format engages elementary-school-age children and adolescents who function cognitively, socially, or emotionally at a latency level. With adolescents, it helps to explain that the workbook is often used with teenagers who went through tough times at a younger age and that the

> **Use of the printed life storybook is not required. In pilot studies, children showed significant improvement without completing all chapters.**

workbook can be modified for adolescents. Or, adolescents can be encouraged to complete the workbook as a model to help younger siblings or other children learn from what they have gone through. Some children may object to the workbook format reminding them of stress they feel at school or that it appears too childlike. Therapists can take workbook pages as activity guides for each session, pulling out pages for each session. Therapists can also substitute activities to match the youth's developmental level, interests, or talents. For example, older youths may be more engaged with video activities in which they function as a writer/director or use of instruments such as keyboards or guitars.

Therapists can also adjust selection of pages. It works best to move progressively through workbook pages and to complete the most important pages, which are marked with a

anywhere on the page. To maintain interest, therapists can also introduce pages and activities from chapters ahead, or go back to complete pages skipped. Since Chapter 1 includes didactic information, it is helpful to provide increased time for centering activities in this chapter. It is also helpful with some children to alternate reading a couple of pages in Chapter 1 with drawings of feelings in Chapter 2. Therapists can adjust the amount of reading about trauma to the child and caregiver's capacity.

Passing the 'Tests'

Traumatized children learn that healing is possible within caring relationships that foster safety and trust that children's worlds have truly changed. Typically, children need to test whether change is real. This often means attempts by children to take control through negative behaviors or to provoke the adults around them to repeat stressful interactions from the past. Testing is more powerful when adults are off guard or struggling with other stressors (e.g., problems with the landlord, at work, the car breaking down, an argument between parents). That's when children often test how much parents, family members, guardians, and mentors really care and what is real.

Therapists and caregivers can welcome or even prescribe 'testing' by children, using their understanding of how trauma works. Testing can be discussed and planned as homework, a way to validate children's need to find out if their lives are really different now. Testing can also be used as a way to practice recognition of 'triggers', feelings, and behaviors that mark the beginning of trauma cycles. No caregiver or therapist should expect to be perfect and it is natural to slip back into old habits. It helps for therapists and caregivers to acknowledge lapses or mistakes, to apologize, and then to reinstitute rules that maintain safety for everyone. Testing can also be encouraged by caring adults to demonstrate their awareness of dangers and 'triggers' for children, their commitment to implement safety plans, how they accept responsibility for what they do, even when they make mistakes, and how they will work to reattach when gaps begin to form between children and adults.

For therapists, testing by children often involves distractions that disrupt progress on the workbook or the sequence of sessions. This is often a test of the 'sanctuary' of therapy sessions and whether therapists can be coaxed or provoked to stop work on overcoming traumas. Therapists need to use their own supports and awareness of trauma patterns. Then, they can demonstrate how safety rules will be maintained and that work on building strengths will continue, even during difficult times for a child, a family, or the therapist.

Maintaining the Session Structure is important to preserve safety and show children that therapists and caregivers are in charge. **This means going through the most important session components** (marked with a check in Table 1.1). It is important to complete at least a page or

> **'CRISIS OF THE DAY'**
>
> **If a child or caregiver comes in with an issue to address, reserve time at the end of the session to work on problem solving. Therapists may want to work with the caregiver separately on this and highlight empowerment of caregivers to manage day-to-day issues.**

two of the *Life Storybook* in every session. This demonstrates that children and caregivers are making progress, page by page, in completing the workbook and making their lives better. If a child or caregiver comes into sessions in the midst of or following a crisis, the session can be adapted to focus on centering activities and discussion of workbook pages can be minimized. It is always possible go back and redo or add to *Life Storybook* pages in later sessions. Children and caregivers can also be told that time at the end of the session (e.g., the last 5–30 minutes) will be saved to work on making things better after whatever happened. This maintains sessions as a sanctuary from ongoing crises. In contrast, sessions can easily become dominated by serial crises if the therapist stops work on skill-building and trauma resolution and focuses entire sessions on the 'crisis of the week or day'.

STEP BY STEP

	OPENINGS
Welcome	Greet children and caregivers with a resiliency-focused and structuring message that shows both respect and curiosity to learn more in a way that allows children to stay within their 'window of tolerance' (e.g. "Great to see you . . . Let's get started . . . Please show me how you are feeling today on the Thermometers.").
	Initial messages make a difference in setting a tone for the session and establishing whether children give this therapy a chance or feel a need to resist the therapist. For instance, if the therapist asks "How are you doing today?" many children who have had previous counseling or disciplinary sessions will experience this as a message that this therapist, like others in the past, is going to assess for problems and label children with vague and sometimes scary words that may mean to children that this therapist sees them as bad or damaged and will try to control them.
	It helps to remember how you felt/acted as a 13-year-old (Baker, 2015) and ask yourself how you'd understand opening messages. Ask yourself what different messages you use to start a session.
	• How would a 13-year-old understand what adults want/expect with this message? • Reminders/triggers that may be activated. • What part of the child's brain are you speaking to? • What would you do if you were 13 and an adult asked you this question?
Safety to Share and Safety Signal	1. Remind children and caregivers of *The Pledge*, how caregivers and the therapist want children to share what they think and feel in this workbook, and that it is their book.
	2. Check with children and caregivers to see if the therapist understands nonverbal safety signals that indicate children (or caregivers) are too stressed to share more about something. Remind children that the therapist will watch and listen for this signal, and ask for children's help in case the therapist misses the signal: "I'm going to count on you to stop me if I ask you to do anything that is too 'nosy' (or stressful)" (Schlosberg, 1989). Therapists can come back to pages or tasks at a later time in the work when children are more secure.
Bookmark/ Progress Notes	Show how the therapist, caregiver, and child can check off what was done in each session on either the *Progress Note* (Session Checklist) or the *Fidelity Progress Note* for 'collaborative documentation.'
	Invite children to color the back of the *Bookmark* (in Part V). The *Bookmark* can then be laminated to preserve it and highlight children's artwork.
	Show how the therapist, caregiver, and child can check off what was done in each session on the *RLH Progress Note* for 'collaborative documentation.' The content of progress notes can also be incorporated into state or funding source mandated progress note formats or electronic case record systems with references to completing RLH pages or components.
My Thermometers	Ask children to scan over their bodies from their toes to the top of their heads, and then mark, or color in, the level on each thermometer from 1–10, indicating how high they would rate that feeling at that moment. Thermometers include: self-ratings of stress (*Knots*), self-control (*Self-Control Power*), and feelings of *Mad*, *Sad*, *Glad*, and *Feel Safe*. Introduce *Knots* as feelings of

tightness, tension, or even aching all over their bodies. *Self-Control Power* means using their whole body. That means being able to sense how you're feeling from the tips of your toes to the top of your head and being able to use the thinking power of your brain. *Self-Control Power* means being able to stay calm enough to use your strength to help yourself and help others.

Thermometers provide a quick check on children's emotional balance and self-awareness and can be used at any time to encourage body and self-awareness. It is also helpful to point out to caregivers and children how practice using thermometers (self-monitoring) activates the left prefrontal cortex and thus promotes self-control and coping skills to manage problems and achieve children's goals. Use of the thermometers also fosters respect for children's feelings, and provides reassurance that the therapist won't push children beyond what they can manage.

ASSESSING MODULATION

The ratio of children's *Self-Control Power* to *Knots* provides a quick measure of their capacity to manage stress at that moment. When children's stress is equal to or greater than their capacity for self-control, it is important to focus work on modulation and safety issues, reducing distress, and enhancing self- and co-regulation.

If desired, an additional thermometer can be used to highlight an important attribute for children. For instance, with children who appear agitated, it may be helpful to encourage a self-rating of their energy level from 'exhausted' to 'hyper.'

Magical Moment	1. In initial sessions, it is very helpful to incorporate a ritual that shows how these sessions can be different than past treatment and to promote curiosity and exploration. Magic, science, or math work well to engage children to look behind what is first seen and find out how the 'trick' works. Latency-age children are especially interested in magic. Providing a magical moment helps children see that they may be able to find solutions to problems in their lives and increases hope for making things better, together with caregivers and therapists. 2. Show children a simple trick e.g., experiment with tonality and sound with a glockenspiel (xylophone), or point out mysteries of snowflakes falling down. Using the German word 'glockenspiel' adds a magical quality to even an inexpensive xylophone. 3. In later sessions, the Magical Moment may be omitted. 4. **Therapists can encourage children and caregivers to make up their own initial ritual to start sessions**—for instance, making up a special dance or movement, starting the session with a special seven-step handshake, blowing a giant bubble, or making a 'fist-bump power-tower' with children's fists alternated between the caregiver's.
	CENTERING ACTIVITIES
Breathing, Balancing, Yoga, and Movement to Increase Self- and Co-Regulation	Introduce centering activities as steps and skills children and caregivers can learn to keep themselves in control to do what they want to do and to make things better in their lives. Centering can be explained as developing a greater sense of balance in the child and caregiver's mind and body. This can be described as similar to how a football player, a tennis player, or a singer position themselves with their feet, legs, and arms, and also with preparation of their minds before the ball is snapped, the whistle is blown to start a game, or the curtain goes up. Select activities matched to children's level of self-regulation and the strength of children's emotionally supportive relationships using Tables 1.2 and 1.3. Adjust the activity to match children's developmental age and level of arousal. **Getting started:** Use of a peacock feather (Macy et al., 2003) is very useful as an initial activity to engage children into centering activities at the beginning of sessions to develop mind and body awareness, balance, slow breathing, and modulation skills. See Centering Activities (in Part V) for a detailed guide to using peacock feathers and other activities.

After the peacock feather, utilize centering activities (in Part V) to develop SOS slow breathing and multisensory awareness. Recommended activities for Chapter 1 include:

- *SOS Slow Breathing with Imagery, Motion, Muscle Tension-Relaxation Practice*
- *Breathe Like a Sleepy Little Bear* (for calming)
- *Breathe Like a Slowly Slithering Snake* (to slow down)
- *Breathe Like a Rabbit* (for increasing energy or waking up)
- *Developing Multisensory Awareness* (for Safety First Card): 'Mindful Eating,' 'Mindful Smell,' 'Mindful Touch,' 'Mindful Hearing,' 'Mindful Sight,' 'Floating Like a Sailboat' (to increase balance, stability)

See the *RLH Strategy and Activity Guide* (in Part V) for additional activities to increase modulation.

	LIFE STORYBOOK
Workbook Pages	Plan to complete 2–5 pages of the workbook each session, depending on the difficulty for children. Chapter 1 is different from all other chapters as it includes didactic psycho-education. Depending on their reading ability, children can be asked to read paragraphs, or alternate sentences or paragraphs with caregivers. Therapists can gauge how many pages to read before interspersing an activity. If children and caregivers appear to be losing interest, the therapist can outline a plan to read '#' of pages each session, then skip ahead and ask children to complete the first page of Chapter 2 and afterwards go back to finish reading the planned '#' of pages in Chapter 1 later in the session or the next session.
Chapter 1:	**Trauma Psycho-education: Normalizing and Healing** Introduce children and caregivers to psycho-educational materials that detoxify trauma symptoms and counter the stigma and self-denigration often accompanying traumatic stress. The "survival" alarm metaphor (Ford, 2005) is very useful to teach children and caring adults how traumatic stress and PTSD lead to a bodily state of alarm, an alarm that never seems to end. Show children and caring adults how traumatic stress can be viewed as a natural way our brains work to protect us when we are threatened with life or death situations (e.g., fears of a beloved sibling dying or parents hurting or killing each other). Staying in hyper-alert and 'alarm' mode can become a habitual response that very likely helped at one point in a child or adult's development. However, being in alarm mode blocks learning, reasoning, and building better relationships. Accordingly, preventing traumatic stress reactions or PTSD means turning down the alarm bells and opening up our abilities to self-soothe, perceive, learn, think, and take charge of our lives (Ford & Russo, 2006). Normalize how our brains continue working on solving problems and that children or caregivers may be reminded of something from the past or in sessions during the week. This can be explained as a part of healing. Children and caregivers can be asked to write these down and bring them to the next session, so they don't have to keep thinking about them. Use of mindfulness metaphors can help. For instance, describing thoughts or feelings like waves rolling into the shore (Marra, 2004), with children sitting far away on a high bluff looking out at the ocean and watching how each wave comes in, some large, some small, some crashing in, and some coming in softly, with all of the waves then slipping back out and a new wave coming in. Or, thoughts and feelings can be seen as leaves floating down a stream, one following another or cars passing below an apartment window, one after another . . . Each thought and feeling comes and then goes. By accepting how thoughts and feelings come and go, children and adults can relax fears and worries about their thoughts or feelings.
Share Trauma Symptoms and the Brain	Briefly outline key parts of this psycho-education addendum with caregivers and adolescents, and use with modification with younger children. Stress how the brain develops from 'bottom-up' and 'inside-out' and how all children develop regulation skills from infancy, with caregivers first providing care (feeding, changing diapers, etc.), regulating children in response to their cries and

	needs, then caregivers co-regulate with children, and later children learn to self-regulate. Highlight how adolescents and adults continue to help each other with co-regulation through life.
SOS Picture Power Cards	Use extra copies from the *RLH Toolkit* (Part V) for caregivers to complete their own SOS *Picture Power Cards*. Therapists are also encouraged to complete their own cards before using these with children and caregivers.
	Practice 'SOS' (adapted below from Ford & Russo, 2006).
	Slow Down: One thought at a time, breathe in and out, slower and slower, filling up your whole body from the tip of your toes to the top of your head. Slowly scan over your body from the tip of your toes through your feet, ankles, knees, thighs, hips, stomach, chest, arms, and up your neck to your mouth, and all over your head to the very top; rate yourself on *My Thermometers* (in Part V).
	Open Your Eyes to who and what can help: Focus on right now, in this place; wiggle your toes, listen to your breathing, notice who's around who could help you, and look for calming objects you can see or feel . . .
	Seek Help and Help Others: Counter feelings of shame and loneliness with lessons from heroes working together.
	To reinforce this, practice developing an 'SOS' ritual adapted for children. For instance, tap in Morse code: • • • – – – • • •, with children gradually slowing the rhythm. Use a glockenspiel or other instruments to practice a note from a chord to match each step: slow down, open your eyes, seek help, and help others, followed by all three notes together.
	Continue practicing 'SOS' skills through the next several chapters until children can slow down and self-orient quickly. These skills will be further integrated and reinforced in Chapters 7 and 8 as part of "*Mind Power*" and "Changing the Story."
Encourage Nonverbal Expression	Use workbook activity pages, such as the SOS Picture Power Card, to encourage nonverbal expression, to create opportunities for validation, and to promote attunement with children.
	For workbook drawings, ask children to respond nonverbally to each activity page beginning with drawings as "silent stories" (Macy et al., 2003) by selecting colors and then experimenting with sketches, accentuating intensity and detail.
	Add rhythm to a drawing by asking children to tap out the drawing as a beat, experimenting and shaping loudness and tempo to match children's images. Children may enjoy constructing their own homemade drums with coffee cans and different covers tightened with string, as well as experimenting with different 'drumsticks,' glockenspiel mallets, etc.
	Experiment with tonality to go along with rhythm and images. This can be done in a simple manner by encouraging children to pick a note on the glockenspiel to go along with the image for each page. Later, children can be encouraged to develop the note into a three-note chord by adding notes to complement the first note selected. This could mean taking the '1, 3, 5' notes for a simple chord progression; however, the emphasis should be on fostering children's safety and creativity to select notes desired to convey a musical 'story.' Afterwards, children could be encouraged to experiment with tempo, rhythm, and patterns with the notes in this chord.
	Creative music can be used as an opportunity to foster bonding with children in much the same way that an infant or toddler learns to coo and make sounds and simple words through attunement with a caring parent who repeats what a child says. Attunement and harmony counter children's feelings of isolation after traumas. It is very helpful for the therapist and, where possible, a caring adult to begin by copying (echoing) children's notes on the

	glockenspiel, then tapping the note in unison. Later, it may be possible to mirror, harmonize, or to accentuate the base note of children's chords while they experiment with notes, chords, and patterns (see Austin, 2002; Macy et al., 2003).

Encourage children to try out a Movement to enact what they have drawn on the workbook page like in a game of charades. They could use a gesture, a look on their face, how they position their arms, hands, or legs, or a short movement.

To facilitate children's comfort with movement, it may help to invite them to think of themselves as actors working with the figures drawn on the workbook page. Actors take on the feeling of a character and show it with their bodies through movement and action.

Children (and parents) can also use action figures to demonstrate an attitude and action using the figures' posture, facial appearance, and positioning their arms, hands, legs, torso, and neck.

Use a mirror (Mullin, 2004) or a camera to help children capture the look of the *Movement*. Remind children how actors also practice with mirrors and movie directors often try scenes several times, asking actors to try different movements to capture what they want to express. Children can also be asked to copy how they look in the mirror as a drawing to highlight what children are showing. Mirrors ideally should be large enough to reflect children's upper bodies, if not a whole-body stance.

Invite children to add verbal responses to describe their drawing, rhythm, tonality, and movement.

Reinforce children's success in conveying images, melodies, and stories, 'silent' or verbal, for each page/task of the workbook. |
| **SOS Slow Breathing** | Practice SOS Slow Breathing with Centering Activities (in Part V) to go along with the SOS Picture Card.

Add imagery and muscle tension and relaxation exercises. |
| **SOS Picture Card** | Encouraging children to develop a detailed image of a safe time and place is very important, and begins in RLH with the RLH SOS Picture Card and is enhanced in Chapter 7 with *Life Storybook* pages devoted to Safe Place imagery. 'Safe Place' imagery may be fostered by having children draw a picture of a time when they felt warm, cared for, and secure. Children can be encouraged to add color and accentuate with details the best parts of this picture. The picture could be laminated, or shrunk on a photocopier.

Safe Place imagery requires practice to make it useful. Ask children to redirect their thoughts away from whatever is going on around them to their own special 'Safe Place.' This can be a homework activity along with in-session practice.

As an alternative, especially for children who enjoy music, invite children to pick one of their favorite songs, and a verse or two that makes them feel upbeat and good about themselves. This can become children's 'safe song,' and again should be practiced in different situations until children can bring it to mind easily, even when stressed. |
| **Safety First Card** | **Promote Multisensory, Multimodal Self-Soothing and Co-Regulation**
Introduce children to more advanced self-soothing skills as part of becoming stronger and learning from heroes. Learning self-soothing skills can be compared to learning to ride a bike. Each one may seem awkward or even impossible at first, but with practice it becomes natural.

Utilize centering activities (in Part V) at the start of the session and during work on chapter pages to help children prepare for Safety First Card.

First, have children learn to self-soothe in all five senses (after Ford, Cruz St. Juste, & Mahoney, 2005): |

Eyes: Look at a photograph of someone or something that makes you feel peaceful; look at plants or flowers, find something in every room that makes you feel good inside . . .

Ears: Listen to relaxing music, or the music in a favorite person's voice, sing along with a 'feel-good' song . . .

Taste buds: Treat yourself to a tasty, soothing drink (e.g., hot chocolate or herbal tea), sip slowly and savor . . .

Nose: Sniff as you sip or pull out your favorite perfume. Sniff flowers, a spice, or a favorite treat . . .

Touch: Smooth a rich peaceful smelling lotion on your hand, take a warm bubble bath, pet a friendly animal, rub a soft piece of fabric . . .

Second, add movement and body awareness:

Take a walk.

Swim, play a sport, or exercise.

Learn and practice yoga.

Third, encourage children to get help from someone they trust:

Talk to a friend.

Hug someone.

Fourth, have children write their favorite self-soothing activities down on the Safety First card (in Chapter 1) as part of their safety plan and put the card in their wallet, backpack, or pocket along with names and phone numbers of people they can call for help.

Identify Activities That Help Child and Caregiver Modulate

Continue assessment in sessions with special attention to what helps the child and caregiver to calm down. Track the use of body movement, and the types of sensoriotor stimulation (Warner et al., 2014) and somatic experiences (Ogden, Minton, & Pain, 2006) children use to self-soothe. Practice using these in a way that helps caregivers learn how to help their children and for children to learn to become aware of how they can self-regulate and also help themselves to get help from safe caring adults to co-regulate.

Additional Self- and Co-Regulation Skill-Building

Utilize the RLH Strategy and Activity Guide and Centering Activities (in Part V) to enhance slow breathing skills, muscle relaxation, imagery, and refocusing.

'Progressive deep muscle relaxation' techniques help children learn with practice to first tense then relax different muscles in their bodies. This usually begins with tensing their toes, holding the tension, counting from one to five, and tying this in with slow 'belly' breathing. This skill requires practice, working up the body from children's toes, to the arch of their foot, through their calf, thigh, back, upper arms, lower arms and fists, neck, and head. Over time, children can increase their ability to calm their bodies from their toes to the top of their heads and to use this skill in different situations.

Music and rhythm can also be used to help children relax. Many children have favorite songs that help them feel calmer. Remembering and humming to themselves a lyric or musical phrase can be used as a signal to help their bodies calm down and refocus their attention away from a preoccupation with danger signs.

	With many children, it is helpful to encourage them to reach into a pocket or their book bag and pull out or touch a special memento (e.g., a stone or laminated picture symbolizing the care children remember from a good and safe time in their lives). Children can be encouraged to practice using SOS for Stress when they pull out their memento.
	CLOSINGS
Repeat Thermo-meters	Repeat thermometers at end of the session, as well as any time during the session, to monitor the child and caregiver's level of modulation. Use these to guide incorporating more Centering Activities into the session.
	IF CHILD'S 'KNOTS' EXCEED 'SELF-CONTROL POWER' Encourage the child to continue to use rhythm, music, or movement along with self-soothing activities ('SOS,' Slow Breathing, Mindfulness, and encourage safe caregivers involved in sessions to support and comfort child in ways child has identified are helpful until child indicates their Self-Control Power Thermometer rating is higher than their Knots. Then, resume work on *Life Storybook* page activities.
Special Time	It often helps to set aside a special time at the end of sessions for children to do what they enjoy in a way that increases development of self-modulation skills. For instance, if a child likes to sing, the last five minutes could be reserved for practicing singing. If a child likes to make up songs on the glockenspiel, the last few minutes could be saved to make up special music that could be developed over time and recorded.
***Progress Note* and Wrap-Up**	Ask child and caregiver's help to complete the required *Progress Note*. Use of the *RLH Progress Note* is recommended to promote fidelity. Ask children to check off what was done, or, if preferred, to help the therapist record what happened accurately. For narrative descriptions, encourage positive attributions and self-direction in reviewing what was done and what children shared. It is important to recognize children's true beliefs and to accentuate the positive aspects of what they like about themselves. This can begin with abilities children illustrate in Chapter 1, as well as abilities they demonstrate to cope with stress and past traumas, skills that can be redirected to help them succeed. Refocusing on positive self-statements (e.g. "I can do this" or "I've done this before") helps children avoid becoming caught up in reactive behaviors that lead to problems.
'Homework' and 'Teamwork'	Encourage children (and caring adults) to practice self-soothing skills daily until they become automatic. This goes along with the dictum in neurobiology that 'Neurons that fire together, wire together' (Hebb, 1949). Skill-building requires frequent practice, as suggested in Chapter 1, regarding how athletes and musicians learn skills. Using the illustration of brain pathways, children and caregivers can be encouraged to think of practicing new skills for managing stress as a way to widen a narrow mountain trail into a 12-lane express highway that can replace what children and caregivers have been doing, on what may be an almost automatic basis, when reminded of trauma events. Urge caregivers and children to practice Centering Activities introduced in sessions at home over and over to make them natural and available to children when needed, like learning to ride a bike. Activities related to workbook chapters can be practiced in additional home-, school-, or clinic-based sessions by safe caregivers, in-home support workers, residential counselors, or teachers. See the RLH Strategy and Activity Guide and Centering Activities (in Part V) and references for yoga and mindfulness listed in the resources at the end of this chapter. Encourage homework for children to practice skill development in a fun way and to recognize their body awareness skills as a signal to use 'SOS' and other self-soothing strategies. Encourage children to watch for feelings of tension they have identified (e.g., tightening of their stomachs or

	finding their fists beginning to clench). And, practice what they can do to keep themselves in control when this happens. Encourage youths to utilize these warning signs as signals to use self-soothing strategies to slow down and calm down (e.g., pull out a memento). The goal is to make skills as automatic as playing an instrument, and to encourage children to develop their favorite ways to relax before fears or anger lead them to become 'out of control.'
	Where possible, in-home support workers, residential counselors, or resource parents can be asked to guide work on additional workbook pages, and then bring these into the next session, where the therapist can encourage sharing with the steps above.
	Recommended activities are listed by service priority in the RLH Session and Homework Strategy and Intervention Guide (in Part V).
Safety Planning	Remind children and caregivers of initial safety plans developed in contracting sessions, and also in Chapter 1, to deal with predictable stressors. These should include what children and caregivers can do and who children can call at different times of the day and week if they feel stressed.
Normalize Feelings after Sessions	Normalize feelings of stress that may come up after sessions. These may be described as ways that children's brains are working on healing Encourage children (and caregivers) to write down thoughts or feelings that come up during the week, store them in a special place (e.g., a lockbox), and bring them to the next session.
'Goodbye' Message	Set a time/date for the next session and encourage participation by safe caregivers therapist believes can support child and increase child's 'window of tolerance.'

➤➤➤ TIPS

➤ Make Chapter 1 fun for yourself as well as children and caregivers.

➤ For Chapter 1, it is helpful to devote more time to Centering Activities than in other chapters to help children discharge energy before (and in between) reading about traumatic stress and to break up work. Use Centering Activities in Part V for session and homework practice on SOS slow breathing and multisensory awareness.

➤ Adapt psycho-education on stress, trauma, and the brain to the reading level and ability to concentrate of children and caregivers.

➤ Use hand-model for brain image and understanding functions of key brain parts (Siegel, 1999). For a video description, see www.youtube.com/watch?v=kH-BO1rJXbQ.

➤ Use children's interests to promote understanding the brain (e.g., visual image tricks, or, for zombie lovers, *A Zombie's Guide to the Human Body* (Beck, 2010)), which includes parts of the brain.

PITFALLS TO AVOID ➤➤➤

➤ Therapists are seen by children as case managers and/or child protective services workers, responsible for monitoring safety in the home and making decisions about what children or caregivers can or cannot do.

➤ Children or caregivers interpret psycho-education to mean they are damaged, bad, or unworthy.

CHAPTER CHECKPOINTS

☐ 1. Establish a ritualized sequence for sessions, demonstrate respect for the child's safety plan, utilize a playful approach to develop skills, enhance expression of feelings and details with creative arts, accentuate important stories of strengths and overcoming obstacles.

☐ 2. Adapt psycho-educational materials to the child's developmental level and review with children and caregivers, emphasizing how 'alarm bells' are learned behaviors that help children (and caregivers) cope with 'tough times' and can later interfere with success at home or school. Help caregivers to use an understanding of their children's developmental level and experiences of trauma and coping strategies to avoid shaming of children or themselves. As appropriate, give caregivers NCTSN handouts on Understanding Trauma or from the Resource Parent Curriculum. Also, provide, as indicated, NCTSN handouts on specific traumas (e.g., helping children after tornadoes, domestic violence, or sex abuse).

☐ 3. Help children develop *SOS Picture Power Card* with Safe Place imagery and practice 'SOS' with six-step breathing, focusing on resources, seeking help, and helping others.

☐ 4. Help children develop 'Safety First' plans to protect children, caregivers, and practitioners from threats of violence, emotional abuse, or neglect, and for known 'triggers' for trauma reactions, including children's signal to safe adults and action plan if *Knots* begin to rise or *Self-Control Power* falls. 'Safety First' plans include who to call for help and self-care, what caring adults can do to help, and what to do if children have 'no words.'

RESOURCES

For additional resources on trauma and resiliency psycho-education, see:

National Child Traumatic Stress Network Resources for Caregivers, www.nctsn.org/resources/audiences/parents-caregivers#q3. On the NCTSN website, see *What Is Complex Trauma? A Resource Guide for Youth*, Complex Trauma Fact Sheets (NCTSN Complex Trauma Workgroup), and handouts from *Caring for Children Who Have Experienced Trauma: A Workshop for Resource Parents*.

Books for parents and caregivers: *Parenting from the Inside Out*—see especially the exercise on pp. 133–134 (Siegel & Hartzell, 2003), *Wounded Angels: Inspiration from Children in Crisis* (Kagan, 2016b), *Working with Traumatized Children* (Brohl, 2007), *Brainstorm: The Power and the Purpose of the Teenage Brain* (Siegel, 2014), and *The Whole-Brain Child: 12 Revolutionary Strategies to Nurture Your Child's Developing Mind* (Siegel & Bryson, 2012).

Encourage development of self- and co-regulation skills for children and caregivers with yoga, mindfulness, music, movement, etc. Recommended books include:

Baker, A. (2015). Personal Communication.

Flynn, L. (2013). *Yoga for children*. Avon, MA: Adams Media.

Guber, T., & Kalish, L. (2005). *Yoga pretzels: 50 fun yoga activities for kids and grownups*. Oxford, UK: Barefoot Books.

Harper, J. C. (2013). *Little flower yoga for kids: A yoga and mindfulness program to help your child improve attention and emotional balance*. Oakland, CA: New Harbinger.

MacLean, K. L. (2009). *Moody cow meditates*. Somerville, MA: Wisdom. (See also *Peaceful piggy*.)

Marra, T. (2004). *Depressed and anxious: The dialectical behavior therapy workbook for overcoming depression and anxiety*. Oakland, CA: New Harbinger.

Schlosberg, S. (1989). Personal communication.

Siegel, R. D. (2010). *The mindfulness solution: Everyday practices for everyday problems*. New York, NY: Guilford Press.

Snel, E. (2013). *Sitting still like a frog: Mindfulness exercises for kids*. Boston, MA: Shambhala.

Stanchfield, J. (2007). *Tips and tools: The art of experiential group facilitation*. Oklahoma City, OK: Wood 'n' Barnes.

NOTES

1. Adapted from Ford and Russo (2006).
2. Adapted from Gordon (2014).

2

A Little about Me

Recognizing and Expressing Feelings

OBJECTIVES

Children and caregivers help each other learn to:

- identify and accept feelings as normal bodily reactions;
- recognize and identify common feelings in others;
- increase affect modulation and self-control; and
- express feelings with color, drawings, rhythm, tonality, movement, and words.

Children and caregivers practice affect identification, expression, and modulation skills in sessions and at home or in group care.

OVERVIEW

Initial activities in Chapter 2 foster recognition of children's strengths and promote recognition and expression of common feelings with modulation. Workbook activities also provide opportunities for children to test whether it is safe to share feelings. Children typically watch faces and listen carefully to the tone of caregivers' and therapists' voices to see whether adults accept their real feelings, perceptions, and thoughts, and how safe it is to share what they really think and feel. It is important for therapists to watch the interactions (Action Cycles) of children and caregivers to assess how safe children feel to share, what is blocking expression of feelings, and what could help promote safety and trust.

Affect dyregulation is a primary concern in Complex Trauma, and Chapter 2 provides opportunities for children to get in touch with feelings in their bodies, to learn that everyone has feelings, and to find ways they can share those feelings with safe caregivers. Activities can also be used to open up discussion of how feelings in our bodies help us by providing clues that we are sensing something. Activities can also be used to help children share the kinds of feelings they often have and where they feel them in their bodies.

Chapter 2 helps children and caregivers recognize how feelings are normal and helpful. Therapists can reduce shame by stressing that feelings are part of what make us human and by helping children to understand that what makes us happy, sad, or angry is important for developing strengths and part of an integrated life story.

Feelings can also be understood as signals to do something. The word 'emotion' comes from the Latin word '*movēre*, to move.'[1] Feelings can remind us of situations we've encountered before and trigger bodily reactions, including movement. This is also very helpful in developing safety plans. For instance, a youth who feels her fist clenching can use this signal to start using multisensory tools that help her slow down and seek help from safe adults she has identified in different parts of her life, at home, at school, in after-school programs, in her neighborhood, etc. Safety steps can build on what helps children calm down, as well as strategies and practices used by family members and linked to children's cultural heritage (e.g., chanting a prayer while touching rosary beads).

Chapter 2 workbook pages promote the integration of drawing, rhythm, tonality, movement, and relationship as a means of increasing regulation. The intent is to facilitate developmental growth after traumas by increasing safety in relationships and increasing nurturing, attuned relationships with creative arts and movement activities linked to expressing and recognizing emotions and children's developmental levels. Hughes (2007, p. 139) described attunement as the "intersubjective sharing of affective states . . .

at the heart of the parent-child attachment . . . There is a realization, often implicit, that the pleasure being experienced is greater because it is being shared with the other."

In RLH sessions, safe caregivers are asked in sessions to copy (mirror) children's rhythm, tonality, and movement to foster attunement. Mirroring promotes attunement, with the adult reflecting children's movement, feelings, and beliefs using nonverbal, facial expressions, tone of voice, eye focus, and emotions along with children's words. With mirroring, children feel heard by the therapist. Mirroring in treatment demonstrates the empathy of the therapist and caregiver to children (Ogden & Fisher, 2015).

Perry (2014) described how multiple pathways can be used to restore regulation, including relational (child and caring adult), somato-sensory (bottom-up brain functions), cortical (top-down brain functions), and pharmacological. Cognitive behavioral strategies typically work top-down, which can be slower than utilizing a combination of relational, multisensory, and cognitive approaches. Sharing feelings in Chapter 2 with drawings, rhythm, music, and movement helps develop attunement between children and caregivers.

The RLH Session Structure promotes patterned, repetitive, multisensory, rhythmic, and fun activities that promote security that may have been lost after traumatic events. These 'healing' activities are then reinforced with practice as part of 'homework' assignments between sessions.

STEP BY STEP

	OPENINGS
Welcome	Thank children (and caregivers, if part of the session) for coming.
	Make the session special and differentiate from the rest of children's days (and, if needed, from previous counseling) with a ritual (e.g., special fist bump, herbal tea, or a magic trick).
My Thermometers	Encourage children to scan over their bodies as they complete *My Thermometers*. Their thermometers can be viewed as a measure of how they are feeling overall, like an internal weather report (Snel, 2013) or how fast a river representing their thoughts and feelings is flowing from a smooth and gentle current flowing over a soft, sandy bottom to rough water with multiple currents and foaming bubbles rushing over large rocks. It may be helpful to point out to children (and caregivers) that we can't change the weather outside (Snel, 2013) or the force of a river. We can instead step back, get the weather report or check how the river is flowing, accept what is happening, and use 'SOS for Stress,' children's Safety First card, or other steps to co-regulate and self-regulate with mindfulness of the weather or river.
	Use children and caregivers' thermometers, and especially the ratio of *Self-Control Power* to *Knots* (stress) to guide time allocation for Centering Activities needed for regulation and type of activities that may be most effective with different levels of movement (see guidelines in *The Pledge* and Chapter 1).
Safety First	Remind children, if necessary, about the safety signal established in Chapter 1.
	Assess safety from children's perspectives as children (and caregivers) share feelings in Chapter 2.
	Encourage children (and caregivers) to practice and to help each other use 'SOS for Stress' from Chapter 1, especially if they indicate moderate to high levels of *Knots*. Children can be encouraged to refocus on their breathing, slow down, become aware of resources that can help them, and then to seek help and help others. 'SOS for Stress' helps counter feelings of being alone and can be used to promote co-regulation by doing it together with safe caregivers and other adults helping children.
	If children appear unsafe, unwilling, or unable to share feelings, review the messages children are getting or have gotten from caregivers, family members, peers, or authorities that may be constricting expression. In these situations, consider:
	• Have viable safety precautions been implemented that match risks for children and the people they love?
	• Are authorities advocating mandates that children return to homes and relationships as treatment goals when children appear fearful of these homes or relationships?

	• Have authorities and service providers voiced the experiences and fears children have shared from past traumas, or have authorities and service providers appeared afraid to 'say the words' and share disclosures of abuse, neglect, family violence, or other interpersonal traumas?
	CENTERING ACTIVITIES
Breathing, Balancing, Yoga, and Movement to Increase Self- and Co-Regulation	Expand skills and use of 'SOS' and Safety First cards developed in Chapter 1 with breathing, balancing, and movement exercises. Recommended Centering Activities (see Part V) include: • *Breathe Like a Little Cat* (for showing feelings) • *Little Cat Breathing with Yoga* (for body awareness and movement) • *Roar Like a Lion* (to increase energy and courage) • *Breathe Like a Hummingbird* (to soothe as you move) See the *RLH Strategy and Activity Guide* (in Part V) for additional activities to increase modulation.
	LIFE STORYBOOK
Workbook Pages	Promote increased creative expression of feelings for workbook pages and reinforce session rituals to promote safety using *RLH Bookmark*: 1. Begin by having children select a special color to sketch each feeling as a free, spontaneous, and simple image, then accentuate details (e.g., asking children what the figure reminds them of, and then encouraging them to accentuate those features, or possibly to shape an initial sketch into a living being, a plant, an animal, or a person). 2. Identify the tone of voice accompanying this image or encourage children to experiment with different intonations. 3. Tap out a rhythm and intensity to match a feeling. 4. Match tone of voice with a note from the xylophone or keyboard. Encourage children to try out two to three other notes that blend with the first note, creating a chord selected by children to match a particular feeling or task from the workbook. Alterations in the notes selected can then be utilized to generate simple, short melodies. Repetitions of two or three chords can also be utilized to create a mood or feeling (see Austin, 2002). 5. Promote bodily awareness of each feeling by asking children and caregivers to imagine having the feeling in the picture (e.g., mad) and to show this by how they hold themselves, how their face would look, and with movement. Then scan over their bodies, from their toes up to their head, and share sensations of feelings (e.g., tense, relaxed, aches, etc.). 6. Identify feelings expressed with drawings, rhythm, chords, and movement using words. Ask how children show feelings (e.g., with a smile, a frown, a clenched fist, etc.). 7. Invite children to extend important stories with drawings, music, or movement. For instance, encourage continuation of movement with enactments involving movement or dance, utilizing children's metaphors and imagery. For instance, a sports move can be tied to a feeling (e.g., a 'happy' dunk shot in basketball, a 'sad' free shot, a 'powerful' soccer kick at goal). 8. Encourage children to add to stories about their drawings, music, or movements, where possible, with open-ended questions that enlarge children's perspectives.
Identify Something Fun	Encourage children and caregivers to identify something fun that they like to do, things that they are good at, and sports or games that they enjoy. This helps to enrich children's positive memories and to demonstrate that the therapist will focus on strengths, rather than problems, as many children expect. Follow up children's drawings of fun events with questions about times that they remember doing one of the things that they enjoyed (e.g., winning a game), as well as something that they may not have enjoyed (e.g., losing at a game). This helps children to see that it is possible to acknowledge and accept both good times and hard times as a normal part of life.

Recognize Feelings in Self and Others	Ask children to recognize feelings in others and within themselves. This may be challenging for many traumatized children. It is important to emphasize that feelings are natural and universal. Everyone feels fear, anger, sadness, and happiness at different times. For instance, children who lose a family member who was murdered may feel an urge to strike back. Feelings are not bad or good. Feelings are not the same as actions that we choose (Cohen et al., 2001). And, feelings change from moment to moment, flowing like waves (Marra, 2004) or leaves floating down a stream. Foster skills in recognizing emotions with role playing and identification of emotions in feeling charts, from photographs, illustrated children's storybooks, or magazines. Or, watch movies with strong emotions with no sound and ask children and adults to identify feelings.
Explore Feelings	Feeling Exercise:[2] Explore feelings with children and caregivers to guide service planning and 'homework': – "What's the feeling you have most?" – "What's the feeling you have the least amount of time?" – "What feelings would you like to have more of? Less of?" Remind children and caregivers that when children or adults go through 'tough times,' it's normal to have intense feelings. And, feelings (see above) can be seen as signals from our body to try to move, e-motions, and these feelings come with power (energy) to help us do things and make things better. Then explore activities with caregivers that can increase feelings children would like to have more of and reduce the feelings children would like to have less of.
Inside Outside Feelings[3]	Chapter 2 includes body outlines (Baker, 2013) for children (and caregivers) to share how they want others to see them feeling and how they really feel inside. Use body drawings to help children identify where in their bodies they experience feelings and to share how they feel in different situations. For Inside Feelings, (Ford & Russo, 2006) ask children who have been hurt physically or emotionally to draw where they feel hurt and stress. Ask them if they feel part of their body trying to move and what that body part would want to do. Ask children how they would like to feel in these parts of their bodies and what could help.
Express Feelings with Modulation	Ask children to tap a rhythm, add tonality, and try out a gesture, movement, or facial look to match each feeling drawn in Chapter 2 or on a feeling chart. Use the additional activities below and in the *RLH Strategy and Activity Guide* (in Part V) as needed to develop and reinforce sharing feelings with modulation: Practice making faces for each feeling. These can be photographed if the child or caregiver has a smartphone or digital camera, or this can be done while children are looking at a mirror (Mullin, 2004). Encourage children to make collages from cut-out photos or combining clips from movies and use these to share feelings chosen by children. Draw hearts and color in feelings showing how children feel at different times. Draw on body outlines where children (and caregivers) feel different feelings. This can be encouraged by asking children to close their eyes and imagine that they are feeling that way in the present time.[4] Ask children to color in a body outline (e.g., copies of the Inside Outside Feeling figures in Chapter 1), where children experience body sensations related to that feeling. Reinforce with children how sensations in our bodies show us feelings and how we can learn how to listen to our bodies and then use the messages our bodies are sending as clues to understand what is affecting us and to make things better. Draw Halloween pumpkins showing how children feel (Pratt, 2005).

	Ask children to make a list of all the feelings they can think of in three minutes (Cohen et al., 2001). Then draw these feelings, add rhythm and tone with glockenspiels, and enact them with a movement, a simple gesture, or a special look.
Encourage Storytelling	For important stories that the child starts, and to learn more to help with assessments, ask children to make up a short story and add a beginning, middle, and end. To enrich use of feelings, ask children to make up a story for important feelings on a feeling chart or shown in Chapter 2
Highlight Positive Beliefs	Elicit beliefs and promote the value of using feelings, stressing strengths, and coping with problems, and links, wherever possible, to the family's cultural and religious heritage.
CLOSINGS	
Repeat Thermo-meters (as Needed)	Use the *Knots* and *Self-Control Power* thermometers to check in with children if they appear to be becoming more stressed. Thermometers can be used at any time. This will help children begin to connect external variables with differences in their internal states. Use of the thermometers also provides a means for the therapist to validate children's abilities to 'stop' work that becomes too stressful, to switch to 'Centering Activities,' or to remind children to utilize self-soothing skills as needed.
'Homework' and 'Teamwork'	Encourage practice during the week of fun child-caregiver activities, recognizing feelings in family members and expressing feelings with modulation.
	Children's choices for fun activities can be utilized to encourage special times with caring adults every day, whenever possible. Therapists can also use children's favorites as reinforcements for working in sessions or as a fun way to end sessions. Therapists can encourage caring adults in separate sessions to do special things with children (e.g., crafts, knitting, origami, paint by number, Legos).
	Ask children and caregivers to take photos of each other showing a wide range of feelings (e.g., using smartphones or inexpensive digital cameras). Then, see if they can identify the feeling that goes with each facial expression. This can also be done with movies or live enactments in which children and caregivers act out feelings like a charades game, and then learn to identify the feeling each one is expressing. The intent of these and similar activities is to increase accuracy in feeling recognition by family members.
	See the *RLH Strategy and Activity Guide* (in Part V) for other activities for identifying feelings in oneself, in others, and expressing feelings with modulation.
Special Time, *Progress Note*, Reminder of Next Session	Continue special time at the end of the session and 'collaborative documentation' by completing *Progress Note* and other required forms together, as appropriate.
	Invite children and caregivers to suggest things they would like to do in the next session, any other supportive and safe caregivers to invite to the session (if appropriate), and schedule a date and time.

►►► TIPS

► Encourage children (and caregivers) to learn how animals use their feelings to cope with different situations, to keep themselves safe, and to calm down after stressful experiences. Build on Centering Activities to learn cat and dog secrets and recommend reading *Cool Cats, Calm Kids* (Williams, 2005), or similar books, with caregivers.

► Pay attention to what children identify as leading up to feelings of anger, fear, sadness, and courage. These often provide clues to both strengths and triggers that will be helpful in later trauma work.

► Discuss with traumatized children how fear helps protect them (Macy et al., 2003). By recognizing how their bodies are signaling an emotion, such as fear, children can become aware of 'early warning signals' of danger and then implement safety plans developed with caring adults.

PITFALLS TO AVOID ➤➤➤

➤ Therapist urges children to reveal or disclose feelings or experiences with parents or other adults in the room who have not met safety criteria.

➤ Therapist is uncomfortable with expression of feelings, or with creative arts (e.g., music or movement), leading children to feel constricted.

➤ Therapist omits strengthening or building attunement and emotional connections through integration of nonverbal creative arts (music, movement) with narratives for workbook pages.

➤ Children are living in an unsafe home and safety plans are not developed, or revised, when initial plans appear inadequate.

➤ Children living in placement have heard a message from parents, extended family members, or authorities that they must return to an unsafe home or participate in unsafe visits.

➤ Children are living in placement and do not have, or are not aware of, a viable 'permanency plan', including a backup (concurrent) plan for finding and strengthening substitute guardians in case primary caregivers are unable or unwilling to do what is necessary to protect and care for children to maturity.

CHAPTER CHECKPOINTS

☐ 1. Ask children to test whether the practitioner will maintain the 'sanctuary' of sessions by checking on how 'Safety First' plans will be implemented.

☐ 2. Guide adults in sessions to share their feelings and experiences in a way that helps children learn from caring adults without overburdening or traumatizing them with adults' experiences.

☐ 3. Ask children and caregivers to practice recognition of feelings in self and others with photos, movies, enactments, drawings, or collages.

☐ 4. Encourage children and caregivers to share feelings in a safe way and to accept feelings as natural without shame.

RESOURCES

Encourage development of self- and co-regulation skills for children and caregivers with yoga, mindfulness, music, and movement using the books listed in Chapter 1. Books that promote acceptance of changing feelings are helpful (e.g., *Double-Dip Feelings* (Cain, 2001), *Alexander and the Terrible, Horrible, No Good, Very Bad Day* (Viorst, 1987), *You've Got Dragons* (Cave & Maland, 2003), and *Visiting Feelings* (Rubenstein, 2014)). Feeling charts are also useful.

NOTES

1. See Merriam-Webster for complete definition: http://www.merriam-webster.com/dictionary/emotion.
2. Adapted from Kinneburgh (2013) (for more information, see Blaustein and Kinneburgh, 2010).
3. From Ford and Russo (2006).
4. Adapted from Cohen et al. (2006).
5. Pratt, K. (2005). Personal communication.

3
Heroes

Restoring Hope, Inspiring Change

OBJECTIVES

- Children and caregivers identify (or learn to identify):

    - people acting as heroes who appeal to children, including popular figures from sports, music, politics, media, fictional characters from books, movies, and real people in their families or communities or with the same cultural heritage as children;
    - attributes and actions of these people that make them heroic; and
    - how these people or characters in stories learned skills, got help and helped others.

- Children and caregivers develop increased self- and co-regulation skills modeled after how their heroes learned skills, got help from others, and practiced skills and problem-solving to become better able to manage difficult situations.
- Children and caregivers become better able to focus their minds and use the energy in their bodies to make things better for themselves and others.

OVERVIEW

Stories of heroes, male and female, can be utilized to renew hope and inspire courage to move beyond the constraints of children and caregivers' fears and to experiment with new strategies to manage problems.

The meaning of heroism can be explored by asking children to draw someone who they admire. Afterwards, discussion can include the different traits that a particular individual possesses that make him or her special and how that person mustered the courage to face adversity in his or her life. For example, if children are interested in sports, a sports hero could be identified who they admire. This would optimally be someone who is similar to the child in some way (e.g., children's experiences, special skills or interests, or their ethnic heritage). Children can then be encouraged to learn about the adversities this person faced, what helped this 'hero' keep going and become successful, who helped this person, what helped him or her develop his or her special skills, and how he or she overcame hardships. Children can be encouraged to explore a hero's strengths and weaknesses, how he or she faced challenges or danger, and what helped him or her stay safe and overcome problems. It is important to highlight how he or she was able to get help along the way (e.g., from mentors, family members, teachers, coaches, etc.) so children can see that all of us can act in heroic ways and real heroes help each other, in contrast to the myths of solo invincible crusaders. This can be used to encourage children to reach out to others to get help, just as the heroes in their lives got help to develop their skills and to succeed in overcoming challenges.

Discussing heroes provides an opportunity to help children learn how ordinary people become heroes. It is important to emphasize how everyone has weaknesses, just like fictional superheroes. Superman had kryptonite. Luke Skywalker was impulsive. Heroes learn to overcome their weaknesses with the courage to be honest with themselves and the courage to change. Stories of famous heroes can be used to emphasize that courage, like other skills, is learned through repeated practice (Miller, 2002). Caregivers can help their children become heroes by encouraging them to practice being brave in safe ways and by asking children to share everyday acts that demonstrate courage.

Encouraging children to help others is an important part of recovery. Helping others builds self-esteem and helps children move beyond images of children themselves as damaged, sick, fragile, bad, or dangerous to others. Caregivers, teachers, therapists, and other caring adults can bring out heroic qualities in children by helping them to identify skills, talents, and interests, and then to develop these skills and use them to help others in their families, schools, and communities. Models of caring and helping others from the child's family and cultural heritage can also be used to promote the value of helping others.

Drawing heroes provides a natural segue to identifying attributes of self-regulation that children admire in heroes, including skills the hero relies on when going through tough times. Real heroes get scared, sad, and mad. To succeed, heroes learn skills and develop relationships that help them remain calm enough (centered) to think about what is happening, to plan strategies to make things better, and to carry out these strategies. Children's heroes can be used as models for developing skills such as focusing, learning, problem-solving, and affect regulation. Affect regulation includes developing the ability to calm oneself with multiple modalities (e.g., imagery, music, rhythm, slow breathing, meditation, progressive muscle relaxation, sports, dancing, yoga, singing, and writing poetry or journals). Focusing allows children to change how their minds are working in order to facilitate problem-solving and change long-standing patterns of preoccupation with hyper-vigilance and reliance on impulsive reactions, fighting, fleeing, freezing, or fainting to cope with reminders of past traumas or current stressful situations.

Chapter 3 activities, such as the *Superhero Band-Aid*, facilitate children sharing what they feel is healing for them. Practitioners and caregivers can build on what helps children (e.g. hugs from dad, grandma's chicken soup, or praying with mom) to foster co-regulation and self-soothing at times of distress. The Superhero Band-Aid also facilitates use of cognitive behavioral techniques, including expanded use of self-monitoring with *My Thermometers*, refocusing one's sight and thoughts on positive, safety resources, and decreasing preoccupation with exaggerated risk factors. The band-aid exercise elicits the child and caregiver's sense of what helps to heal and these strategies can then be incorporated into the child's Safety First Card from Chapter 1 for managing feelings of distress from within or without and further developed in Chapter 4 into the child and caregiver's personal *Pocket Power Cards*.

Key elements of Chapter 3 include learning how heroes had to practice skills (e.g., athletes or musicians practicing multiple hours every day and building skills step by step with mentoring by teachers, coaches, and other safe adults who have mastered skills and were willing to pass along

> **Heroes Seek Help and Help Others**

> **Help children welcome the energy in their bodies, rather than fighting to control it.**

what they have learned). The neurobiological principle that "Neurons that fire together, wire together" (Hebb, 1949) can be used to frame how children and caregivers can develop new and more effective coping patterns, including how they use their senses and their bodies. To do this, however, takes practice. This can start in sessions and be reinforced with 'homework' and in services provided by collaterals.

Children and caregivers can "rewire" (after Siegel, 2011) the way their minds work by learning to refocus their attention. It helps to think of attention as a powerful tool, like a giant telescope that children can focus on different objects. Using a mindfulness perspective, children and caregivers can be encouraged to refocus their attention in different ways (e.g., 'SOS for Stress' refocuses attention on breathing, resources in the environment, getting help, and helping others). By redirecting their attention, children are also 'rewiring' patterns of neural functioning. With practice and support from caregivers, they can change how they use their minds and develop their refocusing abilities. Children's heroes can provide models for refocusing attention (e.g., a batter in a baseball game concentrating on the next pitch) and be used to encourage children to develop the same skills with centering activities in sessions, with caregivers at home, and in skill-building activities such as sports or music.

Chapter 3 can also be used to reframe how children or caregivers perceive their level of arousal. Heroes use their energy to do something to help others. By modeling after heroes, children and caregivers can be encouraged to accept the energy level in their bodies and to learn to redirect it in ways that may be more useful to make things better. For instance, many children with traumatic stress move their hands, arms, or legs a great deal and show symptoms of hyperactivity. Rather than fighting against children's need to move, it helps to provide things for them to do with their bodies. This can include a wide range of fidget toys for their hands or use of movement and yoga activities so they can move in sessions in a safe way.

Children who are constantly moving their hands can be encouraged to use their hands to tap a rhythm on a drum or to create art forms. Children who are thumping their legs may be able to use their legs to express themselves with a dance or bounce while sitting on a Disc 'o' Sit or fitness ball.

Accepting children's arousal levels helps to avoid battles in which children see caregivers, teachers, and therapists as trying to constrict them, leading to defiance, running away, or fighting back. Instead, therapists can encourage caregivers to welcome and accept children's arousal levels and to use modalities in therapy sessions, at home, at school, and in the community to help children express this energy in appropriate ways. Focusing on how heroes use their energy level in Chapter 3 can normalize this perspective on use of our level of arousal and model after what heroes do. This can help caregivers to help their children to use their energy to enhance skills and talents and learn to better manage difficult situations, rather than remaining locked into battles of control.

STEP BY STEP

	OPENINGS
Welcome, Safety Signals, *My Thermometers*	Welcome children and caregivers, reinforce the use of safety signals, if necessary, and ask them to complete *My Thermometers*. Frame feelings on Thermometers as sources of energy that can be used to make things better.
Magical Moment	Children's heroes can be used as guides to help children figure out the 'tricks' behind skills (e.g., how an athlete puts a spin on a basketball or baseball).
	CENTERING ACTIVITIES
Breathing, Balancing, Yoga, Movement, and 'Improv' to Increase Self- and Co-Regulation	Centering Activities for Chapter 3 help children with balance, slow breathing, focused attention, and modulation. Recommended Centering Activities (see Part V) include: • Blowing Bubbles • Mirroring with Music • Fingertip Concentration • Dolphin Inverse Stretch (for increasing flexibility and discharging energy) • Juggling (to increase focused attention) • Back Stretch (for smoothing out stress) • Healing Hands and Breathing Slow (for calming) • Chair Yoga Exercises (for sitting through a long class) See the *RLH Strategy and Activity Guide* (in Part V) for other activities to increase modulation.
	LIFE STORYBOOK
Identify Heroes	Encourage children to learn about a wide range of heroes encompassing the many different facets of their world. Therapists can draw on autobiographies for children about famous and important people, and interviews with prominent athletes, artists, and representatives of different ethnic groups, including the child's own ethnic or cultural group. Learning about heroes from the child's family and community is very helpful. Encourage reading heroes books. The Heroes Library (in Part IV) lists recommended books for children with heroes from different ethnic groups for three reading levels. It is highly recommended that each agency or clinic have a Heroes Library of books to loan matching the ages, reading level, and ethnic heritage of clients. Highlight how heroes develop skills over time through practice, how real heroes have fears and weaknesses, and how heroes must work with others to overcome obstacles. Simply put, any heroes without vulnerabilities and weaknesses would be unreal and boring! Even Superman had to watch out for kryptonite. The same is true for moms and dads, grandmas and grandpas.
Normalize Vulnerabilities	Highlight heroes' reactions (helpful and unhelpful) to danger and tie this to how boys and girls, men and women have very normal reactions to traumatic events. Emphasize the importance of fostering strengths and avoiding shame by recognizing how everyone has sensitivities and vulnerabilities. Reference to popular fictional heroes (e.g., Harry Potter, Luke Skywalker), famous athletes, or singers may be useful to emphasize how heroes learn to accept their weaknesses and work on becoming stronger. This usually means getting help from mentors intensive and extended practice.

Normalize Seeking Help	Encourage children to learn how famous people or characters were helped by relatives, mentors, or friends to develop special skills, to muster the courage to face adversity, to grieve losses, and to endure hardships; use readings from the Heroes Library (in Part IV).
Help Children and Caregivers Accept and Utilize Energy Levels	Focusing can be challenging for children and caregivers with traumatic stress, and frustration completing tasks can increase feelings of shame or depression.
	Help children and caregivers not criticize themselves for having scattered thoughts or difficulty focusing and instead think of our thoughts (and feelings) flowing in and out like waves (Marra, 2004) or flowing like rivers (Harper, 2013). One thought follows another, like leaves floating down a river. Encourage children to:
	"Close your eyes and see if you can imagine a river flowing. See if you can form a photo in your mind of your thoughts and feelings floating down the river. The river may flow slowly or fast in different places and at different times. That's just how rivers and our minds work.
	If you like, draw your own river of thoughts with leaves or branches floating downstream, going fast and slow in different parts of your picture."
Focusing	Encourage children to build their abilities to focus with practice and at the same time respect and accept their minds' need to keep generating thoughts and feelings. Heroes learn to increase their ability to focus their minds (sight, smell, hearing, thoughts), even when stressed. For fans of J. K. Rowling, think of Harry Potter and Hermione focusing energy through their wands. Or, Luke Skywalker using 'the Force.'
	Encourage children and caregivers to develop greater *Self-Control Power*, so they can do what they want to do in different situations.
	Focusing exercises include:
	• Pick something you would like to focus on (adapted from Harper, 2013). This could be a painting, a lamp, or something outside like a tree. • Have an adult ring a bell or singing bowl or tap a drum to signal when to start and stop. • See if you can focus for 15 seconds, then try 30 seconds, 45 seconds, 60 seconds, 90 seconds, 2 minutes . . . • Practice each day and see if you can increase your time. • Adults can practice too . . . • Now try focusing while you do a yoga position like the tree pose (after Harper, 2013). • Try keeping your focus while you balance first on one leg. • Then try keeping your focus while you balance on the other leg. • If you want, try to balance on one leg and then see if you can keep your balance with your eyes closed. This can be difficult. We balance with help from our eyes, the feeling of our feet planted on the floor, and parts of our inner ear. Even if you can't see, your other sensory systems, for example feeling the position of your feet on the floor and your inner ear, can help keep you balanced.
	• **Extra challenge:** Try balancing the peacock feather with your eyes open, with one eye closed, and then with both eyes closed. Is it possible?
	Heroes' Capes: Use Hero's Cape Activity (in Part V) to encourage children to explore the qualities that comprise a hero and identify individuals that they feel are heroes in their families and communities. Children will identify their own strengths, interests, character traits, and resiliencies in effort to create a 'Hero's Cape' and identify themselves as a hero to themselves and others.
	Caregivers can also be asked to create Hero's Capes showing how they see hero qualities in their children.
	Similarly, siblings can be asked to create Hero's Capes showing how they see hero qualities in each other.

	CLOSINGS
'Homework' and 'Teamwork'	Inspire children to recognize and develop hero qualities in themselves. Encourage children to write, draw, or enact what they did to help others and what helped them develop the strength to keep going when things got bad.
	Children may wish to create their own storybook, song, or sports move (movement) named in honor of a particular hero.
	See the *RLH Strategy and Activity Guide* (in Part V) for other activities for recognizing and developing hero qualities.
Continue Closing from Earlier Chapters	Repeat Thermometers, if needed, and provide special time at the end of the session and 'collaborative documentation' by completing *Progress Note* and other required forms together, as appropriate. Invite children and caregivers to suggest things they would like to do in next session and schedule a date and time.

➤➤➤ TIPS

➤ Use stories of people who experienced similar traumas as children.

➤ Help children see how real heroes feel frightened but learn how to utilize their reactions and get help to overcome hardships.

➤ Respect the child and adult's need to stay on guard and not become too relaxed (Straus, 2013) given what the child experienced and ongoing dangers that therapists may not be aware of.

PITFALLS TO AVOID ➤➤➤

➤ Glorifying heroes as superstars, as perfect, or near perfect.

➤ Presenting heroes as good versus bad and ignoring how everyone has weaknesses and makes mistakes.

➤ Minimizing how heroes develop skills slowly with extensive practice, instruction from mentors, and support from key people in their lives.

➤ Reinforcing myths of solitary 'heroes' as an ideal.

CHAPTER CHECKPOINTS

☐ 1. Help children recognize how heroes have skills, resources and weaknesses, make mistakes, and work together, relying on other people to help them overcome hardships and succeed.

☐ 2. Help children identify real people in their lives who have acted as heroes.

☐ 3. Help children identify how they have acted as heroes, helping others.

RESOURCES

Consider fun learning games such as *Spot It* for concentration and *Jenga* for fine motor coordination, balance, and frustration tolerance.

It is very helpful to utilize books about heroes from the child's community and ethnic heritage. Recommended books about heroes include:

McDonough, Y. Z. (2002). *Who was Harriet Tubman?* New York, NY: Grosset & Dunlop.

McDonough, Y. Z. (2010). *Who was Rosa Parks?* New York, NY: Grosset & Dunlop.

Meltzer, B. (2010). *Heroes for my son.* New York, NY: HarperStudio.

Obama, B. (2010). *Of thee I sing.* New York, NY: Knopf. (This book encourages parents to identify hero qualities in their children.)

Pascal, J. B. (2008). *Who was Abraham Lincoln?* New York, NY: Penguin.

See the Heroes Library for a guide to books about heroes listed by reading level with links to ethnic groups.

4

Power Plans

Resilience-Centered Safety Plans for Children and Caregivers

OBJECTIVES

- Children complete and practice use of the *Youth Power Plan* to prevent or reduce traumatic stress reactions.
- Caregivers complete and practice use of *Caregiver Power Plans* to prevent or reduce traumatic stress reactions.
- Practitioners complete *Caregiver Power Plans* to prevent or reduce secondary traumatic stress reactions.
- *Power Plans* identify skills and supportive relationships, triggers to traumatic stress reactions and safety plans built on re-establishment of attunement with caregivers, multsensory co-regulation, development of more effective responses, and practice with caregivers in a range of situations.

OVERVIEW

Chapter 4 provides a structured worksheet for youths to develop a resiliency-focused and multisensory safety plan to help prevent and reduce traumatic stress reactions. A separate *Caregiver Power Plan* (in Part V) guides caregivers and practitioners to develop their own safety plans to prevent or reduce primary and secondary traumatic stress reactions and to use their understanding of traumatic stress and resilience to help the children in their lives. Multisensory skill-building and relationship enhancement developed in Chapters 1–3 provide the framework for developing a written plan that emphasizes child, family, and collaborative strengths and resources. In RLH, *Power Plans* provide the planning structure to build Relationships and Emotional Self- and Co-Regulation to improve Action Cycles. Safety plans are especially important when children are frequently reminded of previous traumas or have experienced recurrent traumas.

Traumatic events perceived by children or adults as life-threatening, or leading to severe injury or loss, have been described as blocking the child or adult's capacity to do something, to move in a way that could make things better. For instance, a 5-year-old may be cowering in the corner of the kitchen shaking with terror as he watches his parents fight and his mother stab his father with a knife. He feels trapped, helpless, and torn between the urge to help and his fears. The child naturally wants to stop his parents fighting but may be terrified to do so, or forced to stay away. After the fight, when the child tries to reconnect, a distressed parent may send him away out of shame or anger. The child may feel alone, or like he made his parents fight and his mother or father hate him because he is so terrible.

Empowering Caregivers: Converting Behavior Problems into Learning Opportunities

Power Plans bring out skills and strengths in children, and guide work to rebuild (or build) connections and change interactive patterns. Caregivers play a central role in this process and can use the *Caregiver Power Plan* to identify their children's strengths, what leads to cycles of problem behaviors, and what can help their children to become more successful in managing reminders of past problems and other stressors. The *Youth Power Plan* asks children what adults do that helps them and what makes things worse. This is condensed into the *Pocket Power Plan*. Caregivers can pull out copies of the youth's *Pocket Power Plan* or post it in the house (e.g., on the refrigerator) to remind themselves and children of steps that can help. Caregivers can also use their own *Pocket Power Card* to help keep themselves composed to implement effective and trauma-informed discipline when children become dysregulated.

Empowering caregivers builds on an understanding of the brain and how to increase self-regulation introduced in Chapter 1 and *Trauma Symptoms and the Brain* (Caregiver Addendum in Part V). Behavior problems are often old coping behaviors that children developed to help them survive stressful or traumatic experiences. Behavior problems typically reflect a breakdown in children's integration within themselves (Siegel & Bryson, 2012) and with caregivers and other critical relationships. To help children, a four-step discipline approach is outlined that builds on an understanding of the brain and encourages caregivers to determine first if a behavior is important, and if so, then:

1. Use 'SOS' for caregivers.
2. Decode the behavior:

   • How does it help children cope?
   • Brain modulation level: 'secure,' 'alarm mode,' 'reacting'
   • Developmental level: emotional age, cognitive functioning
   • Arousal level: hyper . . . modulated . . . hypo

3. Connect with children nonverbally with your eyes, facial expressions, tone of voice, posture, gestures, timing, and intensity.[1] Ask yourself, "What could I do to help my child if I had no words?"[2] Ask, "What happened?" Offer to help make things better together.
4. Make it a learning experience (4 R's): **R**e-do's, **R**eframe (as coping), **R**estitution (matched to cultural heritage), **R**eplace (reactive behavior patterns with adaptive skills).

Chapter 4 Centering Activities provide opportunities for caregivers to experiment with matching modulation activities with children's levels of arousal. This can be augmented by home-based services and assistance to caregivers to access or utilize space and tools. Providing a safe space, freedom to move, and attuning messages from therapists (and caregivers) helps children to decrease levels of arousal or agitation.

Low lights, soft colors, soft sounds, lotions with calming scents, rocking, swinging, and being with a safe person can help. Gentle but firm (deep tactile) pressure is also comforting and reduces arousal. For instance, if you stub your finger, it helps to squeeze it gently but firmly. Gentle but firm tactile pressure appears to calm children, reducing their heart rate and decreasing the arousal level of their parasympathetic nervous system (Warner et al., 2014). In contrast, ruffling children's skin or tickling (light pressure) increases arousal.

Most parents understand that children (and adults) need to get outside and play. Children who feel locked up in a house become irritable, especially if stressful events are taking place. Getting outside, or to a gym, provides opportunities for physical play and helps everyone calm down. For families who lack safe neighborhoods or parks, assistance in getting to a community center can be a great help.

Co-Regulation to Tame Serial Crises

Children's dysregulation and behavioral problems can provide opportunities for caregivers to demonstrate to children how *Power Plans* will be implemented to restore safety and how the family has changed interaction patterns (Action Cycles) building on skills, resources, and family pride. Children can be expected to test whether their caregivers and families have truly changed or whether increased stress will prompt repetitions of past neglect, violence, or crises for children, families, and communities. Caregivers can help children calm down and learn new skills by using their understanding of children's reactions and matching interventions to children's level of arousal, security, and attachments.

For hyper-aroused children, more intensity in activities, increased repetitions, or a longer time may be needed to calm down (Warner et al., 2014). For example, a child triggered by reminders of abuse in her family may need to toss a large fitness ball vigorously for several minutes before continuing to draw pictures in her *Life Storybook*. Slow, steady bouncing calms with vestibular and proprioceptive input. Similarly, rocking with a slow, steady rhythm, for instance with the child prone over a fitness ball, can help decrease arousal level, and help calm the child. This can be guided by a safe, emotionally attuned caregiver in a safe space. Children may need to repeat an activity vigorously to get sufficient sensory input to satiate their need for that type of input (Warner et al., 2014). Practitioners can watch for children developing a steady rhythm in their movement.

For hypo-aroused children, gradual shifts in pressure with prolonged moderate sensory input are recommended to increase arousal level (Warner et al., 2014) (e.g., a safe caregiver rolling a physioball over a child's back with gradually faster patting motions over 20 minutes may help the child's arousal increase gradually to a more comfortable level, within the child's 'window of tolerance'). In contrast, a sudden, strong input (e.g., yelling, pushing, poking) could lead to increased dysregulation (Warner et al., 2014).

Caregivers need to demonstrate over time that they are replacing any unavailability of caring adults, violence, or unpredictability of the past with consistency. This can mean rebuilding family rituals, from getting up in the morning, breakfast, going to school, returning home, afterschool activities, dinner, to bedtime rituals designed to calm and reassure. Caregivers also play a central role in building pride in oneself, one's family, one's cultural heritage, and one's community to counter shame and isolation following traumatic events.

When children misbehave, trauma-informed caregivers learn to reconnect before they redirect (Siegel & Bryson, 2012). Caregivers can re-attune to dysregulated children, right brain to right brain, holding off on trying to reason or make verbal demands when children are dysregulated. Caregivers can use their own modulation skills to understand their own stress reactions, to understand what is leading to children's dysregulation, and to implement simple steps that help avoid battles and repetitions of past conflicts. This means working from the emotional level of development of children when triggered (e.g., a 13-year-old may start acting like a 3-year-old when reminded of living for years with serial family violence, emotional abuse, and witnessing sexual assaults).

Offering choices geared to children's developmental level at the time of the traumas can help avoid caregivers inadvertently increasing children's feelings of being trapped and unsafe. So, a parent could offer a child acting like a 3-year-old two choices (worked out ahead of time), then ask the child to take one to five minutes to decide what he or she wants to do and keep the child in sight. Choices to foster regulation could include taking five minutes to calm down reading a favorite book or balancing a peacock feather while walking around the living room.

Once the child has calmed down sufficiently, the caregiver can help the child to explore 'what happened'. This helps the child integrate powerful feelings with words and opens up possibilities of reasoning with his or her left prefrontal cortex and the help of the caregiver. The child can be encouraged to tell the story in his or her own words of what happened and what was so distressing (Siegel & Bryson, 2012). Then, the child and caregiver can work out strategies to handle similar situations better next time and practice these to make them more likely to happen.

This approach to discipline avoids common cycles of increasing crises in which caregivers feel they must control the child by demands or threats, leading the child to feel more alone, shamed, and desperate. Instead, caregivers can join with the child, brain to brain, working with thechild's level of arousal and safety to jointly figure out better solutions. Discipline can thus be used to help to repair disrupted attachments.

> **Avoid discipline that increases a child feeling trapped. Even cute little chipmunks will bite if pressed against a wall.**

STEP BY STEP

	OPENINGS
Welcome	*My Thermometers* plus *Safety reminders* and *Magical Moment*, if needed.
	CENTERING ACTIVITIES
Breathing, Balancing, Yoga, and Movement to Increase Self- and Co-Regulation	Centering Activities for Chapter 4 help children with balance, energy discharge, and modulation, and include more gross motor activities. Recommended Centering Activities (see Part V) include: • Disc 'o' Sit and Balance Discs (for increasing focus and balance and child-caregiver attunement) • Fitness balls (for balance and child-caregiver attunement) • Sensorimotor Activities for Smaller Spaces and Larger Spaces(to promote use of sensory resistance, touch, sight, pressure, and movement for modulation) • Bear Stretch and Relax • Beach Rest See the *RLH Strategy and Activity Guide* (in Part V) for other activities to increase modulation.
	LIFE STORYBOOK
Practitioner Power Plan	Complete your own *Power Plan* for the practitioner separately and share that you did this. Use ProQOL (Stamm, 2009) to help assess overall Compassion Satisfaction, Secondary PTSD, and Compassion Fatigue. Identify common types of triggers associated with children or families that led to stress experienced in treatment.

	Identify sources of 'Compassion Satisfaction' and resources to help prevent secondary traumatic stress. Own your attachment and temperament patterns and incorporate in healing and preventive strategies secondary traumatic stress. For instance, for highly driven, anxious practitioners, it helps to normalize how high-drive work habits are reinforced in many countries and equated with high achievement. Highly driven and anxious people may tend to ruminate more than others (e.g., "What if . . . ?"). Neurobiologists have described a biological predisposition to worry and generalized anxiety marked by higher norepinephrine and less active GABA in the basal ganglia nerve system. It is also possible to develop higher norepinephrine from under-sleeping and too much caffeine. Stress reactions for highly driven and anxious people are like a well-traveled major highway that your brain takes when experiencing 'tough times'. You can get stuck on this speeding highway seemingly going in circles and making little progress. The more worry, the stronger the worry pathway, and the more likely you are to find yourself stuck in an eight-lane speedway with no exits. To change this pattern means learning, practicing, reinforcing, and then more practicing of a healthier pathway, not the eight-lane worry-way. *RLH Power Plans* for practitioners, just as for children and caregivers, include multisensory, multimodal steps: • Breathing, reminders of being cared for (e.g., images or pictures or videos of someone who has cared for you and who you care for), movement, and use of our senses: eyes, ears, nose, taste, and kinesthetic and proprioceptive awareness. • Enhancing images of what makes you feel good. • Seeking help for yourself from someone you trust. Once you have developed strategies to prevent secondary PTSD, the hard part, of course, is to implement them. Getting a 'buddy' to help you stay on track can help. Practicing your strategies in many different situations helps to generalize. Playing a music clip on a smartphone or tablet or PC can remind you to do your 'SOS for Stress' or pull out and implement your *Pocket Power Plan*.
Youth Power Plan	Introduce *Power Plans* as tools to build on the child, family, and cultural strengths to achieve the goals set out by the child and caregiver. Normalize problems or crises as expected, given long-standing patterns and stressors around the family. Ask children if they prefer working on their *Power Plan* with the practitioner alone or with identified safe caregivers. **Intersperse Centering Activities as needed to help children and caregivers stay modulated and able to focus on materials.** For example, ask children and caregivers to complete two pages of the *Power Plan* and then do a Centering Activity or do an activity after every page. Aim, wherever possible, to complete *Power Plans* in one session. Reinforce resiliency factors (skills, talents, motivation to help, relationships) to help children become stronger than reminders of traumatic events. Highlight and help children share with safe caregivers how cycles of stress reactions work, early warning signs, and ways children have identified that adults can make things worse and how they can make things better. Then, help children and safe caregivers to prepare for reminders with safety plans. This can be developed into a playful game (e.g. "What would you do if _____ happened?" (Siegel & Bryson, 2012). Therapists or caregivers can write the child and caregiver's answers into *Power Plans*.

Caregiver Power Plans	Ask caregivers to complete their own *Power Plans* as children complete their Power Plans.
	Review the use of *Trauma Symptoms and the Brain* (in Part V), introduced in Chapter 1.
	Help caregivers identify triggers to stress reactions.
	Help caregivers understand that children's stress reactions are often not about the caregiver, and instead reflect entrenched coping behaviors for survival developed during traumatic events.
	Help caregivers to identify children's brain mode, developmental levels, attachment pattern, and arousal level in stress reactions.
	Then, help caregivers to develop strategies to connect to children, right brain to right brain, and show children that the caregiver can hear and accept their experience (attunement and validation).
	Help children co-regulate with multisensory centering activities matched to them.
	Once children are calm enough for verbal processing, help them figure out what happened, identify triggers, and jointly work out plans to be more successful when stressed again.
	Incorporate effective self- and co-regulation steps into *Youth* and *Caregiver Power Plans* and *Pocket Power Plans*.
Pocket Power Card	Condense *Power Plans* into *Pocket Power Cards* for use by children and caregivers when children sense signals of stress reactions.
	Incorporate components of 'SOS for Stress' and the 'Safety First' cards from Chapter 1 into the *Pocket Power Plans*.
	Make a copy of children's *Pocket Power Card* for caregivers and encourage posting in the kitchen (e.g., on the refrigerator or another easily accessed site).
	Arrange practice times for *Pocket Power Plans* with support from caregivers identified in children's primary environments: home, school, after-school programs, neighborhood, and extended family.
	Practice strategies for self- and co-regulation in a wide range of situations to strengthen and promote generalization.
	CLOSINGS
'Homework' and 'Teamwork'	This chapter could be guided by a home-based support or intensive-in-home services worker who is part of a trauma-informed team serving children using the RLH workshop and model to help coordinate treatment by different service providers.
	Use *Power Plans* to develop service plans.
	See the *RLH Strategy and Activity Guide* (in Part V) for other activities for developing safety plans and increased modulation.
Special Time, Thermometers, Progress Note, Reminder of Next Session	Continue special time at the end of the session, if helpful, and 'collaborative' *Progress Note*, as appropriate. Invite children and caregivers to suggest things they would like to do in the next session and schedule a date and time. Consider anyone else to invite to support children. Repeat Thermometers and Centering Activities if necessary.

▶▶▶ TIPS

➤ Match caregiver responses to children's arousal levels, children's developmental levels, and co-regulation strategies that have proven successful for children.

➤ Remind caregivers to 'connect' before they 'redirect' (Siegel & Bryson, 2012) and that it takes time and extensive practice to change long-standing trauma reaction patterns.

➤ Practice use of *Power Plans* for a wide range of problems and situations to increase adaptations and value.

➤ Use problems that develop as opportunities to improve *Power Plans*.

PITFALLS TO AVOID ▷▷▷

➢ Caregivers continue to use disciplinary strategies that remind children of past traumas and increase children's fears or sense of isolation (e.g., use of time-outs or threats of placements for children with insecure attachments).

➢ Caregivers and practitioners reinforce children's beliefs that children must change on their own in order to earn caring and security in their families.

➢ Caregivers and authorities rely on verbal direction and demands for highly aroused children.

➢ Caregivers and children expect perfection to avoid shame.

CHAPTER CHECKPOINTS

☐ 1. Help children complete *Youth Power Plans* using an image of their heroes to encourage development of skills and resources.

☐ 2. Help children complete *Pocket Power Cards* and identify what they and others can do to help them stay calm and prevent traumatic stress reactions.

☐ 3. Help primary caregivers complete *Caregiver Power Plans* identifying their own triggers and developing plans to keep themselves and their children calm when reminded of traumatic events.

☐ 4. Guide children and caregivers in the practice of self-soothing skills, including 'SOS for Stress,' six-step breathing, muscle relaxation, 'Safe Place' imagery, Mind Power, and 'thought-shifting.'

RESOURCES

See the handouts for parents and caregivers from NCTSN (www.nctsn.org) on helping children with challenging behaviors who have experienced traumas (e.g., domestic violence, http://www.nctsn.org/sites/default/files/assets/pdfs/childrenanddv_factsheet_7.pdf).

Recommended books include: *No-Drama Discipline: The Whole-Brain Way to Calm the Chaos and Nurture Your Child's Developing Mind* (Siegel & Bryson, 2014), *The Whole-Brain Child* (Siegel & Bryson, 2012), *Brain-Based Parenting* (Hughes & Baylin, 2012), and *Therapeutic Parenting: A Handbook for Parents of Children Who Have Disorders of Attachment* (ATTACh, 2008).

For parenting adolescents, see *Brainstorm: The Power and the Purpose of the Teenage Brain* (Siegel, 2014).

Residential counselors and home-based workers can utilize *Working with Traumatized Children: A Handbook for Healing* (Brohl, 2007).

NOTES

1. Adapted from Siegel and Bryson (2012).
2. Adapted from Abbuhl (2006).

5

My Family

Remembering People Who Cared

OBJECTIVES

- Children and caregivers complete a family tree, indicating a broad range of important relationships in children's lives that give the tree roots for stability.
- Children and caregivers share and learn about positive memories of caring family members and how they helped children and caregivers learn skills and cope with challenges.
- Children and caregivers share and learn about parts of their family and cultural heritage that inspire courage and commitment to make things better.

OVERVIEW

Chapter 5 renews and expands memories of people who cared for children. Children who have suffered through traumatic events often lack the resources to remember both positive and negative events without becoming distressed. Working with children in the safe environment of a therapeutic relationship can help them to recall and strengthen positive memories, especially the images and affects associated with family members and other important people who affirmed their importance and value in the past. These memories can be reinforced. In addition, identifying caring adults from the past can provide a guide for rebuilding emotionally supportive relationships. Formerly close relationships can be renewed and, when necessary, the types of relationships that were lost can provide a model for building new supportive relationships. For instance, if children felt valued and protected by a now deceased grandmother, they may be more amenable to developing a new supportive relationship with an older woman.

Caring adults serve as mentors and guides in children's quest to rebuild a positive view of their lives. Children often respond well when the therapist and caring adults work with them as detectives. Activities can be presented as detective work to recover positive events and especially positive acts of caring. The therapist can use activities to elicit support from adults in children's lives to help them rediscover strengths from the past and resources for the future.

Centering Activities in Chapter 5 are designed to increase attunement and connections with caregivers and family members. *Life Storybook* pages and Centering Activities are also designed to develop comfort with storytelling. Improv-style activities and other games are facilitated when therapists set a tone in sessions that is playful, respectful, curious, and aligned with the child and caregiver's level of modulation and capacity (Hughes, 2011) to promote growth in relationships.

STEP BY STEP

	OPENINGS
Welcome	*My Thermometers* plus *Safety reminders* and *Magical Moment*, if needed.
	CENTERING ACTIVITIES
Breathing, Balancing, Yoga, Movement, and 'Improv' to Increase Self- and Co-Regulation	Centering Activities for Chapter 5 utilize child-caregiver yoga exercises and improv games to build or strengthen attunement and trust and to promote sharing and storytelling. Yoga activities promote conjoint slow breathing, attunement, and modulation. Recommended Centering Activities (see Part V) include: • Breathing Together (to increase attunement and modulation) • Back to Back (to increase connections and safe touch with caregivers) • Child and Caregiver Trust Exercises: Seesaw (to increase safe touch, proprioceptive resistance, vestibular balance) • Two-Person T Balance (to increase safe touch, proprioceptive resistance, vestibular balance) • 'Up We Go' (to increase safe touch, proprioceptive resistance, vestibular balance) • Build a House (to increase connection, trust, support, balance) • Secret Messages (to increase attunement and communication) • Lean Forward 'Ski Jumper' (to increase balance and trust with caregiver) See the *RLH Strategy and Activity Guide* (in Part V) for other activities to increase modulation.
	LIFE STORYBOOK
Detective Work	Identify people who can help children learn about what happened in the past, identify strengths, and open up possibilities for future positive relationships. Ask extended family members for help in learning about people who cared for children that they cannot remember (e.g., caregivers when children were under 5 years old and memories of caring obscured by later traumatic events). Engage relatives and service providers to provide information by asking for their help to help their children, showing respect for what they have done and their special roles as aunts, uncles, grandparents, coaches, clergy, etc. Sharing questions or types of questions in advance can also help to alleviate concerns over intrusion in private family affairs. It is also helpful to ask family members to use some of the same safety tools established with children and caregivers (e.g., asking them to signal if questions become too difficult or upsetting and indicating that the therapist will stop questions whenever asked). It often helps to remind extended family members that you know that if children are hurting, then adults who care about the child are also hurting. To reduce anxiety over being asked questions, it helps to introduce by saying, "I'm a [psychologist, social worker, etc.] and as you probably expect, I tend to ask a lot of nosy questions. I'm going to count on you to tell me if I'm getting too nosy" (Kagan & Schlosberg, 1989).
Family Tree	Encourage thinking broadly to include past and present resources for children (e.g., foster parents, mentors, teachers, coaches, clergy, and pets, as well as biological family members).
Caring Memories	Highlight people who cared for children when they were hurt or sick. Strengthen memories of caring by inviting children to add details and to make pictures into 'Three-Chapter' Stories with a beginning, middle, and end. Accentuate details of positive memories: smells of cooking, the taste of grandma's fried chicken, the look on a caregiver's face, the warmth of a 'Safe Place.' These activities can provide openings to strengthen children's self-soothing abilities.

	Along with drawing a 'Safe Place,' encourage children to try out and then practice a rhythm and tones to reinforce this image. Ask children to look at the 'Safe Place' drawing, then tap out a rhythm that matches the picture. Next, pick one to four notes on the glockenspiel to go along with the picture and tap the rhythm on those notes. Similarly, repeat this process for a rhythm and notes to match both the highest *Self-Control Power* level on the thermometer and the lowest *Knots*.
	These notes, chords, and rhythm patterns can then be practiced along with imagery of a 'Safe Place,' and used as reminders to bring to mind, to help children calm inside their minds and bodies, and to remind them of soothing and powerful music that can drive away noise or anxiety-provoking perceptions.
	In place of drawings, it is helpful with some children to encourage the use of photos, movies, or collages. This can also provide a segue to ask extended family members for help in learning more about family members who cared for children in the past but may have been lost over time due to deaths, illness, incarceration, or moving away.
Rebuilding (or Building) Emotionally Supportive Relationships	Chapter 5 provides a great opportunity to enlist potentially safe caregivers who have not played a major role in children's lives to become significant resources for children. Similarly, Chapter 5 can help caregivers who played a significant role in previous years but lost that role, to return and re-establish emotionally supportive relationships.
	When rebuilding or building attachments are goals, gradually include safe caring adults in work during sessions. The amount of shared work should be based on the comfort of children and the ability of caring adults to foster the creativity and spontaneity of children.
	Once caregivers have met safety criteria, conjoint work can begin by having children share their work on Chapters 1–4 and have caregivers share their own work on these chapters or similar materials.
	Next, involve caregivers to help gather information for the *Life Storybook* and to answer other questions children may have (e.g., who helped them when they were sick as toddlers).
	Include caregivers in work on understanding and normalizing how trauma affects children and adults.
	Encourage caregivers to explicitly acknowledge to children how it is normal to have both positive and negative memories, beliefs, and feelings about key people and events, including the caregiver or family members with whom the caring adult has had conflict-ridden relationships.
	Encourage caregivers to share stories of family members overcoming hardships and to point out skills and family, religious, and cultural values that helped family members succeed.
	Encourage caregivers to utilize steps for promoting creativity with children, including use of a xylophone, keyboard, or other instruments to mirror and harmonize with children.
	Encourage the use of art, music, and movement to express losses and grief shared by children.
	Encourage caregivers to validate children's feelings nonverbally by matching tones, literally showing that children are heard, as well as with verbal validation of lost people, time, etc.
	CLOSINGS
'Homework' and 'Teamwork'	Encourage detective work by family members and team service providers to capture stories of caring and integrate them into children's *Life Storybooks*.
	See the *RLH Strategy and Activity Guide* (in Part V) for other activities.
Special Time, Thermometers, Progress Note, Reminder of Next Session	Continue special time at the end of the session, if helpful, and 'collaborative' *Progress Note*, as appropriate. Invite children and caregivers to suggest things they would like to do in the next session and schedule a date and time. Consider anyone else to invite to support children. Repeat Thermometers and Centering Activites if necessary.

 **T I P S**

➤ Look for stories of caring that can be developed into strong memories and Safe Place imagery that children and caregivers can pull up to help calm themselves in times of stress.

➤ Note how caregivers helped children deal with distress in the past and use these strategies to help develop *Power Plans* for the future.

P I T F A L L S   T O   A V O I D ➤➤➤

➤ Inadvertent messages to children that reinforce expectations that parents, guardians, or other important adults are either all-good or all-bad; lack of validation for how parents and caregivers may have been caring and neglectful, abusive, or abandoning at different and often unpredictable times.

➤ Lack of respect, validation, or detective work to help children recover the caring parts of parents and other caregivers who may have been abusive or neglectful at times (e.g., when intoxicated or when triggered into their own traumatic stress responses).

C H A P T E R   C H E C K P O I N T S

☐ 1. Help children identify at least three adults who cared for them in the past and three adults who children would like to get help from or become closer to in the future.

☐ 2. Ask caregivers to keep children safe by:

___ giving children support and permission to share what they experienced;
___ validating children's experiences, including traumas involving the caring adult;
___ committing themselves to protecting children from anyone, even other family members;
___ identifying how adults see children as special and part of their lives;
___ demonstrating to children that caring adults are able to manage exposure to reminders of past traumas and manage their own reactions without re-traumatizing children; and
___ sharing adults' life stories in a way that helps children learn from caring adults without overburdening or traumatizing them with adults' experiences.

RESOURCES

Look for resources within families, including family members who keep the family history alive, photo albums, and chronologies. Home visits can reveal resources and strengths that may not be apparent, for example pictures hung on walls, and symbols of achievements by family members: plaques, trophies, newspaper articles about successes, a child's fourth-grade story published in the local paper or, religious symbols. Each of these can open up possibilities to explore and strengthen skills and relationships that can help children develop the safety to reintegrate after multiple traumas.

6

Important People

Promoting Emotionally Supportive Relationships

OBJECTIVES

- Children and caregivers recover and reinforce memories of good times and achievements that may have been obscured by traumas.
- Children and caregivers share positive memories reinforcing strengths and relationships.
- Children can identify important people in their lives who helped them develop skills and solve problems.

OVERVIEW

Chapter 6 helps children recall positive events in their lives involving relationships with other people and then to utilize these events to shape positive beliefs about children's competence and identity within important relationships. This chapter can be used to enhance children's pride in their accomplishments and to tie this into how they would like to make their world better, for instance with a campaign slogan if they were running for president. Activities promote images of children's lives as a journey or quest, in which they can help others, and by so doing, build a positive identity, rather then remain feeling stuck, 'damaged,' like a 'victim,' unwanted, or as unforgivably 'bad.'

Remembering some of children's 'best times' also provides clues for identifying people who helped them in the past and who could possibly help them in the future. Rebuilding connections with allies and mentors help children feel secure enough to grieve losses and overcome hardships. Chapter 6 renews children's hopes for connections, for example by imagining the power to create their own special holiday (adapted from Evans, 1986) and other activities that accentuate relationships with important people for them. Reinforcing memories of good times from the past fosters the confidence and memories of positive relationships that can help children take risks to develop new relationships or recover former relationships and enjoy good times in the future. Documenting good times from the past also facilitates children's courage to

reintegrate not-so-good times and traumatic memories in Chapter 10 of the *Life Storybook*.

Centering and *Life Storybook* activities focus on reintegration of children with caring adults and positive peers in their extended family, school, religious organizations, and broader community. Activities in sessions and 'homework' are intended to increase or restore fun (and learning) times with important people. Therapists have an important role in this process by fostering the safety for children and caregivers to risk sharing feelings and thoughts. Increasing relationships can be very difficult for children and caregivers who have experienced relational traumas. And, children with Complex Trauma are typically far behind their chronological age level in development of social skills. Therapists can watch for clues to what types of relationships or specific relationships increase a child or caregiver's distress and which relationships promote security. This can help to guide further work on building or rebuilding positive relationships. For instance, a boy in residential treatment who had been abandoned by his parents and had no documented family relationships replayed over and over stories in a sandbox about a boy-figure and an older woman. By contacting the county's department of social services, the author learned that he had been cared for in his early years for extended periods by a babysitter before placement. The boy had had frequent violent outbursts. He was reunited with his old babysitter in visits and his aggressive behaviors markedly decreased.

'Improv' exercises (included in Centering Activities in Part V) are a fun way to generate sharing and increase the scope of relationships. 'Rules of improv' help create attunement, focused attention, concentration, sharing, and comfort with storytelling. The 'Yin Yang' exercise reinforces understanding that everything has different sides and that nothing is all one way or another. 'Improv' Centering Activities also provide opportunities to children to open up areas of concern (e.g., feeling scared in a new class and not knowing what to do) and then to hear suggestions from safe caregivers or others participating in a group or family activity.

Relationships, of course, are never always positive. Exploring relationships provides opportunities for children to learn how conflicts can be used to help strengthen trust that relationships can endure through good times and 'tough times.' Therapists can use memories of conflicts to help children (and, at times, caregivers) to learn to see other people's perspectives, to recognize nonverbal cues, to look for openings for collaboration, and creating 'win-win' situations. Looking from a safe distance at past conflicts can also provide opportunities to help children learn important social skills, including how apologizing for one's mistakes can be a strength, how forgiving can promote healing for oneself, and how making amends or restitution for things done wrong can help restore relationships and reduce feelings of shame.

TABLE 6.1
Four Rules of 'Improv' for Trauma Therapy[1]

1.	"Always Agree . . . Start with a YES and see where that takes you . . ."
2.	"The second rule of improvisation is not only to say yes, but YES, AND. You are supposed to agree and add something of your own . . . YES, AND means don't be afraid to contribute . . . Always make sure you're adding something to the discussion."
3.	"MAKE STATEMENTS . . . Don't ask questions all the time . . . Whatever the problem, be part of the solution."
4.	"There are no mistakes, only opportunities . . . In Improv there are no mistakes, only beautiful happy accidents."

STEP BY STEP

	OPENINGS
	OPENINGS
Welcome	*My Thermometers* plus *Safety reminders* and *Magical Moment*, if needed.
	CENTERING ACTIVITIES
Breathing, Balancing, Yoga, Movement, and 'Improv' to Increase Self- and Co-Regulation	Centering Activities for Chapter 6 help children and caregivers work together to increase collaborative skills, focused attention, communication, problem-solving, attunement, and storytelling. Recommended Centering Activities (see Part V) include: • Coffee Can Pass (to increase attention and collaboration) • Countdowns (to increase attention, concentration, and collaboration in groups or families) • Musical Family (focused attention, attunement) • Circle Time (sharing with three or more) • 'Improv' Fun (to promote sharing, collaboration, and storytelling) • Word Games (to increase eye contact, memory, storytelling) See the *RLH Strategy and Activity Guide* (in Part V) for other activities to increase development of relationships.
	LIFE STORYBOOK
Memories of Good Times	Engage children to share interests and activities they enjoy, including who they enjoy playing with and learning from in the present time as well as in the past. Help children to add details to memories of success, including what helped them succeed and their beliefs about skills and talents. Engage children to recall and share memories of times when they felt good, even in small ways, with others. Help children to add details, including who else was there, what their faces looked like, what they did, what children did, how did children feel, etc. If needed, continue detective work from earlier chapters to build up children's record of 'good times.'

	Arrange safe interviews with caring adults in extended family and community, record interviews, develop a visual record of children's past successes with drawings, photographs, or video, and help them obtain concrete symbols of past successes and 'good times' such as lost trophies or photographs of them holding a fish caught, batting, at a family party, etc.
	Accentuate images and memories of children with caring adults highlighting positive beliefs about them.
Special Holiday	Encourage children to add details and enrich this drawing and look for clues to important people.
Strong Supportive Relationships	Look for strong memories when children felt cared for and safe. Reinforce these with music and movement, photos, and movies, and practice bringing up memories of these good times at times when children start to feel stressed. This can be incorporated in the 'O' of 'SOS,' opening children's memories to relationships from the past that generate feelings of security and hope.
Helping Others	Workbook pages eliciting memories of pride or running for president elicit ways children have helped or would like to help others. These can be reinforced.
CLOSINGS	
'Homework' and 'Teamwork'	Encourage family fun activities that promote safe sharing and skill development with games (e.g., charades, board games, etc).
	Home-based service providers can help children to learn about past experiences through contacts by phone or visits and build new lasting relationships. This can include visits to past schools, religious organizations, foster families, departments of social services, and residential counselors.
	See the *RLH Strategy and Activity Guide* (in Part V) for additional activities.
Special Time, Thermometers, *Progress Note*, Reminder of Next Session	Continue special time at the end of the session, if helpful, and 'collaborative' *Progress Note*, as appropriate. Invite children and caregivers to suggest things they would like to do in the next session and schedule a date and time. Consider anyone else to invite to support children based on their stories of past caring and support. Repeat Thermometers and Centering Activities if necessary.

▶▶▶ T I P S

➤ Learning about good times is part of detective work.

➤ Watch for clues in children's relationships to important types of relationships or relationships with specific people that can be recovered or recreated with safe caring adults in their extended family and community. Consider inviting emotionally supportive adults to sessions to enhance relationships.

➤ Use clues about past experiences of pride and children's wishes to help others to link children to mentors and community or school-based activities that can increase their skills and confidence.

➤ Promote opportunities for children to use their strengths to help others.

➤ Have fun with sharing activities, such as 'improv' games that promote storytelling.

PITFALLS TO AVOID >>>

➢ 'Rushing' through Chapter 6 without development of sufficient support from caring adults to confront 'tough times.'

➢ Children perceive nonverbal messages from therapists or caregivers that they are only comfortable dealing with happy or positive memories.

➢ Children with Complex Trauma are expected to demonstrate social or problem-solving skills at their chronological age level without help developing these skills.

➢ Children are instructed by adults that mistakes are not allowed and that making mistakes means they are 'damaged,' 'sick,' or 'bad.'

CHAPTER CHECKPOINTS

☐ 1. Help children share positive memories where they felt supported by other people with the practitioner and with safe, caring adults.

☐ 2. Help children share two or more memories of how they helped other people.

RESOURCES

Look for school- and community-based resources to encourage development of skills and build positive peer relationships through sports, drama, music, arts, and religious activities.

NOTE

1. Excerpted from Fey (2011, pp. 84–85).

7

Mind Power

Making Things Better with Mindfulness and Self-Regulation

OBJECTIVES

- Children and caregivers increase mindfulness skills to help themselves to stay modulated and increase their ability to focus their minds on what they want to pay attention to.
- Children and caregivers develop the capacity to remind themselves of times and relationships when they felt safe and emotionally supported, Safe Place imagery.
- Children and caregivers reduce expectations of being perfect and shame reactions.
- Children and caregivers develop the capacity to remind themselves of strengths and resources in their family and cultural heritage that inspire courage to keep going in 'tough times.'

OVERVIEW

Chapter 7 begins with the fun of magic tricks to highlight the power of the magician and then invites children to develop their *Self-Control Powers*, as they learn the tricks behind the 'magic' of self-control and courage. By using the image of the magician, therapists can engage children to learn and practice mindfulness and self-soothing skills to help them increase self-control and develop the capacity with caregiver support to reintegrate memories of tough times in Chapter 10.

Mind Power

Children are encouraged to think about how magicians learn the skills and art to perform magic tricks and then to explore ways they can develop their own skills through Mind Power to make things better for themselves and other people they care about. Mind Power[1] is the capacity to focus attention where you want it and to utilize self- and co-regulation, awareness, and thinking to achieve goals. Daniel Goleman (2014) described how we can develop our "concentration muscle" with basic skills, including focusing our attention, refocusing our attention when we are distracted, and learning to let go of thoughts and feelings that are not helpful. Chapter 7 builds on Goleman's concep-

tion of using our eyes and our brain like an astronomer uses a telescope. Children (and caregivers) are encouraged to strengthen their skills to focus their attention, like telescopes, on what they want to pay attention to. This appeals to traumatized children's need to gain control. Focusing and concentration are presented as skills that can be strengthened in much the same way as you would strengthen muscles, senses, or skills. Chapter 8 helps children to let go of thoughts and feelings that are not helpful and to use more constructive thinking to better manage problems.

Mind Power provides a segue for therapists to develop mindfulness concepts and skills at a latency level. This includes acceptance that we will become distracted and our focus will wander or be drawn to other things. The more we bring our attention back from distractions, the stronger we grow our Mind Power to concentrate and focus.[2] And, the stronger we grow our Mind Power, the better our brains work to succeed at figuring out how to handle different situations.

The concept of Mind Power can be used to help children (and caregivers) learn how their brains work and how to use this understanding to make things better. Children and adolescents are not too young to learn about ways to use their brain to calm down, to think, to plan, and to solve problems. Caregivers can use their understanding of the brain to help calm themselves and their children. Mindfulness activities can become a strong skill. Neurobiologists have demonstrated that "Neurons that fire together, wire together" (Hebb, 1949). Calming and focusing requires repeated practice, just like a gymnast learns to do a difficult move or a guitar player learns to master a complex riff.

Practitioners can utilize Siegel's hand model of the lower brain (Siegel, 2011) or videos online to help children concretely see where they are developing their Mind Power to modulate and focus. This can be highlighted as the lower center part of the prefrontal cortex, the ventromedial prefontal cortex that connects the left and right sides of the brain.

Mind Power skills help us to calm ourselves down sufficiently to focus our attention, to swing the telescopes of our minds back to what we want to focus on, rather than becoming consumed with paying attention to multiple stimuli in our environment. Refocusing attention helps a youth pay attention to a teacher's assignments rather than provocative chatter from another youth or worries about what might be happening at home. Calming down also enables our brains to think about what is happening and to get help when it is needed. Focusing and calming helps improve relationships with family members and others. Children develop greater *Self-Control Power*, which, in turn, helps them to achieve their goals.

Safe Place/Safe Relationship Imagery

Children are encouraged to develop strong images of a time when they felt safe and pictures of someone that helped (or helps) them feel warm and good inside. For each of these images, children are asked to practice focusing their minds and concentrating to develop the details of each image. And, when they become distracted, children are encouraged to practice gently bring their minds back (refocusing) on their image of a 'safe place and time' or comforting relationship to strengthen their focusing skills so they can bring up these images when they start to feel stressed.

To make Safe Place imagery stronger, it is helpful to accentuate key factors in children's art, music, or movement that promote feelings of peace, the ability to concentrate, and positive beliefs about children's skills and abilities to contribute and succeed at home, at school, or in activities (e.g., sports or music). These can then be practiced and reinforced, so that children can remember, visualize, touch, or enact whatever helps them. 'Safe Place' imagery can be enhanced by tying this to concrete symbols children can carry with them (e.g., laminated photos of people who cared about them, necklaces from important people, a polished stone given to children by a favorite uncle, the favorite scent of a beloved guardian, etc.). It is also helpful to reinforce these images by asking children to practice the music they develop for each picture hundreds of times so these melodies become so strong that children can bring them up in different situations (e.g., at school). To further strengthen Safe Place and Relationship imagery, children are encouraged to develop these pictures into 'Three-Chapter' Stories with a beginning, middle, and end.

Reducing Shame

Emotional abuse, neglect, and blaming are associated with self-denigration and intense shame, a critical factor in development of Complex Trauma (Herman, 2014). Shame typically involves detachment from others that may follow externally or self-imposed chastisement, humiliation, or shunning. A 5-year-old boy was forced to stand outside his house on the front porch with soiled underwear over his head by his mother and stepfather. A 14-year-old girl was told that she was dangerous to her family and could never return home. Children with Complex Trauma have often gotten into serious trouble and may feel responsible for problems impacting their families. For these children, shame often means feeling unlovable like they have a monster inside and if other people truly knew what children had done, they too would be appalled, hate them, and shut them out of their lives.

Many children with Complex Trauma confuse shame and guilt. Guilt refers to feeling regret or remorse for something the person has done (e.g., "I disappointed my mother by forgetting to take out the trash", "I got into trouble at school today for yelling at my teacher"). Shame involves denigration of one's identity (e.g., "I am bad, damaged, sick, evil . . ."). With shame, children, and caregivers, often feel there is nothing they can do to make things better.

Herman has described pride as the antidote to shame (Herman, 2014). Pride is shaped by developmental and cultural factors. For infants, feeling a parent's love and attunement, eye to eye, face to face, and the way the parent's face lights up when he or she sees the infant. For preschool and latency-age children, pride comes from doing things with caregivers and feeling their support and appreciation. For adolescents, pride often comes from doing things with peers, teachers, coaches and other influential adults, getting their respect, and feeling a sense of belonging with others outside the family.

In RLH, work on building pride is coupled with efforts to reconnect children to emotionally supportive caregivers, caring adults, mentors, and positive peers. Increasing pride is also linked to the hero's journey to solve problems and to find a way to give back and help others, to bring back the "boon" (Campbell, 1968).

Working on Chapter 7 with a safe, supportive caregiver can help counter common beliefs of traumatized children that they are primarily responsible for the horrible things that have happened or that nothing can be done to make things better. Working on the section on perfection is ideally done with children and safe caregivers so that children see that caregivers accept that no one is perfect, everyone makes mistakes, and that, together, they can work out ways to make things better. Wherever possible, children should be guided to apologize and make up for what children did that hurt someone else with some form of restitution. Chapter 10 also includes pages devoted to helping youths find ways to acknowledge things they have done that have hurt others, to apologize, to find ways to give back to those who were hurt and to take steps to prevent future harm to others.

Readiness for Trauma Experience Integration

Recovery from chronic and severe traumas requires reprocessing the demons, fears, and reaction patterns that have plagued children and families, sometimes for generations. Re-experiencing past traumas for short intervals may strengthen traumatic stress reactions. Establishing safety, developing emotionally supportive relationships, and developing self- and co-regulation skills need to come first so that tough times from the past can be re-experienced long enough with children remaining regulated to allow reduction in trauma reactions and desensitization to triggers. Building skills, support, and self-confidence help prevent rekindling or strengthening trauma reactions. Use of graduated exposure and structured rituals that emphasize 'moving through' tough times to safety makes it possible to elicit trauma stories without provoking trauma reactions (see Chapter 10).

Chapter 7 ends with a brief self-rating of how each child is managing stress that can be combined with the *Knots* and *Self-Control Power* thermometers and other measures to indicate whether he or she is able to work on changing beliefs in Chapter 8 and reintegrating more painful memories in Chapters 9 and 10. If children are not ready, additional work is often needed to foster their trust in caring adults, including taking time to search for and engage adults willing and able to commit to supporting and guiding them. Children may also need more practice in developing skills or to see how other children and adults have confronted their tough times and became stronger. In some cases, children do not appear ready to work on trauma reintegration because their families or communities are unsafe. This may be due to factors that the therapist is not aware of (e.g., a sex abuse perpetrator secretly visiting or living in the child's home).

The goal in RLH, as in other trauma treatments, is for children to develop sufficient resources, inside and outside themselves, to manage graduated exposure in therapeutically guided treatment without becoming unsafe. Sufficient stability includes continuity in living arrangements and primary relationships. Children should also have developed sufficient self-regulation skills and sufficient support within their relationships with caregivers and service providers (co-regulation) to manage exposure to traumatic memories. *My Thermometers* can be repeated periodically to see if work on re-establishing safety, strengthening supportive relationships, and skill development for self- and co-regulations provides sufficient security to move ahead with Chapters 9 and 10.

Therapists can build children's confidence by maintaining the expectation that they will 'move through' the remainder of the workbook with additional work and support, just as real heroes in real life move forward, step by step, in their quests to make things better. The therapist's responsibility is to respect children's readiness, the viability of safety plans, and the progress of caring adults in rebuilding, or building, trust after traumas.

A Resource Checklist is provided in Part V to help therapists assess whether children have developed necessary skills and resources before desensitization of traumas, and to identify areas where further development of skills, safety, and supportive relationships is needed. If more work is needed, therapists can keep children moving forward developing coping and creative arts skills, as well as efforts to find and strengthen relationships with caring adults and to establish viable safety plans.

STEP BY STEP

	OPENINGS
Welcome	*My Thermometers* plus *Safety reminders* and *Magical Moment*, if needed.
	CENTERING ACTIVITIES
Breathing, Balancing, Yoga, Meditation to Increase Self- and Co-Regulation	Centering Activities for Chapter 7 help children with balance, slow breathing, focused attention, and use of meditation as part of mindful modulation. Recommended Centering Activities (see Part V) include: • Breathe Like a Happy Elephant (to increase self-care) • Tree Yoga (to increase balance) • Glider Airplane (to increase balance and good feelings) • Mindful Motion (to increase focus, body awareness, and modulation in daily activities) • Mindful Meditations (to increase use of meditations for modulation) See the *RLH Strategy and Activity Guide* (in Part V) for other activities to increase modulation.

Mental Challenges, Nine Dots, T Puzzle, Latin Cross Puzzle	Use puzzles, tricks, or math games to help children and caregivers develop skills. Two favorites are listed below: **Nine Dots** Challenge children to connect nine dots with four consecutive straight lines, not lifting their pencils. The Nine Dot Puzzle (see Figure 7.1) has been used to encourage children to utilize 'breaking out of the box' perspectives to overcome obstacles. Introduce the **T and Latin Cross puzzles** (see Figure 7.2) to reinforce looking at puzzles, or 'tough' situations, from different perspectives in order to find solutions. Draw a large letter T and a cross about two inches wide, cutting them into different pieces (see Figure 7.2) and ask children to reassemble the 'T' and the cross. Using puzzles also provides opportunities to practice skills in using calming, centering, and 'SOS' skills to manage frustration and to increase perseverance.	
	LIFE STORYBOOK	
Magic	Enhance skills and resources by imagining powers through magic using basic card or other tricks that match children's developmental levels. Encourage children to learn new tricks and take pride in sharing them. Use the metaphor of magic to expand possibilities for figuring out difficult situations that seem, on the surface, to be impossible to solve. Learning how the magician hides the trick reinforces children's abilities to figure out solutions.	
Looking behind the Curtain	**Developing Mind Power by Learning How Our Brains Work** Invite children and caregivers to 'look behind the curtain' to learn tricks on how to use their brains to increase their ability to achieve goals. By learning how our brains work, we can increase our Mind Power to make things better. Adapt a brief overview of the brain to the developmental level of the child. Introduce the 'hand brain' model by Daniel Siegel with reference to books (e.g., Siegel, 2011, pp. 14–22), or on YouTube search for "Dan Siegel hand model of brain." Highlight how the limbic system, represented by the thumb (anterior cingulate, amygdala, hippocampus), drives much of our automatic responses to perceptions and bodily sensations, including impulsive and learned reactions. The amygdala works like an early warning system or alarm bell (Ford & Russo, 2006). The limbic system can generate high arousal states quickly to protect children (or caregivers). The prefrontal cortex can help 'pause' and calm down the limbic system. The ventromedial prefrontal cortex, in particular, has been described as helping to regulate the amygdala and is important in Emotional Regulation. Demonstrate how we can turn on our prefrontal cortex with *My Thermometers*. To complete thermometers, children and adults turn on their prefrontal cortex and scan over their bodies and then convert this into a measure, a number on the thermometer's scale. Point out how mindfulness also activates the prefrontal cortex. And, repeated practice of mindfulness develops strong skills that youths and adults can utilize to manage difficult situations with greater modulation. Neurobiologists have found that reflection within caring relationships stimulates development of neural pathways in the prefrontal cortex. And strengthening these pathways can enhance emotional self- and co-regulation. Show children, using the 'hand model of the brain,' how mindfulness activities can strengthen the prefrontal cortex and especially the power of the center part of the prefrontal area, the	

	middle two fingernails, to help them focus, to reflect, and to modulate feelings. This center part of the brain, the ventromedial prefrontal cortex, integrates impulses from the brain stem, limbic system, and relationships between children and others. Practicing mindfulness activities helps strengthen this area and develop skills for staying 'cool,' just like a magician learns to do a series of magic tricks with lots and lots of practice.
Mind Power 'Telescope'	Describe Mind Power as a set of skills, like muscles in your brain that can increase your ability to focus on one thing and ignore distractions. Encourage children to imagine their eyes, ears, and brain working like a telescope. They can aim their telescope to focus on whatever they want. Encourage children to be aware of how they decide what to focus on. Help children and caregivers to accept that everyone's minds drift and become distracted. Feelings and thoughts change. One thought or feeling follows another, just like waves rolling one after another on to a beach (Marra, 2004). To test this, invite children to change the feelings in their bodies. Tap on different parts of their bodies: their forehead, cheeks, ears, shoulder bones, chest, stomach, wrists, etc. Next, ask children to use their fingers to put pressure on different places, then try little finger swirls or tickles. Ask how their skin feels. If children are comfortable being touched in these ways by a safe caregiver, ask them if they would like the caregiver to do the taps, swirls, or tickles. Remind children of safety messages in case they want to stop at any time. Highlight for children how each time they bring their minds back to focus on what they want to focus on, they are increasing the strength of their Mind Power. And, increasing their Mind Power increases their self-control and thinking power. Ask children to focus their minds like aiming a telescope as they practice 'Slow Breathing' in 'SOS for Stress,' breathing in rhythmically as they count to themselves: "1, 2, 3, 3, 2, 1." Ask children to focus on the air coming in through their mouths, into their throats, down to their lungs, and pushing up their bellies. Placing one hand on their belly and one hand on their chest can help them to focus on feeling the air coming in. Encourage them to imagine the air moving in and out as they breathe. *Note*: For younger children or developmentally delayed children, placing a teddy bear or similar object (Deblinger, 2005) on their bellies can be helpful. *Encourage children to gently bring back their focus when their minds drift away.* This is the most important part of this exercise. Encourage children to think of the effort to bring their focus back as similar to athletes in training. Each refocus is like practicing a successful jump shot or lifting a weight one more time. With each repetition, children's Mind Power grows stronger and stronger. Link Mind Power to children's heroes whenever possible (e.g., the concentration of a pitcher staring at the plate, a tennis player getting ready for the next volley, or Harry Potter battling Voldemort) (Rowling, 1999). Help children experience intensity in the moment as they concentrate on a task (e.g., balancing a peacock feather on a fingertip).
Safe Place/ Safe Relation-ship Imagery	Help children remember and accentuate memories of when they felt safe, highlighting what helped, who was there, and what they did with detailed drawings. Ask children to enrich details for pictures by expressing interest (after Deblinger, 2005); for instance, "I'd like know more about that . . . " Ask about multisensory perceptions: "What sounds did you hear?" "What smells?" Ask children to add feelings in their bodies in the safe place and time (e.g., "If you scanned over your body from your toes to your belly to your head, what were you feeling?" What was your heart doing? Your stomach?"

	If children draw a picture where they are alone, ask, "Who would you want to have with you in this special place?"
	Similarly, on the next page of the workbook, help children remember and reinforce memories of how they felt warm and good inside with someone who was emotionally supportive.
	Reinforce these images by asking children to practice the music they develop for each picture so these melodies become so strong children can bring them up in different situations (e.g., at school) and in stressful situations.
'Three-Chapter' Story	For the strongest image of children feeling safe with emotional support, ask children to share a 'Three-Chapter' Story to go along with images where they felt safe. "What happened next, right after the picture you just drew? Draw a picture of that. That picture could become the end of your story. What happened right before the first picture you drew? Draw a picture of that. That could become the first chapter in your story. Now you have a 'Three-Chapter' Story!"
Shame and Perfection	Encourage children to learn about mistakes one of their favorite heroes made, what the hero learned from making mistakes, and how the hero tried to make up for what he or she did and prevent future mistakes (see Tips below).
Family Shield	Ask children to develop symbols from their family, cultural heritage, and their own successes that can remind them of strengths and resources they can carry with them wherever they go.
	Encourage children to draw symbols that are strong and enrich with meaning by adding details and stories.
Resource Checklist and Thermometers	Review Resource Checklist in Part V for sufficient skills and resources for children to remain in their 'window of tolerance' with the support of therapists and caregivers as they work to reintegrate 'tough times' in Chapter 10. The goal in RLH, as in other trauma treatments, is for children to have just enough resources, inside and outside themselves, to manage graduated exposure in therapeutically guided treatment without becoming unsafe.
	Check children's balance of *Self-Control Power* to *Knots* (Stress). Continue to build children's relational supports and self- and co-regulation skills until they are sufficiently stable to maintain adequate modulation while using creative arts and other modalities to 'move through' memories of 'tough times.'
	Continue to build family and community supports as necessary.
CLOSINGS	
'Homework' and 'Teamwork' Practice:	**Safe Place/Safe Relationship Imagery, Mindful Motion** Practice Safe Place/Safe Relationship imagery in different environments (e.g., home, school, community).
	Reinforce the importance of caregiver-guided practice with reminders of how our brains work and the need to steadily grow the strength of positive coping skills. "Neurons that fire together, wire together" (Hebb, 1949). Emphasize importance of daily practice to foster skill development
	Encourage mindfulness activities outside of therapeutic sessions with a safe caregiver or activity counselor. See Mindful Motion in Centering Activities (Part V).
	See the *RLH Strategy and Activity Guide* (in Part V) for additional activities.
Special Time, Thermometers, *Progress Note*, Reminder of Next Session	Continue special time at the end of the session, if helpful, and 'collaborative' *Progress Note*, as appropriate. Invite children and caregivers to suggest things they would like to do in the next session and schedule a date and time. Consider anyone else to invite to support children. Repeat Thermometers and Centering if necessary.

➤➤➤ TIPS

➤ Make Safe Place and Safe Relationship imagery so strong that children can bring up the pictures, sounds, and feelings anywhere, any time. To do this, ask children to practice bringing up images, sounds, smells, and feelings multiple times a day and then practice bringing up imagery while they do something else (e.g., balancing peacock feathers, getting tickled by a caregiver, doing push-ups). Ask, "Can you still see the picture (of the Safe Place/Safe Relationship)?"

➤ To strengthen Safe Place/Safe Relationship imagery, it is helpful to remind Harry Potter fans of how the "Patronus Charm" (Rowling, 1999) can be used to drive away Dementors. Instructions can be replayed on YouTube videos; search for 'Harry Potter and the Prisoner of Azkaban – Expecto Patronum.' Accentuate for children how this needs to be a strong image and they need to let it fill them up and absorb the good feelings in their bodies. A strong Safe Place/Safe Relationship image can drive away reminders of traumas just as the Patronus Charm drives away Dementors. Dementors, in the *Harry Potter* series, work in many ways like overwhelming traumas, with dementers sucking away all the good feelings and memories.

➤ Encourage children to carry reminders of the Safe Place/Safe Relationship with them 24/7. Match reminders of the Safe Place/Safe Relationship with children's developmental age and use multisensory reminders. For children who are emotionally stymied at a 1–2 age level, ask caregivers to help them to carry a fabric with the scent (e.g., cologne or perfume) of someone who has cared for them. For more mature youths, photos or gifts of jewelry that symbolize a relationship can help.

➤ Many children blame themselves for bad things that happened in their families, especially when they did something wrong. Help children to differentiate feeling sorry for what they did (regret) with being responsible (Griffin, Cohen, Kliethermes, & Mannarino, 2014) for what happened, including what led up to their doing something that may have hurt other people or themselves. For example, a 12-year-old girl goes to a friend's home without permission and is raped; she then blames herself and becomes depressed. In such cases, it often helps to ask the youth to consider what he or she would tell a friend who blamed him or herself if it happened to him or her.

PITFALLS TO AVOID ➤➤➤

➤ Accepting children's assertions that they can bring up Safe Place/Safe Relationship imagery without practice or testing that they can reliably do this when feeling stressed.

➤ Not addressing the need to develop safety plans for shaming messages or other forms of emotional abuse that continue to denigrate children or caregivers.

➤ Treating youths as too fragile to address shaming.

➤ Asking children to reduce level of arousal and awareness of real dangers when this is not safe.

CHAPTER CHECKPOINTS

☐ 1. Help children expand focusing skills and increase self-regulation with mindfulness activities practiced every day, ideally with safe caregivers.

☐ 2. Help children develop and share a 'Safe Place memory' involving a relationship with a caring adult and practice bringing up imagery until they can reliably do this when feeling stressed.

☐ 3. Help children develop a 'protective shield' that integrates strengths in their family, cultural heritage, and themselves.

RESOURCES

Resources for promoting mindfulness with children and caregivers include:

Biegel, G. M. (2009). *The stress reduction workbook for teens: Mindfulness skills to help you deal with stress.* Oakland, CA: New Harbinger.

Gilbert, P. (2009) *The compassionate mind: A new approach to life's challenges.* Oakland, CA: New Harbinger.

Kabat-Zinn, M., & Kabat-Zinn, J. (1997). *Everyday blessings: The inner work of mindful parenting.* New York, NY: Hyperion.

Maclean, K. L. (2009). *Moody cow meditates.* Somerville, MA: Wisdom.

Marra, T. (2004). *Depressed and anxious: The dialectical behavior therapy workbook for overcoming depression and anxiety.* Oakland, CA: New Harbinger.

Siegel, D. J., & Bryson, T. P. (2012). *The whole-brain child: 12 revolutionary strategies to nurture your child's developing mind.* New York, NY: Random House.

Siegel, R. D. (2010). *The mindfulness solution: Everyday practices for everyday problems.* New York, NY: Guilford Press.

See also YouTube videos on mindfulness and brain development presented by Daniel Siegel and videos on focus and the 'concentration muscle' by Daniel Goleman.

NOTES

1. Adapted from Goleman (2014).
2. Adapted from Goleman (2014).

8
Changing the Story

Changing Beliefs and Action Cycles to Achieve Goals

OBJECTIVES

- Children and caregivers understand the linkage between thoughts, feelings, and behaviors; how traumatic experiences lead to negative thoughts, fear, anger, and failures; and, conversely, how positive beliefs, self-awareness, and calming/centering skills lead to more success in reaching their goals.
- Children and caregivers strengthen and increase skills to slow down, reflect on what is happening, shift distressing thoughts and images to Safe Place imagery and constructive thoughts, get help when needed, and develop more effective strategies to manage stressful situations.
- Children and caregivers decrease the power of dysfunctional beliefs linked to traumas and increase positive perceptions of themselves and their family and cultural heritage.

OVERVIEW

Chapter 8 engages children and caregivers to change cycles of behavioral interactions by boosting their use of Mind Power to think about what is happening in stressful situations and to solve problems more effectively. Children and caregivers are encouraged to think of themselves as directors in their own movies and then to change how they view situations, to open up possibilities for change, and to try out new beliefs and perspectives with more adaptive behaviors.

The ABCs of Trauma provide a structured exercise to integrate children's skills of centering, increased capacity to focus, getting help when needed, and use of positive beliefs in order to better manage low-level stressors. The chapter begins with an outline of how stress affects thoughts, behaviors, and feelings, building on the introduction to traumatic stress in Chapter 1. This worksheet helps children understand how trauma can lead to catastrophic thinking and failures. Conversely, children learn and practice how they can utilize an understanding of the 'ABCs of Trauma' to increase the power of their thinking skills, switch to courageous thinking, and avoid being trapped in a trauma pit.

Children are encouraged to use their full brain instead of just their self-defense reactions as a means of pulling themselves out of trauma reactions. Triggers are identified, as well as bodily reactions, feelings, beliefs, and behaviors. Children (and caregivers) are then asked to evaluate what they really want (goals), to try out more constructive beliefs, and to open up new strategies for succeeding.

Chapter 8 also includes practice in shifting distressing thoughts and images to Safe Place/Safe Relationship imagery and more constructive thoughts and beliefs. In RLH, children are encouraged to accept and use the energy of feelings, images, and thoughts, and then convert these into more productive forms of problem-solving. Image control has been described as important in promoting resilience with traumatized children (Wolmer, Hamiel, Barchas, Slone, & Laor, 2011).

Using the ABCs of Trauma helps children build increased self-esteem and prepares children to decrease the power of their tough times. After changing their stories, children are invited to continue working on the Hero's Challenge by moving ahead through Chapters 9 and 10 of the workbook.

STEP BY STEP

	OPENINGS
Welcome	*My Thermometers*, Safety First if needed.
Magical Moment	**'Jumping Rubber Band' Magic** Demonstrate the 'Jumping Rubber Band' magic trick, shifting a rubber band placed on your first two fingers to your next two fingers. Then demonstrate switching one rubber band from the first two fingers with another rubber band (of a different color) that was originally placed around the next two fingers. See YouTube videos or magic books for instructions by searching for 'jumping rubber band magic.' **Show children how this is like shifting thoughts and images. "You just have to know the trick."** Encourage children and caregivers to make up a good story to go with the magic.
	CENTERING ACTIVITIES
Breathing, Balancing, Yoga, Movement, and 'Improv' to Increase Self- and Co-Regulation	Centering Activities for Chapter 8 help children with focused attention, sharing with safe caregivers, problem-solving, and developing kindness, caring, and a more positive identity. Recommended Centering Activities (see Part V) include: • Disc 'o' Stories (to develop problem-solving strategies and support) • Solution Circle (to foster getting help from others to develop solutions/strategies to difficult problems) • Kindness Circle (to increase focus and sharing of kindness and positive regard) See the *RLH Strategy and Activity Guide* (in Part V) for other activities to increase modulation.
	LIFE STORYBOOK
ABCs of Trauma	Make sure children understand the connection between thoughts, feelings, and behaviors, and how we can be triggered into 'fight' or 'flight' modes, losing the capacity to think and figure out how to succeed. Help children understand 'triggers' as reminders of things that happened before. In the past, children may have needed to jump into an alarm state and fight or run away to survive. Now, children are older, wiser, bigger, and can get help. Children can respond to 'triggers' with their skills of centering, calming, slow breathing, and thinking about how they can now manage to do what seemed impossible at a younger age. Watch for dysfunctional beliefs and help children overcome self-blame for things that adults did (e.g., for parent/guardian neglect or abuse). Encourage children to take more control of how their own thinking can lead to success and avoid repeated failures.
Involving Caregivers	When possible, encourage children to share their worksheets with safe caring adults. Prepare adults in advance by asking them to complete the 'ABCs' themselves and to become aware of how this process works for in their own lives as well as for their children. Then, ask adults to: • show children that they understand how tough times have led to their reactions; • validate that the caregiver can understand what led children to act in a certain way (i.e., the 'ABCs of Trauma' for that child); and • see that children are using the power of their own thinking, Mind Power, to succeed. Encourage caring adults to share memories of good times and bad times as normal parts of their lives, stressing how they, other family members, and heroes from their ethnic group and community have faced and overcome hard times. Ensure that work is tailored to respect children's cultural heritage.

Thought- and Image- Shifting	Ask children to practice changing a stress-provoking train of thought or image by saying a favorite word or command (e.g., "Let it go") or utilizing a physical action, such as tapping their forehead or taking a slow breath and practicing 'SOS for Stress' from Chapter 1.
	Encourage children to imagine themselves absorbing the energy of the stress-provoking thought and then shifting it to something else, thought-shifting. This means respecting and accepting the energy and bodily sensations to move or do something and then transferring the energy to be used for something more positive. (*Note*: Thought-shifting is not the same as 'thought-stopping.')
	Then, practice substituting relaxing or 'Safe Place/Safe Relationship' images and thoughts (e.g., getting a hug from grandma, mastering a basketball shot, or imagining what will happen next in a book they are reading). Or, children can 'open their eyes' to who and what is around them that can be helpful.
	Highlight for children that this is like the 'Jumping Rubber Band' trick and practice trick again, if helpful.
	Practice 'thought- and image-shifting' with slow breathing and body tension/relaxation:
	– "Tense your toes as tight as you can. Then, take a slow breath, counting '1, 2, 3,' and tighten up from your toes through your legs, all the up to your shoulders and forehead, squeezing your eyes closed tight [for children who feel safe enough to do so], and holding yourself tighter and tighter."
	– "Now, empty your head and let the air out, counting '3, 2, 1,' and relax your whole body. Let everything go, every thought, all the tension. Let it all go until you feel as loose as a rope with no knots, no knots at all."
	– "Place one arm on your belly and one on your chest."
	– "Take in another slow breath, feeling the air slide into your belly. Feel your belly rise with your breath and fall down again as you breathe out."
	– "Breathe in again and this time fill up you mind with pictures and thoughts of your favorite safe and warm place with someone you feel safe with. Or, if you want, fill your mind with your favorite song that makes you feel warm and good inside. Try to add color and sounds and feelings to the pictures of your safe place."
	– "Take another slow breath, and try to make the picture and thoughts even stronger. Try to keep your mind focused on that picture."
	Afterwards, reinforce children for taking power away from painful thoughts and images and taking control of what they want to think about.
Changing the Story	Engage children to become the directors of their own movies instead of feeling overwhelmed and reacting to reminders of past traumas.
	Use a movie camera in smartphones or digital cameras that the family have; or, if not available, consider use of inexpensive digital cameras in sessions with children and caregivers keeping pictures and movies.
'Letting Go'	Encourage children to imagine filling a balloon up with fears and wishes that can't come true. With each breath, encourage children to imagine putting one more fear or loss into the balloon. Then, when it's full, "let it go."
	Encourage children and caregivers to develop their own ways to grieve lost hopes, lost people, and lost wishes in ways that match their cultural heritage.
Problem- Solving for Difficult Feelings	Encourage children to use their feelings (e.g., sadness, anger) as a cue that it's time to look at what's going on (the 'movie'), and consider strategies (changing scripts) to make things work better.
	Try out a a five-step problem-solving exercise for dealing with specific feelings children are experiencing in situations that are leading to problems: (1) describe the problem; (2) develop strategies; (3) decide which strategy to use; (4) practice acting it out; and (5) now use it.
	Repeat for other problem situations.

	CLOSINGS
'Homework' and 'Teamwork'	Practicing new perspectives, beliefs, and strategies is essential. Caregivers and team members play a critical role in transferring plans into reality. See the *RLH Strategy and Activity Guide* (in Part V) for additional activities.
Special Time, Thermo- meters, *Progress Note*, Reminder of Next Session	Continue special time at the end of the session, if helpful, and 'collaborative' *Progress Note*, as appropriate. Invite children and caregivers to suggest things they would like to do in the next session and schedule a date and time. Consider anyone else to invite to support children. Repeat Thermometers and Centering Activities if necessary.

▶▶▶ TIPS

➤ The 'ABCs' worksheet and plans are a beginning. Practice is essential to change Action Cycles. This is like moving from the script of a movie to the director calling for "Action" after the actors have rehearsed a scene many times and know their lines, their gestures, and what they want to do. Integration of the 'ABCs' means becoming the director of your own 'movie.' And, just like a movie director, children and caregivers can practice managing a situation as many times as they need to get it down the way they want it.

➤ Mind Power also means letting go of expectations and wishes that can't come true. Loss is often a primary trauma for children with Complex Trauma, and 'letting go' of lost hopes may be perceived as too painful to think about (e.g., giving up the wish of a child in placement for multiple years to return to live with a parent who is consumed with drugs and unable or unwilling to change). 'Letting go' and grieving may feel impossible until children develop sufficient security in new or strengthened relationships.

➤ Some children (and adults) are very good at thinking out problem cycles and coping strategies but have great trouble integrating these verbalized plans with feelings and actions. It is important to emphasize the importance of integrating bodily sensations, feelings, thoughts, and behaviors to change Action Cycles.

PITFALLS TO AVOID ▶▶▶

➤ Using words and activities that don't match children's developmental levels.

➤ Asking children to give up wishes for reunion or rebuilding relationships with caregivers who have not demonstrated the willingness or capacity to care for them when they have no one else to help them feel the magnitude of their losses and move forward.

➤ Failure to emphasize the importance of practicing new perspectives, beliefs, and behaviors multiple times every day for several weeks in order to change Action Cycles and leaving the 'ABCs' as simply a paper-and-pencil exercise.

CHAPTER CHECKPOINTS

☐ 1. Help children and caregivers list five positive beliefs about themselves and practice new, more adaptive behaviors based on those beliefs multiple times each day for several weeks to create better endings for stressful situations.

☐ 2. Help children and caregivers accept responsibility for their own behavior and avoid blaming themselves for the actions of others.

RESOURCES

For additional child-friendly exercise workbooks and guides, see:

Verdick, E., & Lisovskis, M. (2003). *How to take the grrrr out of anger*. Minneapolis, MN: Free Spirit.

Whitehouse, E., & Pudney, W. (1996). *A volcano in my tummy*. Gabriola Island, BC: New Society (for activities such as the problem-solving exercise above).

For additional skill-building exercises geared to adolescents and young adults, see Marra (2004) and other workbooks on the application of DBT (Linehan, 1993).

9

Timelines and Moves

Making Sense of the Past

OBJECTIVES

- Children and caregivers develop an organized, sequential record of important events in children's lives that include places lived, important people, children's ratings of how they felt in different places, and how good or 'tough' times were at different ages.
- Children identify important people and times in their lives when they felt supported and cared for.
- Children share losses and experience validation by caregivers, when possible.
- Therapists develop a list of children's traumatic experiences in chronological order and dysfunctional beliefs about traumatic experiences to address in Chapter 10.

OVERVIEW

Creating an Integrated Life Story

Children with Complex Trauma have often moved multiple times and experienced multiple losses, including separations from primary caregivers, deaths, incarcerations, hospitalizations, and placements. Children's lives may feel chaotic and like they are living in a perpetual state of crisis. And, children who have experienced multiple traumas often lose memories of caring and come to feel alone or rejected, especially following repeated and severe experiences of violence, loss, or abandonment.

Chapter 9 helps children develop and organize a fact-centered record of their lives, including important people and places where they have lived. *Life Storybook* pages help children and caregivers to record places lived in chronological order, identify important people in children's lives, and elicit strengths and caring in children, caregivers, family members, and other caring adults who helped children at some time. Helping children remember people who have helped, even in small ways, can highlight resources, strengths, and talents within children, family members, and important people in their lives. Recording facts and identifying caring adults from the past also helps

to diffuse self-blame and accentuates the responsibility of adults to care for and protect children.

Chapter 9 begins with a map that shows moves and can be used to identify primary resources for children, key people who have helped them in the past, and who could help them in the future. Children know that journeys have a starting point and destinations that can be pictured on a map. Maps have a magical quality and can lead to buried treasures. Similarly, life story work can be seen as a process of locating and recovering lost caring relationships (buried treasures) after traumatic experiences. Children also know that maps can keep them from getting lost and far away from dangers.

Life story work is a shared journey. Children and caregivers have the knowledge of past experiences and the information needed to develop the map for the journey and to identify resources and risks that can help or hinder the journey ahead. Therapists guide children and caregivers along the journey building on the therapist's understanding of how to use resources and confidence that there is a way out of the nightmares of trauma.

Identifying Traumatic Experiences

Chapter 9 begins work on children's more stressful experiences, including losses. In this work, it is important to acknowledge that children very likely had both positive and negative experiences with different caregivers, including significant family members. This often led to both positive and negative memories, beliefs, and emotional reactions to reminders of those people or situations. By helping children recall people and places in their lives, therapists and, whenever possible, caregivers validate children's experiences and, at the same time, demonstrate that it is safe to use creative arts, movement, or words to share children's experiences of what happened. This, in turn, provides opportunities for reinforcing good times and reintegrating negative experiences, including bodily sensations, feelings, thoughts, and actions.

> **Life story work can be utilized like a map to guide children in their quest to rebuild, or build, attachments to important people.**

Healing is fostered by promoting acceptance and permission from significant adults in children's life to hold both the good and the bad in their lives and to stop feeling driven to hide or avoid distressing memories. To do this, children need the security of caring, protective adults who are strong enough in their own lives to accept that children may have different, and at times very painful, feelings and memories that adults may wish to forget or ignore.

Caring adults make significant contributions to children's recovery by showing them that it is safe and healthy to learn about both good times and bad times in the past, and to use this understanding to make a better future. Caregivers model acceptance by sharing their own life stories in an appropriate way that children can handle. Caregivers also help bridge the gaps that have formed in children's memories by giving them permission to learn about the facts of the past and to share their own memories and feelings.

> **Completing Chapter Nine with caregiver support shows children that adults in their lives have the courage to face past traumas.**

Acknowledgement and acceptance of children's experiences and perspectives, including both positive and negative memories, is critical for children to feel that caregivers validate their experiences and can be trusted.

Therapists can use children's descriptions of feelings in different situations and ratings of how they felt at different ages to construct a list of experiences to address in Chapter 10. In addition, children's descriptions of memories of what happened and the reasons for different events can help therapists to construct a list of dysfunctional beliefs to address in treatment.

Organizing the list of traumatic memories is recommended in most cases for use in Chapter 10. Deciding what order to process traumatic memories varies by treatment models. Going through stories in chronological order is often used in EMDR (Shapiro, 2001) along with using themes of traumas (e.g., several traumatic hospitalizations or separations from a caregiver). Starting with a later trauma can bring up reminders of earlier traumas, making resolution of the later trauma more difficult, even if the later trauma is rated by children as lower in stress. Reworking the earliest traumas first helps keep the process organized and allows children to work through components of traumas that may be reactivated as reminders by later traumatic experiences. For a discussion of alternative strategies (e.g., using themes of traumas, going in hierarchical order from least to worst trauma, addressing the worst trauma first, or using chronological order), see Greenwald (2013) and Greenwald, McClintock, Bailey, and Seubert (2013).

Recovering Relationships and Grieving Losses

Chapter 9 provides opportunities for children and therapists to engage family members to help children recover their past. This is detective work, with children and therapists working as detectives. Completion of Chapter 9 may require finding relatives and family friends who are able to help children learn what happened, especially during their earliest years. Adults and children can learn from each other what has helped and the skills and courage that helped family members get through 'tough times.'

Chapter 9 fosters an understanding of important family members, foster parents, and other people who children may have had difficulty talking about in previous chapters. This can lead to focused work on rebuilding lost positive connections and grieving losses for children. Inviting children's beliefs about the reasons for moves also helps identify factors involved in traumatic grief, including self-blame, shame, and feelings of failure. After completion of Chapter 9, grief work can be conducted in conjunction with Chapter 10 or separately using guidelines (e.g., Cohen et al., 2006).

STEP BY STEP

	OPENINGS
Welcome	*My Thermometers* plus *Safety reminders* and *Magical Moment*, if needed.
	CENTERING ACTIVITIES
Strengthening Centering 'Make Your Own' Centering Activities	Utilize Centering Activities (see Part V) that were omitted from previous chapters. Strengthen use of activities that resonated with children or caregivers and helped children to modulate. Emphasize the value of daily practice to foster skill development. Encourage children and caregivers to make up their own activities for calming alone and together. **Make a schedule with a special time each day for practicing Centering Activities at home.** It helps to separate this time from anything else that happened. Focus on the activity and attunement with each other. Avoid making Centering Activities contingent on behavior. This can become a special time for children and caregivers, a 'sanctuary' in their daily routine, a time to refocus on what really matters and a fun time for child-caregiver re-attunement. See the *RLH Strategy and Activity Guide* (in Part V) for other activities to increase modulation.
	LIFE STORYBOOK
Detective Work	Remind children that caring adults and other therapists or authorities can help to answer questions. Children are not expected to know what happened. It's OK to keep going back to Chapter 9 over the course of work on the *Life Storybook*, filling in missing sessions as information becomes available. Engage children to work as detectives *with* safe caregivers, extended family, libraries, news media, hospital records, child protective services, and other community resources to discover what family members and other significant adults did or did not do, what was known, and what interventions were attempted to help a family. Recording of facts is especially important for diffusing self-blame and acknowledging the responsibility of adults to care for and protect children. If possible, involve safe caring adults in portions of sessions as sources of information. Children should not be asked to approach an adult alone unless that adult has validated a child and supported healing, including resolving pain from the past as well as the present. Reinforcement of safety rules for sessions and practicing asking questions to these adults may be necessary to reduce children's anxiety. If adults in children's families are not safe, the therapist may be able to get information privately from adults by asking for their help or to approach other extended family members and learn about the unsafe adults through multiple sources. Work with children on recording facts, such as dates and places, as a means of recording key events *without* needing to verbalize painful feelings. Omit map work if this seems childish for an older youth.
Timeline	Point out how feeling states change for all of us over time by turning the timeline horizontally. Connect the ratings in the right column, creating a graph. Turn the timeline chart horizontally and highlight upswings in children's lives, noting how these upswings related to important people and events. Use the timeline and other assignments to highlight positive memories and to foster hope for making things better again. Encourage using different colors to reflect different feelings (after O'Conner, 1983), and coloring in the boxes in the left column for each year. Moving horizontally, children can then elaborate on what happened and use the numeric scale to rate their lives that year.

Help Children Recover Positive Relationships and Grieve Losses	Use Chapter 9 to trace lost relationships and open up possibilities for rebuilding connections to positive caregivers and family members wherever possible.
	
	After completion of Chapter 9, help children to grieve lost relationships and to work on building new relationships. Mourning losses is a critical part of trauma therapy.
	
	To facilitate grief work (Cohen et al., 2001):
	
	• Identify special parts of past relationships that can't be reclaimed: lost futures, what might have been.
	• Identify special parts that can be kept alive.
	• Help children consider ways that events (holidays, achievements) can be made special, even without the lost person present, and honor the contributions of the lost person (e.g., dedicate awards to the lost person and honor what children learned from that person).
	• Create a memory book of the lost person, including his or her favorite pastimes, funniest habits, some of the nicest things the lost person did for children, children's favorite gift from the lost person, and some of the best times children and the lost person had together.
	• Honor special gifts from the lost person in a memorial service, including the child's tribute.
	• Include what the lost person would have wanted for the child in the future and tie to goals.
	• Identify reminders of loss and help the child develop coping skills for reminders (Layne, Saltzman, Savjak, & Pynoos, 1999).
	• Predict future times of sadness as normal and tied to anniversary dates, holidays, etc.
	• Help children give self-permission to feel loss, including emptiness, anger, sadness, and yearning.
	• Normalize reactions as part of grief; being human by definition means to grieve over lost loved ones, not a sign of pathology or weakness.
	• Plan for how to cope when reminded of losses (triggers): who to talk to, self-soothing, imagery, use of life storybook to remember positive lessons.
	• Help children gradually shift relationships to the deceased as a memory that they can keep inside (after Wolfelt, 1991).
	• Help children identify, develop, and commit to new relationships.
	• List significant people remaining or possible in children's lives and how they help children.
	• Help children use losses to develop new strengths and understanding from losses:
	
	  – "If you met another boy/girl who lost someone they loved, like you did, what would you tell them?"
	  – "What would you want them to know that might help them?"
	  – "What would you say to them?"
	
	• Memorialize a lost person with action that builds on positive lessons inspired by that person (e.g., making the world better by raising money for cancer, speaking out against cigarette promotion to children or pressure to use drugs).

Resource Checklist	Recheck children's levels of modulation and supports using the *Resource Checklist* in Part V, *My Thermometers*, and *Chapter Checkpoints* below to ensure sufficient modulation before going ahead with Chapter 10.
	<div align="center">**CLOSINGS**</div>
'Homework' and 'Teamwork'	Caregivers, case managers, in-home support workers, and other advocates for children play a major role in the detective work necessary for many children to learn about what happened in their lives and to organize this information in a meaningful way that they can accept and remain modulated. Children should not be asked to seek help from adults who are not supportive. See the *RLH Strategy and Activity Guide* (in Part V) for additional activities.
Special Time, Thermometers, *Progress Note*, Reminder of Next Session	Continue special time at the end of the session, if helpful, and 'collaborative' *Progress Notes*, as appropriate. Invite children and caregivers to suggest things they would like to do in the next session and schedule a date and time. Consider anyone else to invite to support children. Repeat Thermometers if necessary.

>>> TIPS

➤ By making parts of Chapter 9 a shared activity with a safe caregiver, children learn that they are not alone, that they may be safe enough to share different parts of their traumatic experiences (bodily sensations, feelings, beliefs, actions), and that important people in their lives value caring for one another through good and tough times.

➤ At the same time, children naturally watch adults involved in life story work to see in their facial looks, tone of voice, gestures, and actions whether they support children addressing traumas in the past. If children become reluctant to work on recording life moves, etc., it may be helpful to check on messages children have received from family members or other important people in their lives.

➤ Validation of losses is a key part of work on rebuilding attachments.

➤ Accept children's responses of stressful memories and dysfunctional thinking and organize these for processing in Chapter 10, rather than feeling these need to be addressed as they are shared.

➤ If sharing moves is stressful, intersperse use of 'SOS' or Centering Activities that help modulate children and care-givers to keep children modulated (e.g., after completing every two pages of Chapter 9).

➤ If children share memories that are very stressful (e.g., memories that make their *Knots* scale on *My Thermometers* exceed their *Self-Control Power*), therapists can help children put these memories into a 'lockbox' that will be kept in the therapist's office to address at a later time.

PITFALLS TO AVOID >>>

➤ The therapist expects children to know facts about the past, rather than working together as detectives and pulling in past, current, and future caring adults to help.

➤ The therapist asks children to share feelings in words when they are feeling overwhelmed by reminders of past events.

➤ Children perceive the therapist is afraid to confront details of memories (e.g., frightening aspects of an abusive adult's appearance or sexual abuse), inadvertently reinforcing the power of feared people and events.

CHAPTER CHECKPOINTS

☐ 1. Help children organize information about their lives in a meaningful order, including happy memories and 'tough times.'

☐ 2. Develop a sequential list of trauma events, including resources and positive connections for children, traumatic events, and dysfunctional beliefs about moves or traumatic events to be addressed in Chapter 10.

☐ 3. Check to see that resources below are in place to support trauma event integration before starting Chapter 10:

    __ Children's *Self-Control Power* ratings are higher than their *Knots* in therapy sessions.

    __ Chldren have at least one committed, caring adult with sufficient stability, who is physically and psycho-logically available, willing, and committed to work through traumatic memories with children and provide support after sessions.

    __ Children demonstrate sufficient self-regulation abilities and supports from resources in their family and community to manage distress and stress reactions to trauma reminders and avoid becoming dangerous to themselves or others.

    __ Children have developed, and can bring to mind, a positive 'Safe Place' image of feeling safe with someone who cares, or cared in the past, about them.

    __ The practitioner has experience or support from his or her supervisor, colleagues, or consultants with expe-rience to 'move through' traumatic memory reintegration with children at their developmental age (e.g., *TF-CBT, EMDR, Progressive Counting*).

    __ The practitioner has access to resources (pharmacotherapy, acute crisis evaluation and hospitalization, case management resources, pediatric care) if needed.

RESOURCES

Life stories have been used in foster care and older child adoptions for several decades (Fahlberg, 1991; Jewett, 1978; Kagan, 1996, 2004; Kliman, 1996; Wheeler, 1978) as a way of helping children to grieve losses, to remember their past, and to share their experiences with adoptive families. For further information and guidelines for life story work with traumatized children, see Kagan (2004, Chapter 8).

10

Through the Tough Times

Trauma Experience Integration

OBJECTIVES

- Children and caregivers develop the security for children to share stories of traumatic experiences, including bodily sensations, feelings, actions, beliefs, the worst parts, what helped, and what made things worse.
- Children experience that caring adults can tolerate children's affective experiences related to traumatic memories.[1]
- Children integrate bodily sensations, feelings, thoughts, and actions within 'Five-Chapter' Stories of 'moving through' tough times that include children and caregivers helping each other. Children and caregivers strengthen images of *Real Life Heroes* working together to grow stronger, instead of children or adults feeling alone, ashamed, or overwhelmed.
- Sharing 'Five-Chapter' Stories helps children and caregivers strengthen attunement, bridge gaps formed during traumatic experiences, increase trust and augment skills for self- and co-regulation.
- Sharing 'Five-Chapter' Stories while remaining sufficiently modulated helps children and caregivers to desensitize stress reactions to reminders of traumas while reintegrating fragmented memories.

OVERVIEW

Tough times are introduced as something everyone experiences. No one can change what happened; however, children and caregivers can help each other to reduce the distressing power of traumatic memories and help free themselves from reliving past traumas in their bodies, minds, and interactional behaviors (Action Cycles). The workbook structure counters expectations and messages that children or caregivers should have been able to do better in the past to overcome hardships, to 'put the past behind them,' or that they have failed, hurt other people, and therefore defined themselves forever as bad, mentally ill, or dangerous. Chapter 10 invites children and caregivers to work together to grow stronger than the traumas that afflicted parts of their lives.

Caregivers play a central role in trauma experience integration. For children, the threat to the relationship with the caregiver is often worse than the traumatic event itself (Alexander, 2013). The storytelling process can help chil-

dren experience that caring adults can tolerate children's affective experiences related to traumatic memories. This is a critical component in helping children feel secure enough to share traumatic experiences, including their bodily sensations, perceptions, beliefs, feelings, and actions. Caregivers serve as guardians, mentors, and models of courage to face traumas. By supporting children's expression of mind-body experiences, caregivers help children to master what was impossible to face in the past and demonstrate that children will not be left feeling alone and vulnerable to repeated traumatic events.

Finding a Pathway through the Maze

Traumatized children often feel like they are trapped, stuck, and unable to face "unspeakable terrors" (van der Kolk, 1996). In some ways, this is like living in a maze anticipating horrors around every corner, especially if past attempts to escape led to re-traumatization. Traumatized children may feel hopeless that there is any way out of the maze. Caregivers may feel equally traumatized or feel constricted by their own overwhelming fears of what may lie ahead if traumas are faced.

Resiliency-focused trauma treatment enlists the support of caregivers, therapists, home-based support workers, care managers, residential counselors, teachers, and many others to help traumatized children find a pathway out of traumas. This means helping children become safe enough and strong enough to explore other ways of living and to develop the confidence to take risks to find a way out of the maze so they do not have to live on guard, as if trauma is all around them, 24/7, or that they are stuck living in a dark corner of a foreboding maze.

RLH Chapters 1–9 help children develop and see the strengths they carry inside, strengths honed by the ordeals of their journeys through good times and tough times. Attunement and body-mind self- and co-regulation (centering) activities help children and caregivers experience that they do not have to hide their perceptions, feelings, or beliefs. Children and caregivers typically share previously hidden traumatic memories as they 'move through' the workbook.

With the support of caregivers and the guidance of therapists, children learn that they can 'move through' the pain and use the resources they gain along the way. Just as in stories of heroes, children learn to use what they gain from facing challenges (ordeals) to develop ways to give back to others (sharing the boon). In the process, children can transform themselves from feeling they are hopeless victims who feel shame, damaged, no good, sick, rejected, or abandoned, into heroes who feel stronger by giving back to others and because of the attunement and increased trust they have developed with caregivers, mentors, therapists, and other caring adults.

Trauma experience integration in RLH means reintegration of children's mind-body experiences (bodily sensations, feelings, thoughts, beliefs, actions) and their connections to important people in their lives, as well as their families and cultural heritage. Children and caregivers grow larger together than the bad things that happened that split them apart.

The RLH structured storytelling process promotes safety and provides a map for 'moving through' the maze. The storytelling process highlights how children and caregivers can 'move through' each traumatic memory to images and feelings of safety and emotional support at a time following the trauma experience. This can be the Safe Place or Safe Relationship imagery developed in Chapter 7, or another memory of children feeling safe and emotionally connected to someone who cares (or cared) for them. Since most children with Complex Trauma have

> **Re-integration of traumatic experiences includes integrating relationships, the child's mind-body experiences, and skills for self and co-regulation, all of which are reflected in the RLH Life Storybook.**

experienced relationship traumas, it is important that the Safe Place or Safe Relationship memory be a time when children were not experiencing danger to their primary relationships. The memory needs to be strong, rich, and detailed. And, children and caregivers need to have practiced eliciting the memory as a multisensory experience (e.g., with pictures, rhythm in multiple types of situations, tonality, movement, feelings, and verbal descriptions).

Practice in sharing stories helps children experience that they do not have to remain trapped and feeling like they are reliving trauma experiences, or that they need to hide their traumatic memories, and often feelings of shame, from safe caregivers and other safe caring adults committed to helping children grow stronger than traumatic experiences. With each story, children (and caregivers) experience that they can venture forward and that they can use the emotional support, the skills they have developed, and a structured format to highlight pathways through the maze to feelings of safety within themselves and their primary relationships.

'Five-Chapter' Stories

Chapter 10 provides a 'Five-Chapter' multimodal storytelling format that is designed to boost a child and caregiver's confidence and to counter the helplessness, lack of self-control, and confusion (van der Kolk, 2014) that follows serial traumas. The *Life Storybook* provides outlines for children to share six[2] 'tough times' with the 'Five-Chapter' format, starting with their earliest memory of a stressful time. (See Chapter 9 for tips and options

---

MAZE AND TRAUMA STORYTELLING TIPS

1. It's okay to make mistakes. We don't have to repeat the same thing again and again. We can learn from mistakes what skills and resources help; and we can try something new.

2. It helps to work as a team with caregivers and children helping each other check out pathways through the maze and sharing a trauma story.

3. Testing out strategies in therapy sessions is like checking out a maze path with your finger before drawing in a line. Trauma therapists can help children and caregivers explore in a safe way.

4. Each time you solve a maze or share a story of a 'tough time', it becomes easier to do it again. You can use similar strategies to help you solve other mazes and make it easier to share other traumatic experiences in a way that makes things better.

for organizing a list of trauma memories in chronological order.) If traumas occurred before children were able to remember (e.g., before age 4–5), safe caregivers can be asked to help him or her recall what happened and to co-create trauma stories (Lieberman & van Horn, 2011). Additional pages of the 'Five-Chapter' format can be copied from Part V of the *RLH Toolkit* for children who have more than six major trauma experiences.

The 'Five-Chapter' format expands on the 'Three-Chapter' Stories with a beginning, middle, and end that were introduced in Chapter 5. 'Five-Chapter' Stories begin with: What happened (Chapter 2); What helped children and people they loved get through (survive) the 'tough time' (Chapter 3); A safe time and place after the traumatic event when children felt cared for and protected (Chapter 4); What led up to the traumatic event (Chapter 1); and How children could prevent or reduce 'tough times' now that they are older, smarter, and stronger with help from caring adults (Chapter 5). The additional two 'chapters' elicit memories of what helped children and caregivers in the past and accentuate what children and caregivers could do in the future to prevent or minimize future traumas in the future.[3] Chapter 3 of children's stories helps caregivers (and other caring adults) understand how they learned to cope and how this may be related to their behaviors. Chapter 4 can be used to highlight for children how their home, family, school, or community has changed and how things are different now than when the 'tough times' were happening. Encouraging children to visualize or enact Chapter 4 helps to reinforce how caregivers, other caring adults, and children have made their lives safer since the traumatic experiences took place.

The 'Five-Chapter' format builds on principles of therapeutic exposure (Berliner, 2005; Briere & Scott, 2014; Cohen et al., 2006) and the goal of helping children to share trauma experiences, including bodily sensations, feelings, perceptions, beliefs, and actions, while remaining sufficiently modulated with the child and caregiver's level of Self-Control on *My Thermometers* higher than their level of *Knots* (stress). Modulation is facilitated in RLH by the structured 'Five-Chapter' storytelling protocol that promotes safety and helps children stay within the 'therapeutic window' (Briere, 2002), a middle range between overwhelming and inadequate exposure.

Stories follow a now-familiar and ritualized structure for children and caregivers that elicits emotional processing skills, multimodal expression, and emotional support developed in earlier chapters. Drawings, questions, and use of *My Thermometers* help elicit details, perceptions, feelings, beliefs, and actions to promote multimodal trauma exposure (Lanktree & Briere, 2016). Directions encourage children to utilize imagery, movies, and other creative arts activities to show how problems from the past can be managed with the broadened perspective and increased skills that children have developed along with help from caring adults.

Emphasis in each story is placed on what helped children get through each 'tough time' and what they learned from that experience, now that they are older and wiser. Storytelling focuses on solutions and development of "healing stories" (adapted from Figley, 1989) for difficult times, including what children saw, heard, thought, and did, what was most difficult, and emphasizing what children and caregivers would now do, as a story or a movie, to prevent or better manage repetition of past types of traumas (e.g., domestic violence, emotional abuse). Stories provide opportunities for children to share what they have learned and for caring adults to reinforce changes that have been made to prevent or minimize future 'tough times.' With each 'Five-Chapter' Story, children become progressively more and more able to experience images and reminders of traumatic events without becoming overwhelmed.

Helping Others, Increasing Pride, and Reducing Shame

Chapter 10 provides multiple activities to create openings for children to share their 'tough times' in a safe way. Following the 'Five-Chapter' Stories, children are asked to share a lesson they learned about what can help them and their families get through 'tough times' and how they would deal with a similar situation if it happened again. Children are also encouraged to envision themselves on games cards in a series of three drawings. The first drawing shows children in their toughest time. The second card shows children as heroes who faced the same 'tough time' again. And, the third card shows children growing larger and larger (Rojano, 1998) with greater abilities to handle problems. Children are then encouraged to describe how they would help someone they cared about who was experiencing one of their 'tough times.'

Chapter 10 also reminds children of how heroes, in real life, feel scared and make mistakes, including hurting others, and how heroes transform themselves by developing courage, owning what they did, and by helping others. Since traumatized children are often constricted by feelings of guilt and shame, children are encouraged to share ways they've hurt others and take steps to apologize and make up for what children did. This should include a safety plan to prevent children from repeating past harm to others. Developing forms of apology and restitution works best when it's possible to link this to the child and family's cultural heritage, and how their family or religion has provided a means to learn from mistakes and promote healing for everyone involved.

Eliciting Trauma Stories

The workbook format frames trauma story integration as simply another part of a structured curriculum that builds sequentially on the relationship and mind-body skill-building exercises in previous chapters. Structured questions utilized in cognitive behavioral trauma desensitization treatment (e.g., TF-CBT) (Cohen et al., 2006) help elicit details of traumatic memories and reinforce children's resilience. Creative arts, thermometers, and movie-making questions facilitate children sharing details of bodily sensations, feelings, thoughts, and what they and others did.

Trust in a therapist, and any caring adults present, is essential for trauma processing. Therapists and caring adults connect to children and build trust by demonstrating over time that they truly want to know what they experienced. With child traumatic stress and Complex Trauma, this often means witnessing (Herman, 1992b) children's unfolding disclosure of fragmented memories, including their conflicting emotions, intense feelings of intimacy and pain, and good times that led into violence, terror, and shame.

Children often respond well when they see, feel, and hear nonverbal and verbal messages from therapists that demonstrate (e.g., "I want to know more about what happened . . . What were you feeling? . . . What were you saying to yourself inside your head? . . . " (Deblinger, 2005). It helps for children to experience that the therapist wants to know children's whole experience, the good parts and the 'tough times,' *and* that the therapist can experience children's sharing of the experience without shaming or abandoning them. Direct messages building on the therapist-child relationship often work well to elicit children's complete experience. Deblinger (2005), for instance, will invite children to share a more complete story by expressing caring and curiosity (e.g., "I'd like know more about that . . . What happened next? What happened right before? . . . Then what happened?" It is also helpful to use body image questions to help children share their physical experience of an event (e.g., "If you scanned over your body from your toes to your belly to your head, what were you feeling? What was your heart doing? How was your stomach feeling? What were your hands doing?").

Since traumatized children are particularly sensitive to nuances in adults' tone of voice, posture, gestures, and facial expressions, therapists need to develop the ability to both attune to hurt children (and adults) and at the same time keep themselves safe. Therapists must feel secure enough to truly 'want to know.' Part of this comes from training and understanding that facing and reintegrating painful memories is essential for trauma therapy. Therapist self-protection, as in all trauma work, is essential, including support from supervisors, administrators, and consultants. In order for a therapist to create a 'sanctuary' in therapy sessions for trauma processing to occur, the therapist needs to work within an environment that is safe and supportive, the opposite of the neglect and abuse that fractures family relationships and spurs traumatic stress. Implementation of principles of the Sanctuary® model (Bloom & Farragher, 2013) are highly recommended in mental health and child and family service organizations to create safety for staff as well as children and families.

Therapists' confidence plays a major role in fostering the courage of children and caring adults to reduce the toxicity of traumas. Confidence can be enhanced with an understanding of how exposure therapies have been proven highly effective when clients are able to experience images of past traumas long enough to reduce distress (Rothbaum & Schwartz, 2002). At the same time, repetition of short exposures to traumatic memories may increase threat avoidance and trauma reactions if they do not allow time for habituation and lead to reduction of anxiety.

Effective exposure therapies involve repetition of exposure (Rothbaum & Schwartz, 2002) with modulation and foster self-control by clients in setting the pace for work. Asking children for details can be minimized in the early phases of sharing a trauma memory, when the child is not yet feeling safe with the therapist and distress is typically the highest.

Children can guide how much they share and how fast they work through the 'Five-Chapter' Story to complete a first draft. However, over the course of sessions, it is helpful for the therapist to elicit as much detail as possible, especially about children's *toughest times*, in order to promote habituation (Cohen et al., 2006). Details include sounds, smells, words, tone of voice, dress, and children's reactions. Avoiding painful details may seem kind but prevents emotional processing and reintegration of traumatic memories.

Children can be asked to make a first draft of the 'Five-Chapter' Story and then to go back and add more details in a series of drafts of the story until the story includes an integration of bodily sensations, feelings, thoughts, and actions. After completing each draft, it is important to assess how children are feeling on *My Thermometers*. The goal is to help children have *Knots* (Stress) ratings of 0–2 and *Self-Control Power* of 8–10 after reviewing each draft of the story. Repeating reading and adding to stories with emotional support and modulation typically leads to reductions in *Knots* (Stress) levels and increases in *Self-Control Power*.

To promote children sharing and re-experiencing trauma stories, it can be helpful to invite children to control how fast or slow they re-experience stories. Children are familiar with fast forwarding, slowing, pausing, rewinding, and playing videos on TVs or computers. Similarly, they can be encouraged to use the Self-Control and Mind Power they have developed in Chapters 1–9 to adjust how fast or slow they 'move through' their trauma stories and to stay modulated (adapted from Siegel & Bryson, 2012). Children can be invited to share their trauma stories in a variety of ways e.g., with drums, as a song or music with a piano, xylophone, or guitar, with puppets, as a cartoon strip, or a short movie.

Using the 'Five-Chapter' format allows for children to quickly draw pictures for their Chapters 2, 3, 4, 1, and 5, and then to stop and do a Centering Activity, if needed, before completing the story. Completing the story includes answering questions and sharing bodily feelings in drawings and *My Thermometers* linked to each chapter in their story. This can be seen as children hitting the 'pause' button on their remote control (after Siegel & Bryson, 2012), using a Centering Activity to modulate, and then returning to complete the story. Centering Activities can be brief (e.g., looking at a picture of the child with caregivers on a beach vacation and touching a sand tray to feel the texture of the sand) or involve more movement (e.g., standing up to balance a peacock feather). It is also important to help children relax before the end of every session, and, if possible, to end sessions with a fun activity.

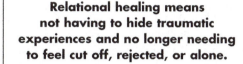

Relational healing means not having to hide traumatic experiences and no longer needing to feel cut off, rejected, or alone.

Sharing the full trauma experience in a safe way with emotionally supportive adults helps put trauma stories within children's control, rather than reinforcing its power as something, or having some parts, that they do not dare say out loud or remember for fear of something terrible happening again (e.g., a parent becoming so overwhelmed that he or she hurts him or herself or rejects the child).

Reintegration of traumatic memories is promoted by sharing with safe, caring adults who show children they can validate their experience. Sharing also reinforces caring adults as protectors for children in the future as part of *Power Plans*. Children learn that previously unbearable memories can be managed with help from caring adults and that bodily sensations, feelings, thoughts, and behaviors can be modulated when reminded of traumatic events.

When 'Five-Chapter' Stories Are Not Working

Children's reluctance to share traumatic memories may indicate that children are experiencing dangers or stressors unknown to therapists or caregivers. It is important to check on whether the traumatic experience is truly over (Greenwald, 2013), whether children are experiencing threats to their primary relationships, or whether they are sufficiently stable in their lives to do trauma experience integration. If traumas are still happening, attempts at trauma experience integration are not likely to be very effective. Children need to stay on guard, at a high arousal level, for survival and protection of people they love. In these situations, repeating trauma and resiliency assessment tools can be helpful, along with checking individually again with children on how safe they feel with different people, including caregivers or therapists. Safety plans and skills may need to be adjusted, strengthened, and practiced. In some cases, children may simply not be safe enough to share traumas given the external and/or internal threats they are experiencing. Further work on centering activities, building more secure relationships, and incorporating *Self-Control* and *Mind Power* may be needed. In

other situations, children may be able to do trauma experience integration at a later point when transitions in their lives have been completed (e.g., return home from placement or a family's move to another community and away from a dangerous neighborhood where the children were targeted).

If children can draw pictures, but appear to be stuck cognitively (e.g., blaming him or herself), it can help to ask them to imagine what they would do or say to help another child who had similar beliefs that were contributing to feeling distressed or stuck (adapted from Greenwald, 2013).

If children appear too anxious to share details of a story, it may help to explore adding resources. For instance, ask children who they would like to have in the session to support them when they re-read or work again on the story (adapted from Greenwald, 2013). It can also help to remind children of how much bigger, stronger, and smarter they are now than when the trauma took place and how they now have caregiver support and protection. Reinforcing and accentuating Chapter 5 of children's stories can be helpful, especially how they would get help from caregivers and other caring adults if the traumatic events started to happen again. It is also helpful to increase support from safe caregivers in ways that help children to modulate. This may include having a caregiver hold the child's hand, putting his or her arm around the child's back, or just sitting close.

For anxious children, it can also help to practice use of detachment (distancing) techniques, in which children, for example, are guided to:

- Imagine watching a memory like a scene on a movie screen from the back of a large theater or through a thick window with five inches of bulletproof glass, while children sit comfortably in a speeding train (Shapiro, 2001).
- Utilize superhero or game card images to help him or her feel protected from stressful memories and empowered with the help of allies to remain safe. For example, "If (the child's favorite hero) was with you now, and you saw _____ , what would you do?" Boundaries around cards can be painted with dark, wide ink.
- Visualize strong images of sitting close to friends, protective family members, and other caring adults, while imagining a 'tough time.'
- Use creative storytelling techniques that children enjoy with music, video, movement, puppet or family doll enactments, or act out themes from their memories in different ways (e.g., mini-dramas).
- Explore how children's heroes would have handled similar situations.
- Play out different endings to children's stories.

If children bring up additional traumas before processing the targeted story, it can be helpful to thank them and tell them that the additional traumas will be added to the list of traumas to be addressed and put in a 'lockbox' kept by the therapist for future sessions.

If children refuse to add more details or to work on more stories, it is important to congratulate them for sharing as much as they have and to point out that they will have other opportunities to share more when they are ready. With each story, children become stronger and stronger together with people they care about. It is also helpful to check and see if anything has changed that has led to children stopping sharing. Do caregivers or other family members appear distressed about children sharing traumas or some other stressor that is impacting the family? In many cases, it may simply be a bad time for the family and waiting a few weeks can lead to sufficient stability for trauma processing.

The *RLH Life Storybook* can be utilized with models of desensitization that do not include verbally sharing traumatic memories. Detailed guides to the use of Progressive Counting (Greenwald, 2013) and EMDR (Shapiro, 2001) are available (see Resources below). The movie imagery in RLH meshes well with movie-making in Progressive Counting and the emphasis on getting *through* traumas to a safe time when the danger is over. With Progressive Counting, safe, emotionally supportive caregivers can demonstrate to children that they can support children 'moving through' each trauma story in progressively longer periods of time, even though they are not sharing out loud in words what they are visualizing.

Completion of Trauma Memory Reintegration

Trauma processing is not magical, clear-cut, or demonstrated by total remission of distressing feelings about a traumatic event. What happened cannot be changed, and entrenched response patterns don't just stop. Neural pathways warning children of renewed traumas can be respected and used in helpful ways. Children and caregivers can develop skills to identify warning cues, to remain modulated when reminded of traumas, and to move on developmentally in their lives without needing to relive the traumas in their bodies and actions every day.

Criteria for desensitization in many trauma treatment models includes the youth feeling at a '2' or less on stress scales. Other signs of trauma desensitization include: the youth being able to experience reminders of traumas without significant distress (Griffin et al., 2014); the youth being able to differentiate reminders of past traumas from real and current dangerous situations (Griffin et al., 2014); the youth not needing to shut down or avoid reminders of traumas (Lanktree & Briere, 2016); and the youth being able to allow themselves to experience disturbing thoughts, feelings, or memories without needing to fight them off or become preoccupied with them (Lanktree & Briere, 2016), and youths develop a stronger sense of themselves as coming through traumas and being able to thrive as well as survive. In RLH, meaning-making includes youths finding a way to understand what happened in trauma events as parts of their lives and also developing an understanding of how they can use their experiences to help themselves and others. In this way, traumatized children and caregivers transform themselves and their families from victims to heroes, sharing what they learned with others.

STEP BY STEP

	OPENINGS
Welcome	*My Thermometers* plus *Safety reminders* and *Magical Moment*, if needed.
	CENTERING ACTIVITIES
Breathing, Balancing, Yoga, Movement, and 'Improv'	Strengthen the use of Centering Activities that resonated with children or caregivers and helped them to modulate.
	Encourage children to do a maze geared for their developmental level, first alone, and then with a caregiver and with strategy tips from the therapist. Afterwards, ask children to repeat these mazes. Share tips for mazes and trauma storytelling above.
	See the *RLH Strategy and Activity Guide* (in Part V) for other activities to increase modulation.
	LIFE STORYBOOK
Desensitization Checkpoints for 'Sufficient Stability'	Avoid re-exposure to traumatic memories where there is not an established means of keeping children safe, and also identification of signs, reminders, and triggers for the trauma happening again. This allows creation of a "healing theory" (Figley, 1989), which is highlighted in Chapter 5 of the 'Five-Chapter' storytelling format

	Ensure that children can bring up strong imagery and feelings in Safe Place or Safe Relationship stories that help them stay regulated and can be used as end points (Chapter 4) in 'Five-Chapter' stories.
	Safe Place/Safe Relationship imagery stories are about times, however long, when children were not in danger of losing their primary relationships.
	Strengthen Safe Place/Safe Relationship imagery, if necessary, and arrange to bring reminders to session (e.g., photos of a dog that comforts a child, or the actual dog).
	Check for sufficient continuity in living arrangements and stability of primary relationships.
	Check for sufficient self-regulation skills combined with support within children's relationships with caregivers and service providers (co-regulation) to manage exposure to traumatic memories in sessions.
	Enlist the help of emotionally supportive caregivers in sessions to comfort children in ways that help (e.g., sitting close).
	Repeat the use of *My Thermometers* to check for level of stress (*Knots*) compared to *Self-Control Power* and '*Feeling Safe*' in sessions after children share stories. Utilize *Centering Activities* and *Power Plans* as needed to promote modulation.
'Five-Chapter' Stories	Help children desensitize memories of 'tough times' by sharing details and feelings with the therapist and trusted adults of traumatic events or themes of traumatic events in 'Five-Chapter' Stories that emphasize 'moving through' traumas and staying within children's 'window of tolerance.' **Ask children to start with their earliest traumatic memory using the list developed with children and caregivers during work on Chapters 1–9.** 'Five-Chapter' Stories include: What happened (Chapter 2); What helped children and people they loved get through (survive) the 'tough time' (Chapter 3); A safe time and place after the traumatic event when children felt cared for and protected (Chapter 4); What led up to the traumatic event (Chapter 1); and How children could prevent or reduce 'tough times' now that they are older, smarter, and stronger with help from caring adults (Chapter 5). **After children have drawn all five pictures, ask them to go back and utilize sounds from the glockenspiel and movement to share how they felt and what they did in each picture.** **Afterwards, ask children to share in words what happened in each story, highlighting the end when they felt safe in their relationships.** **Ask children to describe feelings and thoughts: "What was the worst moment, the worst part?" (after Cohen, Mannarino, & Deblinger, 2003).** **For each story, invite children to elaborate and expand on solutions (Chapter 5): "What could prevent (trauma) from happening again? What could make things work out better?"** Children's narratives can be written down or recorded. Children can adjust how fast they work through the story. Complete stories in drafts, going back and adding more details with subsequent drafts, just as an author writes a book. Continue drafts until children have included bodily sensations, feelings, thoughts, and actions. This can be shown in drawings, in written or verbalized narrative, in gestures, in rhythm, in music, or in movement. **After each draft, encourage children (and caregivers) to take a slow breath, and then 'let it go.'** It may help to imagine the slow breath exhaled going into a balloon and then letting the balloon go. This can also be enacted with a real balloon, with children imagining that they are filling the balloon up with the trauma story, and then 'let it go.' **Check children's feelings of stability at the end of sharing stories.**

	Generally, if *Knots* is higher than a '2' or *Self-Control Power* is lower than a '7' or '8,' repeat the story, gradually increasing the time spent on the story with continued self- and co-regulation until going through the story has lower *Knots* and higher *Self-Control Power* scores.
	If more time is needed in sessions than possible, stories can be kept in a 'lockbox' to be addressed at a later time.
	It is important to save time to end sessions on a positive note with a special centering or special time activity.
'Three-Chapter' Stories for Younger Children	Stories can be shortened to three chapters if children are unable to handle the 'Five-Chapter' format (e.g., for younger children). 'Three-Chapter' Stories include: What happened (Chapter 2), A safe time and place after the event when children felt cared for and protected (Chapter 3), and What led up to the event (Chapter 1). In 'Three-Chapter' Stories, questions linked to Chapter 3 of children's stories can highlight what helped them get through traumas and how caregivers and children can prevent or minimize future traumas.
Validation and Support	Encourage caregivers to demonstrate understanding and acceptance of what led children to act as they did in the past and to work with them to develop the resources necessary to make a strong Chapter 5 for each story in which children and caregivers prevent or minimize the impact of children's toughest times.
Important Lesson, Power Card, and Regret Stories	Use additional stories in Chapter 10 to integrate what children have learned and how they have grown stronger.
	Highlight *Power* card and encourage children to draw themselves with all their skills and powers and with everyone they can think of who could help them.
	Use 'Regret' stories to find ways children can acknowledge and make amends as much as possible for what they did that hurt others, and take steps to prevent recurrence of them hurting others as they did in the past.
'Toughest Time' Story	**Before completing Chapter 10, ask children if the stories completed include their 'toughest time.'**
	If not, ask children to sketch a story of themselves and caring adults getting through their 'toughest time ever' using another 'Five-Chapter' Story form (e.g., from Part V of the *RLH Toolkit*).
	Remind children to practice *Power Plans* and *Mind Power* skills (e.g., "Think of who could help you. What can keep you calm? What tools and skills would you bring with you? How is your life different now?"). Guide children to add details, color, and strong rhythm, intonation, and a movement to enrich drawings.
	Next, ask children to draw a picture of their 'toughest time ever.' Children can use a simple pencil for this.
	In Chapter 5 of the story, it may help to ask children to sketch a picture of themselves and all of their allies fighting off the toughest time. This picture will ideally show how caring adults and children have implemented a safety plan and will accentuate their skills and power. Encourage children to make this drawing their strongest, most detailed picture, accentuating symbols of strength.
	A title sheet can be added (e.g., MY TOUGHEST TIME), and these pictures can be preserved as a separate booklet to accompany the *Life Storybook* or kept in a special safe place.
Completion of Trauma Memory Reintegration Checkpoints	Criteria for desensitization in many trauma treatment models include:
	• Youths feeling at a '2' or less on stress scales.
	• Youths being able to experience reminders of traumas without significant distress (Griffin et al., 2014).
	• Youths being able to differentiate reminders of past traumas from real and current dangerous situations (Griffin et al., 2014).

	• Youths not needing to shut down or avoid reminders of traumas (Lanktree & Briere, 2016). • **Youths being able to allow themselves to experience disturbing thoughts, feelings, or memories without needing to fight them off or become preoccupied with them (Lanktree & Briere, 2016).** • **Youths finding a way to understand what happened in trauma events as parts of their lives.** • **Youths developing an understanding of how they can use their experiences to help themselves and others.**
Additional Trauma Processing	If 'Five-Chapter' Stories are not sufficient, or children are unwilling or unable to utilize this format, check for current dangers (see overview above). Consider the use of *Progressive Counting* (Greenwald, 2013) or *EMDR for Complex Trauma* (Wesselman & Shapiro, 2013) with support and validation of caregivers.
	CLOSINGS
'Homework' and 'Teamwork'	Encourage family activities that promote sharing of experiences and memories (e.g., asking each family member to share the 'best' and 'worst' part of each day, playing memory games on car trips, eliciting details of shared experiences). See the *RLH Strategy and Activity Guide* (in Part V) for additional activities.
Special Time, Thermo-meters, Prog-ress Note, Reminder of Next Session	End each session with calming relaxation and, whenever possible, a fun activity. Continue special time at the end of the session, if helpful, and 'collaborative' *Progress Note*, as appropriate. Invite the children and caregivers to suggest things they would like to do in the next session and schedule a date and time. Consider anyone else to invite to support children. Repeat Thermometers if necessary.

➤➤➤ TIPS

➤ 'Move through' a complete 'Five-Chapter' Story each session, if possible, and highlight Chapter 4 and Chapter 5 of children's stories before ending each session. Additional details can be added to stories in later sessions.

➤ Accentuate how children and caregivers can feel safe in the present time, that traumas were finite points of time in the past, and that children and caregivers can find a way to be safe in the future.

➤ Keep the focus in stories on relational healing. This includes being aware of how caregivers and other family members are managing their own feelings of stress and adjusting interventions to boost caregivers' capacity to support children sharing stories and becoming stronger. It also means being aware of children's levels of fear of losing a caregiver's love (Lieberman & van Horn, 2005). The goal of storytelling is to strengthen relationships, not to write a story (Lieberman & van Horn, 2005).

➤ Trauma processing includes much more than what is written down (Griffin et al., 2014). Trauma processing is often shown more in what children share in facial expressions, gestures, tonality of their voice, rhythm, music, movement, and verbal communication (Lieberman & van Horn, 2005).

➤ Trauma stories can merge with each other and are often presented as fragmented and imperfect (Lieberman & van Horn, 2005). Uncovering recurring themes of stories is helpful to pull these together.

➤ Children and caregivers may have different memories of the same event. Therapists can respect these differing memories, adding context and meaning (e.g., highlighting developmental issues and different experiences). Therapists can also help to find a way to bring these memories together (Lieberman & van Horn, 2005).

➤ Use stories to counter feelings of shame and isolation by highlighting emotionally supportive relationships, lessons learned, and how children and caregivers would prevent or minimize future 'tough times.'

➤ End sessions with a fun and relaxing centering or 'special time' activity.

PITFALLS TO AVOID >>>

➤ Children perceive therapists as too anxious, rushed, or detached to help them overcome 'tough times.'

➤ Leaving stories constricted or one-dimensional (e.g., narratives without integration of bodily sensations, feelings, beliefs, actions, and relationships).

➤ Ending sessions or work on trauma stories before children have an opportunity to work with tough times and experience how they can feel safe.

➤ Repeated short exposures to difficult memories that do not allow sufficient time for children and caregivers to practice affect modulation skills to reduce the distress tied to specific memories and to gain a sense of self-control and feeling of emotional support.

➤ Children repeat the same traumatic experience over and over without learning how they can modulate how they remember what happened and develop images of themselves as heroes overcoming tough times.

CHAPTER CHECKPOINTS

☐ 1. Help children to desensitize memories of 'tough times' by sharing details and feelings with the therapist and trusted adults of traumatic events or themes of repeated traumatic events in 'Five-Chapter' Stories that emphasize 'moving through' traumas and staying within children's 'window of tolerance.' 'Five-Chapter' Stories include: What happened (Chapter 2); What helped children and people they loved get through (survive) the 'tough time' (Chapter 3); A safe time and place after the traumatic event when children felt cared for and protected (Chapter 4); What led up to the traumatic event (Chapter 1); and How children could prevent or reduce 'tough times' now that they are older, smarter, and stronger with help from caring adults (Chapter 5). (*Note*: Stories can be shortened to three chapters if children are unable to handle the 'Five-Chapter' format. 'Three-Chapter' Stories include: What happened (Chapter 2); A safe time and place after the event when children felt cared for and protected (Chapter 3); and What led up to the event (Chapter 1).)

☐ 2. Help children to stay regulated by using their growing skills and relationships. Highlight what is different now in their lives that could prevent re-traumatization.

☐ 3. Help children express remorse and implement plans for apologizing and making appropriate restitution for at least one thing they regret doing.

RESOURCES

See detailed guides to trauma desensitization and reintegration, including:

Briere, J., & Scott, C. (2014). *Principles of trauma therapy.* Thousand Oaks, CA: Sage.

Cohen, J. A., Deblinger, E., & Mannarino, A. P. (2006). *Treating trauma and traumatic grief in children and adolescents.* New York, NY: Guilford Press.

Greenwald, R. (2013). *Progressive counting within a phase model of trauma-informed treatment.* New York, NY: Routledge.

Shapiro, F. (2001). *Eye movement desensitization and reprocessing: Basic principles, protocols, and procedures* (2nd ed.). New York, NY: Guilford Press.

van der Kolk, B. (2014). *The body keeps the score: Brain, mind and body in the healing of trauma.* New York, NY: Viking.

Wesselman, D., & Shapiro, F. (2013). Eye movement desensitization and reprocessing in D. Ford & C. A. Courtois (Eds.), *Treating Complex Traumatic stress disorders in children and adolescents* (pp. 203–224). New York, NY: Guilford Press.

NOTES

1. Adapted from Lieberman (2011).
2. This matches the mean number types of traumas found in surveys of children in foster care programs with Complex Trauma (Greeson et al., 2011).
3. Adapted from Figley (1989).

11

Into the Future

Identifying Goals and Important Relationships

OBJECTIVES

- Children develop positive beliefs about themselves at different ages, extending into the future.
- Children develop images of themselves at different ages involved in enduring positive and nurturing relationships.
- Children incorporate images of themselves helping others as part of their identity.

OVERVIEW

In heroic stories (Campbell, 1968), the transformed hero returns with newfound knowledge or wealth, the 'boon,' that can benefit the community in the future. Chapter 11 provides an opportunity for children to incorporate skills and positive beliefs about themselves into images of their hopes for the future. Children are encouraged to continue to help others, a key factor in building self-esteem and countering shame. The Greek definition of hero, "to serve and protect" (Vogler, 1998), can be reinforced and utilized to strengthen ties between children and people they care about. Similarly,

elements of children's favorite heroic stories involving helping others can be stressed (e.g., "With great power, comes great responsibility" from *Spider-Man*) (Lee, 1963). In this way, therapists and caregivers help children to grow into caring adults integrated as a productive member of their families and communities. Chapter 11 can also be used to bring out children's responsibilities for helping others with models of contemporary heroes (e.g., Malala Yousafzai, the 17-year-old Pakistani survivor of an assassination attempt who risked her life to be an education advocate for girls).

STEP BY STEP

	OPENINGS
Welcome	*My Thermometers* plus *Safety reminders* and *Magical Moment*, if needed.
	CENTERING ACTIVITIES
Breathing, Balancing, Yoga, Movement, and 'Improv'	Utilize Centering Activities (see Part V) that were omitted for previous chapters.
	Strengthen use of activities that resonated with children or caregivers and helped them to modulate. Encourage daily practice of Centering Activities with safe caregivers.
	See the *RLH Strategy and Activity Guide* (in Part V) for other activities to increase modulation.
	LIFE STORYBOOK
Looking Back, Looking Ahead	Encourage children to visualize their lives as a whole, beginning from the time they were born and extending into the future. Review the timeline from Chapter 9, and turn sidewise so children see the 'ups' and the 'downs.'
Future Selves	Ask children to draw or enact themselves utilizing desired skills and attributes in the future.
Helping Others	Accentuate how children see themselves helping others.
	Use children's heroes and heroes in their family and cultural heritage to inspire giving back and sharing lessons learned. For instance, Malala Yousafzai said it was her "duty" to speak out for girls' education.
	CLOSINGS
'Homework' and 'Teamwork'	Enlist caregivers and other team members (e.g., home-based support workers and case managers) to help children develop skills needed to achieve their goals and to develop and strengthen enduring emotionally supportive relationships.
	Develop opportunities for work with mentors and participation in skill development programs linked to children's goals.
	See the *RLH Strategy and Activity Guide* (in Part V) for additional activities.
Special Time, Thermometers, *Progress Note*, Reminder of Next Session	Continue special time at the end of the session, if helpful, and 'collaborative' *Progress Note*, as appropriate. Invite children and caregivers to suggest things they would like to do in the next session and schedule a date and time. Consider anyone else to invite to support children. Repeat Thermometers if necessary.

>>> TIPS

➤ Highlight important relationships in children's stories.

➤ Use children's identified important relationships to help guide work on finding or strengthening emotionally supportive relationships that can last into the future.

➤ Encourage children to incorporate strengths gained from 'moving through' and becoming stronger than past traumas.

➤ Encourage children and caregivers to accept that everyone goes through 'tough times' and everyone makes mistakes. The important thing is how we choose to deal with 'tough times' in the past and the future, and how we learn to acknowledge, learn from, and make up, as best as possible, for our mistakes: "Pain is what happens to us; suffering is what we do about it" (Briere, 2014).

➤ If children present unrealistic goals, encourage development of more realistic alternatives in addition to idealized goals.

PITFALLS TO AVOID >>>

➤ Children perceive messages from family members or service providers that despite all their work, they remain 'victims' forever, or they are entitled to special treatment 'forever more' because of how they were so 'damaged.'

➤ Future stories focus on children alone without positive, enduring relationships or children dependent on fragile or risky relationships.

➤ Children present unrealistic goals without more realistic alternatives; for instance, children having a perfect life without any more 'tough times' or any mistakes made by children or caregivers.

CHAPTER CHECKPOINTS

☐ 1. Help children develop positive images and beliefs about themselves, extending into the future, including goals and helping others.

☐ 2. Help children identify important relationships to maintain or build in future years.

RESOURCES

Encourage children to read age-appropriate books and see age-appropriate movies about famous people who have overcome adversity to achieve important roles, especially people from their own cultural heritage. In the United States, stories of contemporary and historical figures, for example Presidents (Abraham Lincoln, Teddy Roosevelt, Franklin Roosevelt, John F. Kennedy, George H. W. Bush, Bill Clinton, Barack Obama), Supreme Court Justice Sonya Sotomayor, Eleanor Roosevelt, Rosa Parks, Maya Angelou, and Oprah Winfrey, describe how these famous people experienced similar traumas as children in treatment (deaths, domestic violence, alcoholism, wars, depressed parents, severe illnesses) and found ways to overcome challenges and to succeed. See books such as *Of Thee I Sing: A Letter to My Daughters* (Obama, 2010), *Who Was Harriet Tubman?* (McDonough, 2002), and the HEROES Library for Children (Part III of the *RLH Toolkit*).

12

'My Story'

Creating an Integrated Life Story with a Past, Present, and Future

OBJECTIVES

- Children and caregivers develop an organized story of their lives that integrates how past experiences in both good times and 'tough times' led to feelings, thoughts, actions, and relationships. Children and caregivers share how they can use these past experiences, the special skills they have developed, and relationships they have formed to achieve their goals for the future.
- Children become able to share their life stories with safe caregivers and other caring adults.
- Children's life stories include how they will apply lessons learned and skills gained to help others.

OVERVIEW

After completion of Chapters 1–11, it is helpful for children and caregivers to pull together what they have learned into an integrated life story. This can be presented as part of the 'hero's journey,' sharing what children and caregivers have gained in a way that helps children, family members, and other people in the child's community.

Children's narrative life stories provide a measure of whether they have been able to integrate painful events into their lives. Therapists can help children to see that traumatic events, even repeated traumas, were limited to certain times, places, and relationships, a small part of children's entire experiences leading up to their current ages, and an even smaller part of their entire lives, looking ahead into the future. The objective is not for children to forget what happened, but rather to be able to share a coherent, integrated account of their lives in which traumatic events are no longer all-consuming. From a concrete perspective,

children's *Self-Control Power* becomes much stronger than the *Knots* associated with specific, and even multiple and repeated, traumas.

Completion of the book can be celebrated with a ceremony honoring children as authors of their books, including autographing copies for the family to save in a special location. A parent can offer to put the book away in a secure place, to be read again whenever children wish. Certificates can be framed and combined with photographs of children and caring adults who helped them.

Children may also be honored by asking them to share their life stories with younger children or children who have recently experienced similar 'tough times' (after Freedman & Combs, 1996; White & Epston, 1990). With consent from children and guardians, this could include donating a copy to a special library after names and other identifying details have been changed.

STEP BY STEP

	OPENINGS
Welcome	*My Thermometers* plus *Safety reminders* and *Magical Moment*, if needed.
	CENTERING ACTIVITIES
Breathing, Balance, Yoga, Movement, and 'Improv'	Utilize centering activities (see Part V) that were omitted for previous chapters.
	Strengthen the use of activities that resonated with children or caregivers and helped them to modulate. Encourage continued practice with safe caregivers after completing Life Storybook.
	See the *RLH Strategy and Activity Guide* (in Part V) for other activities to increase modulation.
	LIFE STORYBOOK
Message to Other Children	Ask children to write a message that could be shared with other children about what they learned about getting through 'tough times,' a message that could help other children who are going through 'tough times.'
	Invite children and caregivers, where possible, to share de-identified messages, and portions of life stories, to help younger children going through similar experiences.
Integrated Life Story	Ask children and caregivers to write or put together a narrative, audiotape, or videotape about their lives from birth to their current age that pulls together some of the things they learned about themselves. A word-processing program or the blank pages at the end of the workbook can be used. The narrative can be of any length and can be presented in many ways (e.g., a written movie or a videotaped interview, a musical story, a videotaped enactment).
	Utilize the life events chart from Chapter 9 as an outline to events experienced.
	Encourage children and caregivers to include how experiences in their lives contributed to their feelings, beliefs, actions, and relationships in the past.
	Accentuate how children and caregivers have been able to learn from these experiences to shape a better future for themselves and important people in their lives.
	Encourage children and caregivers to highlight both good and bad times, emphasizing what was learned, strengths that helped them overcome problems, how they helped others, their goals for the future, what they want to learn, and how they will help others.
Cover, Dedication, and Photograph	Invite children to create their own title page, dedication, and 'about the author' pages, like books in the library. Remove published title page, Introduction for Caregivers and About the Author, to make this book the child's own.
	The blank title page for children can be used. This is located after the 'About the Author' page in the *Life Storybook*. Or, children can create a separate page and paste it over the published *Life Storybook* cover. Heavy paper is recommended. Title pages can also be laminated.
	Encourage children to include a dedication as a way of thanking special people in their lives. Encourage children to add photographs of themselves to the back cover with a brief paragraph under the heading "About the Author."
	Youths can also create their own bound edition of a Life Storybook. To create an attractive book cover (Scheele, 2005) with bound editions of the Life Storybook, bind the pages together between two pieces of process board using book thread and a child-safe stitching needle with no sharp point. Prepare the covers in advance by having an adult punch three holes into the pages using a pushpin. After the board and pages are stitched together, a child-safe glue can be added to help secure the outside binding. Cloth book tape can then be added to the whole length of binding while the glue is still wet.

'Relapse Prevention'	Review safety and coping steps to deal with predictable problems and reminders of traumas in the future. Reinforce acceptance that no one is perfect, that everyone makes mistakes, and ways that children and caregivers can heal after mistakes or 'tough times' in the future.
Certificate of Completion	Have safe caregivers, therapists, and other caring adults involved in life story work sign the *Certificate of Completion*.
Sharing and Protection of *Life Storybook*	Maintain a backup copy of the *Life Storybook* in a safe place. The original can be laminated and bound. Keeping two or three copies is highly recommended in order to preserve children's memories and provide a resource for them in later years.
	Invite children to share their storybook with safe, validating adults and children in their families and, as appropriate, with other service providers, mentors, and clergy. Introduce storybooks as including both good times and tough times, and how books highlight the importance of caring, safety, courage, and commitment with respect and thanks for caring adults who helped children along the way.
Completion of *Life Storybook* and RLH Treatment	Invite children and caregivers to share their perspectives on life story work: what they liked, didn't like, best parts, hardest parts.
	Invite children and caregivers to share how they feel about completing life stories and saying goodbye to the therapist (adapted from Cohen et al., 2006). This can be done as a narrative, in a picture, as a craft object, or as a movie.
	Therapists can share resiliency seen in children and caregivers, challenges addressed, safety plans, ways therapists will remember children and caregivers' accomplishments (e.g., with pictures or keeping a backup copy of the *Life Storybook*), lessons learned by therapists as part of this work, and how therapists can use these lessons to inform their work and help other children and families.
	Memorialize the completion of work. This can be done in many ways. Examples include:
	• Children decorating a rock or planting a shrub or perennial in a school or program's special garden, a 'healing garden.' • The therapist selects a gift for children from a 'collection' (e.g., a teddy bear, puppet, special necklace, or gem) that fits with children.
	CLOSINGS
'Homework' and 'Teamwork'	Protect the *Life Storybook* in a safe place in the family's home where it cannot be accessed by family members or others who do not meet safety criteria, or people who children and caregivers have not given permission to see the *Life Storybook*.
	Assist children in completing parts of the *Life Storybook* that children and caregivers see as appropriate to foster self-esteem and promote children sharing what they have learned and how they have grown stronger and stronger.
Special Time, Thermo-meters, *Progress Note*, Reminder of Next Session	Continue special time at the end of the session, if helpful, and 'collaborative' *Progress Note*, as appropriate. Repeat Thermometers if necessary.

►►► T I P S

► Have children share important lessons learned in the course of completing the workbook.

► Help children incorporate the skills and sensitivities developed to survive and overcome trauma as special attributes that they can use to help others in the future.

PITFALLS TO AVOID ►►►

➤ Life stories focus on negative traumas rather than accentuating how children and caregivers overcame past traumas and reinforcing the strengths of children, caregivers, their families, and their cultural heritage.

➤ Children's life stories are shared with adults or family members who do not meet safety criteria or without permission of children or guardians.

CHAPTER CHECKPOINTS

☐ 1. Encourage children and caregivers to create messages to help other children and caregivers who have experienced similar 'tough times.'

☐ 2. Help children and caregivers create life story narratives with words, art, or music, integrating their growth through good times, 'tough times,' and into the future.

RESOURCES

See Siegel and Bryson (2012, pp. 143–144) on developing an integrated life story for caregivers that shows how caregivers have come to understand how their experiences in the past, including with their own parents, have contributed to how they have acted in their own lives and affected their relationships with their children.

Part II

Adaptations

13

Adaptation for Adolescents

The *Real Life Heroes Life Storybook* has worked well in pilot studies with adolescents who function with emotional, social or cognitive development in the 6–12 age range with just a few adaptations. The challenge *and* the appeal of using the workbook with adolescents with traumatic stress centers on adolescents' natural drive to free themselves from their families and establish their own identities at the same time that they are often struggling with childhood traumas and unmet dependency needs. Most of the troubled youths I've met have desperately wanted to be validated, protected, and loved by caregivers. The *Life Storybook* provides a useful tool to address this dual challenge, especially with adolescents who function developmentally at a younger age, including adolescents who were traumatized as children and whose social and emotional development was stymied.

Engaging Adolescents

The *RLH Life Storybook* can be presented as a workbook that was written for children who went through 'tough times' between ages 6 and 12, and has also been used by teenagers who went through hard times in those years and earlier. For instance, therapists can say, "This workbook was originally developed for youths in elementary school who went through some of the same things you did. I'd like you to take a look at it (since you went through some tough times when you were that age). We can modify it to fit a teenager who is ___ years old."

To engage adolescents, it has often been effective to appeal to their greater understanding and abstract reasoning ability as teenagers: "Now that you are ___ and can understand things in ways that you couldn't at age 8 (when the trauma happened), it helps to look back at what happened and use your understanding and help from others to figure out what happened." The *RLH Life Storybook* can be enhanced with multiple forms of creative arts that are geared for adolescents. The combination of art, rhythm, tonality, movement, yoga, 'improv,' and mindfulness appeals to adolescents' interest in trying out new things,

creative expression of feelings, learning skills, and connecting to others.

If youths object to the child-centered format, therapists can develop activities modified for each page of the workbook, using activities that address the themes without using the workbook as a whole. Pages of the *Life Storybook* can also be pulled out and used separately so they don't appear to be part of a workbook.

Additional strategies to engage adolescents include:

• Encourage youths to take the *Life Storybook* and recreate it in their own way (e.g., making a movie, writing a series of rap songs, or writing a journal, poetry, or an autobiography, such as "My World, My Way"). The chapters and tasks can serve as an outline to break up the work into pieces, just as the author of a book, the director of a movie, or a student working on a thesis divides up a project into segments. The 12 chapters of the *Life Storybook* can be presented as a draft outline for a movie or an autobiography.

• Invite youths to let themselves go *back in time* and imagine themselves at a younger age, respond to workbook exercises, and then work on the book at their current age. For instance, they could imagine themselves as 6 *and* 15, completing pages the way they *used* to feel and think when things were very hard. Then, invite youths to contemplate how they feel and understand situations from the vantage point of their current age, now that they are much older, wiser, and stronger in so many ways.

• Ask youths to complete the book as a gift for younger siblings or as a way of helping younger children who have experienced situations resembling what happened in their lives. At the same time, use the workbook to develop special competence in an area of strength or interest (e.g., singing, art, sports). This can lead to mentoring relationships and opportunities for adolescents to help others, while at the same time boosting their own self-esteem.

- Invite youths to 'try out' something written for younger children, children who went through what they did when they were younger, *even though* they are *much* older now.
- Substitute age-appropriate puzzles and engaging science or math for the more child-centered magic tricks in the workbook.
- Present materials from the *Life Storybook* to youths in a white folder (Peacock & Hawkins, 2004) and provide materials to decorate it, encouraging self-expression and identity. Youths could be asked to decorate the front when they start and the back when they finish, creating a beginning and ending ritual.

Group Activities

As part of growing up and establishing their own identities, adolescents become very sensitive to peers and their behavior is shaped a great deal by their involvement with positive or negative peers and informal or formal groups. Adolescents often learn with peers how to utilize abstract reasoning skills to find new ways to master old problems. Therapists can utilize adolescents' affinity for peers to shape understanding and coping skills.

Group exercises on learning to understand and overcome trauma, manage feelings (affect regulation), and develop assertive communication and problem-solving skills can be very effective (see Cloitre, Koenen, Cohen, & Han, 2002; DeRosa et al., 2008; Ford & Russo, 2006; Ford, Mahoney, & Russo, 2001, 2003; Ford & St. Juste, 2006; Miller, Rathus, & Linehan, in press; Saltzman, Layne, & Pynoos, 2003). Therapists can also use pages from the *Real Life Heroes Life Storybook* as a guide for group activities in which adolescents choose their own modality or work together with painting, sculpture, choreography, or theater arts.

Group arts and crafts projects can be used to engage adolescents to identify significant people in their lives and resources they can call upon for help to achieve their goals and manage stressful situations. For example, in groups (Rappaport, 2006), use photographs or drawings of favorite people to create three-dimensional frame cubes and make shields with drawings of symbols of strength and important people who can help youths (to obtain 3D Frame Cube and shields, see, e.g., www.ssww.com).

Use of contemporary music in adolescent groups is another great way to engage youths, normalize traumatic experiences, promote expression, and create opportunities for youths to help each other using mediums they enjoy. Many popular songs address themes of overcoming traumas. Peacock and Hawkins (2004) used songs including "Losing My Head" (Grandmaster Flash and Furious Five, 1982, *The Message*, Sugar Hill), "Hyper Drive" (India Arie, 2002, *Slow Down. Voyage to India*, Motown Records), "Trapped" (Black Eyed Peas, 2003, *Anxiety. Elephunk*, Interscope Records), "Pain" (India

Arie, 2002, *Get It Together. Voyage to India*, Motown Records), and "The Anger Inside Me" (Lauryn Hill, 1998, *The Miseducation of Lauryn Hill*, Columbia) in the Sanctuary® program at the New York Jewish Board of Children's and Family Services. For additional suggested music, see Heroes Library (in Part IV). Adolescents can be invited to bring in some of their favorites, screening out, as necessary, any music that promotes violence, ethnic debasement, or self-abuse. Similarly, caring adults can be invited to share music that inspires them. See, for instance, "In My Daughter's Eyes" (Martina McBride, 2003, *Martina*, BMG).

Helping Others

Adolescents can also be engaged to help each other develop solutions to difficult situations in their lives (e.g., being insulted by a storekeeper, being accused by a peer of trying to take away his or her boy or girlfriend, pressure to engage in unsafe behavior, being questioned by police). This can be done with enactments, dance, music, and arts, even creation of short movies or plays. It is very important in these activities to help youths move beyond misinterpretations of other people that lead to trauma reactions, especially perceptions that other people are attacking or targeting the youth with little or no recognition of other possibilities. For instance, the belligerence experienced from a police officer questioning youths late at night may stem from the officers receiving urgent calls for help regarding other youths who had been violent in the same neighborhood, the officers' own traumatic experiences, or deep-seated prejudice against people who look like the youth, rather than anything having to do with a particular youth.

Discussions that promote understanding of sexual, economic, or ethnic victimization can also be used to engage older youths and to help them redirect their anger into active steps that foster competence and strength and help a youth to break out of self-shaming. Active involvement in advocacy groups such as NOW, the NAACP, "Take Back the Night" marches, protests against sexual harassment, etc. with caring adults and peers can promote empowerment and counter feelings of helplessness and persecution.

Self-Respect

The hero framework can be addressed with a focus on individuation and adolescents' drive to develop self-respect (Peacock & Hawkins, 2004) (e.g., "What will it take for you to become a hero?"). Emphasizing self-control goals and choices is very important with adolescents, including identification of:

- What has helped you make good choices in the past?
- What has gotten in the way of making good choices?
- Who can you count on to tell you when you are wrong and help to make things better?

- Who helps you make good choices and do the work necessary to succeed?
- What would it take for you to become a person you respect?

In individual or group sessions, youths can be asked to make a list or draw people they respect (e.g., "Who I respect and why"). Adolescents could then be asked to discuss: "In what ways are they similar to the people they respect? And, what would it take to become the 'best possible you'?" (Peacock & Hawkins, 2004).

Conversely, youths can be asked to respond to questions about people who give mixed messages, pressure others to get into trouble, or show disrespect to themselves or other people. Discussion questions could include (Peacock & Hawkins, 2004):

- What examples do you see in the news or in movies, stories, etc. about people who say they care but do something very different?
- Are there people in your life who said they cared but then treated you or others disrespectfully or hurt them?
- How can people manage overt disrespect?
- What can help with covert disrespect?

Restoring Hope and Relationships

Fantasy activities and discussions related to the future are especially helpful with adolescents who have experienced chronic trauma and given up hope for change. It's helpful to expand upon Chapter 11 activities with imagery exercises about what they hope to be doing at different ages. Solution-based therapy exercises can be very useful. Youths can be asked to imagine themselves at an older age: What would help them succeed? What would they have learned? What would they advise to themselves at a younger age (after Dolan, 1991)? What would be their greatest dream for the future? What would it look like? Who would be with them, helping them? What would be the smallest step toward making their dream come true? What would be a second step . . . ? These exercises can lead to step-by-step plans for making adolescents' goals come true.

It is very important to ensure that each youth has positive roles in his or her community through involvement in areas of interest and talent and with the active support of family members, mentors, coaches, etc. Development of adaptive living skills (e.g., cooking, paying bills, getting cars repaired, etc.) works best by having youths work with the close guidance of a caring adult (Cook, 2005).

An attachment-centered focus is essential in effective work with adolescents, just as with latency-age youths. Relationships change over the years and caring adults need to find ways to keep bonds and close ties with young people as they mature. Close family ties may be lost after traumatic events, especially when family members who the youth had been close to become disabled or die. It's easy then for adolescents to become detached, withdrawn, or pressed by remaining family members to grow up and move on with their lives. This increases adolescent vulnerability to further traumatization. At the same time, social, mental health, or educational service systems may regard adolescents as less vulnerable than younger children, or more culpable for family conflicts, and this can lead to reduced funding for adolescents.

Adolescence is a time of great risk, demonstrated by the high rate of victimization of adolescents compared to other age groups. This is also a time of great opportunity to help adolescents overcome traumas and shape positive identities as successful young adults, future parents, and citizens contributing to their communities. Neurobiologists have documented how adolescents' brains are going through a period of rewiring that presents great opportunities for healing (Siegel, 2014). Life story work can play an important role in this transformation.

Completing the *Life Storybook* can be viewed as another point in a youth's journey in life, rather than an end point. The therapist's role as a guide and mentor can be linked to one part of this journey. And, therapists can help youths identify who will be continuing to help as they mature and continue the journey of their lives.

Heroes: Developing Courage

Adolescents can be engaged to discuss what it means to be a hero in a much deeper manner. To start a discussion, ask youths to consider these quotations:

> You don't develop courage by being happy in your relationships everyday. You develop it by surviving difficult times and challenging adversity.
>
> (Epicurus, Greek philosopher)

> "To serve and protect" represents the ancient Greek definition of heroes.
>
> (Vogler, 1998)

> "It is not the critic who counts; not the man who points out how the strong man stumbles, or where the doer of deeds could have done them better. The credit belongs to the man who is actually in the arena, whose face is marred by dust and sweat and blood; who strives valiantly; who errs, who comes short again and again, because there is no effort without error and shortcoming; but who does actually strive to do the deeds; who knows great enthusiasms, the great devotions; who spends himself in a worthy cause; who at the best knows in the end the triumph of high achievement, and who at the worst, if he fails, at least fails while daring greatly, so that his place shall never be with those cold and timid souls who neither know victory nor defeat."
>
> (Theodore Roosevelt Excerpt from the speech "Citizenship In A Republic," delivered at the Sorbonne, in Paris, France on 23 April, 1910)

Then, ask youths to share how this fits with their own experiences.

Discussion questions could include:

- Are people born brave or do they develop courage as they grow up?
- What would it take to help children become courageous men or women when they grow up, people who would value their convictions, assert themselves, and devote themselves to making things better?
- What could you do as a parent to help your children develop courage?
- What could schools do to foster courage?
- Do heroes today 'serve and protect'?
- If you devote yourself to serving and protecting others, is it important to also take care of yourself?

Discussion points to bring out include the role of emotional support for children and how to help children who lack emotional support at home.

Review Conferences

In review conferences, it is helpful to focus on: the adolescents' primary goals; progress toward goals; anything getting in the way; and what can be done to help the adolescent overcome obstacles and achieve his or her goals. With this strength- and goal-centered framework, adolescents are often willing to encourage caring adults to participate in activities, and, in turn, caring adults can be engaged to help monitor, coach, and guide adolescents, including serving as resources to help adolescents identify, prevent, and, if necessary, cope with 'triggers' to chronic trauma behavior cycles. These caring adults can also provide encouragement for adolescents to utilize their understanding and strengths to accomplish their goals and move away from repetitive behavior cycles that reactivate traumatic reactions.

RESOURCES

Biegel, G. M. (2009). *The stress reduction workbook for teens: Mindfulness skills to help you deal with stress.* Oakland, CA: New Harbinger.

Briere, J., & Lanktree, C. (2013). *Integrative treatment of traumatic stress-A (ITCT-A) treatment guide* (2nd ed.). Los Angeles, CA: University of Southern California. Retrieved from http://keck.usc.edu/Education/Academic_Department_and_Divisions/Department_of_Psychiatry/Research_and_Training_Centers/USC_ATTC/~/media/KSOM/Education/Academic%20Department%20and%20Divisions/attc/ITCT-A-TreatmentGuide-2ndEdition-rev20131106.pdf.

DeRosa, R., Habib, M., Pelcovitz, D., Rathus, J., Sonnenklar, J., Ford, J., Sunday, S., Layne, C., Saltzman, W., & Turnbull, A. (2008). *Structured psychotherapy for adolescents responding to chronic stress.* Manhasset, NY: Northshore Hospital-Long Island Jewish Health System.

Siegel, D. J. (2014). *Brainstorm: The power and the purpose of the teenage brain.* New York, NY: Penguin.

14

Adaptation for Preschool Children and Children with Disabilities

The workbook can be adapted for younger children and children with moderate developmental delays or learning disabilities. This typically involves making activities simpler, with fewer directions and choices, more use of visual guidance, and less use of verbal directives or requests. For some children, narrative responses may only be a single word, while more verbal children may want to generate longer stories in addition to pictures. Children can also substitute drawings in many places for words. On the *Circles of Caring*, children can sketch in faces of people in each circle. And, instead of using *My Thermometers*, children can identify feelings using larger and larger faces (e.g., for feeling unhappy or stressed):

Additional guidance and help is needed for children with cognitive abilities under age 6. Therapists or caring adults may need to read text to children and help them to write or spell words, working carefully to reflect children's responses without bias. Adults can also write out children's dictated stories on notepaper or on a word processor. Then, either the adult or the child can copy the story on to the appropriate page of *Real Life Heroes Life Storybook*.

Often, children with limited writing skills do better by dictating answers into a tape recorder that can later by typed and inserted into the *Life Storybook*. It sometimes helps for therapists to take on the role of a radio or TV show interviewer, or to become a TV host children admire, and then use the questions on each worksheet as a mock interview that can be taped for later transcription, and, if desired, shared with caring adults.

Other children may prefer to use word-processing programs geared to their developmental age to facilitate writing and editing narratives that can be pasted into the book or printed directly on the bottom of pages under pictures. Audiotapes or videotapes can also be made to accompany the pictures, page by page.

Puppet Stories

Younger children often can be engaged to utilize puppets for storytelling, and therapists or caring adults can transcribe the story enacted. Simple puppets can be constructed by having children sketch images of family members or other figures, cut them out with child-safe scissors, and tape the images to a piece of folded cardboard, such as the back of a legal pad, cut to match the size of children's drawings and folded along two vertical lines approximately an inch from the left and right edges to form a U shape that can hold up children's drawings. The result can be a group of puppet figures that children own and with which they can play out stories from their own experience. Children can change their stories as they develop broader perspectives about family members and other important people in their lives. Desensitization exercises and activities designed to boost self-esteem help children reduce the power and intensity of frightening images while increasing the size, power, and strength of pictures of themselves, caring family members, and other positive people in their lives.

RESOURCES

For children under 6, see: *Psychotherapy with Infants and Young Children: Repairing the Effects of Stress and Trauma on Early Attachment* (Lieberman & van Horn, 2011).

15

Adaptations for Youths and Adults with Intellectual and Developmental Disabilities

Youths and adults with intellectual disabilities have higher-than-average rates of adverse childhood experiences (Horner-Johnson & Drum, 2006), including interpersonal traumas such as abuse, neglect, and family violence along with disrupted attachments and family relationships, leading, in turn, to a high risk of Complex Trauma. RLH can be easily adapted to engage youths and adults with intellectual disabilities by slowing down the pace of treatment, breaking it into smaller pieces, modifying some vocabulary for adolescents and adults with intellectual disabilities, and including more repetition (Marcal, 2015). From a developmental standpoint, an adult with a mental age of 10 can probably learn things a 10-year-old can learn. But what might take a 10-year-old of average intelligence one session, might take three (Marcal, 2015). RLH can also be adapted to work well with the NCTSN's training curriculum for supporting children with intellectual and developmental disabilities (Ko, Griffin, Vanderbilt et al, 2015).

Adapted Introduction to *Real Life Heroes*® for Adults with Intellectual Disabilities

To engage adults to work with RLH materials, the following introduction has proved helpful (Marcal, 2015):

Heroes know that being hurt is part of real life. Bad things do happen. Sometimes good people get sick or get hurt or lose people they love. I think that you are a real life hero because _____ . [Insert personalized info, e.g., "Even though some bad stuff happened to you, you are doing pretty well. You are brave and you are working with me to make things better."]

Heroes work to make sure that the bad times don't take over what is good in our lives, so we don't have to live with the stress from those things. That stress is sometimes called traumatic stress. This is stress that comes from bad things happening to us.

Heroes learn to use their minds and bodies to think and act, so they can make the world a little better for everyone. Heroes keep on trying, even when tough times seem horrible or impossible to change. [Insert personalized example, e.g., "Like when your housemate accused you of going in his room this morning and it made you think of other times when someone didn't treat you well or didn't believe you. And, you kept doing what you needed to do this morning. And, then you came and told me about it."] Heroes keep on working, just like you did, to find ways to make things better and stop traumatic stress from taking over.

A hero knows that staying calm and in control is a skill that can be learned and improved step by step, day by day, year by year. It's very much like learning to shoot a basket or _____ . [Insert personalized example, e.g., work in the machine room or learn a new math skill.] It may seem hard or even impossible at first, but then, with a lot of practice, it becomes easy. You can grow your *Self-Control Power* and keep traumatic stress from taking over your mind and body by practicing skills using your breathing, your eyes, ears, and other senses, and your mind. Today, we practiced another way to deal with your housemate or anyone who accuses you of something. By staying calm when you are wrongly accused, you will help people believe you. And you can keep on making things better for you and the people you care about.

Adaptation of 'Best Practice' Component-Based Treatment

Recommended 'best practice' treatment for children and adolescents (Cook et al., 2003; Ford & Cloitre, 2009) with Complex Trauma can be utilized with adults, as well as youths with intellectual and developmental delays. These include addressing: developing safety and stability; relational engagement of children, caregivers, and therapists; assessments and services are always relational, strengths-focused, and developmentally informed; all phases of treatment promote self- and co-regulation for children, adults, and primary caregivers; increasing self-reflective information processing; increasing positive emotions and a positive self-identity; trauma memory reintegration matched to the youth, adult, and caregiver's capacity; and prevention and management of disruptions of primary relationships and crises, including trauma reactions. These components have been summarized below, along with suggested guidelines for implementation with youths and adults with a range of intellectual and developmental disabilities.

TABLE 15.1

Developmentally Targeted, Trauma, and Resiliency-Focused Treatment for Youths and Adults with Developmental Disabilities and Complex Trauma

'Best Practice' Components of Treatment for Complex Trauma (Cook et al., 2003; Ford & Cloitre, 2009)	Strategies, Tools, and Interventions Utilizing RLH Tools
Developing safety and stability	Safety plans include concrete steps youths, adults, and caregivers can take to reduce stress, remind youths and adults of supportive relationships, and prevent trauma reactions.
	Use of concrete, visually, and body-oriented safety plans.
	Practice of safety plans on a daily basis and as needed to increase use. Much more practice may be needed than would be expected with children or adolescents with average intellectual abilities.
	Tangible reminders, including *Power Plan* cards for safety plans, and practice using them with caregivers.
	Examples include the *Real Life Heroes*® SOS *Power Plan* and RLH *Power Card*.
Relational engagement	Service providers, therapists, and care managers work to connect with youths, adults, and primary caregivers to create a sense of 'we' and 'us' working together from referral to discharge in treatment programs with a consistent plan and message.
	Adults utilize multimodal activities geared to the youth or adult's developmental level. Examples from RLH include creative arts activities that emphasize attunement of youths, adults, and caregivers with drawings, rhythm, music, and movement in each treatment session.
Assessments and services are relational, strengths-focused, and developmentally informed	Examples include the use of the RLH Trauma and Resiliency-Focused Service Plan, *Circles of Caring*, and *My Thermometers* to assess feelings of youths and adults with important people and environments.
Developing self- and co-regulation	Expanded practice developing skills. Practice slow breathing, yoga, and mindfulness using activities geared for the youth or adult's cognitive, social, and emotional age. Examples include RLH Centering Activities, including adaptations of yoga activities for children.
Increasing self-reflective information processing	Practice changing words and images using drawings and role plays.
	Rehearse more positive self-talk.
	Examples include Chapter 8 of the *RLH Life Storybook* with youths, adults, and caregivers acting as directors changing a brief story or movie in a step-by-step process.
Increasing positive emotions and a positive self-identity	Fun activities using creative arts and movement that promote skill-building, success, and pride to counter feelings of shame.
	Stories drawn or enacted showing positive acts of caring by the youth or adult.
	Examples include bringing out hero qualities in children, adults, and caregivers with the *RLH Life Storybook* (see especially Chapters 3, 6, and 12).
Trauma memory reintegration	Step-by-step storytelling that emphasizes drawings, pictures, and 'Three-Chapter' or 'Five-Chapter' Stories with a beginning, middle, and end that shows how the youth or adult and caregivers can manage previous traumas in a better way now.
	Examples include Chapter 10 of the *RLH Life Storybook*, which can be adapted for adults with intellectual disabilities using simple, concrete language, drawings, symbols, or expressions through music.
Prevention and management of disruptions of primary relationships	Reminders and responses to behaviors emphasize how caregivers and practitioners reinforce youth or adult's primary relationships.
	Examples include sharing how 'we' can work this out (e.g., "We can do our SOS *Power Plan*", "We can do our slow breathing (yoga, walk and talk . . . , whatever works for children, adults, and caregivers)").

RESOURCES

Ko, SJ, Pynoos, RS, Griffijn, D, Vanderbilt, D & NCTSN Trauma and IDD Expert Panel (2015). The road to recovery: Supporting children with intellectual and developmental disabilities who have experienced trauma. Los Angeles, CA and Durham, NC: National Center for Child Traumatic Stress.

16

Adaptations for Families with Foster Care, Kinship, or Adopted Children

Real Life Heroes® has been used successfully with children who have been or are in the process of being placed into kinship, foster care, or pre-adoptive homes and with children who have been adopted after experiencing multiple moves or traumas in their lives. The workbook allows children to share their past with their new caregivers, parents, and relatives, to get help in answering questions, and to find out if their new families will accept their past experiences, affection, loyalty, grief, and wishes.

Making Sense of the Past

Children adopted as infants can also grow up with questions, doubts, and, at times, deep-seated insecurity, if their past is shrouded in secrecy or if caregivers show anxiety about sharing what they know about children's biological parents or pre-adoptive experiences. Life story work provides a structure to normalize sharing and reduce stress. The *Life Storybook* process helps children and parents to transform non-verbalized feelings of tension, fear, or sadness into pictures and words. The RLH Session Structure provides a means for adoptive parents to connect with children, to show children they can validate their experiences, to help them grieve losses, and to help them strengthen attachments to their adoptive families.

By working with their children on the *Life Storybook*, adoptive parents can validate typical concerns of children and demonstrate courage and commitment to their children. Parents who adopt can show that they respect children's natural curiosity and feelings of loyalty by helping them learn as much as possible about their birth parents, or first family (or families). Ideally, this should be done in an age-appropriate manner from children's earliest years, with more complete sharing of information available by age 10–12 to prevent children, as adolescents, feeling that things were kept hidden.

Adoptive parents may be tempted to block out information on lost parents out of anger or fear of losing children, or as a way of protecting children from dealing with birth parents' medical problems, criminal actions, addictions, neglect, or rejection of children. Other adoptive parents may feel a need to make up some excuse or justification for what biological or previous foster or adoptive parents have done. Neither is helpful for children (van Gulden & Bartels-Rabb, 1995). Similarly, if adoptive parents tell children that they 'chose' to adopt them, children will naturally want to know why their previous biological or foster parents chose *not* to keep them.

Adoptive parents should be encouraged to provide a balanced view with respect for their children, birth parents, and birth family members. Dichotomies, such as the 'good' versus the 'bad' parent, may be initially comforting, but often lead later on to idealization and expectations of perfection in parents and the children themselves. Children who learn to think in 'black or white' terms often flip back and forth and may begin responding to their new parents as 'good or bad,' but never 'real.'

Life story work is about honesty and courage. Deep inside, children have experienced what really happened and they carry the impact of past traumas in their bodily sensations and reactions (van der Kolk, 2014). Distortions confuse children and teach them that their parents are afraid to address and overcome what really happened. In contrast, life story work can help children and adoptive parents reintegrate children's experiences, including confusing bodily sensations, feelings, beliefs, and behavior patterns learned from before their adoptions.

Seeking Control

It helps for adoptive parents to remember that children who have felt abandoned or rejected often desperately feel a need to assert control of what may have been experienced as a dangerous and chaotic world and experiences that relationships are tenuous and can lead to distress. Defiance and testing may be part of children's struggle with a conflicting wish to trust again and, at the same time, deep-seated trauma-based reactions that push them to fear and avoid any sense of dependence on caregivers.

This cycle of interaction is most evident when children tell adoptive parents, "You're not my real parents," or when children threaten to leave: "I hate you. I want to go to my 'real' parents." By overtly challenging adoptions, or adoption plans, wounded children test their beliefs, often proven from multiple past rejections, that "deep down, these new parents *want* me to leave. I am too awful for anyone to love . . . " The adoptive, or pre-adoptive, parent's responses to children's challenges can prove the parent's commitment over time or conversely confirm children's deepest fears.

When children who have experienced traumatic stress 'act out' excessively, the strength of children's defiance or troubling behavior often matches the level of the traumas experienced. It's as if children are warning and testing 'would-be' parents, "Do you dare to enter my world?" Children's behaviors push parents away, but at the same time challenge parents to face children's deepest secrets and help them find a way to reintegrate unknown or unspeakable fears.

Adoption as a Life Journey

Adopted children go through the same developmental phases and behaviors as children growing up with their birth parents. It is important for adoptive parents to understand developmental norms and not to overreact to common behaviors (e.g., 2-year-old temper tantrums or 4-year-old night terrors). At the same time, children who are adopted after experiencing multiple traumas bring with them the bodily sensations, feelings, beliefs, and behavior patterns that were developed during the time they lived with previous families, and these complex feelings shape how children perceive and react to new challenges.

For traumatized children, entering an adoptive family can mark the beginning of a 'new world,' a special world, which incorporates new possibilities for healing or perpetuating relationship patterns from the past. In this special world, the greatest fears of parents and children are often tested through a series of ordeals to determine whether this family will *only* prove to be a variation of past losses or abandonments, or whether this new reformed family will foster a parent-child bond that can include and help reintegrate children's experiences.

Accepting the challenge of adopting traumatized children means opening oneself to children's pain and bringing their struggles into one's own home. This takes tremendous courage. "To serve and protect" represents the ancient Greek definition of heroes (Vogler, 1998). Parents who adopt wounded children are truly heroes who 'serve and protect,' transforming the lives of hurt children and their communities.

RESOURCES

See educational curricula and guides for foster, kinship, and adoptive parents, including an excellent 12-hour training curriculum, *Caring for Children Who Have Experienced Trauma*, with handouts available at no charge, from the National Child Traumatic Stress Network (www.nctsn.org).

For children in foster care, see *Maybe Days* (Wilgocki & Wright, 2002).

17

Integrated Trauma-Informed Services

Real Life Heroes® can be used as part of an integrated trauma-informed system of services in a wide range of child and family service programs. The RLH Assessment and *Service Plan Review* system can be used to guide service planning and to coordinate, review, adjust, and evaluate services. The step-by-step guides for each chapter include suggested activities to integrate services by therapists with home-based support staff, residential counselors, or other service providers. The *RLH Life Storybook* and *RLH Toolkit* provide a portable treatment system that can go with children who are moved from program to program and therapist to therapist to promote continuity of treatment.

The HEROES Project (Kagan et al., 2014) demonstrated that RLH could be used successfully in seven interconnected treatment programs, including clinic-based, school-based, placement, and home-based services. To integrate services across disciplines and programs, the HEROES Project provided all service providers with the same framework, "The Essential Elements of Trauma-Informed Parenting" (Grillo et al., 2010) to use in service planning and treatment. Residential counselors, foster and kinship parents, home-based support workers, and educators received training in the NCTSN curricula, *Caring for Children Who Have Experienced Trauma* (Grillo et al., 2010). County social services workers were training in the NCTSN curricula, the Child Welfare Toolkit (Chadwick Trauma-Informed Systems Project, 2013), and therapists in seven programs were provided training in *Real Life Heroes*®. These training programs ensured that team members shared a common understanding of Complex Trauma and core components for trauma-informed services.

Suggestions are provided below for implementing RLH in conjunction with groups, school-based programs, and residential treatment and home-based services.

Use with Psychotherapeutic Groups

RLH has been incorporated into group activities as outlined above in "Adaptations for Adolescents" and in more

TABLE 17.1
Essential Elements of Trauma-Informed Parenting

1.	Recognize the impact trauma has had on your child.
2.	Help your child to feel safe.
3.	Help your child to understand and manage overwhelming emotions.
4.	Help your child to understand and manage difficult behaviors.
5.	Respect and support the positive, stable, and enduring relationships in the life of your child.
6.	Help your child to develop a strength-based understanding of his or her life story.
7.	Be an advocate for your child.
8.	Promote and support trauma-focused assessment and treatment for your child.
9.	Take care of yourself.

concrete ways suitable for latency-age children in residential treatment. Combining group skill-building and awareness training with child-caregiver treatment can promote incorporation of change into the different parts of youths' lives. Children can develop many skills in groups while they work on rebuilding attunement and trust and reintegration of traumatic memoires in child-caregiver treatment.

Psychotherapeutic group work can be used for skill-building activities in Chapters 1–4, parts of Chapters 5–6, and Chapter 7. This can include Centering Activities and chapter content.

To do this safely, children need to feel free to share only what they feel is safe. Therapists guiding groups need to protect children from sharing too much. Confidential information and trauma experiences should be reserved for child-caregiver treatment sessions.

Groups can bring in the power of peer support and validation. Children can see that they are not alone. Groups can also provide a structure for learning and practicing skills and bringing youths together to work for change as part of the 'hero's journey' (e.g., to work together to make things better for a school, a community, or a people in distress).

Use in School-Based Programs

Counseling in school-based programs may mean limited time for sessions (e.g., 25 minutes) or lack of access to caregivers. Children may have to go back to large group classes at the end of sessions. In these situations, it may be best to limit use of the *RLH Life Storybook* to Chapters 1–8 and arrange for children to work in a clinic setting on reintegration of traumatic memories.

Use with Residential Treatment and Home-based Services

Residential counselors and home-based support workers can provide guidance, support, coaching, and safety for children to learn and practice skills, and it can be a great help to involve them in sessions when children feel supported by these staff. Residential counselors and home-based support workers can then carry over session skill-building to group living or home visits. In addition, residential counselors and home-based support workers can use one-to-one time to work on related skill-building, bringing out youths' talents, and helping youths to find ways to help others.

Community-based workers can play a critical role in coordinating youths' involvement in community programs and making arrangements for long-term mentoring in areas of strength, as well as assistance in building up skills needed for youths to succeed.

Part III

Resources

18

Creative Arts Supplies and Books

Start-Up Kit

The following guide emphasizes use of inexpensive materials that can be utilized to make therapy sessions a special time and place where children can become free to explore, to create, and to develop skills. Creative arts materials also foster attunement activities involving caring adults and children. Please also see the accompanying list of items, approximate prices, and vendors in Table 18.1.

FOR CHILDREN

- Deluxe sets of washable markers and colored pencils stored in an attractive case, ideally including both large and fine-pointed markers, and at least a dozen colors, including different skin shades.

- Xylophone (glockenspiel) with two mallets and a two-octave scale; ideally, one for the child and one for the therapist or caring adult (e.g., LMI 25 Note Bell Set with Case G-G, approximately $20 from Amazon and other online stores).

- Peacock feathers, sterilized, stem-dyed tail with full eyes, 35–40 inches long, shed naturally by peacocks (available for approximately $80 for 100 plus shipping, e.g. www.featherplace.com).

- Rhythm instruments (e.g., homemade or store-bought drums from different countries or ethnic groups).

- Craft materials: beads, clay, ribbons, children's scissors.

- Collage materials: teen and sports magazines appropriate for often over-sexualized youths.

- Copies of *Real Life Heroes Life Storybook* (3rd ed.) (2016), available from amazon.com, bn.com, routledgepress.com, and other book sellers.

- Digital camera for photos and recording enactments of stories, music, and 'interviews' for children who do not have access to a smart phone in their families.

- Mirror (large enough to capture children's faces).

- Charts showing a range of feelings (e.g., see *Childswork/Childsplay*) (GuidanceChannel.com).

- *Reference materials*: books, movies, and CDs about heroes matched to each child's ethnic background, sex, age, and reading level (see Heroes Library in Part IV of the *RLH Toolkit*).

- Case or bag to carry supplies for home and community-based work.

FOR CAREGIVERS

- Handouts for parents from the NCTSN and from *Caring for Children Who Have Experienced Trauma* (ww.nctsn.org).

- Books such as *Yoga Pretzels* (Guber & Kalish, 2005), *Yoga for Children* (Flynn, 2013), *The Whole-Brain Child* (Siegel & Bryson, 2012), *No-Drama Discipline* (Siegel & Bryson, 2014), and *Wounded Angels: Inspiration from Children in Crisis* (Kagan, 2016b).

- Caregivers may complete their own copy of the *Real Life Heroes Life Storybook* or use separate pages that can be compiled or attached to their children's *Life Storybook*.

TABLE 18.1
Suggested Creative Supplies, Books, and Vendors

Item	Estimated Price	Sample Vendors	Website
SKILL-BUILDING			
Balloons (bag of 144)	$14.99	Oriental Trading	www.orientaltrading.com
Colored pencils	$1.90	Oriental Trading	www.orientaltrading.com
Markers (box of 200)	$21.99	Oriental Trading	www.orientaltrading.com
Bubbles	$0.69–1.00	Party City	
Lyons or Angel 25-Note Glockenspiel	$18–20	Amazon	
Peacock feathers, 35–40 inches (100 natural)	$53–70	Zucker Feathers	www.featherplace.com
Play-Doh (10 pack small)	$4.49	Target	
Play-Doh (24 pack large cans)	$12.89	Target	
Play-Doh (4 pack large cans)	$1.99	Target	
Jumbling game ('Jenga')	$4.99	Target	
Puppets	$6–30	Folkmanis Puppets	www.folkmanis.com
Dragonfly	$22	Vietnam crafts and vendors	
Poppin Peepers, see brain, also IPOP monsters	$3.20–		officeplayground.com
Zen sand gardens	$16		officeplayground.com
Hoberson Mini Sphere	$12	Amazon	
Fitness ball sizes 55 cm diameter, 65 cm diameter	$20	Amazon	
Everlast weighted exercise ball (silver, 5 pounds) (note: requires safe space)	$6	Amazon	
Reebok balance disc (note: requires safe space)	$20	Amazon	
Reebok air stability wobble cushion	$15	Amazon	
BOOKS			
Alexander and the Terrible . . . Very Bad Day	$6.95	Scholastic	www.scholastic.com
Cool Cats, Calm Kids	$8.05	Amazon, Barnes & Noble	www.amazon.com, www.bn.com
Double-Dip Feelings	$8.95	Amazon, Barnes & Noble	www.amazon.com, www.bn.com
A Volcano in My Tummy	$11.81	Amazon, Barnes & Noble	www.amazon.com, www.bn.com
Maybe Days (Foster Care)	$8.95	Amazon, Barnes & Noble	www.amazon.com, www.bn.com
A Terrible Thing Happened	$8.95	Amazon, Barnes & Noble	www.amazon.com, www.bn.com
Of Thee I Sing	$18.00	Amazon, Barnes & Noble	www.amazon.com, www.bn.com
Who Was Hariet Tubman?	$5.00	Amazon, Barnes & Noble	www.amazon.com, www.bn.com
Pet Heroes	$4.00	Scholastic	www.scholastic.com
Something Small		Sesame Street	www.sesamestreet.org/parents/topicsandactivities/topics/grief

19

Resources for Caregivers and Therapists

Recommended books and other resources are listed below on: Attachment Research and Treatment, Child and Family Services, Organizations Supporting Traumatic Stress Treatment, Parenting and Healthy Development, Storytelling and Narrative Therapies, and Trauma Therapies.

ATTACHMENT RESEARCH AND TREATMENT

Ainsworth, M. D. S., Blehar, M. C., Waters, B., & Wall, S. (1978). *Patterns of attachment: A psychological study of the strange situation*. Hillsdale, NJ: Lawrence Erlbaum.

Becker-Weidman, A., Ehrmann, L., & LeBow, D. H. (2012). *The attachment therapy companion: Key practices for treating children and families*. New York, NY: Norton.

Beringen, Z. (1994). Attachment theory and research: Application to clinical practice. *American Journal of Orthopsychiatry, 6*(3), 404–420.

Bowlby, J. (1988). *A secure base: Parent-child attachment and healthy human development*. New York, NY: Basic Books.

Delaney, R. (1997). *Healing power*. Oklahoma City, OK: Woods 'n' Barnes.

Delaney, R. (1998). *Fostering changes*. Oklahoma City, OK: Woods 'n' Barnes.

Delaney, R. (1998). *Raising Cain*. Oklahoma City, OK: Woods 'n' Barnes.

Hughes, D. A. (1997). *Facilitating developmental attachment*. Northvale, NJ: Jason Aronson.

Hughes, D. A. (1998). *Building the bonds of attachment: Awakening love in deeply troubled children*. Northvale, NJ: Jason Aronson.

Hughes, D. A. (2011). *Attachment-focused family therapy: Workbook*. New York, NY: Norton.

James, B. (1994) *Handbook for treatment of attachment-trauma problems in children*. New York, NY: Lexington.

Kagan, R. (2004). *Rebuilding attachments with traumatized children: Healing from losses, violence, abuse and neglect*. New York, NY: Routledge.

Levy, T., & Orlans, M. (1998). *Attachment, trauma, and healing*. Washington, DC: CWLA.

Mahler, M., Pine, F., & Bergman, A. (1975). *The psychological birth of the human infant*. New York, NY: Basic Books.

Pastzor, E. M., Leighton, M., & Blome, W. W. (1993). *Helping children and youths develop positive attachments*. Washington, DC: Child Welfare League of America.

Peterson, J. (1994). *The invisible road: Parental insights to attachment disorder*. Self-published manuscript.

Schore, A. (1994) *Affect regulation and the origin of the self: The neurobiology of emotional development*. Hillsdale, NJ: Lawrence Erlbaum Associates.

CHILD AND FAMILY SERVICES

Finkelstein, N. E. (1991). *Children and youth in limbo: A search for connections.* New York, NY: Praeger.

Kagan, R. (1996). *Turmoil to turning points: Building hope for children in crisis placements.* New York, NY: Norton.

Kagan, R. (2000). "My game": Rebuilding hope for children in placement. In C. E. Schaefer & S. E. Reid (Eds.), *Game play: Therapeutic uses of childhood games* (pp. 73–95). New York, NY: Wiley.

Kagan, R., & Schlosberg, S. (1989). *Families in perpetual crisis.* New York, NY: Norton.

Kaplan, L., & and Girard, J. L. (1994). *Strengthening high-risk families: A handbook for therapists.* New York, NY: Lexington Books.

Klass, C. S. (1996). *Home visiting.* Baltimore, MD: Brookes.

Painter, W. (n.d.). *White Paper: Family Centered Treatment: An evidence based model of home based treatment developed by practitioners.* Institute for Family-Centered Services. Retrieved from http://familycenteredtreatment.com.

Schorr, L. B. (1998). *Common purpose: Strengthening families and neighborhoods to rebuild America.* New York, NY: Doubleday/Anchor.

Steinhauer, P. (1991). *The least detrimental alternative: A systematic guide to case planning and decision-making for children in care.* Toronto: University of Toronto Press.

ORGANIZATIONS SUPPORTING TRAUMATIC STRESS TREATMENT

American Psychological Association Resource Guide: www.apa.org/topics/trauma

David Baldwin Trauma Information Pages: www.trauma-pages.com

Annie E. Casey Foundation: www.aecf.org

Chadwick Trauma Informed Systems Project: www.ctisp.org

Child Welfare League of America: www.cwla.org

International Society of Traumatic Stress Studies: www.istss.org

International Society for the Study of Trauma and Dissociation: www.isst-d.org

National Child Traumatic Stress Network (NCTSN): www.nctsn.org/resources/audiences/parents-caregivers#q3

See: *Caring for Children Who Have Experienced Trauma*, materials on understanding trauma, how to help children with traumatic stress plus specific resources for: Childhood Traumatic Grief, Domestic Violence, Medical Trauma, Military Children & Families, Physical Abuse, Sexual Abuse, Substance Abuse, Terrorism and Disaster.

Sidran Foundation: www.sidran.org

PARENTING AND HEALTHY DEVELOPMENT

ATTACh (2008). *Therapeutic parenting: A handbook for parents of children who have disorders of attachment.* Lake Villa, IL: Association for the Treatment and Training in the Attachment of Children.

Brazelton, T. (1974). *Touchpoints.* New York, NY: Perseus Press.

Butterfield, P. et al. (1997). *Love is layers of sharing.* Brighton, CO: How to Read Your Baby, Inc.

Faber, A., & Mazlish, E. (1999). *How to talk so kids will listen and listen so kids will talk.* New York, NY: Avon Books.

PARENTING AND HEALTHY DEVELOPMENT—*continued*

Hughes, D. A. (2009). *Attachment-focused parenting: Effective strategies to care for children.* New York, NY: W. W. Norton.

Kabat-Zinn, M., & Kabat-Zinn, J. (1997). *Everyday blessings: The inner work of mindful parenting.* New York, NY: Hyperion.

Lansky, V. (1991). *101 ways to make your child feel special.* Chicago, IL: Contemporary Books.

Lansky, V. (1992). *Practical parenting tips.* New York, NY: Meadowbrook Press.

Morin, V. (1993). *Messy activities and more.* Chicago, IL: Chicago Review Press.

Siegel, D. J. (2014) *Brainstorm: The power and the purpose of the teenage brain.* New York, NY: Penguin.

Siegel, D. J., & Bryson, T. P. (2012). *The whole-brain child: 12 revolutionary strategies to nurture your child's developing mind.* New York, NY: Random House.

Siegel, D. J., & Bryson, T. P. (2014). *No-drama discipline: The whole-brain way to calm the chaos and nurture your child's developing mind.* New York, NY: Bantam.

Siegel, D., & Hartzell, M. (2003). *Parenting from the inside out: How a deeper self-understanding can help you raise children who thrive.* New York, NY: JP Tarcher/Putnam.

STORYTELLING AND NARRATIVE THERAPIES

Bettelheim, B. (1975). *The uses of enchantment: The meaning and importance of fairy tales.* New York, NY: Vintage Books.

Combs, G., & Freedman, J. (1990). *Symbol, story, and ceremony: Using metaphor in individual and family therapy.* New York, NY: Norton.

Duhl, B. (1983). *From the inside out and other metaphors.* New York, NY: Brunner/Mazel.

Evans, M. D. (1986). *This is me and my two families.* New York, NY: Magination Press.

Freedman, J., & Combs, G. (1996). *Narrative therapy: The social construction of preferred realities.* New York, NY: Norton.

Gardner, R. (1975). *Psychotherapeutic approaches to the resistant child.* New York: Jason Aronson.

Gardner, R. (1986). *Therapeutic communication with children.* New York, NY: Jason Aronson.

Jewett, C. (1978). *Adopting the older child.* Cambridge, MA: The Harvard Common Press. (See chapter on life stories.)

Kagan, R. (1982). Storytelling and game therapy for children in placement. *Childcare Quarterly, 11*(4), 280–290.

Kagan, R. (2016a). *Real life heroes life storybook* (3rd ed.). New York, NY: Routledge.

Lankton, C., & Lankton, S. (1989). *Tales of enchantment.* New York, NY: Brunner/Mazel.

Munson, L., & Riskin, K. (1995). *In their own words: A sexual abuse workbook for teenage girls.* Washington, DC: Child Welfare League of America.

Roberts, J. (1994). *Tales and transformations: Stories in families and family therapy.* New York, NY: Norton.

Suddaby, K., & Landau, J. (1998). Positive and negative timelines: A technique for restorying. *Family Process, 37*(3), 287–297.

Wheeler, C. (1978). *Where am I going? Making a child's life storybook.* Juneau, AK: The Winking Owl Press.

White, M., & Epston, D. (1990). *Narrative means to therapeutic ends.* New York, NY: Norton.

TRAUMA THERAPIES

Blaustein, M., & Kinneburgh, C. (2010). *Treating traumatic stress in children and adolescents: How to foster resilience through attachment, self-regulation, and competency.* New York, NY: Guilford Press.

Briere, J., & Lanktree, C. (2013). *Integrative treatment of traumatic stress-A (ITCT-A) treatment guide* (2nd ed.). Los Angeles, CA: University of Southern California. Retrieved from http://keck.usc.edu/Education/Academic_Department_and_Divisions/Department_of_Psychiatry/Research_and_Training_Centers/USC_ATTC/~/media/KSOM/Education/Academic%20Department%20and%20Divisions/attc/ITCT-A-TreatmentGuide-2ndEdition-rev20131106.pdf.

Briere, J. N., & Scott, C. (2014). *Principles of trauma therapy: A guide to symptoms, evaluation, and treatment.* Thousand Oaks, CA: Sage.

Cloitre, M., Koenen, K. C., & Cohen, L. R. (2006). *Treating survivors of childhood abuse: Psychotherapy for the interrupted life.* New York, NY: Guilford Press.

Cohen, J. A., Deblinger, E., & Mannarino, A. P. (2006). *Treating trauma and traumatic grief in children and adolescents.* New York, NY: Guilford Press.

Deblinger, E., & Heflin, A. H. (1996). *Treating sexually abused children and their non-offending parents: A cognitive behavioral approach.* Thousand Oaks, CA: Sage.

DeRosa, R., Habib, M., Pelcovitz, D., Rathus, J., Sonnenklar, J., Ford, J., Sunday, S., Layne, C., Saltzman, W., & Turnbull, A. (2008). *Structured psychotherapy for adolescents responding to chronic stress.* Manhasset, NY: Northshore Hospital-Long Island Jewish Health System.

Figley, C. (1989). *Helping traumatized families.* San Francisco, CA: Jossey-Bass.

Ford, J. D., & Russo, E. (2006). A trauma-focused, present-centered, emotional self-regulation approach to integrated treatment for post-traumatic stress and addiction: Trauma adaptive recovery group education and therapy (TARGET). *American Journal of Psychotherapy, 60*(4), 335–355. (See also www.ptsdfreedom.org for TARGET materials.)

Ford, J. D., & Cloitre, M. (2009). Best practices in psychotherapy for children and families. In C. A. Courtois & J. D. Ford (Eds.), *Treating Complex Traumatic stress disorders: An evidence-based guide* (pp. 59–81). New York, NY: Guilford Press.

Ford, J. D., Blaustein, M., Habib, M., & Kagan, R. (2013). Developmental trauma therapy models. In J. D. Ford & C. A. Courtois (Ed.), *Treating Complex Traumatic stress disorders in children and adolescents: Scientific foundations and therapeutic models* (pp. 261–276). New York, NY: Guilford Press.

Gil, E. (1991). *The healing power of play.* New York, NY: Guilford Press.

Gil, E. (1996). *Treating abused adolescents.* New York, NY: Guilford Press.

Greenwald, R. (1999). *Eye movement desensitization and reprocessing (EMDR) in child and adolescent psychotherapy.* Northvale, NJ: Jason Aronson.

James, B. (1989). *Treating traumatized children.* Lexington, MA: Lexington Books.

Kagan, R. (2004). *Rebuilding attachments with traumatized children: Healing from losses, violence, abuse and neglect.* New York, NY: Routledge.

Kolko, D., & Swenson, C. C. (2002). *Assessing and treating physically abused children and their families.* Thousand Oaks, CA: Sage.

Lieberman, A. F., & Van Horn, P. (2005). *"Don't hit my mommy!" A manual for child-parent psychotherapy with young witnesses of family violence.* Washington, DC: Zero to Three Press.

Lieberman, A. F., & van Horn, P. (2011). *Psychotherapy with infants and young children: Repairing the effects of stress and trauma on early attachment.* New York, NY: Guilford Press.

Macy, R. D., Barry, S., & Gil, N. G. (2003). *Youth facing threat and terror: Supporting preparedness and resilience.* San Francisco, CA: Jossey-Bass.

Ogden, P., Minton, K., & Pain, C. (2006). *Trauma and the body: A sensorimotor approach to psychotherapy.* New York, NY: Norton.

Parnell, L. (2013). *Attachment-focused EMDR: Healing relational trauma.* New York: Norton.

Saxe, G. N., Elis, B. H., & Kaplow, J. B. (2007). *Collaborative treatment of traumatized children and teens: The trauma systems therapy approach.* New York, NY: Guilford Press.

Schore, A. N. (2003). Early relational trauma, disorganized attachment, and the development of a predisposition to violence. In M. F. Solomon & D. J. Siegel (Eds.), *Healing trauma: Attachment, mind, body, and brain* (pp. 107–155). New York, NY: Norton.

Shapiro, F. (2001). *Eye movement desensitization and reprocessing: Basic principles, protocols, and procedures* (2nd ed.). New York, NY: Guilford Press.

Shapiro, F., & Forrest, M. S. (1997). *EMDR: The breakthrough therapy for overcoming anxiety, stress, and trauma.* New York, NY: Basic Books.

Siegel, D. (1999). *The developing mind.* New York, NY: Guilford Press.

Siegel, D. (2003). An interpersonal neurobiology of psychotherapy: The developing mind and the resolution of trauma. In M. F. Solomon & D. J. Siegel (Eds.), *Healing trauma: Attachment, mind, body, and brain* (pp. 1–56). New York: Norton.

Tinker, R. H., & Wilson, S. A. (1998) *Through the eyes of a child: EMDR with children.* New York, NY: Norton

van der Kolk, B. (2003). Posttraumatic stress disorder and the nature of trauma. In M. F. Solomon & D. J. Siegel (Eds.), *Healing trauma: Attachment, mind, body, and brain* (pp. 168–195). New York, NY: Norton.

van der Kolk, B. (2014). *The body keeps the score: Brain, mind and body in the healing of trauma.* New York, NY: Viking.

van der Kolk, B.A., McFarlane, A.C., & Weisaeth, L. (Eds.) (1996). *Traumatic stress.* New York, NY: Guilford Press.

TABLE 19.1
Heroes Library: Suggested Books, Movies, and Music for Children and Adolescents Listed by Age, Reading Level, Ethnic Background, and Challenges in Their Lives

Title	Author	Subject Matter	Reading Level	Description	Ethnic Group	Comments
PRESCHOOL						
The Little Engine That Could	**Piper, Watty**	Child hero story, overcoming obstacles	Preschool	A little train carrying oodles of toys to all the good boys and girls is confronted with a towering mountain; he overcomes and finds his way to the other side.	N/A	"Models determination."
PRESCHOOL–GRADES K-4						
Goodnight Moon	**Brown, Margaret Wise**	Child fear	Preschool, Grades K-4	Children overcome fears of dark by saying goodnight to everything.	N/A	"Uses attention to details in a ritualized manner to create a feeling of safety at bedtime."
Today I Feel Silly	**Curtis, Jaime Lee**	Moods	Preschool, Grades K-4	This book takes the reader through 13 different moods, and helps explain mood swings to children.	N/A	
It's My Body (Children's Safety and Abuse Prevention Paperback)	**Freeman, Lory**	Recognizing sexual abuse	Preschool, Grades K-4	Informative paperback that explains good and bad touch to children.	N/A	
I Can't Talk About It: A Child's Book about Sexual Abuse (A Corner of the Heart)	**Sanford, Doris**	Talking about sexual abuse	Preschool, Grades K-4	Young girl reveals her sexual abuse to a dove who helps her heal and learn to trust again. The book also lists guideline for adults to help sexually abused children.	N/A	
Horton Hatches the Egg	**Dr. Seuss**	Parenting	Preschool, Grades K-4	Horton is persuaded to sit on and hatch an egg while the mother takes a break.	N/A	"Teaches the meaning of parenting."
GRADES K-4						
Runaway Bunny	**Brown, Margaret Wise**	Child hero story	Grades K-4	A little rabbit who wants to run away tells his mother how he will escape, but she is always right behind him.	N/A	"For children who are interested in nature and animals."
Stellaluna	**Cannon, Jannell**	Children's adversity story	Grades K-4	Story of a bat who overcomes separation, foster care, racial differences, and reuniting with mother.	N/A	
Alexander and the Terrible, Horrible, No Good Very Bad Day	**Cruz, Ray**	Overcoming adversity	Grades K-4	Story of Alexander's very bad day, and how he overcomes feeling horrible about it.	N/A	"Is an engaging story of frustration with the lesson that some days are just like that."
Hansel and Gretel	**Grimm, Jacob**	Children's adversity story	Grades K-4	Clever children overcome fears and triumph over evil.	N/A	
Elephant in the Living Room: A Children's Book	**Hastings, Jill M.**	Child trauma, substance abuse	Grades K-4	Children's story that uses an elephant to illustrate the experience of having a relative in the house who is a substance abuser.	N/A/	"Demonstrates overcoming secrecy supporting addictions."
A Terrible Thing Happened: A Story for Children Who Have Witnessed Violence or Trauma	**Holmes, Margaret M.**	Trauma	Grades K-4	Story of Sherman, who sees something terrible, and becomes anxious and angry. After seeing a counselor, he talks through emotions and feels better.	N/A	Young raccoon experiences something terrible and his behavior changes. His parents send him to a therapist, and he overcomes his fears.

TABLE 19.1
Heroes Library—*continued*

Title	Author	Subject Matter	Reading Level	Description	Ethnic Group	Comments
			GRADES K-4—*continued*			
Little Red Riding Hood	**Hyman, Trina**	Children's adversity story	Grades K-4	Little Red Riding Hood lessons: keeping promises, to stay on the path, mind her manners, and avoid talking to big bad wolves.	N/A	
Ray Charles	**Mathis, Sharon Bell**	Real life hero story	Grades K-4	Life story of Ray Charles, African-American jazz musician without sight.	African American	African-American musician who lost his sight at age 7.
There is a Nightmare in My Closet	**Mayer, Mercer**	Overcoming fears	Grades K-4	At bedtime, a boy confronts the nightmare in his closet and finds him not so terrifying.	N/A	"A great example of a child mastering his fears."
We Are All in the Dumps with Jack and Guy	**Sendak, Maurice**	Child hero, overcoming adversity	Grades K-4	Sendak takes old nursery rhymes and illustrates hardships of today's world, and the life of orphans living on the streets that are being watched over by the moon. A headline from the book says it all: "Leaner Times, Meaner Times, Children Triumph."	Orphans, street kids	This book should be read by an adult to children to aid in discussion of the illustrations (which arguably tell the story more than the words).
Where the Wild Things Are	**Sendak, Maurice**	Child hero stories	Grades K-4	Story of Jack, who, after mischief, is sent to his room. His room turns into a forest, where he meets a series of monsters, who are scary-looking without being scary.	N/A	"About a defiant child's dream that incorporates becoming like monsters, starting a voyage (courage), and returning to the smell of a hot meal prepared by his mother (reunification)."
			GRADES 4–6			
Double Fudge	**Blume, Judy**		Grades 4–6		N/A	
Freckle Juice	**Blume, Judy**		Grades 4–6		N/A	
The One in the Middle Is a Green Kangaroo	**Blume, Judy**		Grades 4–6		N/A	
Otherwise Known as Sheila the Great	**Blume, Judy**		Grades 4–6		N/A	
Tales of a Fourth Grade Nothing	**Blume, Judy**		Grades 4–6		N/A	
Mouse and the Motorcycle	**Cleary, Beverley**		Grades 4–6		N/A	
Muggie Maggie	**Cleary, Beverley**		Grades 4–6		N/A	
Ramona Boxed Set	**Cleary, Beverley**	Child hero story, overcoming diversity	Grades 4–6	Four stories of Ramona learning life lessons, including: being patient with her sister, her first crush, staying out of trouble, learning bravery, overcoming fears, gaining maturity, and meeting expectations.	N/A	

TABLE 19.1
Heroes Library—*continued*

Title	Author	Subject Matter	Reading Level	Description	Ethnic Group	Comments
GRADES 4–6—*continued*						
Runaway	**Cleary, Beverley**		Grades 4–6		N/A	
James and the Giant Peach	**Dahl, Roald**	Child hero, overcoming diversity	Grades 4–6	James loses his parents, and is forced to live with his wicked and abusive aunts. He becomes the saddest and loneliest boy you could find. He meets a man who gives him magic crystals that fall onto his aunt's peach tree. The tree develops a peach of enormous proportions and he climbs inside, where he finds an assortment of characters who help him through his pain.	N/A	Also made into a movie. This is a great book for children who feel abandoned or neglected by their parents. It also helps aid in coping with the death of a parent.
Matilda	**Dahl, Roald**	Child hero, overcoming	abuse	Grades 4–6		
Revolting Rhymes	**Dahl, Roald**			Grades 4–6		
Joey Pigza Loses Control	**Gantos, Jack**	ADD, overcoming diversity	Grades 4–6	Joey wants a six-week visit with father to count and show him that he can control his ADD. His father makes up for past wrongs and shows Joey how to be a winner and take control of his life.		
Joey Pigza Swallwed the Key	**Gantos, Jack**	ADD, overcoming diversity	Grades 4–6	Joey can't sit still, can't pay attention, can't follow rules, and can't help it. He was born with ADD. He wreaks havoc on class trips and swallows his house key. Joey knows he is a good kid, and no matter how hard he tries to do the right thing, everything goes wrong.		
What Would Joey Do?	**Gantos, Jack**	ADD, divorce, overcoming diversity	Grades 4–6	Joey learns that settling down isn't good for anything if he can't find a way to stop the people he cares about from winding him up all over again.		
Odds on Oliver	**Green, Constance C.**	Child hero	Grades 4–6	Oliver, desperate to be a hero, after many attempts and failures, triumphs when held hostage in a grocery store and finding the solution.	N/A	
The Best of Girls to the Rescue	**Lansky, Bruce (Ed.)**	Overcoming diversity, child hero story	Grades 4–6	Girls featured in the *Girls to the Rescue* series are smart, and save the day.	N/A	
The New Captain Underpants Collection: Box Set (Books 1–5)	**Pilkey, Dav**	Hero stories	Grades 4–6	Five books with stories of Captain Underpants and his adventures.	N/A	After working in the library for several years, I found these books almost never stayed on the shelves. They are funny, and kids love them. They also have a hero figure who conquers many obstacles.

TABLE 19.1
Heroes Library—*continued*

Title	Author	Subject Matter	Reading Level	Description	Ethnic Group	Comments
GRADES 4–6—*continued*						
Shiloh	**Reynolds, Phyllis**		Grades 4–6	Boy befriends abused dog	N/A	
Holes	**Sacher, Louis**	Child hero story	Grades 4–6		N/A	Teaches kids to persevere and builds confidence.
Marvin Redpost: Alone in His Teachers House	**Sacher, Louis**		Grades 4–6		N/A	
Sideways Stories from Wayside School	**Sacher, Louis**		Grades 4–6		N/A	
Sixth Grade Secrets	**Sacher, Louis**		Grades 4–6		N/A	
Falling Up	**Silverstein, Shel**		Grades 4–6		N/A	
A Light in the Attack	**Silverstein, Shel**		Grades 4–6		N/A	
Where the Sidewalk Ends	**Silverstein, Shel**	Children's poetry	Grades 4–6		N/A	
GRADES 7–10						
Hatchet	**Paulsen, Gary**	Child hero stories, overcoming adversity	Grades 7–10	After a plane crash, 13-year-old Brian spends 54 days in the wilderness with only a hatchet to survive. He is also learning to deal with his parents' divorce.	N/A	"A boy who crash lands and must learn to survive in the wilderness."
YOUNG ADULT						
The Children's Homer: The Adventures of Odysseus and the Tale of Troy	**Colum, Padraic**	Hero, mythology	YA	Book tells the story of Odysseus and his adventures in Troy, as well as his journey home to his wife and kingdom. A classic epic of a journey through hardships and obstacles to achieve goals.	Ancient Greek	
Freak the Mighty	**Philbrick, Rodman**	Child hero	YA	Story of two boys that do not fit the norm, and are outcast by peers—one for being big and having a criminal father, the other due to crippling illness. They befriend each other, and make Freak the Mighty, more powerful together then alone. Together, they face adventure and danger. In the end, Mighty copes with the death of Freak, and learns a powerful lesson about himself.	N/A	Wonderful book for children with differences that may make them feel accepted by their peers. It encourages education, reading, and imagination to triumph through it. Made into a movie called *The Mighty*.
Big Fish: A Novel of Mythic Proportions	**Wallace, Danielle**	Modern myth, hero story, father and son relationship	YA	Edward Bloom (Big Fish) and son go through epic story of father's life. Edward spent his life exploring and telling jokes, and stories. Son tries to connect with father during the last moments of his life, and understand who the man is behind the myth.	N/A	Also made into a movie in 2004.
Autobiography of Malcolm X	**X, Malcolm**	Real life hero story	YA	Story of Malcolm X's life	African American	

TABLE 19.1
Heroes Library—*continued*

Title	Author	Subject Matter	Reading Level	Description	Ethnic Group	Comments
YOUNG ADULT–GRADES 7–10 AND UP						
Object Lessons	**Quindlen, Anna**	Coming of ages	YA, Grades 7–10 and up	Child's struggle with her identity and her mother's mistakes.	Irish and Italian communities	"For adolescents grappling with their parents' strengths and mistakes."
Harry Potter Hardcover Box Set with Leather Bookmark (Books 1–5)	**Rowling, J. K.**	Child hero	YA, Grades 7–10 and up	Story of orphaned boy living with abusive relatives who discovers his magical powers (inherited from his parents) and goes off to school to develop them. While there, he has a series of adventures that uncover more of his powers and give him a deeper insight into self.	N/A	Kids love these books (as do adults).
JUVENILE NONFICTION						
Malcom X: By Any Means Necessary: A Biography	**Myers, Walter Dean**	Real life hero story	Juvenile nonfiction	Life story of Malcolm X	African American	
Please Tell: A Child's Story about Sexual Abuse	**Ottenweler, Jessie**	Child hero, overcoming sexual abuse	Juvenile nonfiction, ages 4–8	Life story and illustrations of 9-year-old Jessie to help let other sexually abused children know it's OK to talk about their feelings.	N/A	
JUVENILE NONFICTION–GRADES 4–6						
Bury My Heart at Wounded Knee: An Indian History of the American West	**Brown, Dee Alexander**	Real life hero story	Juvenile nonfiction, Grades 4–6	Life story of Sioux Indians at Wounded Knee in South Dakota. It tells how Indians lost their lives and land to white society and how they endured the suffering of their people and the abolishing of their cultures and community.	Native American	Native American perspective of American history.
A Boy Called Slow: The True Story of Sitting Bull	**Bruchac, Joseph**	Real life hero story	Juvenile nonfiction, Grades 4–6	Life story of Sitting bull, Lakota Sioux Indian.	Native American	
The Leroy Butler Story: From Wheelchair to the Lamseau Leap	**Butler, Leroy**	Real life hero story	Juvenile nonfiction, Grades 4–6	Tells the story of Leroy Butler, former Green Bay Packer, overcoming childhood health problems and moving onto college and becoming a football hero, eventually winning Super Bowl XXXI.	African American	
Go Free or Die: A Story about Harriet Tubman	**Ferris, Jeri**	Real life hero story	Juvenile nonfiction, Grades 4–6	Life story of Harriet Tubman and her role in helping slaves escape bondage.	African American	
Brave Bessie: Flying Free	**Fisher, Lillian M.**	Real life hero story	Juvenile nonfiction, Grades 4–6	Life story of Bessie Smith, African-American female aviator	African American	Two years before Amelia Earhart, Bessie Smith became the first African-American aviatrix to receive her flying license.

TABLE 19.1
Heroes Library—*continued*

Title	Author	Subject Matter	Reading Level	Description	Ethnic Group	Comments
JUVENILE NONFICTION–GRADES 4–6—*continued*						
Brother Eagle, Sister Sky: A Message from Chief Seattle	Jeffers, Susan	Real life hero story	Juvenile nonfiction, Grades 4–6	Adaptation of a speech given by Chief Seattle at treaty negations in the 1850s.	Native American	
A School for Pompey Walker	Rosen, Michael J.	Real life hero story	Juvenile nonfiction, Grades 4–6	Inspired by the true story of a young freed slave, who, with the help of a white man, sells himself back into slavery 39 times to raise money for school.	African American	Story of Gussie West.
When Justice Failed: The Fred Korematsu Story (Stories of America)	Tamura, David	Real life hero story	Juvenile nonfiction, Grades 4–6	Story of Fred Korematsu, born in California, volunteered for military service but rejected because of Japanese ancestry. The book covers his battle with the Supreme Court after refusing to leave his home to live in an interment camp.	Japanese American	
JUVENILE NONFICTION–GRADES 4–6, AND 7–10						
Kids Write Through It		Children's adversity story	Juvenile nonfiction, Grades 4–6,and 7–10	Kids ages 7–12 write about overcoming their challenges on a variety of issues, including mental illness and death.	N/A	Stories by kids, for kids
YOUNG ADULT NONFICTION, GRADES 7–10						
Kids with Courage: True Stories of Young People Making a Difference	Lewis, Barbara A.	Child hero stories	YA nonfiction, Grades 7–10	Eighteen young people respond to heroically overcoming crisis in their lives.	N/A	
YOUNG ADULT NONFICTION, GRADES 7–10 AND UP						
I Know Why the Caged Bird Sings	Angelou, Maya	Real life hero story	YA nonfiction, Grades 7–10 and up	Life story of Maya Angelou and her struggles to overcome abusive childhood.	African American	
A Child Called "It"	Pelzer, Dave	Real life hero story, overcoming adversity and trauma	YA, adult nonfiction, Grades 7–10 and up	Life story of Dave Pelzer and his overcoming of childhood abuse.	N/A	Part of series of four books: "*A Child Called It* and its sequel to expand a youth's understanding and perspective of how people survive and grow despite neglect, violence or abuse."

TABLE 19.1
Heroes Library—*continued*

Title	Author	Subject Matter	Reading Level	Description	Ethnic Group	Comments
MOVIES						
Finding Forrester		Child hero story, over-coming obstacles, caring adult	Adolescent	Young gifted black male befriends sick introverted author and develops his writing talents.	African American	
Finding Nemo		Child hero story, overcoming obstacles	Ages 10 and up	Young Nemo, defiant to father's overbearing paranoia, accidentally gets caught and put into a dentist's fish tank. Father faces his own fears to find his son. During his journey, he meets others who help him along the way, and help him further overcome his paranoia.	N/A	
The Land before Time		Child hero story, over-coming obstacles	Ages 4 and up	Orphaned dinosaur has to make his way to the great valley in order to survive a plague. Along the way, he meets up with others from all different dinosaur species. They bond and travel together, finding ways to deal with the obstacles that lay in their path.	N/A	
Lilo and Stitch		Family/foster care, child hero story	Ages 5 and up	Story teaches that a family can be assembled or born into.	N/A	
Shrek		Hero story, epic adventure	Ages 5 and up	Shrek, misunderstood ogre, makes a deal with the king to rescue the princess to get his land back. During this excursion, Shrek learns to make friends, fall in love, and overcomes many obstacles to achieve his goal.	N/A	
Star Wars Trilogy		Hero story, epic adventure	Adolescent	Luke Skywalker struggles to discover his Jedi powers, find his father, and defeat the Dark Side.	N/A	"In which an orphaned hero, Luke, is guided by a Jedi master, Obi Wan Kenobi, to calm, center himself, and develop his skills, and elicit powers to help others."
Whale Rider		Overcoming diversity	Adolescent	Legend of Paikea overcoming adversity she faces as a youth trying to lead the Maori tribe in New Zealand	Maori	
What's Eating Gilbert Grape	**Based on a novel by Peter Hedges**	Overcoming diversity, families, and mental illness	Caring adult	Gilbert handles running the family, caring for a brother with mental disabilities, caring for an obese bedridden mother, and death in the family. He eventually breaks free and finds a new role in life.		
White Oleander		Neglectful parents, foster care	Adult	Story of abuse, and a child growing up in foster care.		

TABLE 19.1
Heroes Library—*continued*

Title	Singer	Subject Matter	Reading Level	Description	Ethnic Group	Comments
MUSIC						
Follow Me	**Uncle Cracker**	6 and up		Caring person	N/A	
Hero	**Mariah Carey**	6 and up			N/A	
I Will Survive	**Gloria Gaynor**	Adolescent		Overcoming hardships	N/A	
I'll Be There	**Mariah Carey**	6 and up		Caring person	N/A	
I Am Beautiful	**Chritstina Aguilera**	6 and up		Overcoming taunts	N/A	
One	**U2**	6 and up		Overcoming pain	N/A	This song is about finding love for others.
Wind beneath My Wings	**Bette Midler**	6 and up	Hero song	Caring person	N/A	
You've Got a Friend	**Carol King**	Adolescent				

Part IV
Strategies for Overcoming Challenges

20

Strategies for Overcoming Challenges

Challenges (obstacles to treatment) are welcomed in RLH as part of any trauma treatment, especially when working with children and caregivers who have become accustomed to feeling hurt, unsafe, and unable to trust, and may have experienced previous treatments as unhelpful, stigmatizing, or making things worse. Children and caregivers may hold expectations and memories of past treatment that lead to withholding, denying, or testing therapists to see if they can be trusted enough to share feelings or beliefs. In RLH, these are seen as coping behaviors that may have been very important to help children and caregivers in the past.

The *Life Storybook*, Session Structure, and Toolkit provide an easy-to-use structure for engaging often hard-to-reach children and families. At the same time, RLH is intended to be adaptable to meet the goals and needs of diverse children and caregivers and maintain their involvement in a wide range of treatment programs with different resources and constraints.

Strategies (listed below) can help promote safety and enlarge the "window of tolerance" (Siegel, 1999) to allow development of stronger relationships, self- and co-regulation skills, and Life Story Integration. Strategies for common challenges in trauma treatment are organized below by phase of treatment:

- Assessment
- Service Planning
- Safety
- Session Structure
- Affect Recognition, Expression, and Modulation
- Heroes
- Caregivers and Other Important Relationships
- Mind Power
- Changing the Story: Changing Beliefs and Action Cycles to Achieve Goals
- Timelines and Moves: Organizing a Life Chronology
- Trauma Reintegration
- Building a Future
- Creating an Integrated Life Story

20.1 ASSESSMENT

Challenges	Strategies
Caregivers balk at sharing or being asked to participate	Emphasize from the start that therapists need family members' help to help their children. Look for and accentuate signs of caring and pain shared by children and adults. Begin with caregiver and child goals and use to drive assessment and service planning. Utilize engaging messages, including affirmation of rights to choose other treatment programs, to work with other therapists, and openness about the purpose of sessions. Invite children and parents to share their expectations for the assessment. Share how the therapist asks 'nosy' questions and will count on family members to stop him or her if this becomes too sensitive (Kagan & Schlosberg, 1989). For detailed guidelines for engaging and assessing families referred after abuse and neglect, see *Families in Perpetual Crisis* (Kagan & Schlosberg, 1989). See sample protocol below.
The child does not want to complete trauma exposure or symptom surveys	Normalize the use of surveys as a standard part of initial assessments for service planning. See the protocol example in *The Pledge* in Step by Step—Safety Messages. Use to show that the therapist and other program staff can talk about good times and 'tough times.' Link the use of surveys to understanding that many children and caregivers have experienced hard times and the purpose of these surveys is to help the therapist or team develop the most effective services to help children and caregivers achieve their goals. Use a message such as: "I work with many youths and their families who have experienced very hard times as well as very good times. This is a brief survey I use to help find out what has happened and to help develop the best treatment plan in _____ program." Use what the youth shares to help engage. For example, an adolescent indicated "No" for all items except "severe injury or illness" and shared a concern about a teen female friend who had a rare, life-threatening disease. The therapist said he'd bring in information on that illness and used that to help engage the youth.
Children become severely agitated easily whenever sensitive topics are raised	Introducing trauma exposure and symptom surveys in the first two or three sessions helps to get these done efficiently and demonstrates this is just a standard part of a program's services. If this isn't possible, surveys can be done in clumps, with a few questions at a time followed by a centering activity.
Children will complete *My Thermometers* but share little else	Use *My Thermometers* as a primary assessment tool to explore what is happening, what helps, and alternative patterns of behavior: *My Thermometers* **Coping Activity**[1] – Ask children to imagine that they are feeling a '0' on *Knots* and an '8' on 'Self-Control' thermometers. – What would be happening to make you feel that way? – Ask children to imagine feeling a '3' on *Knots* and a '7' on 'Self-Control' thermometer. – What would be happening to make you feel that way? – Repeat questions, increasing *Knots* by '1' and decreasing Self-Control by '1' (e.g., *Knots* at '4' and other 'Self-Control' thermometers at '6'). – This can also be used to develop enriched *Power Plans* and children can be asked to practice preferred coping skills, to make these coping behaviors into 'eight-lane neural highways.'

20.2 SERVICE PLANNING

Challenges	Strategies
Caregivers block participation in services	Check for shame-based messages perceived by caring adults. Reinforce resiliency focus of proposed treatment and using an understanding of trauma as a framework to move beyond shame and blame. See *Families in Perpetual Crisis* (Kagan & Schlosberg, 1989) for detailed guidelines and case examples for engaging family members through home-based family therapy and in-home family support programs. See *Turmoil to Turning Points: Building Hope for Children in Crisis Placements* (Kagan, 1996) for guidelines and case examples illustrating engagement of family members when children are in foster care, crisis, or mental health placements.
Caregivers resist participation in treatment planning or treatment sessions and ask for treatment of children alone	Stress the critical role of family members to help children heal from trauma by modeling the courage to share. Also, stress the important role of family members to help children learn from the family's heritage. Ensure that family members experience respect from therapists and agency staff for the importance of parents, grandparents, family values, a family's religion, and ethnicity. Watch for unspoken concerns about sharing family secrets with the therapist and assess the need for court orders of protection when adults or children have been threatened.
Children remind caregivers of their own traumas	When adults are triggered by children, offer individual trauma therapy for adults regarding their own traumatic life experiences. Work with caring adults to accentuate how they have made their lives different from the past and how they can utilize their understanding and resources as adults to keep themselves and their children safe. Use *TARGET* (Ford & Russo, 2006) curriculum with its emphasis on skill-building. Encourage caregivers to assist youths, building on wishes for their children to succeed when possible. Refer for individual therapy if individual work with adults is not possible.
Caregivers find it too difficult to talk about their own past but are supportive of their children finding a way to heal after traumas	Encourage caregivers to support children's life story work, including helping children learn about strengths from their family heritage and examples of family members' courage and efforts to overcome adversity. Encourage caregivers to work separately in individual treatment if that is more comfortable.
Children do not trust caregivers and repeatedly test or provoke caregivers	Watch for secret fears of children requiring additional safety plans. Help caregivers understand that children need to see that these adults are different than the adults who hurt them, or, if the same people, that caregivers have truly changed. Help caregivers practice how to respond to children in order to rebuild trust by: • listening to children and showing respect for their perceptions and memories; • attunement to children's feelings; • validation of children's experiences; • stressing how their lives are different now; • safety messages; • supportive tone of voice, facial looks, and touch; and • modeling adding words to feelings.
Children are in placement and lack a permanency plan including responsibilities for caregivers in treatment	Trauma therapy often requires work by caregivers on building safety from domestic violence, physical abuse, sexual abuse, and neglect. Trauma work also requires time frames for necessary changes to take place and an understood plan for how children, adults, therapists, and authorities will monitor and know if changes are taking place. Therapists need to be well versed in permanency work and how to engage authorities, law guardians, and family court judges to implement an attachment-centered therapy that meets the requirements of the Adoption and Safe Families Act (see Kagan, 2004, Chapter 5).
Parents or other designated guardians are unsafe	Within the context of state and federal requirements and mandates from family courts and child protective services (CPS), therapists should respect the right of adults to voice their own needs and their right to establish their own pace on working to provide

SERVICE PLANNING—*continued*

Challenges	Strategies
	safety for children and overcome problems that have led to placement, court orders, or CPS monitoring. Parents have to keep themselves safe. At the same time, it is important for everyone to hear in meetings, conferences, and sessions that children need to be protected by other designated adults until parents can rebuild connections and demonstrate to CPS and family courts that they are keeping children safe. And, authorities have responsibilities to implement state and federal laws (e.g., ASFA) with timelines for parents or guardians to make necessary changes and establish safe homes for children.
Parents or other designated guardians are unable to care for child safely over extended period of time	Respecting the right of parents to choose what they can and will do is coupled with recognition of children's inability to wait for long periods of time for parents to change and become capable or willing to parent children to maturity. As part of trauma therapy, therapists need to be strong enough to help children and parents grieve when parents are unable to raise their children and carry out basic parenting, to "protect, provide, and guide" (James, 1994). Children may need to be raised to maturity by a substitute guardian if birth parents cannot do what is necessary. Attachment and trauma therapy means voicing children's need for permanency and making that a priority in treatment (see Kagan, 1996, 2004; Kagan & Schlosberg, 1989).

20.3 SAFETY

Challenges	Strategies
Children appear anxious	Therapists and caring adults can help children relax by learning what helps each child. A hug from a trusted family member, a pat on the back, and praise for children's courage may be all that is needed to help children begin this work. Facial expressions, gestures, and the tone of a caring adult's voice are critical in establishing permission to work with a therapist. For other children, frequent breaks, physical activities, or repeated practice in slow breathing, imagery, and relaxation techniques with a therapist may be necessary. In other cases, children's fears may reflect real dangers. Watching how children self-regulate is a key means of finding ways to help children (Warner et al., 2014) self- and co-regulate.
Children are not safe to share fears	Focus work with children in individual sessions on developing affect management skills and learning from children's heroes (workbook Chapters 1–4) until risks can be identified and safety established. Use workbook Chapters 5–6 to help search for caring adults who can help children become safe enough to share.
A comprehensive assessment is not available	Refer for comprehensive psychological evaluations to identify attachments, risks, unspoken threats, obstacles, subtle triggers, and to develop viable safety plans and services.
Implementation of safety plans is not certain	Check on whether safety plans have been implemented by asking if everyone involved, from children to parents, grandparents, extended family members, school officials, and authorities, can share what will be done to keep children (and adults) safe from repetitions of past traumas at home, in their neighborhoods, and at school: • Who will do what? • What will signal that a crisis cycle is starting again? • Who can serve as protectors from outside the nuclear family to guard against any further abuse or neglect? • Who is committed to protecting the children, even if it means confronting parents or calling child protective services? • How can protectors be contacted? Do children have their phone numbers? • Who will check on children to maintain safety, and how often must this happen in order to keep children safe?

SAFETY—*continued*

Challenges	Strategies
Caregivers cannot manage affect regulation or reactions to reminders of traumas	Often, caregivers need to show children they are working on overcoming their own traumas in order to help their children. This may involve extended therapy. The use of *TARGET* (Ford & Russo, 2006) materials can help adults work on their own skill development. Adults can also work on their own life stories as part of RLH work.
Parents care about their children but are not able or willing to validate their children's experiences	Parents who care about their children but are not able or willing to validate their children's experiences may still be able to give support for therapeutic work in concrete ways (e.g., giving permission for children to work on the *Life Storybook* privately with the therapist, purchasing colored pencils or markers or providing paper for drawings, helping children contact relatives who will share their memories of what happened, pulling out old photos, etc.).
Parents appear unable or unwilling to take on the full task of raising children or to overcome the impact of traumas on children	It is important to respect how parents demonstrate their choices hour by hour and day by day in terms of making the changes necessary to create safe homes, rebuild attachments, and care for children. Reassessing commitments of family members can also be helpful to clarify capacity to change, obstacles to change, perceived mandates from the family, their culture, communities, and authorities, and assistance that could be provided. Children and team members need to be regularly informed about how their parents are doing to accomplish changes needed for the safety and well-being of all family members.
Parents stop working on changes needed for the safety of children or fail to make necessary changes within ASFA time limits for children in placement	Parents may feel they need to avoid change or move slowly over many years to stop risky behaviors and overcome traumas in their lives. Children, however, don't have the time to wait long periods without suffering extensive impairment of their own development. Therapists can help parents, children, extended family members, and caring adults to voice both successes and failures, to grieve what cannot be changed, and at all times to promote the best possible relationship between a parent and a child. See Kagan and Schlosberg (1989) and Kagan (1996) for detailed guidelines for permanency work.
One parent insists another parent is all bad and blocks children from learning about the other parent ('parent alienation syndrome')	Watch for signs in the child or parent's nonverbal reactions that talking about a missing parent is not allowed. Use workbook Chapters 5 and 6 to open up learning by children about other parents. Stress how research has shown that children need to know the good things each parent has done, as well as the bad, or children suffer. When parents separate, children do best when they can have the best possible relationship with each parent and when children's needs are placed above the grievances of either parent.
A parent will not allow child to be seen alone and child is not fully safe with adult	Attempt to meet with the parent alone to address concerns and develop safety plans that reassure the parent that the therapist respects the caring parent, and will support the 'caring' expressed by the parent while helping the child to overcome presenting problems and achieve the goals the parent and child want for the child. Divide the sessions between the parent and child, meeting first with the parent, and then the child. If necessary, limit individual time at first to a few minutes and gradually expand. Focus conjoint time on skill and safety development.
The parent limits what children can say or talk about	Address injunctions to not talk about certain issues as important communications from the parent about where safety plans are needed. Injunctions may stem from the parent's own history of being hurt and rules the parent developed to protect him or herself and children from abuse or abandonment. If possible, work with the parent to frame goals as promoting children's strengths, including the ability to see, hear, and voice what is real while maintaining respect and caring for the parent. In some cases, it may be helpful for parents to complete the workbook themselves with the therapist before starting work with children.
Children fear the parent will relapse, especially during certain times in the year	Children's distress and 'threat avoidance' will naturally escalate during time periods when parents have relapsed in the past, returning to drug use, neglect, etc. Holidays and anniversary dates of losses often mark times when children become especially anxious and preoccupied with recurrence of past traumas. When this occurs, it is helpful to focus directly on what can help children to know that a parent is safe

SAFETY—*continued*

Challenges	Strategies
	(after Macy et al., 2003). What could help children to relax, even for a second, knowing that their parents are safe?
	Signals of relapse can be built into safety plans (e.g., number of cigarettes or cups of coffee, ability of the parent to laugh when tickled by a feather, the parent fixing breakfast for the child, the parent spending time with positive friends, going to NA, or having random drug checks by an authority).
Children lack any safe and validating parent	Introduce *Real Life Heroes®* as a means to search for caring adults, especially adults willing and able to parent children to maturity. After identifying possible caring adults, the next step is to develop and implement viable safety plans. Invite children to work simultaneously with *Real Life Heroes®* materials and a supportive team of therapists and hopefully extended family members, to identify and find two or three caring adults who can support children, even if some can't raise children in their homes. Working on pages of the *Life Storybook*, especially Chapters 5 and 6, is very useful in providing information on who a therapist can contact. The emphasis in this work should not be on children finding caring adults, but rather the therapist, collaterals, and extended family members, where possible, working with information children share to find and strengthen potential caregivers for them.
Children in placement have only one identified caring adult who they can count on for support, validation, and protection	Tell children that it's important to identify at least two possible caregivers, so that if the first adult can't do what is necessary to help, the therapist (and other staff) will work on helping children develop a relationship with another adult. Children can be asked, "Who could help _____ [primary parent-figure] to take care of you?" Or, "Who would you like to live with, if _____ [primary parent-figure], for some reason, can't take care of you?"
Children are living in placement and lack a permanency plan that they can believe will lead to a safe, nurturing home	Introduce *Real Life Heroes®* as a means to identify and find caring adults for children, people willing to work on building trust with them. This can include invitations to parents, extended family members, and other adults to work on validating children and helping them to become stronger. Viability of permanency plans should be assessed from children's perspectives and include safety plans to prevent or protect them from repetitions of previous traumas. For detailed guidelines on permanency work and case examples, see *Rebuilding Attachments with Traumatized Children and Turmoil to Turning Points: Building Hope in Crisis Placements* (Kagan, 1996, 2004).
The youth cannot manage living in a family, or the older adolescent refuses to consider family living	Group care or independent living programs are never sufficient as a backup plan by themselves; however, for adolescents who have demonstrated over multiple years and family placements that they cannot manage family living (e.g., 15–16-year-olds who refuse to consider family living), *Real Life Heroes®* materials can be used to identify caring adults who would be willing and able to support a youth living in such a supervised program. This should include building sustainable relationships with adults who would be willing to help the youth in a crisis, someone he or she could call, if necessary, in the middle of the night.

20.4 SESSION STRUCTURE

Challenges	Strategies
Children are reluctant to start	Accentuate how these sessions are different than other types of relationships children may have had in the past by encouraging children to utilize nonverbal creative arts modalities to illustrate different emotions that they feel. Therapists can foster experimentation rather than production by working creatively themselves with modalities they enjoy and by respecting children's responses. Encourage children and caregivers to see themselves as artists and to let themselves express themselves freely without evaluating or judging what they have done. Creativity is fostered by emphasizing the process rather than focusing on achieving results.
Children lack self-soothing and affect modulation skills	Provide extended practice sessions on developing self-soothing skills in sessions, with help from other service providers and with caregiver guidance. This can be combined with affect regulation skill-building beginning in Chapter 1. Additional skills can be fostered in work with caring adults with yoga and self-comforting exercises (e.g., cross arms up to shoulders, squeeze gently, rock self gently, tap shoulders lightly).
Children appear constricted in their ability to express themselves	Check for secrets, unresolved safety risks, or threats. Mentoring in art or music and participation in art or music classes or projects is helpful to foster the comfort and basic skills needed for this work. This can also be encouraged for caring adults.
Children have been abused or neglected by parents	Placement is needed when children have been severely abused or neglected and parents or guardians fail to take necessary steps to validate children's experiences and to develop and implement viable safety plans. Safety plans should include monitoring by safe caring adults children can trust to protect them, even if that means calling authorities and confronting parents or guardians. In these cases, it is important to identify at least three supportive and protective adults who will monitor and assure safety for children, 24/7, until parents rebuild trust over an extended period of time. Monitoring needs to include checking privately and individually with children along with the establishment of signals they can use and test to bring in help. Monitoring may be needed for long periods of time depending on the type and repetition of abuse or neglect. For severe and repeated abuse or neglect by parents and parents' refusal or failure to work on making necessary changes, children need to understand how state and federal laws (e.g., the Adoption and Safe Families Act) will be enforced by authorities and that they will not be sent back to violent homes or forced to go on visits that reinforce traumas. For more information on permanency work with abuse and neglect, see Kagan (2004).
Conflicts develop between parents, foster parents, and other caring adults	Avoid 'splitting' and fragmented work by involving parents, caring adults, therapists, and mentors in *collaborative planning*, beginning with contracting sessions and continuing with regular scheduled review conferences. Providing a common framework for understanding trauma through training programs (e.g., the "Essential Elements of Trauma-Informed Parenting") (Grillo et al., 2010, pp. 1–17, 19) can help prevent this.
The therapist has responsibility for both case management and trauma therapy for children in placement	Try to get another practitioner to take one of these roles. If this is not possible, clarify with the children how the therapist will separate these important roles and, wherever possible, schedule a separate time and day for weekly *Real Life Heroes®* sessions and use a different location. When that is not possible, the therapist can tell children that in each meeting time, the therapist will split the session. It usually works best to do the *RLH Life Storybook* first. It also helps to bring in a caring adult who will work on attunement and support for children in sessions. When no safe family members are available for this work and children are in placement, residential counselors or foster parents can play a vital role as caring adults in sessions.
Children are excited or distressed about something that happened or is about to happen	If children are too distressed, work on safety issues, including safety related to what happened or what children fear. However, reserve time to continue *Life Storybook* work in order to show children this is important. If children are not overly distressed, tell them that the therapist will save time at the end of the session to work with them on

SESSION STRUCTURE—*continued*

Challenges	Strategies
(e.g., a fight at school or an upcoming visit with a family member)	what happened, or is about to happen, after their special time to work on the *Real Life Heroes®* materials.
Children begin the session with a dramatic story that leads the caregiver to intervene to discipline or protect them	Children may begin sessions with a story of an event or behavior that provokes caregiver intervention. For instance, children may talk about how the principal or a police officer came to see them in their classroom that day, or how they needed to run away from a gang of kids on the way home from school. It is helpful to acknowledge children's stories and then encourage the child and caregiver to slow down and utilize some of the calming and centering skills developed in earlier sessions (e.g., 'SOS for Stress'), assuring both children and caregivers that the therapist will save time to deal with the issue at the end of the session. Therapists can gauge how much time to save based on the severity of the issue.

For critical issues, RLH work may be limited to Centering Activities, with the rest of the session focused on an urgent issue (e.g., homelessness or violent threats). In these situations, a caregiver may need to assert rules and control to keep children safe. Children may also be testing whether a caregiver who had neglected, abused, or abandoned them in the past would be able to maintain safety rules when challenged, or whether a dominant crisis mode will continue, even on days with therapy sessions. Therapists can utilize the goals of *Real Life Heroes®* work to emphasize 'safety first' and work on rebuilding trust and respect, including caregivers guiding children to be safe. |
| Children do not trust adults to believe them | Often, children will test adults to see if they will allow them to share or believe them. More frightened children will often test adults in covert or even sneaky ways, reflecting their experience that sharing has not been safe. Caring adults need to know that the process of testing is both normal and necessary for children to find out if it is safe to open up their feelings and beliefs. Children need to find out if adults will criticize them in a shaming manner or become too stressed to deal with real situations and experiences. Testing can be facilitated by allowing young children to dictate stories to adults. Therapists or caring adults can help by carefully writing down exactly what children say, using children's words. Children can then see that the adult is truly hearing their story and not trying to change it to fit the adult's perspective or wishes. |
| Children fear recurrence of traumas | Encourage caregivers to point out how children's lives are different now and reinforce safety plans. Practice safety plans and check for unknown threats or additional steps needed to increase safety.

Open up possibilities to prevent any future traumas by asking children to consider questions such as:

– "How would [child's heroes] have handled this?"
– "What could have made it just a little better?"
– "What could have helped you and [other people in the story]?"
– "Who could help?" |
| Children want to work alone on pages in sessions | Some children prefer to do sections by themselves and then share their work with their therapist and later with family members they can trust. This is fine; children can be encouraged to share as much as they can safely with caregivers. This is common with adolescents and young adults. Other children may be signaling that they do not feel truly safe with caregivers. Conjoint sessions are not recommended when children are feeling unsafe to share. Separate sessions can be used to work on helping caregivers show children they will validate and protect them. |
| Children balk when asked to consider possible solutions to problems or | Work on solutions should not be forced. Rather, a therapist can ask questions such as:

– "What would you say to a younger child you cared about if the same thing happened to him or her?" |

SESSION STRUCTURE—*continued*

Challenges	Strategies
alternative ways to think about tough times that counter dysfunctional beliefs	– "What would you say to a younger child who was hurt like you were and blamed him or herself?" – "Who could have helped [parents, aunts, uncles, grandparents, friends, neighbors, police, teachers, doctors, etc.]?" – "Who was responsible?" – "Who could help now?" This is similar to the cognitive interweave approaches described by Shapiro (2001) and Parnell (1999). Such questions can elicit children expressing their beliefs that they were responsible for abuse, family violence, addictions, etc., and therapists can encourage alternative perspectives.
Children blame themselves, taking on adult responsibilities and accepting harsh punishments	Challenge inappropriate beliefs with questions that build on children's sensitivity and caring for others, such as: – "Do you know any children [at the age of the child during the incident in the story]?" – "Would a ___-year-old child, like the child you know, be responsible for what happened?" – "Who in the child's family and community could have helped him or her?" Therapists can also challenge these beliefs by inviting children to consider what other children and adults children respect would say about this situation or a similar situation with similar levels of abuse defined by adults as discipline (e.g., "Would your coach [or best friend's mother] say that an 8-year-old was responsible for being burned with hot water and beaten by her stepfather because she left a mess in the kitchen sink?").
Children or the therapist want to target an important skill for development to counter trauma patterns	An additional thermometer can be used to monitor work on specific goals or skills. For instance, to assess development of children's levels of trust and attachment to a parent or caring adult, therapists could ask the child to rate: – "How much of your story does a parent or primary caregiver know?" – "How comfortable would you be if _____ [a potential caring adult] was here right now?" – "How would you be feeling right now if _____ knew the whole story?" Or, the added thermometer could be used to monitor children's ability to replace aggressive reactions to identified 'triggers' with calming and constructive actions by rating (e.g., "How much power did you have today to ask _____ [resource] in your class to take a break and . . . [implement anger safety plan]?"). To make another thermometer, simply trace one of the thermometers in Part V or invite children to make their own.
Children appear to be superficial, or to show little feeling about workbook activities	Elicit a greater range of perspective and feeling with different art materials (e.g., paints, clay), musical expression with a different instrument (e.g., a bongo drum), or movement activities (e.g., enactments of scenes children create or sculpt). Invite children to compare their own stories to books, movies, and stories they enjoy.
Children appear anxious outside their homes or therapy sessions	Check for fears reflecting unspoken traumas. When children have experienced violence or threats outside their homes, safety plans can be developed to counter these threats with the help of community resources. The challenge is to create safety plans children are willing to try out and test and improve and test again can be effective. If perpetrators or other dangerous individuals are present in the community, safety plans need to include ways children and others will work together to stay safe in each part of children's lives: home, on the way to school, at school, after-school activities, going home, etc. Alarm systems for apartments or houses may be needed or escorts to and from school. Bringing a dog into the home that children can trust to watch over them in the night can help children to sleep. Encourage caregivers to point out how steps such as these can make their lives safer than in the past.

SESSION STRUCTURE—*continued*

Challenges	Strategies
Children appear too distressed in a session to work on pages of the book	Consider using this session to work nonverbally on creating materials that foster a sense of safety in children's relationships and ability to self-regulate. Examples include designing a *Pocket Power Card*, inventing a musical instrument, making a shield from cut-out cardboard decorated with symbols representing strengths and powers, or making a photo cube with pictures of people children like and feel close to.
A parent or guardian disrupts sessions by screaming at children for past misbehavior (e.g., "You're grounded!")	Therapists need to assert the importance of sessions to accomplish family goals and the need for boundaries. This is especially important when therapists are working in homes or with caregivers or children who feel pressured to go to counseling. Engagement of parents, guardians, and children requires therapists to be strong, respectful, *and* real. Therapists can tell caregivers that they will save the last _____ minutes of the session to meet with the caregiver and work on ways to help them help their children learn more successful behaviors. Caregivers can be reminded that devoting most of the sessions to day-to-day discipline problems will prevent addressing skill-building and reducing the power of past traumas. No therapy can take place when sessions are used as a time for parents, or any one else, to berate children, or when therapists and other caring adults do not keep sessions safe. At the same time, therapists can respect the positive part of a parent or guardian's efforts to guide or protect children. Parents and guardians may benefit from help to get a break for themselves and to learn more effective ways to set limits and guide children that avoid repeating trauma behavior cycles, especially 'triggers' for the child or the adult. See four-step discipline in Chapter 4 overview and Siegel and Bryson (2014).
The caregiver routinely asks for special time to meet to address problems	Establish a structure in sessions (Mormile, 2005), with an opening for the first 15 minutes to talk with the parent alone, followed by the recommended Session Structure, and then reserving time at the end of the session for conjoint work to address any problems raised by the caregiver. Seeing needy or agitated caregivers first may be necessary to get their support.
Therapists feel anxious or uncomfortable with the use of trauma therapy protocols, creative arts, or life story work	Therapists can develop comfort in the use of trauma therapy protocols and creative arts modalities by practicing in consultation and with ongoing supervision in trauma and attachment therapy. Just as with children, it's helpful take a relaxed playful attitude and explore your own creativity. Taking yoga or dance lessons, movement exercises, art and music lessons can also be helpful as well as rewarding. Working on therapist well-being pays off in being able to be present and stay modulated with clients.
Children become distracted when soothing themselves in response to the sounds of other children or family members and resume threat-avoidant behaviors	Check on reminders and triggers for unresolved safety issues that may be present in the environment (e.g., a home, a residential program, or where the session is taking place). Look for a place where children can feel removed from reminders of threats. This may mean using a room at a church, synagogue, or school as part of home-based work or taking children outside a residential living area. Work with children to practice daily on building skills in concentrating and balance with fun activities (e.g., juggling Nerf balls or balancing peacock feathers, with the therapist or peers trying to distract children with progressively increasing sounds, words, calls, or movement).
Difficulty arranging a special space in home-based work	Establish the special nature and structure of sessions. This can be done, for instance, by laying out a special sheet or blanket on the floor, establishing where everyone will sit, using the glockenspiel to sound the beginning of the session, 'checking in' with thermometers, and then moving on with the Session Structure (Mormile, 2005).
Children refuse to do one part of a sequence (e.g., tapping a rhythm or a movement)	Therapists can encourage children to come up with preferred alternatives for mind-body integration. No aspect of this work should be forced. It is important, however, to find ways to help children remain feeling safe and emotionally regulated long enough with each workbook page in order to reduce the intensity of any traumatic memories. This may mean very little time for many pages but longer for others.

20.5 AFFECT RECOGNITION, EXPRESSION, AND MODULATION

Challenges	Strategies
Children show a limited range of responses on thermometers	Many children initially indicate on their thermometers a narrow band of responses (e.g., 3–4 in every situation), or, conversely, an all-or-nothing perspective (e.g., marking 1's or 10's for every situation). To help children develop a greater ability to sense their own feelings, ask them to tap a rhythm, to vary intensity, and add notes on the glockenspiel to show a low *Knots* rating, then the highest *Knots* possible, followed by a *Knots* level 'in between.' Similarly, ask children to tap out a rhythm, varying intensity, and add notes for low *Self-Control Power*, the highest possible *Self-Control Power*, and 'in between.' Children can also be invited to enact these feelings with a gesture, dance step, or safe athletic/ gymnastic move. Children can also be asked what would have to happen to lead them to feel just a tenth more or less then the level they have indicated on a thermometer.
Children have a limited range of feelings	Hang feelings charts showing children displaying a range of different feelings in the therapy room to foster a sense of acceptance and permission for children to try out different feelings and to associate visual images with words. It is helpful to practice identification of feelings with visual imagery, rhythm, tonality, facial looks, gestures, and words.
Children have difficulty developing the ability to recognize or express feelings	For many children, this may require practice, as recognition and especially expression of feelings have been severely constricted with traumas or perceived threats. Some children may need extended time to work on developing these skills and can come back to these pages as they continue to work on expanding resources and strengths.
Children need additional practice learning to identify feelings	Games (e.g., *Emotional Bingo* (Mitlin, 2008) and the *Story Game* (Black, 1984)) for older children and teens are useful to help children learn to identify feelings.
Children are action-oriented and reluctant to draw or write	Encouraging children to act out different emotions or guess different emotions that the therapist acts out may provide a more engaging and active way of exploring different emotions. For other children, it may be helpful to encourage movement or dance. The therapist could then be responsible for making notes or recording other salient elements during a session, while children remain free to use dance or other movements to illustrate feelings.
Children have difficulty managing multiple tasks	Limit children to what they can handle (e.g., one or two tasks at a time) and divide up tasks to make them more manageable during sessions. The therapist could be responsible for jotting down children's narrative responses.
Children have difficulty or dislike one or another modality (e.g., drawing)	Providing choices to children is important to foster means of moving beyond constraints associated with trauma. Accordingly, if children appear to be having trouble with one form of expression (e.g., drawing), it's fine to encourage the use of other modalities. Some children may be more comfortable acting out different emotional states, while others may be most comfortable sketching with charcoal or selecting colors from a color wheel or fabrics with different textures to express feelings. The goal is for children to build strengths with different expressive mediums, to have fun with activities they can enjoy, and to promote special talents in creative arts of interest to them. For disturbing memories, the goal is also to engage children long enough in safe activities that promote attunement so that their anxiety can be reduced before they move on to something else.
Children become tense or agitated when asked to share	Children's behavior often reflects unresolved fears involving a specific adult, and they should not be required to share with that person. Children may prefer to share with other significant parent-figures. They can also be encouraged to express their feelings, wishes, and concerns in a safer or more comfortable way through letters, tapes, or in conjoint or subsequent sessions. If sharing is unsafe for children in placement, they need to be given a sense of hope that authorities understand their predicament and will work to protect them from being forced to return to unsafe situations or a dangerous home.

AFFECT RECOGNITION, EXPRESSION, AND MODULATION—*continued*

Challenges	Strategies
Children refuse to draw and share feelings	If children are unwilling to draw or share in the first chapters, they may be experiencing current threats or believe, based on past experiences and messages (verbal or nonverbal), that they, or people they love, are unsafe. This is especially true if they are worried about identifying or sharing feelings. Careful assessments of a child and family's safety are essential, including the use of projective tests and play during individual evaluations to check for mandates or messages, often nonverbal, received by children to block expression. An attachment and trauma-centered psychological evaluation is essential to develop effective interventions and viable safety plans. Evaluations can uncover the caring and strengths of family members that can, in turn, lead to their involvement in strength-based trauma therapy which can increase chldren's 'window of tolerance.'.
Children have been threatened or appear intimidated	If children have been threatened, or appear intimidated, by a family member or another person, they can be reassured that disclosures in life story work will remain confidential within the limits of the law and ethical practice. Therapists need to acknowledge their responsibilities to bring in authorities if children were neglected or abused, or if someone is in danger of being harmed. Success in these situations often requires orders of protection, supervision of any contacts with perpetrators, and transfer of custody of children to someone who can be trusted to protect them from any threats with monitoring by authorities (e.g., child protective services) and reports to family court.
Children refuse to see the therapist or tell the therapist to leave in the home-based session ("I don't want to see you")	Children will often test a therapist's commitment before sharing painful memories such as traumatic events. Therapists have been successful in maintaining engagement by persisting over time ("I'll keep calling"). In many situations, therapists can continue working with parents and caring adults while persevering in asking reluctant children to resume sessions. The key to engaging such children often lies in reducing shame involving children's attributions of self-blame and fears of distressing parents they fear losing. Working to help parents and guardians understand how trauma works and their influence in helping children overcome fears can be useful to engage adults to lead the way for their children, to reassure children that parents and guardians will be OK, and to insist that children work on healing and recovery.

20.6 HEROES

Challenges	Strategies
Children appear hesitant, or too blocked, to describe someone they admire as a hero	Check to see if children are setting unrealistic expectations for perfection or whether they are sharing experiences of finding out 'heroes' in their lives had deceived them, increasing their distrust.
	Encourage children to draw a picture of a hero they would like to have or make up a hero's comic book featuring their own hero, mastering some challenge, or, if preferred, develop hero images with puppets, papier mâché, clay, etc.
	Enact stories or compose music, rap songs, or drum beats that inspire hope and courage.
	Develop a hero's game, including obstacles and resources that are similar to children's lives.
Action-oriented children cannot verbalize how 'heroes' could help in real life	Practice 'moves' of children's heroes from sports, theater, movies, etc. to help children see how this feels; then, explore, through fantasy and enactments, how these 'powers' could be used to handle different situations including solving problems, mastering fears and helping others.

HEROES—*continued*

Challenges	Strategies
Children do not identify heroic qualities in family or community	Write out traits children admire on cards and match these traits to a stack of cards identifying people from their lives, including family members, teachers, coaches, clergy, etc.
Children lack understanding of cultural strengths from their heritage	Check on who in the family or community could help children learn about their ethnic heritage. Visit historical sites commemorating 'heroes,' especially men and women from children's ethnic backgrounds. Bring in books and movies about heroes from children's ethnic backgrounds. Encourage listening to videos of positive role models from children's ethnic backgrounds.
Children lack recognition of people in the community helping others	Ask caring adults to take children to visit community organizations to see or interview people making a difference in the lives of people in their community. Go online and look up advocacy and service organizations that address areas of interest or concern for children (e.g., animal care, hunger, human rights, safety for women, child abuse, racism, etc.).
Children lack appreciation for how they can help others	Assist children or arrange mentoring to enhance their interests or skills in ways that can also be used to help others (e.g., teaching sports or music skills to younger children). Involve youths in activities that offer opportunities to help others (e.g., mentoring younger children, helping senior citizen centers, caring for animals in veterinary hospitals and shelters or farms).

20.7 CAREGIVERS AND OTHER IMPORTANT RELATIONSHIPS

Challenges	Strategies
Children lack memories of three caring adults	Think broadly over time and use fantasy exercises, check past records, and ask to look at photo albums and other family records. Identify past therapists, collateral support, and caring adults who could be involved to help children search for lost extended family, mentors, coaches, teachers, employers, and clergy. Utilize the *Attachment Ecogram* (included in the Trauma and Resiliency-Focused Assessment, Part V), the *Important People* survey (in Part V), family drawings, family figure play, and the *Roberts Apperception Test* (Roberts, 1986) to help identify past caregivers.
Caregivers appear reluctant or 'resistant' to help	Check for misunderstanding of purpose of life story work and offer to meet with prospective caring adults to share information on *Real Life Heroes®*, including workbook. Emphasize the importance of children understanding strengths in family. See also the guidelines for engaging family members and service providers from *Families in Perpetual Crisis* (Kagan & Schlosberg, 1989).
The therapist and children are unable to find three safe caring adults within the extended family	Promote safe, positive, and long-term connections with mentors, coaches, Big Brothers/Sisters, clergy, staff from outreach centers, volunteers from the organizations related to children's religion, social service organizations, foster families, etc.
Children lack understanding or appreciation of cultural strengths	Promote pride in the heritage of children's family, including race, ethnicity, and celebrations of culture, with visits to historical sites, exploring music, food, and readings, contacting community leaders, and visiting relatives with a strong positive cultural identity.

CAREGIVERS AND OTHER IMPORTANT RELATIONSHIPS—*continued*

Challenges	Strategies
Family members are not able or willing to help children	Provide help to children in grieving losses of adults who are not able or willing to care for them. Differentiate grief over lost love, commitment, and caring from children's loyalty to family members and respect for family members, especially elders, as part of children's culture and upbringing. Children can still respect a family member while at the same time grieving the loss of what they hoped for from that family member. Normalize grief reactions, seek validation from caring family members of appropriateness of grieving lost love and caring, develop grief rituals with family members, if possible, and help children to see how significant people in their families, in their cultures, and heroes from sports, arts, etc. have become stronger over time by facing hardships and developing strengths to persevere.
Parents and children remind each other of past traumas	Before involving family members and children together in sessions, it is important that intra-familial triggers to trauma reactions are identified and diffused, wherever possible. These include environments (e.g., a grandparent's home where abuse occurred), emotional feelings, and anniversary dates. Safety plans need to be developed and practiced for each family member who has upset children.
	This is especially important when parents and children remind each of other of people who hurt them in the past. This can include the parent's memories of traumas around the age of a same-sex child or victimization as a child by another child who looked like or was the same age as the parent's own child at the current time. A child may also remind a parent of a violent spouse, especially if the child is of the same sex or develops some of the same facial or behavioral responses.
	At the same time, non-offending parents may remind a child of past traumas that the parent did not prevent, and, of course, parents who have hurt a child in the past, emotionally, physically, or sexually, will trigger a child's traumatic responses. In each case, a look, a gesture, or an intonation may be enough to trigger a traumatic response. Recognition of how reactions are natural and practice reinforcing safety plans can help reduce distress.
Parents or guardians provide material support but appear unable to validate children's experiences or talk about 'family business'	Adults who are committed to providing physical or financial support but cannot validate children may be willing to help by providing materials for sessions (e.g., photo albums, birth certificates, immigration documents, special markers, or colored pencils). Encourage parents and guardians to share positive stories of strength as a way of teaching values and important life skills. Simply giving permission out loud for children to go and work with a therapist on life story materials represents a positive message. When possible, these adults can be encouraged to work on overcoming obstacles in therapy. If possible, bring in supportive family elders or clergy who would support parents and guardians validating children's experiences.
	Seek to identify and bring in other safe adults who will provide emotional support, help children recognize strengths in their families, and become safe enough to share and reintegrate experiences of traumatic stress.
Children and parent/guardian are too uncomfortable to work together	If a parent/guardian or children are too uncomfortable to work together on sharing their experiences, it may be helpful to bring in a trusted relative or a friend who can provide emotional support and increase safety. The caring adult may make it possible for children and a parent to feel safer together.
Family members and caring adults are living at distant locations	Arrange telephone calls or videoconferences.
Positive memories lead repeatedly to loops of negative memories and increasing distress	Check on feelings of shame or self-denigration. If so, help children develop stronger self-esteem (e.g., by helping others and saving traumatic memories to be addressed in Chapter 10). Help children learn to use self-soothing skills, 'SOS for Stress', and 'thought-shifting' (see Chapter 8). Practice watching for signs of stress, scanning

CAREGIVERS AND OTHER IMPORTANT RELATIONSHIPS—*continued*

Challenges	Strategies
	from the tips of toes to the top of children's heads, then utilizing children's favorite self-soothing activities and 'SOS.' Encourage children to accept positive memories and positive strengths and to grow these stronger than the 'tough times' with repeated practice.
Children's favorite activities are immature for their age, causing discomfort for caring adults or other service providers	Help caring adults to recognize how traumas impair development and how children can be helped to grow developmentally by developing skills and positive beliefs and by overcoming fears associated with traumas in a progressive developmental process. This means developing skills and reintegrating at each stage of development, often beginning with the stage of development when traumas began to overwhelm the child or caregivers.

20.8 MIND POWER

Challenges	Strategies
Children are not able to sufficiently manage affective responses in order to think about difficult situations without becoming dysregulated	Continue work on developing affect management skills until children can work on materials and stay below a '3' on the stress scale and over '7–8' in *Self-Control Power* in sessions. Utilize activities amenable to children, including: breathing exercises with imagery individualized for children; deep muscle relaxation with changes in environment, including lighting, scents, and background music; refocusing on comforting stimuli identified in every setting; use of 'time-out' spaces in different situations that children can utilize; developing and practicing 'Safe Place' imagery, including sounds, smells, and scenes; practicing songs as meditation; developing sequencing and tonal range with simple musical instruments; and trying out gestures and developing these into movements and simple action movements or dances. Review the guidelines in Chapters 1–4 for building affect management skills.
Children need extra help to develop self-control abilities	Arrange mentoring in areas of interest or enroll children in programs that foster self-control and confidence, such as karate, dance, music, 'Project Adventure' programs, and theater arts.
Children appear too frightened to reintegrate past traumas without severe distress, even after completing Chapter 7	Enhance or create comforting objects associated with protective and caring adults (e.g., photos, jewelry, special stones, tiny flashlights, perfume, soft fuzzy stuffed animals, etc.). Add comforting music to meditation and imagery skills and help children practice bringing up soothing tones by memory to counter stress. Check for other potentially positive and supportive relationships that could encourage children. Check on unknown threats and the need for developing, implementing, and practicing additional safety plans.

20.9 CHANGING THE STORY: CHANGING BELIEFS AND ACTION CYCLES TO ACHIEVE GOALS

Challenges	Strategies
Children appear frightened and lack support from caregivers	Anxious or avoidant children may be responding to fears they experienced in the past or present from guardians or other adults. It is important to check safety plans for children's homes, schools, and communities. Caring adults can foster courage in children and provide more authentic validation after they have developed their own understanding of what happened in their lives and strengthened their own coping skills. Completing a *Caregiver Power Plan* can be helpful to encourage caregivers to reflect on factors leading to children's behaviors, their own reaction patterns, and how they can use an understanding of trauma and resiliency to develop more effective ways to reassure children and strengthen children's security in relationships.
Children lack a sense of past, present, or future	Reading and discussing books such as Dr. Seuss' *Oh the Places You Will Go* and *My Many Colored Days* is helpful to normalize experiences of good times and bad times.
Children continue hyper-vigilant behaviors	Highlight differences in children's worlds by encouraging them to dramatize, draw, or write out messages and actions by important adults 'before' compared to the present time (Sutton, 2003).
Children blame themselves for parent or guardian's failures, neglect, abuse, drug use, or violence	Often, traumatized children blame themselves for violence or accidents. Blaming themselves provides a sense of control but at the cost of shame and self-denigration. Therapists should watch for negative attributions (e.g., children blaming themselves for a fight between mom and dad). It helps to point out that this is a belief that children developed, very likely, in the middle of a 'tough time,' for instance the parents' fight. A belief may be right or wrong. Would they blame another child for a similar fight? Did they really have the power, at the age they were, to make dad hit mom or mom stab dad?
Children bring up specific problems leading to distress	Play out possibilities to solve problems children bring up with puppets, family dolls, or through role plays utilizing understanding and skills from Chapter 8.
Children demonstrate anger control problems	Utilize activities from *A Volcano in My Tummy* (Whitehouse & Pudney, 1996). Draw what makes children feel angry, how their anger would look, and what force would be strong enough to calm their anger. For anger problems, help children draw or play out how their anger affects others and what happens afterwards (consequences). Help children learn to recognize the first signs of rising anger and then practice implementing self-soothing and redirecting steps in sessions, and later in their homes, schools, and communities.
Children need more practice to understand the linkage between thoughts, feelings, and behaviors	Use cognitive behavioral therapy games outlined in Appendix G of *Rebuilding Attachments with Traumatized Children* (Kagan, 2004), and see SPARCS (DeRosa et al., 2008) and TARGET materials (Ford & Russo, 2006) (www.ptsdfreedom.org).
Therapists or caring adults do not feel strong enough to move ahead through 'tough times'	Self-care and support is essential for caring adults and therapists, just as for children. Just as airlines tell adults to 'put on their oxygen masks first,' caring adults can best help children by developing their own skills for self-soothing, developing supportive relationships, and reintegrating traumatic memories in their own work with therapists. Enourage caregivers to complete their own *Life Storybooks* and *Caregiver Power Plans* with support from friends and family.

20.10 TIMELINES AND MOVES: ORGANIZING A LIFE CHRONOLOGY

Challenges	Strategies
Past events trigger trauma reactions	Use of Centering Activities and *Power Plans* can help children modulate.
	Triggers can be utilized as valuable clues for identifying needed safety plans and beginning work on overcoming painful memories that impair attachments. With this perspective, signs of avoidance or emotional reactions can be welcomed. Self-soothing activities are helpful along with reinforcement of how children are in different positions now and accentuating safety factors that have been put in place and were missing before (e.g., a new home, a parent aware of the danger, other caring adults watching over children, alarm systems, a guard dog, etc.).
Parents and guardians do not validate their own responsibility for children's losses, moves, or painful events	Parents may have difficulty validating their responsibility for children's losses and moves (e.g., a parent's drinking leading to foster care placement). It may be possible to engage parents to attune to children's feelings by harmonizing on the glockenspiel with children's notes for each loss or move, or by drawing and sharing their own picture, 'blues' chord, or movement to represent the traumatic experience. The parent's drawing, chord, or movement may then provide an 'opening' to foster shared grief, recognizing how the child and the parent/guardian have experienced losses and other painful events.
Children are too uncomfortable to share certain events	Utilize 'blocks' and areas of discomfort shown by children to guide later work (e.g., in Chapter 10) after children have developed greater security and trust with the therapist and caring adults. Once children learn to trust a therapist, mini-dramas can be enacted (after Hughes, 1998; Becker-Weidman, 2002) in which children are invited to ask the therapist, acting as a previous parent-figure, the questions they have never been able to ask (e.g., "Why did a previous foster parent send me away and keep my sister?").
Children are not aware why they moved	Therapists should check with other family members, authorities, and records on what is known, then work to make it safe enough for children to learn what happened.
The parent misrepresents what happened	A parent or guardian may describe what happened in a false manner to cover shame or painful events he or she cannot face honestly. For instance, a father may say that he was repeatedly 'sick' during different years of his life, when he was in fact living on the streets using drugs, incarcerated for a crime, or in a series of drug programs.
	If an adult misrepresents the truth, therapists can ask to talk to the adult privately and point out how facing the truth is an essential part of trauma recovery. And, adults can help children grow stronger by modeling how even painful events can be faced.
	Often, children know when family members are distorting the truth. It is important that children see that therapists can "say the words" (Kagan & Schlosberg, 1989) and handle the truth. Otherwise, children will learn that the therapist, like other family members, cannot deal with what really happened, and thus cannot be counted on to help children and caring adults overcome past traumas.

20.11 TRAUMA REINTEGRATION

Challenges	Strategies
Children hesitate, pull back, look away, or appear to resist sharing the first 'tough time'	The therapist's confidence is crucial in demonstrating that children can become stronger than tough times and that the therapist will guide children, step by step, and that safe caregivers will be available to support children. Check on ways to increase supportive resources for children (e.g., bringing in a comforting dog).
Children believe they are alone or their experiences were never shared by others	Encourage children to read books that normalize specific experiences. See Heroes Library (in Part IV). Consider these references based on Cohen et al. (2003): • Sexual abuse: *Please Tell* (Jessie, 1991) • Parental separation due to child abuse, parental substance abuse, or hospitalization: *All Kinds of Separation* (Cunningham, 1992) • Crime: *All My Dreams, It's My Life* (Alexander, 1993a, 1993c) • Homicide: *It Happened in Autumn* (Alexander, 1993b) • Traumatic death: *When I Remember* (Alexander, 1993d)
Children enact or express beliefs that they are bad, weak, damaged, or evil because of what they did or what happened	Address expectations based on the developmental age of children when traumas occurred. For instance, if a 5-year-old experienced domestic violence, including knife threats to her mother, and the child then adopted beliefs that she needed to always guard and protect her mother and blamed herself for failing to protect her mother, ask the child, for example, "What can a 5-year-old do when a man is holding a knife? Was the 5-year-old really responsible for what a woman did?" Also address children's attributions and accentuate examples of how children have grown physically, mentally, and also expanded their ties to other positive children. Reinforce how different children and their lives are now compared to the time that the traumatic events took place. Bring in positive caring adults, or messages from powerful adults (e.g., clergy, extended family members) who will challenge dysfunctional beliefs and attributions.
Children do not see caregivers as strong enough to ward off fears of renewed traumas	Encourage caring adults to demonstrate how they have grown and have made their lives different. Practicing implementing safety plans may be helpful. Help caring adults to watch for nonverbal signals from the children that they are not yet safe. Bring in additional supportive individuals who children trust.
Children perceive adults as not allowing memories of how adults have failed as well as succeeded, or how adults have abused, neglected, or abandoned, as well as helped, others	Bridging gaps that have formed between caring adults and children requires acknowledgement, and over time acceptance of both positive and negative memories, including feelings associated with parents who both cared for and may at times have hurt children, directly or indirectly. Healing from trauma requires acceptance of what happened, the good and the bad. To do this, children need to have a secure position and support from significant adults to share how significant adults in their lives may have been both caring and abusive at different times. It is very important that children experience that caring adults accept that children may carry conflicting feelings and beliefs about that caregiver or a previous caregiver (e.g., both love and terror, or adoration and rage). This is especially important when children have lived with emotional abuse and developed chaotic, disorganized attachments.
Children present as more anxious than expected	Review the Resource Checklist (in Part V) and check for missing resources, safety plans that are not in place or sufficient, any threats regarding disclosure, or changes that have decreased children's capacities to cope with stressors. Repeat *My Thermometers* to check on children's feelings if he or she was alone with key people in his or her home, extended family, or other important environments.
Children balk at sharing 'tough times'	Cohen et al. (2003) provide detailed guidelines for helping children tell the story of specific traumas. This begins with explaining to children and their guardians how writing a book about the trauma is like cleaning out a cut. It hurts at first, but each time you work on it the pain goes down. And, cleaning out the cut reduces the pain of what happened. The therapist will help children to make sure that they only feel a little pain at any time.

TRAUMA REINTEGRATION—*continued*

Challenges	Strategies
	And, like all stories, the story of what happens has a beginning, a middle, and an end. Children can choose what page of their story to talk about first.
	In this model, children are asked to describe what they remembers happening without interruption. The therapist may write or type children's stories to help children.
	Afterwards, the therapist can ask questions to add details to the story, including questions about what children were thinking and feeling at different points in the story. In the *Real Life Heroes®* format, this can be enhanced by asking children to sketch pictures of their feelings, tap rhythms, and make up chords, movement, and enactments to nonverbally express how they feel.
	Having children read aloud what they have written helps desensitize them and can be used to promote validation and support. After several repetitions, children's emotional distress should go down. The use of relaxation techniques is important in this process.
	After children have added thoughts and feelings to the story (Cohen et al., 2003), ask them to share the 'worst moment.'
	Reinforce children at the end of each session for work done (e.g., with food, praise, and a positive activity).
Children continue to balk at sharing a narrative of 'toughest times' in any modality	Recheck for safety concerns. Children may need court orders not yet in place, resolution of family or criminal court proceedings, return to a now safe home, or placement into a potential adoptive home before trauma processing can occur. See Cohen et al. (2006) and Kolko and Swenson (2002) for other practice recommendations.
Children will not work on 'Five-Chapter' Stories, or continue to become anxious or have trauma reactions to reminders of previous traumas after completing Chapter 10	Utilize additional therapies that incorporate nonverbal trauma processing (e.g., Progressive Counting (Greenwald, 2013) or EMDR adapted for children (Greenwald, 1999; Shapiro, 2001)).
Children share experiences with the therapist but appear too anxious to share experiences directly with caregivers	If children want to express experiences to a caregiver but are too frightened to do this directly, consider non-direct means of sharing. For example, invite children to make a phone call to the therapist's answering machine or tape recorder in which they are invited to talk into the telephone and answer questions from the therapist about more sensitive issues (Purdy, 2003). Children can then listen to the tape and it can be transcribed and shared with people they trust.
Parents, relatives, or other caring adults block expression of 'tough times'	Adults may be coping in their own lives with denial and avoidance and see this as essential for getting by. Or, adults may believe that sharing pain in any way leads to weakness or moral failure. Optimally, caring adults can be reminded of the psycho-education materials presented earlier, stressing how trauma impacts children (and adults). It is often helpful to utilize descriptions and research from studies of soldiers and survivors of natural disasters, as well as family violence. References for adults on the impact of trauma may be helpful; see, for example, *Wounded Angels: Inspiration from Children in Crisis* (Kagan, 2016b). In many cases, it is important to help adults reassess their own fears and goals, and to re-contract to help children become heroes rather than remain stuck reliving traumas without permission to change or too overburdened with fears of upsetting others to risk changing.
Children, or parents, insist that no one talk about 'family business'	Leaving a story untold can be compared to leaving a cut uncleaned and untreated (Cohen et al., 2003). The result is often a chronic infection. Healing cannot occur in this context, and the child and parent's goals for the child cannot be achieved. Children remain living as if traumas are present when caregivers could help them learn to 'move through' these memories to better times when they can feel safe in relationships.

TRAUMA REINTEGRATION—*continued*

Challenges	Strategies
	For many families, an emphasis on building on strengths and caring, when present, can help engage reluctant parents. In other families, neglect may be dominant and court orders will be needed for real change, protection, and healthy development of children.
Additional safety plans, skills, or supportive resources are needed	One of the advantages of following a structured protocol is that assigned activities will bring out unresolved issues that continue to trouble children but were not known by caregivers or service providers. Therapists can welcome children's hesitation, or resistance, and use children's behaviors as clues to what can help increase children's security and strength (*Self-Control Power*) to a level that would allow children to move forward. This may mean developing greater self-soothing skills, but, more likely, dysfunctional beliefs or lingering threats will need to be addressed.
	Often, children may be able to move forward when safe, caring adults are engaged to join sessions. With an arm behind children, and reassurance, children may be able to move forward. Starting with rhythm, tonality, and drawing often helps. In other cases, role plays dramatizing how caring adults will protect children from past perpetrators (see Hughes, 1997) are very helpful.

20.12 BUILDING A FUTURE

Challenges	Strategies
Children have trouble visualizing a future	Encourage children to visualize life as a book or movie, moving from year to year, and highlighting key goals and relationships (see Greenwald, 1999). Remind children how many successful books or movies (e.g., *Harry Potter* or *Spider-Man*) have sequels, and many become better than the first books or movies in the series.
Caregivers treat children as fragile or requiring special treatment with 'kid gloves' forever	Children need to see that parents and other caring adults believe they are 'normal' and can be strong. Children watch for these beliefs in the way they are treated by caring adults. Reinforce how children have grown and have opportunities to continue to grow stronger and stronger.
	Help caregivers let go of any habitual patterns of interaction or reinforcement of children remaining as, sick, damaged, or bad.

20.13 CREATING AN INTEGRATED LIFE STORY

Challenges	Strategies
Children fear that completion of the workbook will mean an end to work with the therapist or other caring adults	When therapeutic relationships must end, it is important to respect the loss this entails and children's fears of losing important people. Completing the book should be viewed as another marking growth in children's lives, rather than an end point. It's important to accentuate who will be continuing to help children as they mature (i.e., committed caregivers and other caring adults).
Children believe the therapist wants to be done with them, leaving them behind	Work with children to strengthen relationships with caregivers, ideally three emotionally supportive adults. The therapist's role as a guide and mentor can be highlighted along with how the therapist will keep the memory of children's accomplishments alive through pictures or a copy of the storybook. Therapists can point out what they have learned from work with children and, if appropriate, invite children to send letters about special events in their lives to the therapist's agency or professional office.
The guardian or funding source requests termination of therapy before completion of the workbook because children have 'stabilized'	Counties and states, grappling with budget deficits, frequently require family and mental health services to terminate as soon as overt dangerous behaviors subside. It is important to advocate for the time and sessions necessary for trauma processing and reintegration. Stopping trauma therapy at the point of behavioral 'stabilization' leaves children and families at high risk of renewed and escalating symptoms, as well as the prospect of much more costly placements or hospitalizations and increasing children's distrust of all service providers capacity or willingness to continue treatment and supportive services as long as necessary.
The parent or guardian becomes too busy for children to finish the *Life Storybook* (e.g., after taking on a new job)	For important and valid reasons, parents and guardians may make changes in their own lives that interfere with therapy (e.g., taking on a new job with greater hours for higher pay or career advancement). It is often helpful to seek the parent or guardian's permission to continue work with children. This way, children and families can complete the process. Parents or guardians may still be able to participate in limited sharing sessions, or by phoning or videoconferencing and thus help children complete work on re-integration. Parents or guardians can also arrange for other safe and emotionally supportive family members or other caring adults to participate in sessions that the parent or guardian cannot attend.

NOTE

1. Adapted from Foster-Green (2014).

Part V

Toolkit

Section A

Model Summaries

21

Model Summaries for Practitioners and Caregivers

Resiliency-Focused Treatment for Children and Families with Traumatic Stress

Real Life Heroes® (RLH) provides practitioners with easy-to-use tools, including a *Life Storybook*, manual, multi-sensory creative arts activities, and psycho-education resources to engage children and caregivers in evidence-supported trauma treatment. Tools and procedures were developed and tested with latency-age[1] children in a wide range of child and family service programs, including children with Complex PTSD who lacked stable relationships with caregivers they could count on to provide a safe home and work with them in therapy, and children referred for high-risk behaviors that threatened the safety of children, families, organizations, and communities. RLH helps practitioners reframe referrals based on pathologies and blame into a shared 'journey,' a 'pathway' to healing and recovery focused on restoring (or building) emotionally supportive and enduring relationships and promoting development of affect regulation skills for children and caregivers. To do this, the model utilizes the metaphor of the 'hero's journey' and stresses the importance of engaging caregivers and a collaborative team of caring adults working together with an integrated trauma and resiliency-centered framework to help children with Complex Trauma. Creative arts and shared life story work provide a means for children and caregivers to develop the safety and attunement needed for reintegration of traumatic memories, coupled with development of increased security and affect regulation.

Real Life Heroes® focuses on four primary components for strengthening resiliency skills and resources: *Relationships*, *Emotional Regulation*, *Action Cycles*, and *Life Story Integration*. These components frame developmentally based assessments, service planning, session structure, fidelity, and evaluation measures. Learning about heroes includes sharing stories of how family members and people with the child's ethnic heritage have overcome hard times and encouraged children to develop their own strengths, resources, and coping skills, building on strengths in their

> **Engages Hard-to-Reach Children Adaptable for Diverse Families & Programs**

family and cultural heritage. In each session, children learn to recognize clues in their own bodies and how to share these safely. Sessions include sharing feelings nonverbally on thermometers for stress, self-control, and feeling mad, sad, glad, and safe. Magic and centering activities utilize movement, sensorimotor integration, focusing, and mindfulness activities to engage children and caregivers to learn and practice skills and to reduce stress. An activity-based workbook helps to engage children and promote the safety needed in sessions for children to work with practitioners and caregivers to build the skills and interpersonal resources needed to reintegrate painful memories and to foster healing after serial traumatic experiences. The workbook helps children share experiences and develop affect modulation skills with art, rhythm, music, movement, and theater arts. Practitioners help children (and caregivers) transform their drawings into 'Three-Chapter' or 'Five-Chapter' Stories (or movies) with a beginning, middle, and end so children learn they can 'move through' 'tough times' and make things better in their lives with the help of emotionally supportive caregivers, instead of feeling helpless, stuck, ashamed, or overwhelmed.

Chapter by chapter, practitioners help children and caregivers strengthen skills and resources to reduce the power

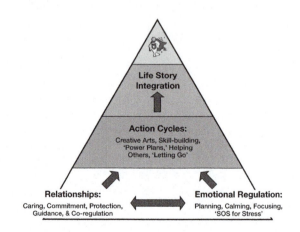

of multiple and serial traumas that have afflicted their past, impaired attachments, and shaped high-risk behaviors. Shared activities help children and caregivers grow stronger than their fears and to change old ways of coping that got them into more trouble. The workbook helps children change how they see themselves, from feeling hurt, unwanted, damaged, or hopeless, to experiences of attunement and security with emotionally supportive adults committed to helping children and preventing re-traumatization.

Real Life Heroes® incorporates the 'Core Components in Evidence-Based Trauma Treatment' and the 'Essential Elements of Trauma-Informed Child Welfare' developed by the National Child Traumatic Stress Center (NCTSN). Chapters in the *Life Storybook* match the phase-based components outlined by the NCTSN Complex Trauma Workgroup (Cook et al., 2003) and recommended practice guidelines (Ford & Cloitre, 2009) for treatment of Complex PTSD in children. Core components include strategies and step-by-step procedures and worksheets

outlined in the *RLH Toolkit* and training curricula to ensure: (1) psychological, physical, and emotional safety for children and their families; (2) strength and relationship-focused assessments and service planning; (3) self- and co-regulation development in all phases of treatment for children and caregivers; (4) trauma memory reintegration matched to the child and caregiver's capacity incorporating components from TF-CBT (Cohen et al., 2006), EMDR (Shapiro, 2001), and Progressive Counting (Greenwald, 2008); and (5) prevention and management of disruptions of primary relationships and crises, including trauma reactions using *Youth and Caregiver Power Plans*. Interventions and activities are prioritized based on children's levels of self-regulation and the strength and availability of emotionally supportive relationships.

> • **Practitioner-Developed** • **Research-Tested** • **Supervisor-Endorsed** •

CHAPTER BY CHAPTER, STRONGER AND STRONGER

Chapter 1: The Hero's Challenge: Trauma and Resilience Psycho-Education and Initial Safety Plans	• Children and caregivers read about how stress can build up inside our brains and our bodies to the point that we feel out of control. • Workbook pages show children how they can build *Self-Control Power* and relationships to help them grow stronger and reduce traumatic stress.
Chapter 2: A Little about Me: Recognizing and Expressing Feelings	• Children and caregivers begin to use workbook pages to develop stories with feelings expressed through rhythm, music, and movement. • Chapter pages encourage children to develop skills and safety to recognize a range of feelings, express feelings appropriately, and change how they feel so they can remain safe.
Chapter 3: Heroes: Restoring Hope, Inspiring Change	• Children and caregivers identify heroes they see in media, popular culture, politics, their cultural heritage, and their families, and learn what helps their heroes succeed, including how heroes get help and help others. • Workbook pages encourage children and caregivers to share stories of overcoming 'tough times' by family members and highlight the importance of caregivers for helping children learn essential skills and developing courage.
Chapter 4: Power Plans: Resilience- Centered Safety Plans for Children and Caregivers	• Children and caregivers build on their awareness of how heroes use skills to look at what has helped them, tough times in their lives, typical reactions to stress, and how they could use skills and support from caregivers and other caring adults to make things better. • Children develop *Youth Power Plans*, strength-based worksheets that focus on helping children share what helps them cope, what doesn't help, and developing a shared safety plan with caring adults to prevent or reduce traumatic stress reactions. • Caregivers are also encouraged to develop *Caregiver Power Plans* that identify their children's triggers, reactions, and interventions, which can prevent or reduce traumatic stress reactions. • *Power Plans* are condensed into *Pocket Power Cards* children can carry with them.
Chapter 5: My Family: Remembering People Who Cared	• Children and caregivers work together as detectives to learn about who helped children in the past and to record memories of caring. • Children's skills and talents are linked with achievements of parents, grandparents, other relatives, and stories of overcoming that are part of children's cultural heritage.

CHAPTER BY CHAPTER, STRONGER AND STRONGER—*continued*

Chapter 6: **Important People:** **Promoting Emotionally** **Supportive Relationships**	• Children and caregivers explore a broad range of people in their lives and identify mentors, protectors, and emotionally supportive relationships. • Memories of support are strengthened to expand children's sense of security and confidence.
Chapter 7: **Mind Power: Making** **Things Better with** **Mindfulness and Self-** **Regulation**	• Children and caregivers develop resources within themselves and with the help of supportive adults to calm down through slow breathing, reminders of caring, comforting images, mindfulness, and movement. • Activities strengthen skills for self-regulation by developing children's ability to become aware of signals in their bodies, how feelings and thoughts can come and go, how they can redirect attention, and how they can open up possibilities for making things better. • Children and caregivers develop skills that help them accept fears and negative thoughts as passing 'waves', elicit positive images of feeling cared for, and try out new behaviors to solve problems. • Children increase development of skills to manage situations that can often trigger traumatic stress reactions, including how to stay safe in relationships, develop positive friendships, and learn from teachers, coaches, clergy, and other safe and supportive adults.
Chapter 8: **Changing the Story:** **Changing Beliefs and** **Action Cycles to Achieve** **Goals**	• Worksheet questions help children and caregivers recognize how stress works in the body and mind, and how changing beliefs about themselves can help children achieve their goals and make things better for themselves and their families. • Children are invited to become the directors of their own 'life' movies as a way to engage them to take control of what happens when they are triggered with reminders that have, in the past, led to problem behaviors. • Activities include breaking apart what happens leading to distress and getting into trouble, and how children can become 'Thought-Shifters to Succeed.' • Working on this chapter with supportive caregivers helps children feel safe enough to share how they felt and acted in the past and how they can feel safe again with caring adults committed to protecting and guiding them to maturity.
Chapter 9: Timelines and **Moves: Making Sense of** **the Past**	• A roadmap and timeline help children and caregivers remember important people and places from the past and to organize what happened in their lives by the years of their lives, from birth to the present time. • Chapter pages encourage children to share how they remember places where they lived, the people who cared for them, how they felt in each place, and how they understand what led to them moving to a new home now that they are older (and wiser). • Chapter 9 helps caregivers and practitioners understand the children's experiences (feelings and beliefs) and develop a list of traumatic events in chronological order to help them reintegrate traumatic experiences with a renewed sense of safety.
Chapter 10: Through the **Tough Times: Trauma** **Experiences Integration**	• Workbook pages help children and emotionally supportive caregivers to safely share what they experienced, what was most difficult, and what they learned can make things better. • Movies and 'Five-Chapter' Stories help children share traumatic experiences stressing how they and supportive adults have developed skills and supports so they can escape feeling trapped in recurrent traumatic experiences. • Activities encourage use of evidence-supported desensitization techniques to help children share undisclosed details and 'move through' traumatic memories to places and times where they felt safe and cared for. • Children and caregivers are encouraged to share experiences of loss and also shame for what they feel they have done wrong and to find ways to make amends for hurting other people. • Before completing Chapter 10, practitioners and caregivers help children practice 'moving through' their worst memories so that reminders of what happened and other hard times will not lead to traumatic stress reactions.

CHAPTER BY CHAPTER, STRONGER AND STRONGER—*continued*

Chapter 11: Into the Future: Identifying Goals and Important Relationships	• Workbook pages encourage children to broaden their sense of time by sharing how they see themselves developing skills and relationships through adolescence and into adulthood. • Activities encourage children to share who they would see as important in their lives and provide opportunities for practitioners and caregivers to build or strengthen positive, supportive relationships with family members, mentors, and other supportive adults.
Chapter 12: 'My Story': Creating an Integrated Life Story with a Past, Present, and Future	• 'My Story' provides an opportunity for children to integrate what they have learned into a life story of overcoming shared in words with photos, drawings, or video. • Children are invited to share what they have learned in a letter to other children who experienced similar 'tough times' as they did, building their sense of themselves as a hero, helping others. • Children are then urged to rip off the *Real Life Heroes®* cover page and substitute their own book cover and dedication to make this book truly their own.

Real Life Heroes® is listed in the National Registry of Evidence-Based Programs and Practices by the Substance Abuse Mental Health Services Administration (SAMHSA), the SAMHSA National Center for Trauma-Informed Care "Models for Developing Trauma-Informed Behavioral Health Systems and Trauma-Specific Services," and as one of the National Child Traumatic Stress Network's (NCTSN) Empirically Supported Treatments and Promising Practices. RLH is also listed as 'high' in Child Welfare System Relevance by the California Evidence-Based Clearinghouse for Child Welfare. The model has been successfully pilot-tested in home-based and placement child welfare services (Kagan et al., 2008) and utilized in a wide range of child and family service agencies in the United States and Canada. The *HEROES Project*, a SAMHSA-funded community practice site of the NCTSN, evaluated use of *Real Life Heroes®* in seven child and family service and behavioral health programs and found significant reductions in traumatic stress and behavioral problems on standardized measures; children receiving RLH did not have placements or psychiatric hospitalizations (Kagan et al., 2014b).

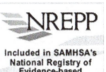

Included in SAMHSA's National Registry of Evidence-based Programs and Practices

For more information on *Real Life Heroes®* research, training programs, and consultation, see www.reallifeheroes.net or email richardkagan7@gmail.com. To obtain *Real Life Heroes: A Life Storybook (3rd edition)*, the *Real Life Heroes Toolkit for Treating Traumatic Stress in Children and Families (2nd edition)*, *Wounded Angels: Inspiration from Children in Crisis (2nd Edition)*, and, *Rebuilding Attachments with Traumatized Children*, see www.amazon.com, www.bn.com, or www.routledgementalhealth.com. Discounts for large purchases are available from Routledge Press.

NOTE

1. Tools and activities are designed for use with children ages 6–12 and have also been adapted and used successfully with adolescents with Complex PTSD functioning at a latency level of social, emotional, or cognitive development.

CAREGIVERS' INTRODUCTION TO TRAUMATIC STRESS AND REAL LIFE HEROES

What Is Traumatic Stress?

Children (and adults) can develop symptoms of traumatic stress when they experience events that threaten severe harm or death to children or someone they love and when a child or adult lacks the ability and supportive relationships to manage these threats. Experiences of natural disasters, deaths, severe illnesses, violence in children's homes or neighborhoods, physical, sexual, or emotional abuse, and neglect can all lead to traumatic stress reactions.

When children feel their lives and the lives of those they love are no longer safe, they may develop long-lasting changes in how they think, feel, or respond with their bodies. Children's heart rates may increase and they may begin to sweat, become agitated, feel tense, feel aches or pains or 'butterflies in their stomachs,' and become hyper-alert. After a traumatic event, children may watch and listen vigilantly for signs that scary or dangerous things could happen again. Children may become emotionally upset with little warning and for reasons that are not noticed by other children or adults. They may also react by withdrawing, isolating, running away, getting into fights, or angrily lashing out at other children or adults.

Traumatic stress reactions are often very distressing, but, in fact, these reactions are also very normal. These are ways our bodies protect us and prepare us to survive dangers. However, children who have experienced traumatic events may develop longer-lasting reactions that interfere with their physical and emotional health, especially if they have experienced multiple traumas that were unpredictable or disrupted children's relationships and security with caregivers. Children cannot learn or develop important social skills when they are always on the lookout for danger and when their bodies are ready to react quickly to any perception of risk for themselves, family members, or other people they love. Attention and memory problems are common reactions along with difficulty making plans or solving problems. Children with traumatic stress may fall behind in school and lack the ability to manage common requests by caregivers, teachers, or others in the community, leading to increased conflicts. Symptoms often include intense and ongoing emotional upset and agitation, chronic anxiety, behavioral changes, difficulties maintaining attention, school problems, nightmares, physical symptoms such as difficulty sleeping and eating, or symptoms of depression.

Traumatic stress may appear in different ways with different children. Reactions are often related to children's age, ability to understand, ability to cope, and feelings of security in their relationships with caregivers at the time that traumatic events occurred. One child in a family may react much more strongly than another child, often depending on his or her ability to cope and the support he

or she experiences during and after traumatic events. The good news is that treatments have been developed that can help children and their families who are suffering from traumatic stress.

What Is *Real Life Heroes*®?

Real Life Heroes® uses a workbook and creative arts activities to help children and caregivers rebuild safety, caring, and resilience after experiences of traumatic stress. Workbook activities help children build the skills and security needed to foster healing, recovery, and the strength to overcome hardships. Children learn about what makes a hero, including learning skills to solve problems, getting help, and helping others. Learning about heroes includes learning about strengths and stories of how family members and people with the child's ethnic heritage have experienced and overcome hard times. Then, with these stories of caring and overcoming, children are encouraged to develop their own skills to succeed with help from caregivers.

In each session, children learn to recognize clues in their own bodies and how to share these safely with practitioners and caregivers. Sessions include sharing feelings on thermometers for stress, self-control, and feeling mad, sad, glad, and safe. Magic and calming activities engage children to learn and practice skills. Workbook pages help children share experiences and develop coping skills with rhythm, music, and movement. Therapists help children take their drawings and make them into short stories with a beginning, middle, and end so that children learn they can 'move through' both good times and later hard times, and make things better in their lives instead of feeling trapped. Every session helps children: (1) build stronger relationships; (2) develop greater abilities to understand and manage feelings; (3) find and practice ways to cope with problems; and (4) overcome feelings of shame or distress and feel good about themselves.

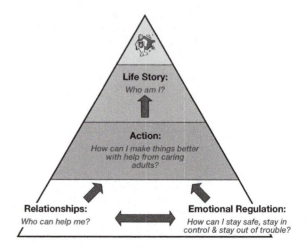

Chapter by chapter, children work with caregivers and therapists to change cycles of behaviors that led to problems. Step-by-step activities help children grow stronger than their fears and to change old ways of coping that got them into more trouble. The workbook helps children change how they see themselves, from feeling hurt, unwanted, unlikeable, damaged, or hopeless, to feeling that they can work through the traumas of the past to experiences of safety with caring adults committed to helping them grow and develop into adulthood.

What's Inside Each Chapter?

Chapter 1: The Hero's Challenge: Trauma and Resilience Psycho-Education and Initial Safety Plans

- Children and caregivers read about how stress can build up inside our brains and our bodies to the point that we feel out of control.
- Workbook pages show children how they can build *Self-Control Power* and relationships to help them grow stronger and reduce traumatic stress.

Chapter 2: A Little about Me: Recognizing and Expressing Feelings

- Children and caregivers begin to use workbook pages to develop stories with feelings expressed through rhythm, music, and movement.
- Chapter pages encourage children to develop skills and safety to recognize a range of feelings, express feelings appropriately, and change how they feel so they can remain safe.

Chapter 3: Heroes: Restoring Hope, Inspiring Change

- Children identify heroes they see in media, popular culture, politics, their cultural heritage, and their family and learn what helps their heroes succeed, including how heroes get help and help others.
- Workbook pages encourage children and caregivers to share stories of overcoming 'tough times' by family members and highlight the importance of caregivers for helping children learn essential skills and developing courage.

Chapter 4: Power Plans: Resilience-Centered Safety Plans for Children and Caregivers

- Children build on their awareness of how heroes use skills to look at what has helped them, tough times in their lives, typical reactions to stress, and how they could use skills and support from caregivers and other caring adults to make things better.
- Children develop *Youth Power Plans*, strength-based worksheets that focus on helping children share what helps them cope, what doesn't help, and developing a shared safety plan with caring adults to prevent or reduce traumatic stress reactions.

- Caregivers are also encouraged to develop *Caregiver Power Plans* that identify their children's triggers, reactions, and interventions that can prevent or reduce traumatic stress reactions.
- *Power Plans* are condensed into *Pocket Power Cards* children can carry with them.

Chapter 5: My Family: Remembering People Who Cared

- Children and caregivers work together as detectives to learn about who helped children in the past and to record memories of caring.
- Children's skills and talents are linked with achievements of parents, grandparents, other relatives, and stories of overcoming that are part of the children's cultural heritage.

Chapter 6: Important People: Promoting Emotionally Supportive Relationships

- Children (and caregivers) explore a broad range of people in their lives and identify mentors, protectors, and emotionally supportive relationships.
- Memories of support are strengthened to expand children's sense of security and confidence.

Chapter 7: Mind Power: Making Things Better with Mindfulness and Self-Regulation

- Children develop resources within themselves and with the help of supportive adults to calm down through slow breathing, reminders of caring, comforting images, mindfulness, and movement.
- Activities strengthen self-regulation by developing the child's ability to recognize signals of stress in their body, increase the child's ability to re-direct attention, and open up possibilities for making things better.
- Children develop skills that help them accept and 'move through' fears and negative thoughts and try out new behaviors to solve problems.
- Children increase development of skills to manage situations that can often trigger traumatic stress reactions, including how to stay safe in relationships, develop positive friendships, and learn from teachers, coaches, clergy, and other safe and supportive adults.

Chapter 8: Changing the Story: Changing Beliefs and Action Cycles to Achieve Goals

- Worksheet questions help children recognize how stress works in the body and mind and how changing beliefs about themselves can help the children achieve their goals and make things better for themselves and their families.

- Children are invited to become the directors of their own 'life' movies as a way to engage them to take control of what happens when they are triggered with reminders that have, in the past, led to problem behaviors.
- Activities include breaking apart what happens leading to distress and getting into trouble and how children can become 'Thought-shifters to Succeed.'
- Working on this chapter with supportive caregivers helps children feel safe enough to share how they felt and acted in the past and to feel safe again with caring adults committed to protecting and guiding children to maturity.

Chapter 9: Timelines and Moves: Making Sense of the Past

- A roadmap and timeline help children remember important people and places from the past and to organize what happened in their lives by the years of their lives, from birth to the present time.
- Chapter pages encourage children to share how they remember places where they lived, the people who cared for them, how they felt in each place, and how children experienced and understand what led to them moving to a new home now that they are older (and wiser).
- Chapter 9 helps caregivers and practitioners understand children's experiences (feelings and beliefs) and develop a list of traumatic events to help children reintegrate traumatic experiences with a renewed sense of safety.

Chapter 10: Through the Tough Times: Trauma Experiences Integration

- Workbook pages help children and emotionally supportive caregivers to safely share what they experienced, what was most difficult, and what they learned can make things better.
- Movies and 'Five-Chapter' Stories help children share traumatic experiences, stressing how children and supportive adults have developed skills and supports so they can escape feeling trapped in recurrent traumatic experiences.
- Activities encourage use of evidence-supported desensitization techniques to help children share undisclosed details and 'move through' traumatic memories to places and times where they felt safe and cared for.

- Children are encouraged to share experiences of loss and also shame for what they feel they have done wrong and to find ways to feel good about themselves again.
- Before completing Chapter 10, practitioners and caregivers help children practice 'moving through' their worst memories so that reminders of what happened and other hard times will not lead to traumatic stress reactions.

Chapter 11: Into the Future: Identifying Goals and Important Relationships

- Workbook pages encourage children to broaden their sense of time by sharing how they see themselves developing skills and relationships through adolescence and into adulthood.
- Activities encourage children to share who they would see as important in their lives and provide opportunities for practitioners and caregivers to build or strengthen positive, supportive relationships with family members, mentors, and other supportive adults.

Chapter 12: 'My Story': Creating an Integrated Life Story with a Past, Present, and Future

- 'My Story' provides an opportunity for children to integrate what they have learned into a life story of overcoming shared in words with photos, drawings, or video.
- Children are invited to share what they have learned and how they would help other children who experienced similar 'tough times' as they did, building their sense of themselves as a hero.
- Children are then urged to rip off the *Real Life Heroes*® cover page and substitute their own book cover and dedication to make this book truly their own.

How Does *Real Life Heroes*® Work?

Real Life Heroes® helps children develop hope, skills, and security with the support of caring adults. The *Life Storybook* highlights each child and family's strengths, including their spiritual and cultural heritage and provides activities that practitioners and caregivers can use to help each child grow strong enough to change problems. Each chapter develops skills and relationships needed for the next chapter, leading up to helping children reduce traumatic stress reactions. The model works like a pyramid for growth, step by step, chapter by chapter.

Creating a
Future

Developing a Life
Story of Overcoming

Moving *Through the Tough
Times with Skills & Support*

Developing the Hero Inside;
Coping and Survival Skills

Strengthening Emotionally Supportive
& Enduring Relationships; *Mentors &*

Rebuilding Security and Co-regulation
with Caring Adults; Creative Arts & Life Stories

Developing Self-regulation and Safety Skills
Inspired by Heroes; *Youth and Caregiver Power Plans*

Learning to Recognize, Express,
and Modulate Feelings; *SOS for Stress*

Real Life Heroes® is listed in the National Registry of Evidence-Based Programs and Practices by the Substance Abuse Mental Health Services Administration (SAMHSA), the SAMHSA National Center for Trauma-Informed Care "Models for Developing Trauma-Informed Behavioral Health Systems and Trauma-Specific Services," and as one of the National Child Traumatic Stress Network's (NCTSN) Empirically Supported Treatments and Promising Practices.

NREPP

Included in SAMHSA's
National Registry of
Evidence-based
Programs and Practices

CHAPTER BY CHAPTER,

STRONGER

AND

STRONGER

Section B
Assessment, Treatment and Service Plans

22

Trauma and Resiliency-Focused Assessment and Service Planning Tools

REFERRAL INFORMATION AND ECOGRAM

Youth/Family:_____ Age:___-___ Assessment-Review Dates:__ __ __ ;__ __ __ ;

__ __ __ ;__ __ __ ;__ __ __ ;__ __ __ ;__ __ __ ;__ __ __ ;__ __ __ ;__ __ __ ;

__ __ __ ;__ __ __ ;__ __ __ ;__ __ __ ;__ __ __ ;__ __ __ ;__ __ __ ;__ __ __ ;

Primary Reasons for Referral/Placement:_____

_____

_____

Previous Evaluations (Medical/Psychological/Education/Parent/Guardian/Child/Siblings/Family/Cultural):

_____

_____

_____

_____

_____

_____

_____

_____

_____

_____

_____

_____

_____

_____

_____

_____

_____

_____

_____

_____

_____

_____

_____

_____

_____

Family Name:
First Names:
Dates of Assessments:
Dates of Birth:
Ages:
Referred by:
For Court: YES/NO   **Needed:**

Focus:

Striking Behaviors/Key Words:

Significant Events – Lived With – Services

Timeline

Age – Date

Community Resources:

Linkage:

.... tentative or partial support past or present

adult believes, nurtures, and protects child in the present

adult committed to nurturing and protecting child until maturity

Strengths/Problems:

Name:

Kagan\Forms\Attachment Ecogram 2005

Basics:
Youth's Goals:_____

_____

Caregivers' Goals:_____

_____

System of Care Goals:_____
Developmental Age: Reasoning/Comprehension___; Emotional___; Social___

Relationships: Who helps or cares? Who does child trust?
Circles of Caring: Most Important: _____

_____

Important:_____

_____

Temporary or Less Important: _____

_____

Supportive Relationships: Validation/Safety by:_____;_____
_____;_____ Nurture-Guidance by:_____;_____
_____;_____ Mentors:_____;_____;_____
Potential:_____
Resources (Family, Cultural, Spiritual Resouces): _____

_____

_____

_____

Primary attachments: Secure___; Anxious___; Avoidant___; Chaotic-Disorganized___; Non-attached___

Emotional Regulation in Context: *My Thermometers* (1-10)
Current:_____

	Knots:	Self-Control Power:	Mad:	Sad:	Glad:	Feel Safe:
With:___						
	Knots:	Self-Control Power:	Mad:	Sad:	Glad:	Feel Safe:
With:___						
	Knots:	Self-Control Power:	Mad:	Sad:	Glad:	Feel Safe:
With:___						
	Knots:	Self-Control Power:	Mad:	Sad:	Glad:	Feel Safe:

Primary arousal level when stressed: Modulated____; Hyper____; Hypo____ Hyper←→Hypo: ____

Action Cycles: What helps & what increases stress reactions?
Trauma Reminders (Family-School-Community) & Traumatic Stress Reactions:

_____
_____
_____
_____
_____
_____
_____
_____
_____
_____
_____
_____
_____
_____

What Helps Child Modulate (Prevention, Co-Regulation, Self-Regulation): _____

_____
_____
_____
_____

What Increases Stress Reactions: _____

_____
_____
_____
_____

Risk: ☐ Self-harm; ☐ Suicidal; ☐ Harm to others; ☐ Drugs/Alcohol; ☐ Dissociation;
☐ _____

Life Story Integration: What happened? Self-concept?
Traumas: ☐ Losses; ☐ Domestic Violence; ☐ Neglect; ☐ Physical Abuse; ☐ Sexual
Abuse; ☐ Sibling Violence; ☐ Medical; ☐ Community Violence; ☐ Disasters ☐

Age	Traumatic & Stressful Events
____	_____
____	_____
____	_____
____	_____
____	_____
____	_____

_____ _____
_____ _____
_____ _____
_____ _____
_____ _____
_____ _____
_____ _____
_____ _____

Youth Strengths (Skills, Talents, Interests): _____
_____

Child's Beliefs about Self: _____
_____

Child's Beliefs about Caregivers: _____
_____

Other Important Factors (Resources, Risks): _____

_____
_____
_____
_____
_____
_____
_____
_____
_____
_____
_____
_____
_____
_____
_____

ASSESSMENTS AND INFORMATION NEEDED

_____

_____

_____

_____

_____

_____

_____

_____

_____

_____

_____

_____

_____

_____

_____

_____

_____

_____

SERVICE PLANNING: PATHWAYS TO RESILIENCE

Relationships:

Building/Rebuilding Committed Caring Relationships with: _____

_____

_____

Mentors: _____

Potential: _____

_____

Permanency Plan: (1.)_____ (2.)_____ Planned Discharge to: _____

Emotional Self and Co-Regulation:

Youth Skill-building:
□ Trauma Psychoeducation; □ Affect Recognition; □ Affect Modulation;
Mindfulness; □ Social; □ Problem Solving; □ Threat Avoidance; □ Focus-
Concentration; □ Memory; □ Reaction to Triggers; □ Drug/Alcohol Treatment; □

_____

_____

_____

_____

_____

Caregiver Skill-building & Co-regulation:
□ Trauma Psychoeducation; □ Affect Recognition; □ Affect Modulation; □
Mindfulness; □ Nurture; □ Developmental Expectations; □ Discipline; □ Validation
of Youth; □ Routines; □ Rituals; □ Re-Attunement; □ Domestic Violence
(Recognition, Protection); □ Drug/Alcohol Treatment; □ _____

_____

_____

_____

_____

Action Cycles (Safety First):

Risk Factors (Trauma Reminders, Reactions and Safety Plans (Who Will Do What in
Each Location, 24-7, to Prevent, Protect, and Co-regulate):

<u>Risk Factors--Signals</u>   <u>Safety Plans</u>

_____

_____

_____

_____

_____

_____

_____

_____

_____

_____
_____
_____
_____
_____
_____
_____
_____
_____
_____
_____

Collaboration (Who Else Can Help? How?): _____
_____

Education Needs: □ Reading; □ Math; □ Writing; □ Test taking; □ Vocational

Activities/Skills/Talents/Interests: □ Art; □ Music; □ Movement/Dance;
□ Sports; □ Spirituality; □ _____
_____
_____

Life Story Integration:
Traumatic Stress Re-integration:
□ Dysfunctional Beliefs; □ Identification of Triggers; □ Desensitization;
□ Life Story; □ Hero's Identity (a new future); □ _____
_____
_____
_____
_____
_____

Community Re-integration: □ Discharge Plan from Placement to _____ ;
□ Family Relationships; □ School; □ Mentors; □ Helping others; □ _____
_____
_____

Additional Priorities: _____
_____
_____
_____
_____
_____
_____
_____
_____

TREATMENT PRIORITIES FOR SESSIONS AND SERVICE PLANS

<table>
<tr><th rowspan="2"></th><th rowspan="2"></th><th colspan="3">STRENGTH OF EMOTIONALLY SUPPORTIVE ENDURING RELATIONSHIPS</th></tr>
<tr><th>High</th><th>Medium</th><th>Low</th></tr>
<tr>
<th rowspan="3">CHILD SELF-REGULATION</th>
<th>High</th>
<td>**Transforming**

Trauma Integration with Caregivers

Self-Image, Identity, Future Goals

Promoting Enduring Relationships

Chapters 1–12</td>
<td>**Integrating**

Attachments, Caregiver Regulation, and Life Story Integration

Strengthen Relationships and Caregiver's Capacity to Manage Stress and Triggers; *Caregiver Power Plan*

Accepting What Happened

Chapters 1–12</td>
<td>**Strengthening**

Attachments and Support

Search for and Strengthen Supportive Relationships; Recover Memories of Caring; Caregiver Skills, Resources, and Modulation; Child Self-Care

With or without Caregiver

Chapters 1–7</td>
</tr>
<tr>
<th>Medium</th>
<td>**Integrating**

Regulation with Caregiver Guidance and Life Story Integration

Stress Management Skills for Triggers, Co-Regulation, Self-Image and Future Goals

Accepting What Happened

Chapters 1–12</td>
<td>**Integrating**

Attachments, Regulation for Child and Caregiver, Life Story Integration

Strengthen Supportive Relationships, Memories of Caring; *Power Plans* to Manage Stress and Triggers; Regulation and Co-Regulation

Accepting What Happened

Chapters 1–12</td>
<td>**Coping**

Attachments, Regulation and Support

Supportive Relationships, Recover Memories of Caring; Affect Regulation Skill-Building; Child Self-Care

With or without Caregiver

Chapters 1–7</td>
</tr>
<tr>
<th>Low</th>
<td>**Strengthening**

Affect Regulation and Co-Regulation, *Power Plans*, Memories of Caring

Chapters 1–7</td>
<td>**Coping**

Affect Regulation and Co-Regulation, Memories of Caring, *Power Plans*

Chapters 1–7</td>
<td>**Restoring Safety**

Safety 'SOS'

Skill-Building, Protective Relationships, Community Support and Hope, Affect Regulation, Child Self-Care

With or without Caregiver

Chapters 1–4</td>
</tr>
</table>

Grid adapted from Saxe et al. (2007). Capacity refers to "window of tolerance" (Siegel, 1999).

NEXT STEPS

ACTIVITY GUIDE
(FOR SESSIONS AND 'HOMEWORK')

PRIORITIES	CHAPTER
	SAFETY 'SOS'
Safety plans to reduce trauma reactions; *Power Plans*	*RLH Life Storybook* **Chapters 1–4 activities:** • Engaging caring adults (see below) as protectors with heroes metaphor • Trauma psycho-education NCTSN handouts (www.nctsn.org) • *Youth Power Plan* • *Caregiver Power Plan* • Use of TARGET (Ford & Russo, 2006) exercises: SOS, FREEDOM, Five Senses Safety Plans • Service Plan Reviews, including review and revision of Safety Plans for each identified trigger that indicate who will do what to help prevent or reduce trauma reactions at different times in the day and night, e.g. at home, at school, after school, during visits to relatives, etc. • Practice implementing safety plans • Safety bags for children to take with them; caring adult practice in evidence-based discipline (see Four-step Developmentally Focused Behavior Management, see Chapter 4 in RLH Toolkit) • Predictable, patterned de-escalating responses by caring adults matched to children's arousal levels (see Perry & Szalavitz, 2006, Figure 3.4; see also Lanktree & Briere, 2008, pp. 55–59)
Safety from sex abuse	*RLH Life Storybook* **Chapters 1–4 activities:** • Books for children: *Let's Talk about Taking Care of You* (Stauffer & Deblinger, 2003); *It's My Body* (Freeman, 1988).
Safety after disasters, terrorism	*RLH Life Storybook* **Chapters 1–4 activities:** • See Psychological First Aid (www.nctsn.org)
Increasing safety after a trauma reaction	*RLH Life Storybook* **Chapters 1–4 activities:** • Keep children and caregivers moving forward, learning from the experience, and improving safety plans. • Revise *Youth and Caregiver Power Plans*, including triggers identified in trauma reaction and safety plans for these triggers, including reducing stimuli, what caregivers can do, and what children can do. • End the session focusing on what helped children calm (what children did, what others did) and how *Power Plans* can help prevent, strengthen, and co-regulate. • Help children develop and implement a restitution plan: what can children do to make up for any harm or damage they cause. • Avoid focusing on shame with repeated questions about how bad/dangerous children were.
	BUILDING/REBUILDING COMMITTED CARING RELATIONSHIPS
Finding caring adults (heroes)	*RLH Life Storybook* **Chapters 5–6 activities:** • Important people questionnaire (Kagan, 2007b, Chapter 18) • Family genogram with play symbols (see Gil, 1991) • Developmental ecogram (Kagan, 2007b, Chapter 17) • Heroes and caring adults chapters of *Life Storybook* (Kagan, 2007a) • Attachment-focused Screening Survey (in Part V); projective play with puppets made from child drawings or family doll figures • Sand play with family figures • Thermometer reactions with different caregivers at the door

Activity Guide (for Sessions and 'Homework')—*continued*

PRIORITIES	CHAPTER
Engaging caring adults	*RLH Life Storybook* **Chapters 5–6 activities:** • Use of the heroes metaphor and journey (Campbell, 1968) • Protector and mentor roles; resilience skill-building framework (see Kagan 2004, Chapter 13; 2007b) • Skill-building activities • Involvement in assessment and service planning • Overcoming fears and obstacles (see Kagan & Schlosberg, 1989, Chapter 4) • Constructing a family shield
Rebuilding (or building) emotionally supportive enduring relationships	*RLH Life Storybook* **Chapters 1–12 activities:** • See Chapter 7 of *Rebuilding Attachments with Traumatized Children* (Kagan, 2004). • The following list of activities was adapted from Vicki Lansky's (1991) wonderful book of early childhood activities and some of my personal favorites (excerpted from Kagan, 2004): – Make matching sets of handprints in plaster of Paris of child *and* parent, and mount together. – Make a family coat of arms with symbols of family strengths (skills, faith, significant people, heirlooms, awards) contributed by the child *and* parent, a family's own Knights of the Round Table, or illustrations of family members vanquishing past problems. – Outline the child and parent's body, color, and hang them up together (also hands, thumbs, feet, etc.). – Plant shrubs, trees, and perennials, and give them special meanings in honor of children's accomplishments (e.g., graduating preschool), an important family event, or as an annual tradition tied in with a religious, cultural, or made-up holiday (e.g., a spring festival to celebrate growth and renewal). – Draw a funny face and a special message on children's lunch bag to take to school or day care *every* day; this can be a single word that reminds children of something fun to look forward to, such as spaghetti for dinner, a planned trip, or simply a heart and kisses. – Sneak up on children with the attack of the 'hug monster' or 'tickle bees,' *and* a reminder, "I'll be back." – Rides on mom or dad geared to children's age (e.g., up and down on a parent's legs, flying through the air as Super Girl, pony rides, or bucking broncos in a swimming pool). These fantasy trips can be expanded into adventure stories of children flying through the air over the neighborhood, zooming through school or day-care centers, or flying over mysterious lands. – Going to the library to get a library card in the child's name, just like dad's. – Face painting to surprise the other parent at the end of the day. – Invite children to name a new pet, a car, or a tree, then family members use this name. – Calling a special party in honor of a made-up holiday and inviting children's friends. – Creating a family newspaper with children's personal column. – Helping children write their own suspense story, make printed copies for grandma and grandpa, and a special laminated edition for the family room bookcase. – Home videos including made-up adventure stories or simply capturing 'a day in the life' of the child. – Reading and rereading baby books and sharing photo albums chronicling children's lives in the family. – Together activities such as riding a bike for two, swinging side by side, swimming, hiking, fishing, or boating.

Activity Guide (for Sessions and 'Homework')—*continued*

PRIORITIES	CHAPTER
	– Dancing together beginning with toddlers in socks or barefoot standing on a parent's feet.
	– Magazines, artwork, foods that show that parents honor the cultural background of children coming into their family from another country or ethnic background and participation by family members in learning about that culture through camp programs or cultural organizations.
	– Marking each child's growth and parents' heights on a *family* height chart placed on a mounted board or backing that can be moved with the family.
	– Saving headline pages from children's birthdays each year.
	– Celebrating birthdays with invitations to family members and children's friends, even if that means two parties; taking photographs of children with family members and friends, and writing a private letter or note to children chronicling some of their accomplishments during the last year.
	– For families celebrating Christmas, add an ornament each year to symbolize a special event or accomplishment for each family member (Johnston, 1999).
	– Creating secret recipes, including 'special' ingredients chosen by children from suggestions by a parent, such as adding white chocolate, a little vanilla, or butterscotch to a cookie or brownie recipe.
	– Hobbies such as foreign money collections, shell collections.
	– Competitions to blow the biggest bubbles in the world, hopping around the yard, or making it through an obstacle course on the sidewalk or driveway.
	– Home theater, beginning with acting like elephants going to a party, dogs going to school, monkeys singing songs, kangaroos on a playground.
	– Composing sounds and melodies just for fun or to entertain mom or dad with pianos, keyboards, children's xylophones, guitars, karaoke, or homemade instruments; holding preschool children on your lap as you compose.
	– Make up mazes and crossword puzzles for children using figures and words that are special to them, such as their favorite activities, a teacher's name, their birthday, etc.
	– Special adventures, such as going to the airport to watch planes taking off, going to an overlook to see trains at a rail yard, checking out cars at an antique auto show, and all manner of museums, including adult-oriented museums with parents helping children imagine what it would be like to sleep in a 1700s bed with three other children, life in a log cabin, or imagining magic in an abstract painting and then making their own artwork to rival the masters.
	– Go on a bus, subway, or train ride around town or to explore another part of a city, sampling favorite foods along the way.
	– Make up a special vocabulary together with funny-sounding words, such as "super-dee-duper."
	– Make a *family* month-by-month calendar with photographs of children and other family members.
	– Follow children's interests (e.g., in fish) and take them to pet stores, book stores, museums, and libraries to learn more, cut out articles in magazines, videotape special shows, go fishing, imagine and investigate with children what could be living in a nearby river or pond.
	– Share special stories from a parent's childhood from photo albums or tied to trophies, crafts, jewelry, etc.
	– Back rubs and foot massages, just 'because . . . '
	– Decorate children's rooms and rearrange the furniture with their help.

Activity Guide (for Sessions and 'Homework')—*continued*

PRIORITIES	CHAPTER
	– Cut children's names out of cardboard or with a jigsaw, paint the pieces, cut out a frame, and create a homemade puzzle children can assemble, or which can be mounted or placed on a bookshelf.
	– When parents travel, collect special objects tied to children's interests (e.g., foreign currency, rocks, basketball team shirts).
	– Use your computer to print or hand-design special note cards, writing pads, and add positive messages with children's names.
	– Arrange for your child to visit you at work and show him or her off to colleagues.
	– Find positive ways that children are like parents (birth or adoptive), such as interests, skills, laughs, etc.
	– Make up stories with stuffed animals, puzzle people, or favorite characters.
	– Create family sculptures with doll collections.
	– Print a family cookbook with favorite recipes from each family member, including children.
	– Mount family photographs with children showing how they grow up from year to year.
	– Make a house out of cardboard or blocks, and create family figures out of paper, cardboard, or clay to enact family stories.
	– Build a dollhouse.
	– Put on a puppet show.
	– Lip-sync a favorite band or create a parent-child dance to go with a favorite song.
	– Create a homemade movie
	– Send special work at every age, school papers, news articles, citations, poetry published in a school journal, and annual photos to grandparents, aunts , uncles, and other relatives.
	– When sending a letter or email to a relative, invite children to add a sentence.
	– Learn something fun to do together, like jump roping, rollerblading, or cross-country skiing.
	– Attend special events for children: assemblies when children are honored, T ball games, soccer matches, school shows, etc., photographing or videotaping the event as well as children with family members, especially visiting relatives, with dinner out at children's favorite restaurants or an ice cream treat afterwards.
	– Teach older children skills in camping, canoeing, reading a compass, setting up a tent, even if it's just in the backyard and going on adventures, carefully planned together (e.g., to climb a mountain, bike a trail in a state park, or take a multi-day hiking or bike trip).
	General strategies:
	• Special times for each child make all the difference. Each child needs one-on-one moments. It's the special quality of the activity that counts for children (e.g., cooking a special food that children love, helping children build a collection of what is special to them, or setting aside a time every weekend, or for younger children every day, to work with children on a special project, such as building a model or adding a new chapter to a story played out with dolls or stuffed animals and recorded in a book, on an audiotape, or filmed with a video camera).
	• Show children that parents want to take children with them to important family events, events that define a family and mark their heritage.
	• The real tests of inclusion vs. exclusion come during the hard times a family faces.
	• Utilize *RLH Life Storybook* with safe, caring adults assisting, completing, and sharing their own workbook (or similar materials).
	• Copy children's rhythm, tones, and movements in each session.
	• Building affect management skills of caregivers and children together.

Activity Guide (for Sessions and 'Homework')—*continued*

PRIORITIES	CHAPTER

	• Establish rituals of calming and healing, and practice daily to prevent anticipated stress and after experiencing stressful events.
	 • Mirroring and attunement activities:
	   – Have children and caregivers face each other and copy each other's movements, taking turns, starting with slow and faster and then slower movements (adapted from Saxe et al., 2007).
	   – Knotted Up Or Free: have children and caregivers enact feeling tight, stiff, and stressed. Then enact feeling loose, free, and unstressed.
	   – Sculpting poses: have children and caregivers take turns guiding each other to take on different poses. This can be done with no touching, or with no words. Over time, increase use of words (adapted from Saxe et al., 2007).
	   – See also Perry and Szalavitz (2006, p. 41, Table 3.1).

Strengthening caring adults (as heroes)	*RLH Life Storybook* **Chapters 1–12 activities:** • Create support groups. • Provide parenting/caring adult sessions after child session, when possible. • Caring adults complete own *Life Storybook* or similar project. • Individual therapy for adults. • Trauma Psycho-education (see below). • *Practitioners*: before leaving work, recall three things that you felt good about that happened that day. • See *Rebuilding Attachments with Traumatized Children*, Chapters 9, 10, and 13 (Kagan, 2004).
Strengthening family relationships (cohesion)	*RLH Life Storybook* **Chapters 5–6 activities:** • Have family members sculpt how each of them sees the family now and how they would like to see the family using Play-Doh figures (Benson, 2011) or cut out puppets, or human figure dolls. Reflect in sculptures closeness and distance, support, conflict . . .
	YOUTH AND CAREGIVER SKILL-BUILDING
Affect recognition	*RLH Life Storybook* **Chapter 2 activities:** • List all feelings you know in three minutes on paper, then draw, enact . . . (adapted, source unknown). • Make a collage of feelings from popular (age-appropriate) magazines; share what your collage shows. • ABCs: Name a feeling that starts with each letter, then enact. Can also ask children to hold that feeling and imagine it filling their body, then letting it go. Share how it feels to hold on to feeling, letting it build, and then letting it go. • For good feelings, ask: "What else helps you feel like that?" • Differentiate main feelings from reactive feelings. • Watch for beliefs associated with feelings. • *Homework*: before leaving school or work, remember three things that you felt good about that happened that day. • Create notebooks with different feelings shown in collages or with cut-out photos from magazines. • Play-Doh: make objects from list (e.g., a bear); have caring adult and child practice guessing (timed); show something you like to do; show something you are good at; show something scary; show something that makes you frustrated (handout: best Play-Doh recipe ever).

Activity Guide (for Sessions and 'Homework')—*continued*

PRIORITIES	CHAPTER

	• Emotional Pumpkins (Pratt, 2004) to show and share feelings.
	
	• *Chiji* Cards: Each pick three cards and tell a story with beginning, middle, ending and cards; then together decide on three cards and tell story together (order from: The Institute for Experiential Education 115 Fifth Avenue South, Suite 503 La Crosse, WI 64501 Telephone: 608-7840789).
	
	• *In session or as homework*: Take photos of different family members showing a range of feelings. Make photos into card games, matching to feeling words, concentration games, etc.
	
	• Watch old movies with no sound and identify feelings expressed.
	
	• Additional activities (from Kagan, 2004):
	
	   – Draw or take photographs of parents and children with funny faces, sad faces, angry faces, scared faces, and put them together on a poster to construct a personalized feeling chart.
	
	   – Take feelings such as being scared and show children how adults and children naturally feel their stomachs tighten, feel prickly, take in a breath of air, look around, etc. when startled, etc. Redefine fear from a negative 'bad' or 'weak' feeling to a natural warning adults and children can use to deal with whatever is happening. Change the connotation of being scared from dread with little sense of self-control to challenges parents and children can prepare for, understand, and master, such as the feeling of riding upwards at the start of a roller coaster ride, the beginning of an obstacle course, the kick-off at a football game with the ball on its way towards you, beginning to make a speech, or the first pitch when children are up to bat. Adults can help children recognize and utilize the energy of fear to take the first and most difficult step in an adventure, a competition, or a performance, recognizing that it gets easier with each additional step.
	
	   – Conduct 'exclusive' radio interviews, including making up stories that are happy, sad, scary, angry, worried, or proud, and sharing with other family members.
	
	   – Practice showing feelings by making faces in a mirror, capturing looks with an instant or digital camera, compiling a feeling photograph book, painting small pumpkins with different feelings, making different sounds, or through puppet shows with hand-held animals or characters from stories.
	
	   – Practice special, parent-modeled words or appropriate phrases from children's favorite television, movie, or story characters to verbalize feelings, even silly responses such as barking like a dog to show friendship, to warn away a trespasser, or to relieve stress
	
	• Books: *Double-Dip Feelings* (Cain, 2001).

Affect expression	*RLH Life Storybook* **Chapter 2 activities:** • Use feeling charts/magnets/posters; pick a feeling to show how you feel today; how you felt when an event happened. • Take photos of yourself showing different feelings. • Body sketches with feelings added to show where felt (parent and child). • Hearts drawings to show different feelings.
Affect monitoring (self)	*RLH Life Storybook* **Chapter 2 activities:** • Introduction to *My Thermometers* or similar stress and affect measures. • Use thermometers to rate feelings when stressed, when calm. • Ask others e.g. your mother to rate how you appear when stressed, when calm. • Feelings drawing (or rhythm/tonality) exercise (from TARGET): (1) show how you feel on the outside; (2) show how you feel on the inside; (3) show how you'd like to feel; and (4) show how you feel with drawings of hearts or bodies or 'Emotional Pumpkins' (Ford & Russo, 2006).

Activity Guide (for Sessions and 'Homework')—*continued*

PRIORITIES	CHAPTER
Affect modulation	***RLH Life Storybook* Chapters 1–4 activities:** • Using the heroes metaphor from RLH Chapter 2 (Kagan, 2007a), frame skill development and daily practice for success. • To enhance slow 'belly' breathing, Saxe et al. (2007) recommend incorporating a "pulse test." Have children find their pulse while breathing normally for 10 seconds and multiply by 6. Do this before starting slow breathing and after slow breathing. • Practice 'SOS for Stress' (see Part I, Chapter 1) daily (adapted from Ford & Russo, 2006). • Practice five senses self-soothing in Safety First Plan (from Part I, Chapter 1) (adapted from Mahoney et al., 2005). • Peacock feather balancing (Macy et al., 2003). • Progressive deep muscle relaxation. • Music and rhythm. • Safe Place imagery. • Sensory activities to evoke feelings: chapstick in different flavors, lotions with different scents, fabrics. • *Homework*: Balance on large exercise ball; balance on balance beam. Games with safe adults and peers: *Twister, Jenga*. • Books for children: *Cool Cats, Calm Kids* (Williams, 2005); *A Volcano in My Tummy* (Whitehouse & Pudney, 1996); *Alexander and the Horrible, No Good, Very Bad Day* (Viorst, 1972). • Rhythm and music as outlet. • Mindfulness meditation: focusing on deep breathing in daily practice (see Lanktree & Briere, 2008, pp. 53–54). • Have parents and children make a CD or playlist for soothing music they both enjoy. • Practice *Youth Power Plan* with emphasis on use 'When you have no words.'
Concentration and focus	***RLH Life Storybook* Chapters 3–6 activities:** • Identify skills of favorite heroes and use to encourage skill development. • Peacock feather balancing (Macy et al., 2003) with distracters and deep breathing like an athlete. • Music and rhythm. • Blow bubbles with competitions for largest bubble, bouncing bubble, or getting bubble through a hoop. • Blow up balloon and imagine you are blowing your fears into balloon, then let it go (Benson, 2010).

Activity Guide (for Sessions and 'Homework')—*continued*

PRIORITIES	CHAPTER
	• Look at fears as a form of energy we can tap. Actors use stage fright for energy. • TARGET activities (Ford & Russo, 2006). • DBT activities (e.g., Marra, 2004). • SPARCS activities (DeRosa et al., 2008) : "snap, crackle, pop." • Tossing ball and counting backwards from 100 by 1's, 3's, 7's with distracters. • Working together with caring adults, pass ball while counting to 0 from 100 (strategies: could count by 10's, hand to hand versus throwing ball). • Pass glass of water from one to another without spilling then faster and faster to reach number targeted of passes in time limit. • Yoga exercises. • Winding oneself to one side, tensing, and letting go. • Slow 'belly' breathing with focus and longer and longer practice. • Blowing bubbles and modulating breathing. • Concentration-movement: roll Nerf ball 5 inches, 10 inches, 8 inches, 18 inches, etc. • Pass feather: time; use breathing, balance, go for one minute; with different movements. • Mindful breathing meditation with caring adult daily (adapted from Lanktree & Briere, 2008). • Introduce mindfulness exercises SOS; focusing on breathing (slow down; focus inside on breath; recognize and accept perceptions from all around children (hearing, seeing) or inside (thoughts, feelings, impulses) coming and going like waves on beach (Marra, 2004); emphasize hero skills in maintaining calm, centered, balanced stance). • *Homework*: Practice meditation with daily SOS and mindfulness meditation (breathing).
Beliefs, thoughts	*RLH Life Storybook* **Chapter 8 activities:** • Thought-shifting with rubber band magic trick (see Part I, Chapter 8) or 'snap out of it' techniques (see Cohen et al., 2003). • Practicing positive beliefs and self-direction.
Problem-solving	*RLH Life Storybook* **Chapters 4–6 activities:** • Puzzles and magic tricks to teach looking at problem from different perspectives. • Heroes' stories from movies, books, cultural heritage, and family members—look at how hero succeeded. • Enact play therapy situations with human figures, puppets, etc. coping with problems.
Strengthening cultural heritage	*RLH Life Storybook* **Chapters 2–3 activities:** • Uncover, write about, and share stories of heroes in family and cultural heritage. • Uncover and highlight stories of overcoming from family and cultural heritage, including community landmarks and historical events (e.g., Underground Railroad sites, Ellis Island, photo albums, religious ties).
Memory	*RLH Life Storybook* **Chapters 3–4 activities:** • Rebuild positive memories of caring by others and how children helped others. • Approach as detective work (Kagan, 2004).

Activity Guide (for Sessions and 'Homework')—*continued*

PRIORITIES	CHAPTER
Self-competence	*RLH Life Storybook* Chapters 1–3, 5–6 activities: • Take photos at home of strengths/abilities for children and caring adults. • Build list of accomplishments day by day, week by week. • Celebrate accomplishments in family and memorialize with mementos, photos. Hang mementos prominently.
Teamwork	*RLH Life Storybook* Chapters 2, 5–6 activities: • Balloon balancing: blow up balloons, have children and caring adults work to keep afloat facing different obstacles; discuss teamwork strategies, emphasize working together to solve problems. • Pass balloon between two to eight people (family or group 2, 5, or 20 times) and find a way to cut time with each trial.
Social skills	*RLH Life Storybook* Chapters 2, 4 activities: • Group or individual practice with typical home, school, and community situations (e.g., late to class, getting permissions, dealing with an irate clerk, getting help with homework, dealing with flirtation, dealing with prejudice or racism, recognizing danger signals, etc). Practice with accurate perceptions of others' verbal and nonverbal communication. Practice expressing self in different situations. For younger children, use play therapy techniques (e.g., toys, human figures, stuffed animals) to practice dealing with difficult situations.
Education	• See *Achievement First* philosophy and curriculum for inspiring success. • See Child Trauma Toolkit for Educators (NCTSN, 2008).
Creative arts: drawing, music	*RLH Life Storybook* Chapters 1–12 activities: • Build on children's talents and interests in creative arts; encourage children to try new or different creative arts (e.g., sculpting with clay, making videos on a digital camera, learning to play a guitar, etc.). • Encourage children to learn about and try out creative arts tied to their family and ethnic heritage.
Body movement: sports/dance/yoga	*RLH Life Storybook* Chapters 1–12 activities: • In offices or small spaces: dancing with peacock feathers; puppet or doll enactments, trying out facial looks and gestures with mirrors or digital cameras. • Use sports and mentoring in skills such as basketball moves. • Use dance instruction where possible. • Provide yoga in groups and classes with daily practice.
	CAREGIVER SKILL-BUILDING
Caring adult modulation of children's reactions	*RLH Life Storybook* Chapters 1–4 activities: • Caring adult de-escalating behaviors matched to children's state of arousal (see Perry & Szalavitz, 2006, Figure 3.4). • Four-step Developmentally Focused Behavior Management (see Part I, Chapter 4 in RLH Toolkit). • Safe touch, rocking, guidance to self-soothing (affect modulation) activities, and children's safety plan. • Caring adult development and practice of interventions for known triggers and children's traumatic stress reactions. • Massage in safe way for children.

Activity Guide (for Sessions and 'Homework')—*continued*

PRIORITIES	CHAPTER
Pet inter-actions for modulating affect	*RLH Life Storybook* **Chapters 1–4 activities:** • Therapeutic use of trained dogs with safe, supervised touch as needed. • Use of dogs and cats to help children feel safe with a pet watching over them and allowing them to relax.
Caring adult emotion processing skills	*RLH Life Storybook* **Chapters 1–4 activities:** • Utilize combined skill-building with children's interventions and activities listed above, along with individual adult therapy when needed.
Caring adult protection from secondary PTSD	*RLH Life Storybook* **Chapters 1–4 activities:** • See www.nctsn.org; *Secondary Trauma Workgroup* and *Caring for Children Who Have Experienced Trauma*. • See www.proqol.org.
	TRAUMATIC STRESS REINTEGRATION
Reinforce Safe Place imagery	*RLH Life Storybook* **Chapter 7 activities:** • Use images from Chapters 2, 3, and 4 in the *RLH Life Storybook*, add details, and reinforce with music. • Ask children to repeat the melody and rhythm for image in daily practice. • Tie Safe Place imagery to photos or symbols children carry for Five Senses Self-Soothing.
Dysfunc-tional beliefs	*RLH Life Storybook* **Chapter 8 activities:** • Encourage expression of story with different tools (e.g., puppets, dolls, sand tray, life storybooks, artwork, music); counter dysfunctional beliefs using children's greater wisdom at current age. • Incorporate psycho-educational information illustrating how abuse, neglect, and family are harmful, and adult responsibilities to provide safety, nurture, and guidance. Encourage validation from caregivers for protecting children from abuse, neglect, and family violence. • Approach beliefs from the perspective of developmental age (e.g., Would you expect a 6-year-old to be to able to stop sex abuse? What would you tell a friend who had this happen to him or her?).
Identification of triggers	*RLH Life Storybook* **Chapters 4 and 8 activities:** • Complete Power Plans for children and caregivers. • Get additional information from guardians, teachers, child care staff, etc. • Encourage youths and caregivers to recognize first bodily signs of being triggered. • Make a list with signs of increasing stress and matching coping and co-regulation strategies. • *Youth Power Plan.* • *Caregiver Power Plan.*
Desensiti-zation to triggers; increase coping skills to manage triggers	*RLH Life Storybook* **Chapters 4, 8, 10 activities:** • Use modalities that have calmed chidren (e.g., use of 'SOS') (adapted from Ford & Russo, 2006), practice use of *Power Plans*, for each trigger; use ABCs of Trauma chapter. • Utilize mindfulness and centering exercises to match the need for calming children and expanding the 'therapeutic window' (Briere & Scott, 2014). • Safety and caring reminders (safety bag, symbols) to take with children. • Normalize memories returning as brain's way of working on overcoming traumas from the past.

Activity Guide (for Sessions and 'Homework')—*continued*

PRIORITIES	CHAPTER
	• Involve safe, caring adults to help keep children safe. • Re-affirm safety plans and test, if necessary.
Threat avoidance	*RLH Life Storybook* **Chapter 6 activities:** • Develop and practice skills for managing problems, challenges, and triggers without running away or dissociation.
Reintegration of traumatic memories	*RLH Life Storybook* **Chapter 10 activities:** • List traumatic memories children and caring adults have shared and organize sequentially in chronological order and rate by level of stress (*Knots*). • Strengthen Safe Place and Relationship imagery for the ending of 'Three-Chapter' and 'Five-Chapter' Stories. • Use Chapter 10 format to structure stories that include what happened before a traumatic event, during the traumatic event, and what helped children get through the traumatic event to a safer time. • Consider *Progressive Counting* (Greenwald, 2008) or EMDR (Shapiro, 2001) or techniques from TF-CBT (Cohen et al., 2006) to calm children while 'moving through' traumas to Safe Place imagery. • Children may want to do something with their hands (e.g., make something they feel good about, such as a rubber band ball). • Titrate exposure to "window of tolerance" (Briere & Scott, 2014), home safety, strength of attachments, relationship safety with therapist, affect regulation skills, community validation and support. • Objective: memories no longer able to trigger distress or negative adaptive behaviors (dissociation, fighting, running away). • Put disturbing memories in a box or garbage bag (e.g., asking children to write down on index cards all the disgusting or disturbing things they can thing of and putting these in a locked box or a garbage bag in the therapist's office) (James, 1989), emphasize how the abuser's actions were disgusting or disturbing, not children's reactions (Lanktree & Briere, 2008). • Adapted *Hatgame* (Lanktree & Briere, 2008): children, caring adult, and therapist write down questions related to traumatic experiences. Children pull questions from the hat and respond using different modalities (creative arts, puppets) to share feelings and beliefs. The therapist emphasizes what helps children get through trauma. The caring adult and therapist emphasize how *different* children's homes are now from the time of traumas. • Write letters to people who hurt children or people who did not protect children with letters destroyed.
Stronger identity and meaning-making	*RLH Life Storybook* **Chapters 8, 10, 11, 12 activities:** • Share strengths and memories of caring, as well as moments of trauma emphasizing how children moved through traumas to safety, caring, and guidance of caring adults. • Share with safe adults.
Apologies, restitution and healing after hurting others	*RLH Life Storybook* **Chapter 10 activities:** • Learn how children's families help each other with apologies, restitution, and making up for hurting others accidentally or deliberately. • Learn how children's families' values and religious orientation help family members with re-connecting to others, making up for wrongdoing, and preventing future transgressions that harm others. • Help families move away from any use of physical punishments or dis-connection, e.g. ostracism, labeling, by re-affirming parents' positive goals and use of understanding of how to help children who have experienced multiple traumas and impaired attachments.

Activity Guide (for Sessions and 'Homework')—*continued*

PRIORITIES	CHAPTER
	COMMUNITY REINTEGRATION
Discharge to foster or adoptive family	**Activities:** • Use *Caring for Children Who Have Experienced Traumatic Stress*, NCTSN Resource Parent Training Curriculum. • Books for children: *Maybe Days* (Wilgocki & Wright, 2002). • Books for resource parents: *Working with Traumatized Children: A Handbook for Healing* (Brohl, 2007); *Wounded Angels: Inspiration from Children in Crisis* (Kagan, 2016b).
Family relationships	*RLH Life Storybook* **Chapters 5–6 activities:** • Reduce problems (triggers, reactions) that led to separations (e.g., special school or placement in foster care). • Increase fun time and positive experiences. • Redefinition of children's experiences with extended family members, including sharing in safe ways experiences of traumas and emphasizing how children are now protected by caring adults, how caring adults have made homes and neighborhoods safer, and how children have developed skills (i.e., how home and family are different now). • Re-establish or strengthen positive and consistent rituals in the home: getting up in the morning, breakfast, school, after school, dinner, going to bed. • Re-establish or strengthen holiday celebrations that reinforce family strengths. • Avoid triggers and implement safety plans.
School	**Activities:** • Develop educational programs that match children's developmental levels, strengths, and needs for guidance, safety, protection from reminders of traumas. • Utilize educational programs that are evidence-supported for children similar to youths. • Encourage caregivers to play strong roles as advocates for their children in educational planning. • Encourage caregivers to follow through with helping with projects and homework, monitoring completion of school work, assisting educational staff in mentoring, providing feedback on progress, etc.
Mentors	*RLH Life Storybook* **Chapters 3 and 6 activities:** • Identify skills and talents of children (RLH Chapters 2–4) and match children with mentors in community for ongoing, long-term (multi-year) guidance (e.g., animal-loving child working with a veterinarian on animal care; basketball mentor for aspiring basketball player; guitar teacher for child who wants to play guitar). • Provide trauma-informed training for mentors e.g. adaptations of the NCTSN Resource Parent Curriculum, Caring for Children Who Have Experienced Traumatic Stress • Religious mentors for interested children and families.
Helping others	*RLH Life Storybook* **Chapters 3, 11, 12 activities:** • Working with talents and interests to help others in family and community in need, caring for older relatives and younger children in safe ways; work for charities; help in schools to guide/teach younger children. • Work with national organizations on causes that enlist children's, and especially adolescents', help.
Hero's identity (a new future)	*RLH Life Storybook* **Chapters 7–12 activities:** • Make a family emblem like a coat of arms showing strengths and values. • Identify successes each day, week, month, school year.

Activity Guide (for Sessions and 'Homework')—*continued*

PRIORITIES	CHAPTER
	• Identify and reinforce how children have helped others in the family and community.
	• Identify positive goals for children (e.g., colleges, occupations, skills that match children's interests and abilities).
	COLLABORATION
Who else can help?	***RLH Life Storybook* Chapters 1, 4, 5–6 activities:**
	• Use chapters to discover possible resources.
	• Consider 'search tools' available to find former caregivers with currently unknown addresses.
	• Involve safe, caring adults in planning meetings or special sessions.
	• Include authorities as part of team (e.g., child protective services, law guardians, and family court judges), even if they cannot make meetings.

ADDITIONAL ACTIVITIES AND INTERVENTIONS FOR CHILD AND FAMILY

SERVICE PLAN REVIEW

Youth/Family:_____   INITIAL OR REVIEW CONFERENCE DATE ___ ___ ___

Guidelines:
1. Review how services are working.
2. Circle Priority Level of Primary Service Goals With Child, Caregiver, and Team Consensus:
   - 1: Not a significant problem at this time (1-2 times a year, little risk, or can be deferred)
   - 2: Occasionally a significant problem (1-2 times a month, low risk, or can be deferred)
   - 3: Frequently a significant problem (1-2 times a week, moderate risk, needs attention soon)
   - 4: Critical problem (almost every day, high risk, or needs immediate attention)
3. Develop Action Plans

Assessment Updates:

Child and Caregiver goals:_____

_____

Developmental Level:_____

Relationships:

Emotional Self & Co-regulation
  Child:_____
  Caregivers:_____
  Prevention of Secondary PTSD:_____

Action Cycles: **What Happens that Helps or Increases Trauma Reactions**
  Triggers & Reactions:_____

_____

_____

  What Helps Child Modulate:_____

_____

  What Increases Stress Reactions:_____
  Risks:_____

_____

Life Story Integration
  Traumatic Events:_____
  Beliefs:_____

_____

  Youth Strengths:_____
  What is Helping Achieve Goals:_____

_____

  Obstacles and Challenges:_____

_____

Additional Information Needed:_____

_____

Prioritization for Core Components and Additional Goals:

CORE COMPONENTS	PRIORITY: 1 2 3 4
Relationships & Permanency	
Emotional Self & Co-regulation: Child	
Emotional Self & Co-regulation: Caregivers	
Emotional Self & Co-regulation; Preventing Sec. PTSD	
Action Cycles: 'Safety First'	
Replace Trauma, Reaction Cycle with Power Plans	
Activities, Skills, Talents, Interests	
Life Story Integration	

Strategies to Overcome Obstacles and Achieve Goals: _____

_____

_____

_____

_____

Action Plans; Who Will Do What By When: _____

_____

_____

_____

_____

_____

Comments from Child, Caregivers, Practitioners: _____

_____

_____

_____

Next Review Date: _____ Invitations to participate to: _____

_____   _____   __ __ __

Practitioner   **Program**   **Date**

ATTACHMENT-FOCUSED SCREENING SURVEY*

Adjust use for each child. Write in names of important people for child in bracketed spaces for names.

Name: _____ **Date:** _____

1. Today I feel_____
2. I get angry when _____
3. School is _____
4. I wish teachers _____
5. People think I am _____
6. My biggest problem is that _____
7. I wish people wouldn't _____
8. I hope I'll never _____
9. I'm afraid of _____
10. What I like to do best is _____
11. The best thing that ever happened to me was _____

    _____

12. The worst thing that ever happened to me was _____

    _____

13. I feel proud when _____
14. The future looks _____
15. I would like to be _____
16. I often worry about _____
17. I wish I could _____
18. I am good at _____
19. What I want most is _____
20. I wish my mother would have _____
21. I wish my father would have _____
22. I wish [_____] would have _____
23. I wish [_____] would have _____
24. My mother would say I am _____
25. My father would say I am _____
26. [_____] would say I am _____
27. ___ would say I am _____
28. I think I am _____
29. If I could, I'd tell my mother _____
30. If I could, I'd tell my father _____

31. If I could, I'd tell [_____] _____

32. If I could, I'd tell [_____] _____

33. The people I care about the most are _____

    _____

34. If you were given $3,000 and a one-week vacation, what would you do? Who would you most like to spend your vacation with? _____

35. Who will really listen to you when you need to talk to someone? _____

36. Who can you count on to help you in a crisis? _____

37. Who would tell you when you are wrong and help you make things better? _____

38. How many times have you felt a strong urge to drink alcohol or use drugs in the last six months?

    ☐ None   ☐ Once a month   ☐ Once a week   ☐ Once or more a day

39. What illegal drugs have you used? _____

    How often?

    ☐ Daily   ☐ Once   ☐ Two or more times a day   ☐ 1–2 times a week   ☐ 1–2 times a month

40. When was the first time you used each drug? _____

41. When was the last time you used any of these drugs? _____

42. Have you ever drank alcohol in the morning?   ☐ Yes   ☐ No

43. How often did you drink alcohol in the last six months?

    ☐ Never   ☐ Once   ☐ Daily   ☐ 1–2 times a week   ☐ 1–2 times a month

    How much did you usually drink? _____

    How much do you think is too much for you? _____

    Did you like to drink by yourself, with others, or both? _____

44. Have you ever passed out?   ☐ Yes   ☐ No

    How often? _____

    What happened? _____

45. If I could, I would change how [_____] _____

46. If I could, I would change how [_____] _____

47. If I could, I would change how I _____

48. Do you think you will be living with _____ next year? In two years?

49. Can you continue living with _____ until you are 18 years old? _____

    Do you want this to be the home where you live until you are grown up? _____

50. If you could live with anyone, who would you live with? _____

    1st choice: _____ ; 2nd choice: _____ ; 3rd choice: _____

*Items adapted from commonly used sentence completion, substance abuse, depression and dissociation scales including Beck (2001), Lazarus (1971), Carlson &Putnam (1986), Burns & Kaufman (1987).

Attachment-Focused Screening Survey—*continued*

	Question	Never True	Some-times True	Often True	Almost All the Time True
1	I am good at lots of things.	0	1	2	3
2	I find myself feeling like crying.	0	1	2	3
3	I have trouble getting to sleep or staying asleep.	0	1	2	3
4	I would like to hide from everyone.	0	1	2	3
5	Nobody really loves me.	0	1	2	3
6	I worry about what will happen.	0	1	2	3
7	Nothing I do helps to make things better.	0	1	2	3
8	Everything I do feels like a strain.	0	1	2	3
9	I have been afraid to tell people about some of the things that happened to me.	0	1	2	3
10	I worry about voices in my head telling me things.	0	1	2	3
11	I feel like no one has ever been able to help me.	0	1	2	3
12	I have had to keep a big secret.	0	1	2	3
13	I see things that are not really there.	0	1	2	3
14	I have heard voices in my head tell me to hurt myself or other people.	0	1	2	3
15	I have been criticized for drinking alcohol or using drugs.	0	1	2	3
16	There are some people that I need to stay away from because I have thought about hurting them.	0	1	2	3
17	I was touched as a child in a way that hurt me or made me feel uncomfortable.	0	1	2	3
18	I have been hurt by someone in the past.	0	1	2	3
19	In the last year, I have felt angry enough to break something or hit someone.	0	1	2	3
20	In the last year, I have thought or daydreamed about hurting someone.	0	1	2	3
21	I have had the experience of finding myself in a place and not knowing how I got there.	0	1	2	3
22	I am not sure whether things I remember really did happen or whether I just dreamed them.	0	1	2	3
23	I find myself staring off into space, thinking of nothing, and not aware of how much time passed.	0	1	2	3
24	I can't remember whether I did something or just thought about doing it.	0	1	2	3
25	There are things people do to me that make me lose control.	0	1	2	3

Attachment-Focused Screening Survey—*continued*

Please draw a picture of a person with a whole body from head to toes.

Attachment-Focused Screening Survey—*continued*

Please draw a picture of yourself doing something with one of the most important people in your life.

Attachment-Focused Screening Survey—*continued*

Please draw a picture of your family doing something.

Thank you for filling out this form.

IMPORTANT PEOPLE QUESTIONNAIRE

INSERT EIGHT 'IMPORTANT PEOPLE' BELOW

_____

_____

_____

_____

_____

_____

_____

Important People Questionnaire—*continued*

Name: _____ Date: _____

Please think about important people in your life and write in their names.

_____

_____

_____

WHEN YOU WERE LITTLE

Who helped you at age 3 or 4, when you were sick? _____

Who helped you at age 3 or 4, if you were scared at night? _____

Who helped you with homework in first grade? _____

Who taught you to ride a bike? _____

Who showed they appreciated what you had done (e.g., a great basketball shot, a good report card, a great painting in school, how have you helped other people)? _____

_____

NOW THAT YOU ARE OLDER

If you were given $3,000 and a one-week vacation, what would you do? _____

Who would you most like to spend your vacation with? _____

Who will really listen to you when you need to talk to someone? _____

Who can you count on to help you if you are in trouble and really need help? _____

Who would tell you when you are wrong and help you make things better? _____

These are the people I care the most about: _____

Who have you helped? _____

_____

Important People Questionnaire—*continued*

FIVE YEARS FROM NOW

Who could you look to for help in a crisis? _____

Who would believe in you? _____

Who would like to be your friend? _____

Who would tell you when you are wrong and help you make things better? _____

Who would you like to help? _____

JUST A FEW MORE QUESTIONS

---

1. How many people can you think of who cared about you *and* helped you from the time you were a baby to your present age? Please circle the closest answer:

   0   1   2   3   4   5–7   8–10   11–15   16–20   20–30   30+

2. When you think about your life, from the time you were a baby until today, how do you feel? Please circle the number that best shows how you feel:

   0   1   2   3   4   5   6   7   8   9   10

   (peaceful)   (upset)

3. When you think about your life, from the time you were a baby until today, how do you think about yourself. Please circle the number that best shows how you would describe yourself:

   0   1   2   3   4   5   6   7   8   9   10

   (terrible)   (good)

4. At your present age, how many people can you think of who care about you *and* would help you if you were in serious trouble? Please circle the closest answer:

   0   1   2   3   4   5–7   8–10   11–15   16–20   20–30   30+

5. What do you think would help make things better for you and the people you care about the most?

   _____

   _____

   _____

THANK YOU FOR COMPLETING THIS QUESTIONNAIRE

CIRCLES OF CARING

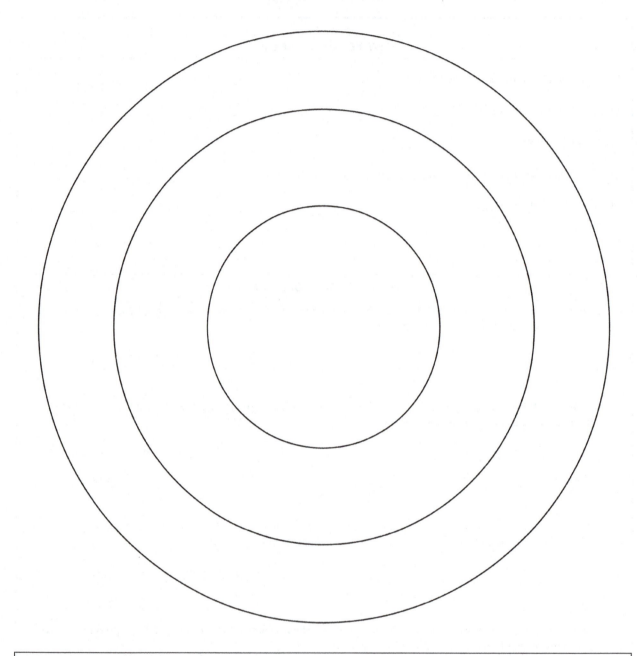

PLEASE WRITE IN NAMES:

Inner Circle: People you feel very close to and are very important to you. People who have cared for you in the past and who you can count on to care about you in the future. People you feel so close to that you can hardly imagine living without

Middle Circle: People who are also important to you and may have cared for you in the past or helped you succeed; but who you feel you are not as close to as the people in the Inner Circle.

Outer Circle: People who are important in your life in a more temporary way and people who could become important in your life.

NEXT: Circle the names of those people in each circle who you trust enough that you could tell them what happened during the best and worst times of your life: what you saw, heard, thought, did, and felt.

Adapted from Antonucci (1986)

My Thermometers

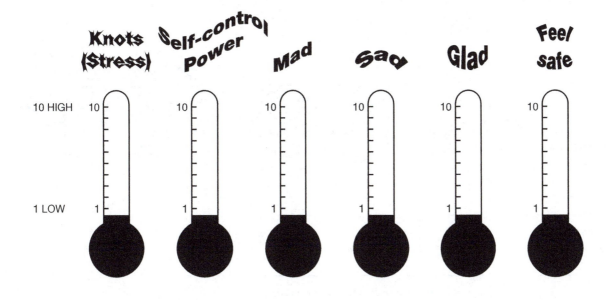

STRONGER AND STRONGER PROGRESS CHART

MY LIFE STORY

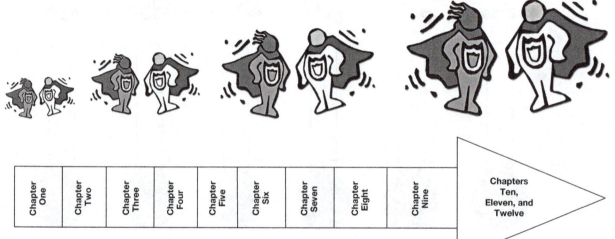

| Chapter One | Chapter Two | Chapter Three | Chapter Four | Chapter Five | Chapter Six | Chapter Seven | Chapter Eight | Chapter Nine | Chapters Ten, Eleven, and Twelve |

(After you complete each chapter, color in the bar)

Section C

Treatment Tools

PRACTITIONER 'CHEAT SHEET' AND FIDELITY TOOL

Child: _____ Practitioner: _____ Program:_____

Supervisor: _____ Consultant: _____

Please check off (✓) items accomplished monthly during supervision or consultation. Items are coded for core components: Relationships (R); Emotional Self- and Co-Regulation (E); Action Cycles (Interaction Patterns) (A); and Life Story Integration (Identity and Desensitization) (L).

Trauma-Informed Systems: *Preparing for the Therapeutic Journey*

☐ 1. Develop trauma- and resiliency-informed service systems in which programs and practitioners (A):

___ routinely screen for trauma exposure and related symptoms;

___ assess child and caregiver goals, strengths, resources, and cultural heritage;

___ use culturally sensitive, evidence-based assessments and treatments for traumatic stress and associated mental health symptoms;

___ make resources available to children, families, and providers on trauma exposure, its impact, and treatment;

___ engage in efforts to strengthen the resilience and protective factors of children and families;

___ address parent and caregiver trauma and its impact on the family system;

___ emphasize continuity of care and collaboration across child-service systems; and

___ maintain an environment of care for staff that addresses, minimizes, and treats secondary traumatic stress, and that increases staff resilience.

☐ 2. Arrange support, training, and ongoing consultation for caregivers, practitioners, supervisors, and agency leaders to sustain trauma-informed services (A).

Phase 1: Using Assessment and Service Planning to Open up Pathways to Change

---

Trauma and Resilience-Focused Assessment: 'A Map and a Compass'

☐ 1. Complete the <u>Trauma and Resiliency-Focused Assessment and Service Plan</u>, including (A):

___ assessment of children's and caregivers' primary goals;

___ child's developmental level;

___ primary relationships and potential caregivers and mentors using *Circles of Caring*;

___ child, family, and cultural resources;

___ Emotional Regulation using *My Thermometers* for children's feelings with primary relationships; and

___ trauma experiences and traumatic stress reactions.

☐ 2. 'Open up' conversations about any traumatic experiences by using trauma surveys such as the *UCLA PTSD Indexes for Children and Parents*.

☐ 3. Assess safety indicators and assure all items are marked with a (✓) below before children are asked to share workbook or other confidential materials with parents, guardians, or other caregivers in sessions (A):

___ Children indicate in private to practitioner that they feel safe to share with caregivers present and want caregivers in sessions.

___ Children demonstrate ability and willingness to signal to practitioner and other protective adults if they, at any time, feel unsafe with caregivers or any other people present.

Practitioner 'Cheat Sheet' and Fidelity Tool—*continued*

_____ Caregiver gives children support and permission to share what they experienced and validates their experiences, including traumas involving the caring adult.

_____ Caregiver demonstrates to children that he or she is able to manage his or her own reactions without re-traumatizing children.

Initial Service Plan and The Pledge: Charting Pathways to Resilience

☐ 1. Share practitioner's assessments and encourage caregivers and children to work together to increase trust and support in relationships, strengthen skills for self- and co-regulation, and decrease traumatic stress reactions in order to achieve child and caregiver goals (A).

☐ 2. Introduce *Real Life Heroes®*, if appropriate, as an evidence-supported treatment for traumatic stress, sharing workbook and Session Structure (*Bookmark*), that focuses on fun activities to build skills to reach goals, to become stronger after experiences of past traumas, and to strengthen or build relationships for children with adults committed to caring for, protecting, and guiding them (A).

☐ 3. Ask caring adults to sign *The Pledge* and commit themselves to respect whatever children share in their *Life Storybook*, even feelings and reactions to the caring adults, and to keep children safe (R).

> **Phase 2: Core Components: Relationships, Emotional Self and Co-Regulation, & Action Cycles (Interaction Patterns)**

Chapter 1: The Hero's Challenge: Trauma Psycho-Education, Multisensory Safety Plans, and the Hero's Challenge

☐ 1. Establish a ritualized sequence for sessions, demonstrate respect for children's safety plan, utilize a playful approach to develop skills and enhance expression of feelings with creative arts, and accentuate important stories of strengths and overcoming obstacles by guiding children to share details and feelings (A).

☐ 2. Adapt psycho-educational materials to children's developmental levels and review with children and caregivers, emphasizing how 'alarm bells' are learned behaviors that help children (and caregivers) cope with 'tough times' and can later interfere with success at home or school. Help caregivers to use an understanding of children's developmental levels and experiences of trauma and coping strategies to avoid shaming of children or themselves. As appropriate, give caregivers NCTSN handouts on Understanding Trauma or Resource Parent Curriculum. Also, provide, as indicated, NCTSN handouts on specific traumas (e.g., helping children after tornadoes, domestic violence, or sex abuse) (E).

☐ 3. Help children develop *SOS Picture Power Card* with Safe Place imagery and practice 'SOS' with six-step breathing, focusing on resources, seeking help, and helping others (E).

☐ 4. Help children develop *Safety First* plans to protect children, caregivers, and practitioners from threats of violence, emotional abuse, or neglect, and for known 'triggers' for trauma reactions, including children's signal and action plan if *Knots* begin to rise or *Self-Control Power* falls. *Safety First* plans include who to call for help and self-care, what caring adults can do to help, and what to do if children have 'no words' (E).

Chapter 2: A Little about Me: Recognizing and Expressing Feelings (Affect Power)

☐ 1. Ask children to test whether practitioner will maintain 'sanctuary' of sessions by checking on how 'Safety First' plans will be implemented (A).

☐ 2. Guide adults in sessions to share their feelings and experiences in a way that helps children learn from caring adults without overburdening or traumatizing children with adults' experiences (E).

☐ 3. Ask children and caregivers to practice recognition of feelings in self and others with photos, drawings, or collages (E).

Practitioner 'Cheat Sheet' and Fidelity Tool—*continued*

☐ 4. Encourage children and caregivers to share feelings in a safe way and to accept feelings as natural without shame (E).

Chapter 3: Finding and Strengthening Heroes

☐ 1. Help children recognize how heroes have skills, resources and weaknesses, make mistakes, and work together, relying on other people to help them overcome hardships and succeed (R).

☐ 2. Help children identify real people in their lives who act as heroes (R).

☐ 3. Help children identify how they have acted as a hero, helping others (R).

Chapter 4: Power Plans

☐ 1. Help children complete *Youth Power Plan* using image of their heroes to encourage development of skills and resources (E).

☐ 2. Help children complete *Pocket Power Card* and identify what children and others can do to help children stay calm and prevent traumatic stress reactions (E).

☐ 3. Help primary caregivers complete *Caregiver Power Plan* identifying their own triggers and developing plans to keep themselves and children calm when reminded of traumatic events (E).

☐ 4. Guide children and caregivers in practice of self-soothing skills, including: 'SOS for Stress,' six-step breathing, muscle relaxation, 'Safe Place' imagery, Mind Power, and 'thought changing' (E).

Chapter 5: My Family: Caring Adults from the Past, Mentors and Guardians for the Future

☐ 1. Help children identify at least three adults who cared for them in the past and three adults whom they would like to get help from or become closer to in the future (R).

☐ 2. Ask caring adults to keep children safe by (R):

____ giving children support and permission to share what they experienced;

____ validating children's experiences, including traumas involving the caring adult;

____ committing themselves to protecting children from anyone, even other family members;

____ identifying how adult sees the child as special and part of his or her life;

____ demonstrating to children that caring adults are able to manage exposure to reminders of past traumas and manage their own reactions without re-traumatizing children; and

____ sharing adults' life stories in a way that helps children learn from caring adults without overburdening or traumatizing children with adults' experiences.

Chapter 6: Important People: Developing Supportive Relationships (Allies and Mentors)

☐ 1. Help children share positive memories where they felt supported by other people with practitioner and with safe, caring adults (R).

☐ 2. Help children share two or more memories of how they helped other people (R).

Chapter 7: Mind Power

☐ 1. Help children expand focusing skills and increase self-regulation with mindfulness (R).

☐ 2. Help children develop, practice, and share a 'Safe Place memory' involving a relationship with a caring adult (R).

☐ 3. Help children develop a 'protective shield' that integrates strengths in their family, cultural heritage, and themselves (A).

Practitioner 'Cheat Sheet' and Fidelity Tool—*continued*

> ### Phase 3: Core Components:
> ### Life Story Integration (Trauma Desensitization & Identity)

Chapter 8: Changing the Story: The ABCs of Trauma

☐ 1. Help children and caring adults list five positive beliefs about themselves and practice new, more adaptive behaviors based on those beliefs to create a better ending (A).

☐ 2. Help children and caring adults accept responsibility for their own behavior and avoid blaming themselves for the actions of others (A).

Chapter 9: Looking Back: Timelines and Moves

☐ 1. Help children organize information about their lives in a meaningful order, including happy memories and 'tough times' (L).

☐ 2. Develop sequential list of trauma events, including resources and positive connections for children, traumatic events, and dysfunctional beliefs about moves to be addressed in Chapters 8 and 10 (L).

☐ 3. Check to see that resources below are in place to support trauma event integration[2] before starting Chapter 8 (L):

___ Children's *Self-Control Power* ratings are higher than their *Knots* in sessions.

___ Children have at least one committed, caring adult with sufficient stability, who is physically and psychologically available, willing, committed to work through traumatic memories with children and provide support after sessions.

___ Children demonstrate sufficient self-regulation abilities and supports from resources in family and community to manage distress and stress reactions to trauma reminders and avoid becoming dangerous to themselves or others.

___ Children have developed, and can bring to mind, a positive 'Safe Place' image of feeling safe with someone who cares, or cared in the past, about them.

___ Practitioner has experience or support from supervisor, colleagues, or consultants with experience to 'move through' traumatic memory reintegration with children at children's developmental age (e.g., *TF-CBT, EMDR, Progressive Counting*).

___ Practitioner has access to resources (pharmacotherapy, acute crisis evaluation and hospitalization, case management resources, pediatric care) if needed.

Chapter 10: Through the Tough Times: Reintegration of Traumatic Memories Memories

☐ 1. Help children desensitize memories of 'tough times' by sharing details and feelings with therapist and trusted adults of traumatic events or themes of repeated traumatic events in 'Five-Chapter' Stories that emphasize 'moving through' traumas and staying within the children's 'window of tolerance.' 'Five-Chapter' Stories include: What happened (Chapter 2); What helped children and people they loved get through (survive) the 'tough time' (Chapter 3); A safe time and place after the traumatic event when children felt cared for and protected (Chapter 4); What led up to the traumatic event (Chapter 1); and How children could prevent or reduce 'tough times' now that they are older, smarter, and stronger with help from caring adults (Chapter 5). (*Note*: Stories can be shortened to three chapters if children are unable to handle the 'Five-Chapter' format. 'Three-Chapter' Stories include: What happened (Chapter 2); A safe time and place after the event when children felt cared for and protected (Chapter 3); and What led up to the event (Chapter 1)) (L).

☐ 2. Help children to stay regulated (e.g., higher *Personal Power* than *Knots* ratings) by using skills and relationships and highlighting what is different now, a protective ending to stories of traumatic events that would prevent re-traumatization (L).

Practitioner 'Cheat Sheet' and Fidelity Tool—*continued*

☐ 3. Help children express remorse and implement plans for apologizing and making appropriate restitution[3] for at least one thing they regret doing (L).

Chapter 11: Into the Future: Reinforcing a Positive Self-Image

☐ 1. Help children develop positive images and beliefs about themselves, extending into the future including goals and helping others (L).

☐ 2. Help children identify important relationships to maintain or build in future years (L).

Chapter 12: My Story: Integrating a Stronger Self-Image as a Hero Helping and Getting Help from Others

☐ 1. Encourage children to create a message to help other children who have experienced similar 'tough times' (L).

☐ 2. Help children create a life story narrative with words, art, or music integrating their growth through good times, 'tough times,' and into the future (L).

Comments/Quotes from Children or Caregivers: _____

_____

_____

_____

_____

Primary Reason for Ending RLH Work: _____

_____

_____

_____

_____

What Helped: _____

_____

_____

_____

_____

Challenges: _____

_____

_____

_____

_____

Recommended Strategies to Overcome Challenges: _____

_____

_____

_____

_____

PROGRESS NOTE (SESSION CHECKLIST)

PROGRESS NOTE
Fidelity Session Checklist

Child:_____ Program:_____ Service Goal (if required):_____ Date:___ ___ ___

Adults and other children participating in session: _____

<u>Check off (√) what was completed:</u>
Assessments: Child Trauma:___ ; Parent Trauma:___ ; Circles:___ ; *Assessment-Treatment Plan:*_____ ;_____ :_____

Openings:

☐ Self-Check Thermometers (1-10): *Knots:___ ; Self-Control Power:___ ; Mad:___ ; Sad:___ ; Glad:___ ; Feel Safe:___*
☐ 'Safety First': safety plans in place; before/during/after reminders for predictable crises; child's signal and action plan if *Knots* begin to rise or *Self-Control Power* falls; plan for practitioner and caring adult self-care
☐ Magical Moment (e.g. herbal tea, cookie, magic trick, skills, special rituals)

Centering Activities:_____ (e.g. slow breathing, imagery, balancing, focusing, humming, bubbles).

Chapter (circled): Pledge 1 2 3 4 5 6 7 8 9 10 11 12; Pages Completed:____ - ____

☐ 1st: Non-verbally, child selects color, sketches image, then taps Rhythm, plays Musical notes, and/or shows Movement to match picture.
☐ 2nd: Child responds to questions listed on page or reflects with thoughts on drawing, rhythm, music, or movement.
☐ 3rd: Therapist highlights strengths, coping skills, positive beliefs and challenges dysfunctional beliefs.
☐ 4th: For important stories and Chapter 10, child develops 'Three or Five-Chapter' stories for pictures with a beginning, middle, and end, utilizing rhythm, music, art, *or* movement, and ending at a safe place or time.

Closings:

☐ End of Session Thermometers (1-10): *Knots:___ ; Self-Control Power:___ ;Mad:___ ; Sad:___ ; Glad:___ ; Feel Safe:___*
☐ Focusing/Centering Activities repeated if necessary or desired by child.
☐ Child's work shared, when possible, with safe, caring adult in sessions; therapist encourages attunement by adults and validation of losses, hardships, adult ownership of responsibilities for what happened.
☐ Reassurance provided to child for: thoughts or feelings to be expected as normal, how your mind is healing and becoming stronger and stronger, how to utilize bodily sensations as messages or reminders, ways to calm and self-soothe using understanding of trauma and positive self-statements; choices; caring adults to call if distressed (on safety cards); plans with caring adults and children to manage reminders of traumas.
☐ Session ended on a positive note reinforcing strengths, helping others, and special activity.
☐ Activities for week planned (fun, skill, and relationship-building activities with modulation practice, related to chapter):_____

Session Narrative & Plans:_____
_____
_____
_____
_____
_____
_____
_____
_____
_____
_____

Date set for next session:___ ___ ___ Time:_____ Adults Invited:_____

FIDELITY PROGRESS NOTE (ABBREVIATED SESSION CHECKLIST)

Client Name:_____ **Session Date:** __ __ __ **Practitioner:**_____

☐ **Openings/Thermometers**
Knots:____ Self-Control Power:____Mad:____ Sad:____ Glad:____Feel Safe:____

☐ **Centering Activity:**

☐ **Life Storybook:** Chapter____ Pages completed (including art, music, movement):
____ – ____

Addressed Core Components (REAL)?

☐ Yes ☐No Relationships (strengthening or building emotionally supportive relationships)

☐ Yes ☐No Emotional Self-regulation and Co-regulation (for youths and caregivers)

☐ Yes ☐No Action Cycles (increasing positive interaction patterns for youths & caregivers reducing trauma reaction cycles)

☐ Yes ☐No Life Story Integration (developing a positive sense of self, family, heritage; integrating trauma experiences and child-family-cultural strengths)

Notes (Themes, Significant Events, Issues to Address in Next Session):_____
_____
_____
_____
_____
_____
_____
_____
_____
_____
_____
_____

Activities for the week; Practice & Power Plans:_____
_____

Supervisor review of Progress Note? ☐Yes ☐No Supervisor signature_____

BOOKMARKS

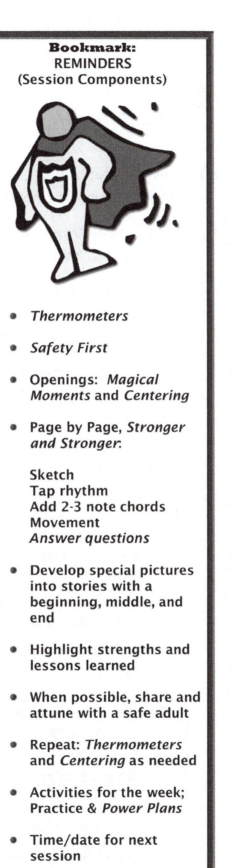

Bookmark:
REMINDERS
(Session Components)

- *Thermometers*

- *Safety First*

- Openings: *Magical Moments* and *Centering*

- Page by Page, *Stronger and Stronger*:

  Sketch
  Tap rhythm
  Add 2-3 note chords
  Movement
  Answer questions

- Develop special pictures into stories with a beginning, middle, and end

- Highlight strengths and lessons learned

- When possible, share and attune with a safe adult

- Repeat: *Thermometers* and *Centering* as needed

- Activities for the week; Practice & *Power Plans*

- Time/date for next session

BOOKMARKS—*continued*

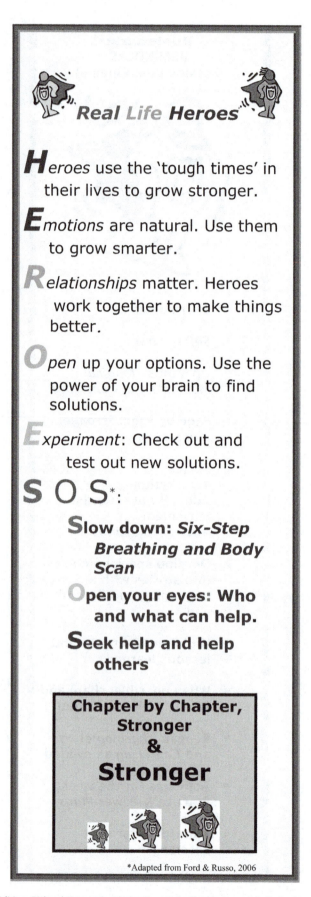

Real Life Heroes

Heroes use the 'tough times' in their lives to grow stronger.

Emotions are natural. Use them to grow smarter.

Relationships matter. Heroes work together to make things better.

Open up your options. Use the power of your brain to find solutions.

Experiment: Check out and test out new solutions.

S O S.:

Slow down: *Six-Step Breathing and Body Scan*

Open your eyes: Who and what can help.

Seek help and help others

Chapter by Chapter, Stronger
&
Stronger

*Adapted from Ford & Russo, 2006

TRAUMA SYMPTOMS AND BRAIN DEVELOPMENT

Psycho-Education Addendum

Understanding brain functions and brain development can help caregivers develop strategies to assist children with traumatic stress.

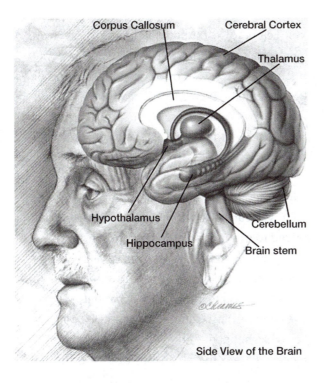

Side View of the Brain

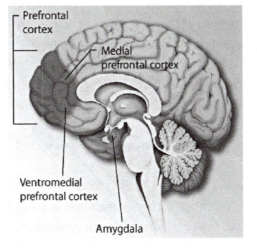

Sources:

Left image: http://www.wpclipart.com/medical/anatomy/brain/human_brain_drawing.jpg.html

Right image: http://www.nimh.nih.gov/health/publications/post-traumatic-stress-disorder-research-fact-sheet/index 34428.pdf

Development of Regulation Capacity

'Bottom Up and Inside Out'

1. Caregiver regulates.
2. Co-regulates with caregivers.
3. Self-regulates.

Goals: Caregiver in charge, providing safety (physical, emotional, relational), nurture, guidance; child learns successful behavior.

> **Brain Functioning by Levels of Stress**
> **Secure: Whole brain**
> **Alarm Mode: Limbic**
> **Reacting: Limbic-Brain Stem (Flee, Fight, Freeze)**
> (Adapted from Perry, 1995)

Four-Step Discipline for Behavior Problems

1. Is it important?[1] If not, ignore. If so, 'SOS' for caregivers.

2. Decode behavior:

   - How does this behavior help children cope with stress? Is it a reaction to a trauma reminder?
   - Brain modulation level: 'secure,' 'alarm mode,' 'reacting.'
   - Developmental level: emotional age, cognitive functioning.
   - Arousal level: hyper . . . modulated . . . hypo

3. Connect with children with your eyes, facial expressions, tone of voice, posture, gestures, timing, and intensity:[2] "What could you do to help the child if you had no words?"[3] Ask "What happened?"

4. Make it a learning experience (4 R's): 'Re-do's,' Reframe (as coping), Restitution (matched to cultural heritage), Replace (reactive behavior patterns with adaptive skills).

   Adapted from Abbuhl (2006) and Siegel and Bryson (2012).

Notes

1. Adapted from John Abbuhl, M.D. (2006) Personal Communication
2. Adapted from Siegel (2012) & Bryson
3. Adapted from John Abbuhl, M.D. (2006) Personal Communication

CAREGIVER POWER PLAN

In order to help children, it helps to start with ourselves. Learning to be better attuned to our own strengths and sensitivities can help us to learn to calm ourselves down when appropriate and become better able to learn what leads to our children's behaviors. This, in turn, can open up ways to help our children get beyond stuck behavior patterns stemming from traumatic events. With an awareness of our own triggers, we can also see more clearly how children's behaviors affect us. Then, we can use that understanding to develop, or reinforce, ways to re-center ourselves so we can attune to children and decode messages children are sending us with their behaviors.

Traumatic events are not limited to one person in a family. When one child or adult is hurt or hurting, emotionally connected family members will feel their pain. We can look at how children's behaviors, and also our own reactions to these behaviors, may be related to past traumas. Some traumas may have been one-time events. Some may have been repeated experiences over a few months or years, adversities experiences over several generations, or dangers that continue into the present time. Multiple traumas that have impacted a child's attachments and regulation require interventions that help rebuild both emotional regulation skills and emotionally supportive relationships. Current dangers call for implementation of safety steps. With a better understanding of what happened that led to behavioral reactions, we can explore antidotes for the distress experienced. Often, these can be ways to bring up opposite feelings or behavioral actions that lead to feeling stronger, more in control, and better about who we are and what we can be. For instance, since shame leads to feeling both isolated and horrible about oneself, an antidote may include ways we can build pride in what we, or our children do, and become more connected, or help our children become more connected, in a positive way with others. Finding ways to apologize, an appropriate form of restitution, and helping other people are important ways to increase pride and decrease shame.

The *Real Life Heroes Life Storybook* includes a Youth Power Plan that is intended to be used in conjunction with the Caregiver's Power Plan. The Youth Power Plan helps engage youths to share their experiences and perspective on what leads to trauma reactions and what helps them calm down and succeed. By using both the Caregiver and the Youth Power Plans, we can put together more effective plans for helping troubled children, including activities for skill development and therapeutic interventions that are informed by a greater understanding of what helps children and caregivers, what happened leading to trauma reactions, and how to engage and build on resources in each family and community and the family's cultural heritage to strengthen resiliency for children and their families.

It is important to do this Power Plan in a way that makes each of us feel safe. Completing this with a therapist is very helpful and especially important when caregivers have experienced traumatic events or find themselves experiencing significant emotional distress.

STEP ONE: Complete a Resilience Survey for Yourself

THESE ARE SOME SPECIAL THINGS ABOUT ME (skills, talents, interests, things I like to do, what I'm proud of)

_____

_____

_____

_____

THESE ARE SOME SPECIAL PEOPLE WHO ARE IMPORTANT TO ME, CARE FOR ME, OR HELP ME LEARN IMPORTANT SKILLS

_____   _____   _____

_____   _____   _____

_____   _____   _____

_____   _____   _____

THESE ARE SOME OF THE BEST THINGS THAT HAPPENED FOR ME AND MY FAMILY

Age   What Happened; Who Was With Me

_____   _____

_____   _____

_____   _____

_____   _____

_____   _____

THESE ARE SOME TIMES I FELT SAFE

Age   What Happened; Who Was With Me

_____   _____

_____   _____

_____   _____

_____   _____

_____   _____

THESE ARE SOME THINGS THAT HAVE MADE ME FEEL STRESSED OR UNSAFE OR REMIND ME OF BAD TIMES

_____

_____

_____

_____

Caregiver Power Plan—*continued*

Some of these things (below) also get me feeling stressed*

☐ Feeling no one listens to me   ☐ Feeling pressured   ☐ Being touched

☐ Lack of privacy   ☐ People yelling   ☐ Loud noises

☐ Feeling lonely   ☐ Arguments   ☐ Not having control

☐ Being alone   ☐ Darkness   ☐ Being stared at

☐ Being teased   ☐ Feeling tired   ☐ Feeling hungry

☐ Being reminded of a very bad time in my life   ☐ Being criticized

☐ Being told 'no' about something I want

☐ Particular people: _____   _____

_____   _____   _____

☐ Particular time of day: _____

☐ Particular time of year: _____

☐ Other things that get me stressed (please describe): _____

_____

_____

_____

THESE ARE SOME THINGS I DO OR FEEL WHEN I AM GETTING REALLY STRESSED AND START TO LOSE SELF-CONTROL (WARNING SIGNS)

_____

_____

_____

I also find some of these things (below) happen when I am getting stressed

☐ Stomach hurts   ☐ Breathing hard   ☐ Racing heart   ☐ Clenching teeth

☐ Clenching fists   ☐ Sweating   ☐ Wringing hands   ☐ Using loud voice

☐ Sleeping a lot   ☐ Trouble sleeping   ☐ Acting hyper   ☐ Swearing

☐ Jittery legs   ☐ Rocking   ☐ Can't sit still   ☐ Being rude

☐ Pacing   ☐ Crying   ☐ Staring at something   ☐ Hurting things

☐ Eating more   ☐ Eating less   ☐ Avoiding people or isolating

☐ Laughing loudly   ☐ Crying out Inappropriately

☐ Other (please describe):

_____

_____

_____

Caregiver Power Plan—*continued*

THESE ARE SOME OF THE THINGS I HAVE DONE WHEN I WAS STRESSED THAT LED TO PROBLEMS FOR ME OR OTHER PEOPLE

_____

_____

_____

_____

I have done some of these things (below) when I was stressed

☐ Losing control ☐ Leaving without permission ☐ Running away

☐ Threatening others ☐ Hurting people ☐ Hurting myself

☐ Attempting suicide ☐ Using alcohol ☐ Using drugs

☐ Getting into fights

☐ Other (please describe)

_____

_____

_____

_____

THESE ARE SOME THINGS THAT HELP ME CALM DOWN AND HELP ME AND OTHER PEOPLE FEEL SAFE IN 'TOUGH TIMES'

_____

_____

_____

_____

These are some of the other things that help me calm down

☐ Talking with family members (who): _____ _____ _____

☐ Talking with adults (who): _____ _____ _____

☐ Talking with friends (who): _____ _____ _____

☐ Time alone in my room ☐ Listening to music ☐ Reading a book

☐ Playing an instrument ☐ Walking ☐ A quiet place

☐ Drawing/art ☐ Molding clay ☐ Jokes/humor

☐ Writing in a journal ☐ Hugging a stuffed animal ☐ Exercising

☐ Cold wash cloth on face ☐ Drinking hot tea ☐ Drinking cold water

☐ Deep breathing ☐ Taking a shower ☐ Playing cards

☐ Video games ☐ Lying down ☐ Meditating

Caregiver Power Plan—*continued*

☐ Getting a hug   ☐ Holding ice in hands   ☐ Using the gym

☐ Rocking chair   ☐ Praying   ☐ Being around others

☐ Being read a story   ☐ Wrapping myself in something warm or soft

☐ Making a collage   ☐ Crying   ☐ Running

☐ Shooting baskets   ☐ Doing chores/jobs   ☐ Yoga

☐ Dancing   ☐ Swimming

☐ Other (please describe):

_____

_____

_____

_____

THESE ARE THINGS THAT MAKE ME FEEL MORE STRESSED AND DO NOT HELP ME CALM DOWN

_____

_____

_____

_____

Some of these things (below) also make me feel more stressed

☐ Being left alone   ☐ Having to be with people   ☐ Sarcasm

☐ Being disrespected   ☐ Not being listened to   ☐ Being ignored

☐ Loud tones of voice   ☐ Peers teasing   ☐ Adults lecturing

☐ Adults giving advice   ☐ Being touched   ☐ Being reminded of 'rules'

☐ Other (please describe):

_____

_____

_____

_____

Caregiver Power Plan—*continued*

STEP TWO: Develop Your Own Self-Control Power Plan

1) These are things I will do to keep myself calm, safe and strong, all day and at night:

_____

_____

_____

_____

_____

And I will do special things to help calm myself:

a. With my eyes: _____

_____

b. With my ears: _____

_____

c. With my nose : _____

_____

d. With my mouth: _____

_____

e. With my hands: _____

_____

f. With my feet: _____

_____

g. With my mind: _____

_____

2) I will watch for these warning signals that tell me when I am getting stressed:

_____

_____

_____

_____

_____

Caregiver Power Plan—*continued*

3) I would like family members, friends, and others who care about me to watch for warning signals like when I:

_____

_____

_____

_____

_____

4) These are people I can call for help, day or night (<u>copy into your smartphone or cut out to take with you</u>):

People I Trust	Names	Phone #'s
Family Members		
Therapists, Clergy, Physicians, Other Professionals		
Friends		

Caregiver Power Plan—*continued*

5) When caring adults notice that I'm getting upset, I would like them to help me feel better and stay safe by:

_____

_____

_____

_____

_____

6) I will help other people feel better and stay safe by:

_____

_____

_____

_____

_____

7) I will develop some of my special skills that can help my family and other people by:

_____

_____

_____

_____

8) I will practice this plan with help from:

_____

_____

_____

_____

Caregiver Power Plan—*continued*

STEP THREE: Help Bring Out the Hero in Your Child by Decoding Your Child's Behaviors in Trauma Reactions

My Child	Clues (key behaviors, repeated behaviors)	What it reflects (reactions to trauma reminders, unresolved fears or shame, unshared experiences)	Stress High–Low	Self-Control Power High–Low
Body (agitation, posture)				
Movement (speed)				
Movement (isolating vs approaching)				
Face				
Voice (loudness, tone)				
Breathing				
Words				
Attention Span				
Concentration				

Caregiver Power Plan—*continued*

DECODE YOUR OWN REACTIONS

Myself	Clues (key behaviors, repeated behaviors)	What it reflects (reactions to trauma reminders, unresolved fears or shame, unshared experiences)	Stress High–Low	Self-Control Power High–Low
Body (agitation, posture)				
Movement (speed)				
Movement (isolating vs approaching)				
Face				
Voice (loudness, tone)				
Breathing				
Words				
Attention Span				
Concentration				

Caregiver Power Plan—*continued*

IDENTIFY REMINDERS OF TRAUMATIC EVENTS FOR YOURSELF AND DEVELOP A PLAN TO STAY MODULATED

Reminders (Triggers)	Reminds Me of _____ at Age _____	Stress Reactions	Antidotes to Stress, Fears, Shame . . . What Can Other Caregivers, Family Members, Therapists, Clergy, Mentors, and The Child Do to Help Adult Stay Modulated?

Caregiver Power Plan—*continued*

Reminders of Traumatic Events for Your Child and a Plan to Help Your Child Stay Modulated with your Support—*continued*

Reminders (Triggers)	Reminds My Child of _____ at Age _____	Stress Reactions	Antidotes to Stress, Fears, Shame . . . Matched to Child's Developmental Age. What Can Caregivers, Family Members, Therapists, Teachers, Clergy, Other Caring Adults and the Child Do to Help Child Stay Regulated?

Caregiver Power Plan—*continued*

Reminders of Traumatic Events for Your Child and a Plan to Help Your Child Stay Modulated with your Support—*continued*

Reminders (Triggers)	Reminds My Child of _____ at Age _____	Stress Reactions	Antidotes to Stress, Fears, Shame . . . Matched to Child's Developmental Age. What Can Caregivers, Family Members, Therapists, Teachers, Clergy, Other Caring Adults and the Child Do to Help Child Stay Regulated?
_____ _____ _____ _____ _____	_____ _____ _____ _____ _____	_____ _____ _____ _____ _____	_____ _____ _____ _____ _____
_____ _____ _____ _____ _____	_____ _____ _____ _____ _____	_____ _____ _____ _____ _____	_____ _____ _____ _____ _____
_____ _____ _____ _____ _____	_____ _____ _____ _____ _____	_____ _____ _____ _____ _____	_____ _____ _____ _____ _____
_____ _____ _____ _____ _____	_____ _____ _____ _____ _____	_____ _____ _____ _____ _____	_____ _____ _____ _____ _____

Caregiver Power Plan—*continued*

Reminders of Traumatic Events for Your Child and a Plan to Help Your Child Stay Modulated with your Support—*continued*

Reminders (Triggers)	Reminds My Child of _____ at Age _____	Stress Reactions	Antidotes to Stress, Fears, Shame . . . Matched to Child's Developmental Age What Can Caregivers, Family Members, Therapists, Teachers, Clergy, Other Caring Adults and the Child Do to Help Child Stay Regulated?
_____ _____ _____ _____ _____	_____ _____ _____ _____ _____	_____ _____ _____ _____ _____	1. Caregiver: _____ _____ _____ _____ _____
_____ _____ _____ _____ _____	_____ _____ _____ _____ _____	_____ _____ _____ _____ _____	2. Child: _____ _____ _____ _____ _____
_____ _____ _____ _____ _____	_____ _____ _____ _____ _____	_____ _____ _____ _____ _____	3. Family & Friends: _____ _____ _____ _____ _____
_____ _____ _____ _____ _____	_____ _____ _____ _____ _____	_____ _____ _____ _____ _____	4. Therapists, Teachers, Clergy, Other Caring Adults: _____ _____ _____ _____

Section D

Centering Activities

23

Breathing, Yoga, Movement, 'Improv,' and Storytelling to Promote Self- and Co-Regulation

Centering activities are listed in order of suggested use matched to chapter content in the *Life Storybook* and phase-based skill development for Phase I of *Real Life Heroes*® (Chapters 1–8). See Chapter 1 in the *RLH Toolkit* for guidelines on selection and adaptation of activities to match child and caregiver levels of development, self-regulation, and strength of children's emotionally supportive relationships. All of these activities can be used to enhance emotionally attuned and supportive relationships. Additional skill-building activities are listed in the *RLH Activity Guide* (in Part V).

Yoga and movement exercises were adapted from multiple sources, including:

Ayres, A. J. (2004). *Sensory integration and the child* (2nd ed.). Los Angeles, CA: Western Psychological Services.

Flynn, L. (2013). *Yoga for children*. Avon, MA: Adamsmedia.

Guber, T., & Kalish, L. (2005). *Yoga pretzels: 50 fun yoga activities for kids and grownups*. Oxford, UK: Barefoot Books.

Harper, J. C. (2013). *Little flower yoga for kids: A yoga and mindfulness program to help your child improve attention and emotional balance*. Oakland, CA: New Harbinger.

MacLean, K. L. (2009). *Moody cow meditates*. Somerville, MA: Wisdom. (See also *Peaceful piggy*).

Marra, T. (2004). *Depressed and anxious: The dialectical behavior therapy workbook for overcoming depression and anxiety*. Oakland, CA: New Harbinger.

Siegel, R. D. (2010). *The mindfulness solution: Everyday practices for everyday problems*. New York, NY: Guilford Press.

Snel, E. (2013). *Sitting still like a frog: Mindfulness exercises for kids*. Boston, MA: Shambhala.

Warner, E., Cook, A., Westcott, A., & Koomar, J. (2014). *SMART: Sensory motor arousal regulation treatment manual*. Brookline, MA: The Trauma Center.

Suggested activities are not meant to replace the guidance of certified yoga teachers, sensory-integration or movement therapists, or medical treatment for specific disorders. Centering Activities should be guided by a therapist trained in trauma treatment and are not meant to be required. See referenced books for pictures of yoga positions and more detailed instructions by experts in yoga, movement, and sensorimotor integration therapies. Recommended books can also be provided to caregivers and team members to continue session activities at home or in home-based support services, group programs, or residential treatment.

Yoga poses and movement exercises require a safe space free from dangerous objects or hard surfaces that a child or caregiver could fall on. Some children or caregivers may find certain exercises to be difficult and some positions may remind children, or caregivers, of previous traumas. Please consult a physician, or ask your clients to consult their physicians, if you or your clients have any concerns about their capacity to do an exercise safely.

After starting use of activities in sessions, encourage children and caregivers to make up their own activities to develop skills for calming alone and together. This can become a special time for the child and caregiver, a 'sanctuary' in their daily routine and, a time to refocus on what really matters.

CENTERING ACTIVITIES

Centering Activities	Self- and Co-Regulation Skills	Page
Chapter 1: SOS AND SAFETY FIRST CARDS		
The Magic of Peacocks	Balance, Focused Attention, Slow Breathing, Modulation	237
SOS Slow Breathing with	Slow Breathing, Focused Attention, Modulation	238
Imagery		238
Muscle Tension Relaxation		239
Practice		239
Breathe Like a Sleepy Little Bear (for calming)	Slow Breathing, Focused Attention, Modulation	240
Breathe Like a Slowly Slithering Snake (to slow down)	Slow Breathing, Focused Attention, Modulation	240
Breathe Like a Rabbit (for increasing energy or waking up)	Breathing, Focused Attention, Modulation	241
Developing Multisensory Awareness (for Safety First Card)	Focused Attention, Modulation	242
'Mindful Eating'		242
'Mindful Smell'		243
'Mindful Touch'		243
'Mindful Hearing'		243
'Mindful Sight'		243
Floating Like a Sailboat (to increase balance, stability)	Balance, Slow Breathing, Focused Attention, Modulation	244
Chapter 2: AFFECT EXPRESSION AND RECOGNITION		
Breathe Like a Little Cat (for showing feelings)	Slow Breathing, Focused Attention, Affect Expression	245
Little Cat Breathing with Yoga (for body awareness and movement)	Movement, Balance, Focused Attention, Affect Expression	246
Breathe Like a Hummingbird (to soothe as you move)	Slow Breathing, Focused Attention, Modulation	247
Roar Like a Lion (to increase energy and courage)	Slow Breathing, Focused Attention, Affect Expression	247
Chapter 3: FOCUSED ATTENTION AND MODULATION MODELED BY HEROES		
Blowing Bubbles	Slow Breathing, Focused Attention	248
Mirroring with Music	Focused Attention, Attunement	248
Fingertip Concentration	Focused Attention	249
Juggling (to increase focused attention)	Focused Attention, Balance	249
Dolphin Inverse Stretch (for increasing flexibility and discharging energy)	Balance, Slow Breathing, Focused Attention, Modulation	250
Back Stretch (for smoothing out stress)	Balance, Slow Breathing, Focused Attention, Modulation	251
Chapter 4: MULTIMODAL POWER PLANS; POCKET POWER CARD		
Disc 'o' Sit and Balance Discs (for increasing focus and balance and child-caregiver attunement)	Balance, Energy Discharge, Modulation	253

Centering Activities—*continued*

Centering Activities	Self- and Co-Regulation Skills	Page
Fitness Balls (for balance and child-caregiver attunement)	Balance, Energy Discharge, Modulation	254
Sensorimotor Activities for: **Smaller Spaces** **Larger Spaces** (to promote use of sensory resistance, touch, sight, pressure, movement for modulation)	Sensory Awareness, Resistance, Balance, Energy Discharge, Modulation	255 255
Bear Stretch and Relax	Beach Rest	256
Chapter 5: CHILD-CAREGIVER ATTUNEMENT AND MODULATION		
Breathing Together (for increasing attunement and modulation)	Slow Breathing, Attunement, Modulation	257
Back to Back (to increase connections and safe touch with caregivers)	Slow Breathing, Attunement, Modulation	257
Child and Caregiver Trust Exercises: Seesaw (increasing safe touch, proprioceptive-resistance, vestibular-balance)	Slow Breathing, Attunement, Modulation	258
Two-Person T Balance (increasing safe touch, proprioceptive-resistance, vestibular-balance)	Slow Breathing, Attunement, Modulation	258
'Up We Go' (to increase safe touch, proprioceptive-resistance, vestibular-balance)	Slow Breathing, Attunement, Modulation	259
Build a House (increasing connection, trust, support, balance)	Slow Breathing, Attunement, Modulation	259
Secret Messages (increasing attunement and communication)	Attunement, Trust	260
Lean Forward 'Ski Jumper' (increasing balance and trust with caregiver)	Attunement, Trust, Balance	260
Chapter 6: FAMILY AND GROUP ATTUNEMENT AND STORYTELLING		
Coffee Can Pass (to increase attention and collaboration)	Balance, Communication	261
Countdowns (to increase attention, concentration, and collaboration in groups or families)	Focused Attention, Communication, Problem-Solving	261
Musical Family (focused attention, attunement)	Focused Attention, Attunement, Memory	262
Circle Time (sharing with three or more)	Attunement, Trust	263
'Improv' Activities	Focused Attention, Communication, Storytelling	264
Word Games (to increase eye contact, memory, storytelling)	Focused Attention, Communication, Memory	265

Centering Activities—*continued*

Centering Activities	Self- and Co-Regulation Skills	Page
Chapter 7: INCREASING MINDFUL MODULATION		
Breathe Like a Happy Elephant (to increase self-care)	Balance, Slow Breathing, Focused Attention, Modulation	265
Tree Yoga (to increase balance)	Balance, Slow Breathing, Focused Attention, Modulation	266
Glider Airplane (to increase balance and good feelings)	Balance, Slow Breathing, Focused Attention, Modulation	266
Mindful Motion (to increase focus, body awareness, and modulation in daily activities)	Balance, Slow Breathing, Focused Attention, Modulation	267
Chapter 8: INCREASING VERBAL PLANNING, THINKING, AND COLLABORATION		
Disc 'o' Stories (to develop problem-solving strategies and support)	Focused Attention, Communication, Storytelling	268
Solution Circle (to foster getting help from others to develop solutions/strategies to difficult problems)	Focused Attention, Communication, Problem-Solving	269
Kindness Circle (to increase focus and sharing of kindness and positive regard)	Kindness, Caring, Positive Identity	269

The Magic of Peacocks

to increase balance, attention, slow breathing, modulation, and constructive beliefs

Experiment balancing a peacock feather in different positions:

1. Stand in a balanced position with knees bent, feet comfortably spread, shoulders centered over hips, eyes on the top of the feather with head upright, and low smooth breathing. Notice how this feels.

2. Now, tense your legs and lean to one side until you feel you could tip over.

3. Try saying a negative belief (e.g., "Everybody hates me" or "I'm bad, really bad") or a secret fear.

4. Try balancing the feather while moving quickly around the room in a hyper manner, breathing fast. Now, try balancing while moving extremely slowly, as if you can hardly move.

5. Try balancing with your eyes darting left, right, up, and down, watching every corner of the room.

6. Try balancing two feathers at once; it's like two competing demands on your time or conflicting goals.

    What feels best? What helps you stay balanced?

Once children have become comfortable balancing the feathers, it is useful to point out lessons or imagery e.g., how looking at the top of the peacock feather keeps our heads centered and we become aware, even without words, when the feather first starts to tilt, and then we can make tiny adjustments; whereas, if we focus down on the bottom of the feather, we are only able to see larger changes and then need to make bigger reactions. Point out how this is similar to how becoming skilled at body scanning and awareness of our bodily reactions helps us to cope better with stressors before things get more difficult.

Children can be encouraged to build their feather skills by gently tossing feathers from one hand to another and later by passing feathers to the therapist or a caring adult. Passing the feather could also be used as a signal to move on to the next phase of the session.

After introducing balancing feathers, children can be encouraged to show on a xylophone or other instrument how their balancing would sound if put to music. If the child is not happy with their balancing, they could be asked to show in tones how they'd like the balancing music to sound and then to make a bridge melody to connect their current balancing with how they would like it to sound.

Adapted from Macy et al. (2005, notes 35–40), feathers are recommended.

SOS Slow Breathing

Practice breathing in slowly through your nose as you count: 1, 2, 3.

Hold for one second and let your breath flow out through your mouth counting: 3, 2, 1.

Repeat this several times and practice every day.

Put one arm on your belly and one arm on your chest. Feel the air slowly lift your belly up as you breathe in and then drop as you let the air out.

If it helps, have someone you trust count or beat a rhythm softly on a drum or glockenspiel with a note chosen by the child. Count approximately one beat per second.

You can also do this while humming or with words using the same rhythm, for example:

• Breathe in Slow

• Hold

• Let It Go

After doing this several times, add a slight smile as you breathe in.

Adapted from Siegel (2010).

Slow Breathing with Imagery

Invite children and caregivers to use a Hoberman Mini Sphere (or similar expansive toy).

Ask caregiver (or therapist) to slowly pull open Mini Sphere and count (1, 2, 3) while children breathe in.

Then slowly close Mini Sphere as caregiver counts (3, 2, 1) and child breathes out.

Repeat with children guiding the caregiver's breathing.

Add hand motion and energy to Slow Breathing.

Have children rub the palms of their hands together vigorously and feel the warmth generated between their hands. Imagine this warmth as energy. If you want, rub your hands together and then press them on your neck. Feel the warmth.

Invite children and caregivers to share the warmth generated with each other, palm to palm, or on each other's shoulders, arms or necks if this feels safe.

Then ask caregivers to rub their hands and then slowly pull open their hands to about the width of the child's body and count (1, 2, 3) while children breathe. Then slowly close their hands as caregiver counts (3, 2, 1) and children breathe out.

Repeat with children guiding the caregiver's breathing.

Imagine the air going in, touching knots in your body, and letting all the tension go like a giant bubble as children breathe out carrying with the bubble all the tension in the child's body.

Slow Breathing with Muscle Tension-Relaxation

Add muscle tension and relaxation with each breath.

Take a breath and count (1, 2, 3) as you tighten up your cheeks, nose, lips, forehead.

Then 'let it go' as you let the breath out (3, 2, 1).

Take another breath and tighten up your chest, arms, belly.

'Let it go.'

Then tighten your hips, legs, feet, and toes.

'Let it go.'

(*Note*: For younger children, focus on one body part at a time.)

SOS Breathing Practice

Practice SOS with slow breathing in different situations every day to make this skill stronger and stronger. Like any skill, slow mindful breathing takes a lot of practice, like learning to play a musical instrument or make a jump shot. Athletes and musicians practice for hours each day to strengthen their skills.

Try using SOS the next time you are about to take a test at school, play in a sports competition like a basketball game, or when you muster the courage to dive off a high diving board, swim to the bottom of a deep pool, or ski down a double diamond ski slope. Use your SOS skills the next time there is a storm warning in your area.

You can use you breathing and power to focus your attention to make things better wherever you are.

To build your slow breathing skills, try the following breathing activities at home with your family or in sessions.

Breathe Like a Sleepy Bear

(for calming)

Imagine you're a bear sleeping peacefully all winter long.

Sit up, lift your head up high with your back straight.

Close your eyes and feel yourself breathe.

Breathe in through your nose very slowly like a sleepy bear as you count: 1, 2, 3. Then hold for a second and let your breath go out slowly: 3, 2, 1. Do this six times and see how you feel.

If you like, try doing this with a caregiver you trust, sitting back to back. See if you can feel each other breathe.

Adapted from Guber and Kalish (2005).

Breathe Like a Slowly Slithering Snake

(to slow down)

Snakes move slowly, gliding over the ground with their eyes open. Try breathing like a snake. Sit up with your head stretching up to the sky.

Wrap your left arm over your belly and your right arm over your chest. Snakes don't need arms.

Breathe in slowly, filling up your belly, as you count: 1, 2, 3. Feel the air push your arm up.

Then breathe out slowly, making a soft, steady hiss for as long as you can.

See how long you can make the hiss go on and on and on and on . . .

If you like, see who can hiss the longest.

Who can hiss the smoothest and the longest?

Adapted from Guber and Kalish (2005).

Breathe Like a Rabbit

(for increasing energy or waking up)

Rabbits are always watching, ready to jump.

Wake yourself up by breathing like a rabbit.

Sit on your knees.

Straighten your back.

Lift your shoulders up high.

Now, lift up your nose and sniff four times, breathing in four big breaths.

Then, let the air go back out your nose as you count: 3, 2, 1.

Try this six times and see how you feel.

Adapted from Guber and Kalish (2005).

Developing Multisensory Awareness
(Safety First Card)

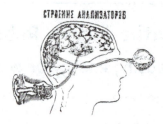

'Mindful Eating'
(to increase use of taste for calming)

When immigrants came to the United States in the 1800s, they had to stop at Ellis Island and wait to be cleared to come into the country. While they waited, boys and girls, men and women, were sometimes presented with food they had never seen before in their native countries. One food that seemed very strange was a banana. Some didn't know how to eat a banana and bit into the skin.

Imagine you are coming from a far away place and presented with different foods. Try feeling the food, smelling the food. Very slowly and carefully taste the food, and let the taste unfold slowly in your mouth.

Foods to try include: dry roasted, unsalted almonds (feel the edges and the sweetness emerge as they melt in your mouth), dark (72% or higher) chocolate, dried fruit (raisins, apricots, etc.), clementines (smell rind as you slowly unpeel), and, of course, bananas.

What foods or flavors (e.g., vanilla, chocolate, mint) help give you energy?

Do any foods or flavors remind you of things that happened in your life? If so, write these down and save them for Chapter 10.

What smells help you calm down? You may want to include these in your Safety First Plan and later (in Chapter 4) in your *Power Plan*.

Mindful Smell, Touch, Hearing, and Sight

Mindful Smell

Place a couple of different 'essential oils' or liquid fragrances (available online or from health food stores) on a piece of paper. Then, slowly bring the paper closer to your nose and sniff the paper. How does it feel in your nose? Is there any taste associated with the smell?

What are some of your favorite smells?

What smells help give you energy?

Do any smells remind you of any good times or tough times? If so, write these down and save them for Chapter 10.

What smells help you calm down? You may want to include these in your Safety First Plan and later (in Chapter 4) in your *Power Plan*.

Mindful Touch

Put a few drops of rubbing alcohol and also different kinds of lotions on your hands.

Focus on how the drops look resting on your hands. Feel the difference in your skin between the areas with drops of rubbing alcohol or lotion and where there isn't any. Slowly smell the drops. What does it remind you of?

Rub slowly in circles, clockwise, then counterclockwise. How does it make you feel?

Mindful Sight

Watch a movie with no sound (e.g., *Casablanca*). Focus on photographs. What feelings do you recognize in the movies or photos? What feelings do you sense in yourself as you watch the movies or look at the photographs?

Mindful Hearing

Listen to the music from a movie without seeing the visual movie, or listen to a range of music suggesting a range of moods. What feelings do you recognize in the music? What feelings to you recognize in yourself as you listen to the music? Use children's or caregivers' favorite music for calming, for energizing, for expressing happiness, anger, sadness.

Make up music and practice remembering music in different places and also reminding yourself of music where possible (e.g., playing music on smartphone apps for pianos, guitars, etc.).

Adapted from Marra (2004).

Floating Like a Sailboat

(to increase balance, stability)

Sit on the floor with your legs stretching out ahead.

Pull your knees up, making an upside down 'V' with your legs.

Move your arms behind your back.

Lean back and place your hands on the floor behind you to support yourself.

Press your toes down and keep your feet planted on floor.

Imagine yourself floating on warm, smooth water.

Breathe in slowly as you count: 1, 2, 3 and let the air go out: 3, 2, 1.

Imagine your breath gently blowing your sailboat forward through the smooth water.

When you're ready, lift up your legs into the air so they are parallel to the floor.

Stretch your arms forward to balance yourself.

Imagine you are floating out on a quiet lake and feel the strength of your belly holding yourself together.

Breathe in and out slowly (1, 2, 3 . . . 3, 2, 1) and let yourself relax.

If you like, do this with a caregiver. Imagine you are floating together down a river or across a lake.

Adapted from Guber and Kalish (2005).

Breathe Like a Little Cat
(for showing feelings)

Little cats can sit quietly, watching as they breathe, saving their energy. They move carefully, quietly, on soft padded feet. Cats can move fast when they need to.

Little cats 'meow' in all kinds of ways to check out if someone is a friend, somebody to run away from, or someone to warn to 'stay away, leave me alone' with a loud 'MEOW.'

Cats can 'meow' in all kinds of ways.

Try breathing like a little cat. Sit on your knees then crouch forward.

Breathe in, filling up your belly, while you count: 1, 2, 3.

Feel how the air gives you energy.

Then breathe out slowly, making a soft warm 'meow' for as long as you can.

See how long you can make the meow go on and on and on . . .

Adapted from Guber and Kalish (2005).

Breathe Like a Little Cat
(Part II)

Try this again, breathe in (1, 2, 3), and this time breathe out a little faster and make your 'meow' sound a little scared, like you are calling for help.

Next, breathe in slow and deep (1, 2, 3) and this time breathe out strong and fast with a loud 'MEOW' to warn anyone who might threaten you to 'STAY AWAY!'

Breathe in slow again and this time breathe out a slow, sad 'meow,' like you missed your mommy or daddy cat.

If you like, breathe like a cat with someone else who appreciates cats and together show all kinds of cat feelings.

See how gently you can 'meow,' how scared, how angry, how sad, and any other feelings you would like to 'meow.'

Adapted from Guber and Kalish (2005).

Little Cat Breathing with Yoga
(for body awareness and movement)

Cats show feelings with their bodies as well as their 'meows.'

Put your hands ahead of you on the floor with your back straight and rest on your hands and knees and the tops of your feet.

Feel your toes stretched behind you and imagine your back as straight as a table top.

Lift up your head, arch your back a little, and smile up at someone or something you like, as you make a 'happy meow.'

Now, arch your back up as high as you can, lift your head up tall, and make a loud, angry 'meow' that could scare a large dog away.

Now sag your head down a little, frown, and make a sad 'meow.'

Lower your head so you are looking back at your legs, and make very, very sad 'meow.'

Try out other feelings with different positions and 'meows.'

Don't forget to have some fun. Cats like to play!

Adapted from Flynn (2013).

Breathe Like a Hummingbird

(to soothe as you move)

Did you ever wonder how hummingbirds keep flying as they hum their way from flower to flower?

Keep your energy going smoothly by breathing like a hummingbird.

First, soften your lips and face so you're ready to feel yourself breathe.

Next, hum, first high, then low, then high again and again low. See how it feels.

Find a humming sound that you like best.

Harmonize with someone you like.

Hummingbirds like to hum together . . .

Adapted from Guber and Kalish (2005).

Roar Like a Lion

(to increase energy and courage)

Sit on your knees.

Place your hands on your knees and lean forward.

Take a huge lion-size breath through your nose.

Open your eyes super wide.

Next, open your mouth as wide as it goes, stick your tongue out, and stretch it down toward your chin.

Now, ROAR out all the air inside you as though you were the king of the jungle.

Feel the strength and courage in your "ROAR."

You can also try this sitting on a chair next to a table.

Lean forward with your arms stretched out and let your inner lion ROAR.

Adapted from Flynn (2013).

Blowing Bubbles

(to increase focus and modulated breathing)

See who can blow the largest bubble.

Who can catch it?

(**Hint**: Blow really slow, smoothly and gently.)

*Adapted from Hubert (2013).

Mirroring with Music

(to build focusing skills and attunement with caregivers)

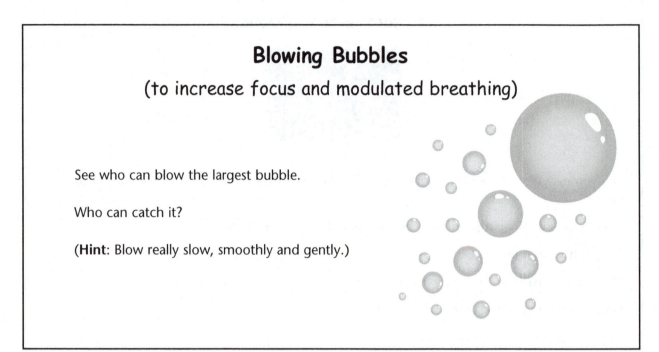

Caregiver (or therapist) taps three different notes, and child imitates.

Caregiver adds a fourth note, and child imitates.

Caregiver adds a fifth note, and child imitates.

Continue to add notes in different repeated patterns to build memory skills. Match number of notes in a repeated pattern to child's capacity. For guitar players, try using notes from a minor pentatonic scale.

This exercise leads to creation of a simple melody.

*Adapted from Hubert (2013).

Fingertip Concentration

(to build focusing skills, including body position)

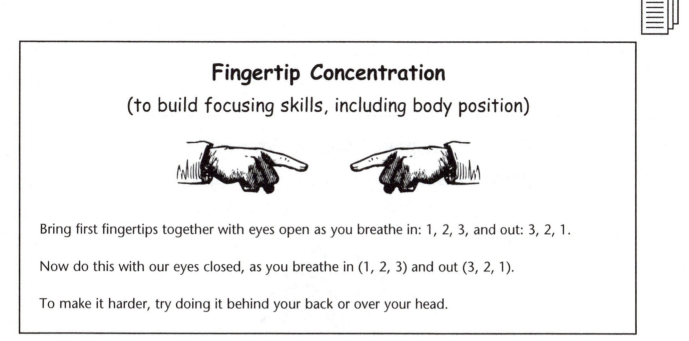

Bring first fingertips together with eyes open as you breathe in: 1, 2, 3, and out: 3, 2, 1.

Now do this with our eyes closed, as you breathe in (1, 2, 3) and out (3, 2, 1).

To make it harder, try doing it behind your back or over your head.

Adapted from Flynn (2013).

Juggling

(to increase focused attention)

Place two small scarves (or two squish balls) in one hand and one scarf (or one squish ball) in the other hand. For scarves, bunch them in your hand so the first is ready to toss.

Throw one scarf up from the hand with two scarves.

Then throw the scarf up from the hand with one scarf.

It helps to use different color scarves.

Try calling out the colors of the scarves when you catch them (e.g., "green, blue, red") and focus your eyes on the scarves.

Juggling tips and guidelines can be found online.

Adapted from Flynn (2013).

Dolphin Inverse Stretch

(for increasing flexibility and discharging energy)

Lie on your belly. Feel the floor support you.

Imagine you are floating in calm water.

Hold your hands together behind your back. This forms the dolphin's fin.

Breathe in slowly (1, 2, 3) and lift up your arms behind your back, holding your hands together and resting them on your backbone. Lift up your legs and your chest as you breathe out (3, 2, 1).

Repeat this as much as you want to stretch out and then imagine you are relaxing back on to your belly a gliding on the floor.

Pretend you are a fast-swimming dolphin as you go up and down. Dolphins are also smart and friendly and like to talk, dolphin-talk.

Is there anyone you'd like to swim like a dolphin with?

What would you say to him or her in dolphin-talk?

If you like, try talking like a dolphin with someone you like to swim with.

Or, make a plan to go swimming with someone you'd like to spend more time with and pretend you are two dolphins swimming together.

Adapted from Flynn (2013).

Back Stretch

(for smoothing out stress)

Lie on your back on a soft mat or carpet.

Imagine yourself floating gently on warm water in a pool with someone you trust next to you and watching over you.

Bring your knees up.

Place your hands on your knees and pull your knees gently against your chest.

Hold your knees against your chest and take a slow breath (1, 2, 3).

Hold your breath for as long as you are comfortable.

Then let your breath out (3, 2, 1) as you slowly place your legs back on the floor.

Repeat this several times and think about who you would like to have next to you and watching over you while you relax.

(*Note*: For some children, lying on their back may remind them of being abused, and this exercise may not be appropriate before trauma desensitization.)

Healing Hands and Breathing Slow
(for calming)

Breathe slow as you count (1, 2, 3), then hold your breath for just a second and let your breath flow out as you count (3, 2, 1).

Close your eyes if that's comfortable and focus on your fingertips.

Imagine them getting warm.

Gently massage in circles below your collarbone 10 small circles with fingers from each hand.

Now, gently massage circles on your forehead and continue up to the top of your head, then down the sides to the back of your neck and in the middle of your back between your shoulders.

Imagine your fingers are making blood flow in your body, spreading warmth and comfort.

Give yourself a slow, gentle hug by crossing your arms and pulling your arms gently toward your belly.

If you like, try this with someone you feel safe with and trust.

Adapted from Flynn (2013).

Chair Yoga Exercises
(for sitting through a long class)

Sit comfortably.

Feel how your back is supported by the chair.

Wiggle toes in your shoes, rock your lower legs, and breathe slow.

Scan over your body.

Breathe in (1, 2, 3) and feel your breath touch tense parts of your body.

Breathe out and let the tension flow out with each breath.

Sit forward in your chair with your back rounded and relaxed.

Breathe slowly (1, 2, 3) as you arch your back straight.

At the count of '3,' slowly breathe out and relax your back again.

Repeat as much as you like.

Adapted from Flynn (2013).

Disc 'o' Sit and Balance Discs

(for increasing focus and balance and child-caregiver attunement)

Use discs to introduce playfulness and permission to move in a safe space with mats for safety from falling.

If you like, try these activities (below) with someone you trust and mirror what each person does:

Sitting Balance:

Balance on Disc 'o' Sit while sitting still or rocking. Have caregiver copy children's movement.

Belly Balance:

e.g., Superman flying, or shark or dolphin yoga positions.

Side Balance:

Place one elbow on disc with forearm extended parallel to the floor. Keep your feet pressed together with side of one foot on the floor. Balance on side with other arm bent with hand on hip.

Sitting Balance:

Gradually extend legs and lean back with hands on floor to support or balance like a seesaw with arms and legs forward. If you can, lean forward and balance with arms extended in front of you.

Standing on Balance Disc (requires safe space with soft mats):

Experiment with arms stretched out to balance. With feet on mat, crouch down slowly as if you were going to sit down with arms extended ahead to balance.

Please follow directions and see pictures included with Disc 'o' Sit and Balance Discs. Safe space required and soft mats for standing. Use away from furniture or other hard objects.

Fitness Balls

Involves multiple sensory inputs:

- Touch with skin receptors: light to deep, variable to steady.
- Proprioceptive through muscle movement and resistance to gravity.
- Vestibular through inner ear balance from movement (e.g., direct line, arcs, up and down).

Activities:

- Sit on, lean to sides or front to back, bounce; keep knees together to make harder.
- Lie on fitness ball in different positions (e.g., on belly, on legs, on chest).
- Slow, smooth sit-ups.
- Caregiver rolls ball back and forth on children lying on soft surface (mat) applying pressure levels directed by children. Encourage caregivers to ask children how much pressure they want and for how long.
- Roll, bounce, spin, toss ball back and forth, and invite children to talk when ready.
- Do tricks with ball.
- Use also to promote attunement with caregivers. Children model movement on ball; caregiver mirrors. Then, reverse with caregiver modeling and children mirroring what caregiver does.

Work with child's energy level to promote attunement and regulation:

For hyper-aroused children:

- More intensity, increased repetitions, or a longer time may be needed to calm down (Warner et al., 2014) e.g., children triggered by reminders of abuse in family may need to toss fitness ball vigorously for several minutes before continuing work.
- Rocking with a slow, steady rhythm. prone over fitness ball can decrease arousal level, calming child; this can be guided by a safe emotionally attuned caregiver.
- Slow, steady bouncing calms with vestibular and proprioceptive input.
- Children may need to repeat an activity vigorously to get sufficient sensory input to satiate their need for that type of input (Hughes & Koomar, 2010).
- Watch for children developing a steady rhythm.

For hypo-aroused child:

- Gradual shifts with prolonged moderate sensory input are recommended to increase arousal level (Warner et al., 2014) e.g., rolling physioball over children's backs with alternate faster patting motions over 20 minutes may help their arousal increase gradually to a more comfortable level, within their 'window of tolerance'. However, a sudden, strong input (e.g., yelling, pushing, slapping) could lead to increased dysregulation (Warner et al., 2014).

Use in a safe space for activity. Avoid sharp corners, hard objects, and breakables. See instructions and pictures included with fitness ball.

Sensorimotor Activities for Smaller Spaces

(to promote use of sensory resistance, touch, sight, pressure, movement for modulation)

- **Chair:** pushing/pulling chair with caregiver (weighted resistance, deep muscle movement). Or, while children are seated in chair, ask them to try to lift chair with arms, hands underneath while seated. Encourage children to push down on arm rests with different levels of pressure: light to hard.

- **Eyes:** scan room, find things that are soft, hard, yellow . . .

- **Tactile:** use Disc 'o' Sit bottom, fabrics, sandpaper, or sand.

- **Hands:**

  - Resistance; squeeze something hard.

  - Press fingertips together.

  - Intertwine fingers in hands, twist outwards and push forward, then twist back to chest. See how many twists you can do.

  - Provide fidget materials for hands (e.g., see Office Playground, Amazon).

Sensorimotor Tools for Larger Spaces and Sensory-Integration Rooms

- **Stepping stones:** create a pathway to walk (to caregiver).

- **Low balance beam:** balance with walking or standing.

- **Bosu:** bounce and balance.

- **Disc 'o' Sit:** bounce while sitting and balance in different positions.

- **Balance board:** or disc balance while standing or gently rocking.

- **Mats:** build forts, hide behind, climb on, climb under.

- **Weighted soft ball:** toss (and talk, when ready) in safe environment to allow strong proprioception, deep muscle movement, and touch.

- **Small trampoline:** jump (and talk, when ready) to allow deep muscle movement, balance, can promote talking while jumping.

- **Weighted blanket:** resistance, reducing stimulation (avoid any wrapping or containment of children by adults and any limitation of breathing).

- **Large pillows or stuffed animal-shaped pillows:** jumping, throwing self into soft resistance.

Ensure safety in spaces available. Avoid sharp corners and breakables. Consider creation of a sensory-integration room and SMART training (Warner et al., 2014). Consultation with an Ayres Sensory Integration O.T. is also recommended to promote development of sensory discrimination and body awareness, coordination, planning, and sensory modulation.

Bear Stretch and Relax
(for calming and rest)

Invite children to lie down if comfortable with this. If possible, ask children if they would like to be covered with a soft or weighted blanket. (Be careful not to cover children's faces.)

Breathe in deeply through your nose, and stretch out your body as tall as you can be. Imagine you are a big black bear getting ready for winter's sleep.

Then, breathe out, saying 'whoooooooo,' or a sound you have made up that relaxes you.

At the same time, let your arms and legs relax, and bring your palms up by your side.

Feel the floor or mat beneath you supporting your body.

Close your eyes if this is comfortable.

Take in another breath, breathe in, stretch, and hold tight again. Breathe out slowly, relax.

Breathe in again without stretching and feel your body become heavier.

Breathe out and repeat.

Feel your body get heavier and heavier each time you breathe in.

(*Note*: It may help to do activities first that expend more energy for high-arousal children. You can also use a fitness ball to gently 'smoosh' down pressure, asking children if they would like caregivers to try this and if they would like more or less pressure.)

Beach Rest

For some children, it may be helpful to ask them to imagine lying on a beach, to feel the warm sand on their bodies, to hear the waves gently rolling in, and to feel people they trust lying next to them on either side.

If you have a sand tray, invite children to move their fingers through the sand.

Breathing Together

Sit with your legs crossed and backs together.

Sit with your backs as straight as you can and lean into each other just a little.

If you feel comfortable, close your eyes and breathe deeply in and out through your nose. Put your hands on your belly and feel the air filling up your body.

Can you feel your partner's breath?

Can you hear your partner breathing?

See if you can match your partner's breathing with your own breathing.

Then, breathe in and out at the same time (1, 2, 3, 3, 2, 1).

Adapted from Harper (2013).

Back to Back

(to increase connections and safe touch with caregivers)

Sit back to back with child.

Breathe in and sit up as high as you can be.

Breathe in again and put your left hand on your right knee.

Breathe in a third time and reach your right hand back and touch the left knee of caregiver.

Breathe in and out twice.

Now let's do it the opposite way:

Breathe in again and put your right hand on your left knee.

Breathe in a third time and reach your left hand back and touch the right knee of caregiver.

Adapted from Flynn (2013).

Seesaw

(increasing safe touch, trust, proprioceptive-resistance, vestibular-balance)

Sit down facing each other with legs extended and feet touching (no shoes or socks if children are comfortable with this). How does it feel? Press gently, firmly, steadily . . .

Lean toward each other and hold each other's hands.

Take turns, one person pulling the other slowly and smoothly while leaning backwards and then letting the other person pull back slowly and smoothly.

Now, try doing this while breathing together as you pull back and forth, counting. Breathe in (1, 2, 3) as you pull one way, and breathe out (3, 2, 1) as you pull the other way.

Adapted from Guber and Kalish (2005).

Two-Person T Balance

(increasing safe touch, trust, proprioceptive-resistance, vestibular-balance)

Face each other and hold each other's hands firmly with your toes almost touching.

Feel the strength in how you grip each other's hands.

Lean backwards slowly, holding each other up.

As you both lean backwards, bend your knees until you are both squatting. The empty space beneath your outstretched arms and your toes should form the shape of a 'T.'

Keep leaning backwards with your arms holding each other and straighten your legs slowly to stand up.

Try this a second time and breathe in slowly (1, 2, 3) as you go down, and then breathe out slowly (3, 2, 1) as you rise up.

How does it feel to balance each other?

Adapted from Guber and Kalish (2005).

'Up We Go'

(to increase safe touch, proprioceptive-resistance, vestibular-balance)

Sit back to back on the floor and imagine yourself forming a two-sided chair.

Bring your knees up with your feet on the floor and hook your elbows together.

Press your backs into each other.

Keep your backs straight and slowly push your legs down so you rise up.

Support each other as you stand up, keeping your elbows hooked together.

Breathe in together (1, 2, 3) and breathe out (3, 2, 1).

See if you can feel your partner breathe along with you.

Feel how you keep each other balanced.

If you wish, practice so you can rise up smoothly together.

Adapted from Guber and Kalish (2005).

Build a House

(increasing connection, trust, support, balance)

Stand up and look face to face with someone you trust, arms at your sides, a couple of feet apart (about the length of children's arms).

Imagine you are the sides of a house.

Press the palms of your hands together ahead of you and bend forward so your arms are stretching out and your palms are still touching.

Lean forward together and gently move your hands up together as though you were pushing a roof over the sides of your house. Visualize creating a strong solid roof that can protect both of you from stormy weather.

Balance and breathe steadily (1, 2, 3) and let it out (3, 2, 1).

If one person is taller than the other, it helps to have the taller person kneel.

You can also do a version of this sitting in chairs.

Adapted from Guber and Kalish (2005).

Secret Messages

(increasing attunement and communication)

Have children sit comfortably in front of caregivers.

Caregivers gently use first finger to draw a shape of something calming or to write a letter, a word, or a message on children's backs.

Ask children to focus on parents' finger and to try to figure out what message the parent is sending.

Messages could include special qualities caregivers see in children.

Reverse and have children write on parents' backs.

Try a gentle massage on children's backs.

Adapted from Flynn (2013).

Lean Forward 'Ski Jumper'

(increasing balance and trust with caregiver)

Have children stand in front of caring adults.

Children stretch arms backwards and caregivers holds children's arms just above wrists gently but firmly.

Caring adults put one foot forward to balance with knees bent just a little.

Children lean forward with adults balancing. Then, adults pull children gently back to standing position.

Repeat with breathing: children and caring adults breathe in as children lean forward and adults count (1, 2, 3). Hold, then breathe out (3, 2, 1) as adults pull children gently back to standing position.

Try this again and pretend you are an Olympic ski jumper flying into the air like a bird flying through the sky.

Your partner can help you land upright on both feet.

Adapted from Flynn (2013).

Coffee Can Pass

(to increase attention and collaboration)

Sit in a circle.

Pass coffee can between feet from one person to another without dropping.

Adapted from Stanchfield (2007).

Countdowns

(to increase focused attention, concentration, problem-solving, and collaboration in groups or families)

Form a circle (or several circles to compete with each other).

Give squish ball to one person.

Instruct group:
"Pass the ball from one person to another, and with each pass count backwards from 100 by 1's (or 3's, depending on developmental level) to the lowest number possible. Let me know when you are done."

Time group and announce winner.

Ask groups to work together to increase speed by collaborating.

Then repeat and make each repetition more difficult by adding others or assigning different people to be distractors who run around group, make noises, block communication, and act, in general, like seventh graders in a food fight. Ask group to count down by more difficult numbers (e.g., 5's, 3's, 7's, 9's, or from 150).

Adapted from Markowitz (2005).

Musical Family

(focused attention, attunement)

Sit with caregivers or other people you trust in a circle.

Imagine you are a family (or group) of troubadours, musicians using drums, xylophones, voices for singing and humming, and any other musical instruments.

Take a slow breath in (1, 2, 3) and let it out (3, 2, 1).

Listen quietly to the sounds in the room with your eyes closed if you feel comfortable.

When the group is ready, take another slow breath in (1, 2, 3) and let it out (3, 2, 1), but this time breathe out with a hum.

Listen to how you harmonize with each other.

Think of something that brings out feelings you'd like to explore, for example, the first snow of the year, a deep forest, a bubbling brook, a scary nightmare, your first day in first grade or middle school . . .

Ask one person to be leader and start playing a rhythm or tune. Then, one by one, others join in and add to what was already shared to create a song.

Keep adding to the song until you feel you've reached an end point.

Then, sit quietly again and breathe in and out.

If you wish, pick a new musical theme and start a new song.

*Adapted from Guber and Kalish (2005)

Circle Time

(sharing with three or more)

Sit in circle.

Close your eyes and breathe in a way that helps you relax.

Or, breathe together, as a family or group: breathing in (1, 2, 3) and out (3, 2, 1).

Scan over your body. Feel how the floor is supporting you.

Now, hold hands in your circle. Notice how it feels to be connected.

Have one person begin sending a message with no words by using a pattern of squeezes (not too hard please . . .).

Gently squeeze the hand of the person to the right and pass the squeeze message along until it gets back to the person who started.

Now, pass a gentle squeeze message along and add a word to share how you feel right now.

Next, pass a squeeze message and a word that shows something you'd like to share with other people in your circle (e.g., courage, play).

'Improv' Activities

(to strengthen connections and promote storytelling)

Eye to Eye,

It's hard to lie.

Four Rules of 'Improv' for Trauma Therapy

1. "Always* Agree . . . Start with a YES and see where that takes you . . . "

2. "The second rule of improvisation is not only to say yes, but YES, AND. You are supposed to agree and add something of your own . . . YES, AND means don't be afraid to contribute . . . Always make sure you're adding something to the discussion."

3. "MAKE STATEMENTS . . . Don't ask questions all the time . . . Whatever the problem, be part of the solution."

4. "There are no mistakes, only opportunities . . . In improv, there are no mistakes, only beautiful happy accidents."

'Improv' Storytelling

- Clap simultaneously with eye contact to the person next to you; that person turns and claps with eye contact with the next person, continue around the circle.

- One-word stories: One word from each person, each person builds on story, second word from next person and so on. Then, when story is complete, nod, bow, with hands together in prayer/respect.

- Sentence stories: Same as above with sentences by each person going around the circle.

- Yin Yang Stories: This activity highlights how there are two sides to everything. Each person builds on evolving story. In pairs, one person, starts: "Fortunately . . . " Second person adds: "Unfortunately . . . " First person: "Fortunately . . . " Second person . . .

*Obviously, there are exceptions for safety but these should be very rare. Liberally adapted from Fey (2011, pp. 84–85). Adapted from Kagan (2010) and other sources.

Word Games

(to increase attention, memory, eye contact, team building, storytelling)

Send a Message:

Start with a three-syllable word, 'Man-hat-tan.' Leader claps hands and points hand to person across circle to continue syllables, who then points to next person.

Next, add a second word (e.g., 'New Jer-sey'). Do two words, going around. Then add a third three-syllable word (e.g., 'Vir-gin-ia'). Go around.

Next, try to speed up.

Repeat with different words or three-part combinations of facial gestures, sounds, and movements.

Sensorimotor option: Try with rolling Disc 'o' Sit or soft ball in safe space.

Adapted from Kagan (2010) and other sources.

Breathe Like a Happy Elephant

(to increase self-care)

Stand up tall.

Let your arms fall down and clasp your hands together in front of you like the trunk of an elephant.

Breathe in deeply through your nose, counting 1, 2, 3, and raise your arms up high over your head like an elephant raising its trunk up high to the sky.

Lean back and hold in your breath for just a second.

Feel how the air fills your body and makes you feel strong.

Then, let the air flow out your mouth as you bring your arms down to your legs.

Try this two more times.

Imagine that each time you blow the air out of your trunk that you are showering yourself with good feelings (love, caring, laughing, playing), just like an elephant showers itself with water from its trunk.

See if you can feel the good feelings falling back down after you breathe.

If you like, do this one more time and shower someone near you with good feelings.

Who else would you like to shower with good feelings?

Adapted from Guber and Kalish (2005).

Tree Yoga

(to increase balance)

Stand up with your arms and hands stretching down.

Imagine you're a tree and your feet are your roots holding you steady into the ground.

Bring your palms together in front of your chest in a prayer-like pose.

Lift up one foot and press it against the opposite leg at your thigh.

Then, reach up like a tree's branches stretching up to the sky.

Place your hands together, palm to palm, up over your head.

Imagine yourself as a strong and beautiful tree enjoying the sunshine.

Now push your hands up as high as they can go and imagine yourself growing taller and taller, bigger and stronger.

As you feel more stable, try bending and imagine you are flowing with the wind while your feet keep you rooted deep and tight to the ground.

Adapted from Flynn (2013), Guber and Kalish (2005), and Harper (2013).

Glider Airplane

(to increase balance and good feelings)

Imagine yourself getting ready to take off like an airplane that needs no engine. A glider plane shaped to flow with the wind.

Stand up tall with your feet spread comfortably apart to balance you.

Slowly breathe in (1, 2, 3) and imagine the air is like the wind flowing under your wings.

Focus your mind and stretch one leg back as you breathe out (3, 2, 1).

Lean forward slowly so you become parallel to the floor with one leg floating back behind you and your chest and head floating into the wind ahead.

Stretch out your arms to your sides and imagine the wind lifting up your wings.

Keep breathing in and out slowly (1, 2, 3, 3, 2, 1) and imagine yourself flying ahead supported by the air under your wings.

Where would you fly? Who would you want to visit?

What makes you feel so good that you feel like you could soar through the skies above, flying wherever your heart wants to go? Imagine taking that feeling and bringing it into your chest. Now imagine sharing that feeling with someone you care about.

Mindful Motion

(to increase focus, body awareness, and modulation in daily activities)

Encourage children and caregivers to focus on breathing and their bodies during activities.

Mindful Swimming

Stand in water at edge of pool. Dive in with arms ahead and feel rush of water around face, neck, chest, legs, and feet. Feel yourself gliding forward underwater without a stroke feeling yourself move through the water.

Take a breath and breathe out slowly. Feel bubbles on your face.

Focus on breathing in and out, feeling the air moving in and out of your chest, neck and mouth, as you swim.

Breathe in slowly (1, 2, 3) and exhale slowly (3, 2, 1) underwater.

Feel the air you breathe out bubble over your face.

Experiment bubbling fast or slow.

Notice how your body feels gliding through water.

What does this remind you of?

Can you picture yourself as a dolphin slipping through the water, or a playful seal?

Put your arms ahead of you with your palms together making an inverted V shape like the bow of a boat.

See how far you can stretch out your arms with the inverted V far ahead.

Kick your feet with a frog kick and feel how your arms stretched ahead balance your body in a glide position. Experiment with having your arms stretched far ahead or close in and wide open.

How does that affect your balance? How does that affect your speed gliding through the water?

Glide forward on your stomach, kicking your feet. Imagine yourself as a sleek boat cutting through the water with your feet like a propeller.

If your mind shifts to another thought, gently bring it back to focus on your breathing, the bubbles on your face, and the feel of the water as you swim forward.

Mindful Walking

Focus on breathing and each step. Feel pressure on thighs or feet. Feel the weight of your body shifting as you move. Focus on the feelings and sensations of all parts of your body as you walk back and forth, beginning with your toes, your feet, your ankles, and moving up your body. Pay attention to your breathing and how your breathing matches the sensations in your legs and feet. If your mind shifts to another thought, gently bring it back to focus on your breathing, sensations in your feet, legs, and body as you walk.

Mindful Meditations

(to increase focused attention and modulation)

Try out these meditations for children: "May I be safe. May I be happy. May I be healthy. May I be filled with kindness and caring."

Try these meditations for adults: "May I be safe. May I be free from suffering. May I be at peace. May I learn to let go. May I be filled with loving kindness."

Then, make your own meditations. Consider use of prayers, words that inspire you, sounds . . .

Practice and see what works best for you.

Adapted from Siegel (2010) and other sources.

Disc 'o' Stories

(to develop problem-solving strategies and support)

Roll Disc 'o' Sit on side from person to person and use for 'improv' stories (rolling a ball or balance disc can also work).

1.   First person starts a story and each person adds to story when disc rolls their way until group feels a sense of an ending or completed message.

2.   Alternate starting story stems with next person continuing, for example:

  • "I get angry when . . . "

  • "What helps me when I'm angry is . . . "

  • "What gets in the way is . . . "

  • "I wish . . . "

  • "I like to . . . "

3.   Generate conversations (e.g., anticipating or reflecting on major events, such as seeing an abusive parent in a visit or on the way to school, anticipating home visits, court sessions). Encourage family or group members to develop situations to address.

Adapted from Siegel (2010) and other sources.

Solution Circle

(to foster getting help from others to develop solutions/strategies to difficult problems)

First person starts a question for other group/family members to complete with an answer: "When I feel ___ (e.g., sad), I . . . " (to next person, going clockwise in the circle, who provides an answer, e.g., "I call a friend"), and then the next person going clockwise adds his or her own answer (e.g., "I go for a walk") and continue on to next person in circle . . . I, . . . and I . . .

Each person in the circle responds until all have finished answering.

First person thanks everyone in the circle.

Next person clockwise in the circle starts a new question for other group/family members to answer in a similar manner:

*   "When I feel ___, I . . . "
*   "When I feel scared, I . . . "
*   "When I need encouragement, I . . . "
*   "When I am happy, . . . "

If you like, you can provide 'improv'-style responses with each member in the circle building on what was said before (e.g., "When I feel sad, I . . . call a friend . . . and meet her to go for a walk . . . and we give each other a hug . . . " This promotes listening, incorporation of ideas, and building connections.

Kindness Circle

(to increase focus and sharing of kindness and positive regard)

First person rolls Disc 'o' Sit disc on side or a ball to another person in the circle and shares one of the special things he or she likes or appreciates about that person.

The person who receives the disc (or ball) then rolls it to someone else and shares one of the special things he or she likes or appreciates about that person.

Continue until everyone has had a chance to roll the disc (or ball) and share something they like about someone else.

If you like, have someone record everything said.

These qualities can also be used in making a Hero's Cape (see Cahpter 24).

Adapted from Snel (2013).

Make Your Own Centering Activities

Make up your own activities to develop skills for calming alone and together.

Then, practice them.

Make a schedule with a special time for activities. It helps to separate this time from anything else that happened. Focus on the activity and attunement with each other. Avoid making Centering time contingent on behavior. This can become a special time for children and caregivers, and to cherish their daily routine.

24
Hero's Cape Activity

Hero's Cape Activity[1]

Activity is designed to take place over two sessions

Objectives

Children will explore the qualities that comprise a hero and identify individuals who they feel are heroes. Children will identify their own strengths, interests, character traits, and resiliencies and come to see how they have acted like a hero helping others.

Materials

- Pencils
- Pom-poms
- Markers
- Felt
- Scissors *(used with supervision/ assistance of staff)*

- Fabric glue *(used with supervision/assistance of staff)*
- Ribbon
- Items brought from home *(future session)*
- Large Post-it paper or flip chart
- Drawing paper

Activity Steps

1. Staff member will discuss with children the concept of heroes and capture responses on flip chart or *Post-it* paper:

   (a) Ask children to identify heroes (real or fictitious). Staff need to get both responses.

   (b) Ask children, "What qualities does each hero mentioned have (real or fictitious)?"

   (c) After discussing heroes' qualities, ask children to brainstorm and identify what makes these people (or characters) heroes . . .

2. Once children have adequately brainstormed these (out loud, on their own, and in writing), the next step is to introduce them to the concept of a 'Hero's Cape.' This could be thought of as a tapestry for older children, if needed.

3. Staff will show children a sample cape or photograph of a cape.

4. Children will then brainstorm the things that they will put on their cape. Ask children to draw a basic sketch of what it will include. Staff should assist individuals as this is done.

5. The last step is to create the cape using material measured and cut by staff. Allow children to bring in personal items to include in the next session.

Developed for Camp to Belong New York by Allison Davenport Continelli (2011) Sidney Albert Training and Research Institute, Parsons Child and Family Center. Used with permission.

Example: Andrea's Hero's Cape

My name is Andrea and my Hero's Cape shows all the things about me that make me a hero for myself and for others. At the center of the cape is my first initial, A.

Music notes shoot out from the bottom of the letter A because music gives me a lift and makes others feel good too. I like to sing, especially with other people, because it makes everyone feel fantastic.

At the bottom of my cape is laughter. I love to make people laugh and I love to laugh. Laughing makes everyone feel better. I am especially proud of myself when I get my brother to laugh.

My grandma and my brother are very important to me. I live with my grandma and my older brother at my grandma's house. We all get along very well. My grandmother is funny and kind and plays the piano. She has a small piano in her house and we sing new songs together, as well as old favorites too.

A picture of me is on my cape. I am holding a big heart because I am told that I am caring and have a big heart. My grandma says that it is one of her favorite things about me.

There is a picture of my dog Alvin on my cape. Alvin is the best dog in the world. He understands me and always knows what to do. If I am happy and want to do something fun, he is right there with me and up for anything. If I am sad and want to lay on the couch and read or nap, he is right there too. Whenever I come through the door at my grandma's house, he is there ready to give me 1,000 kisses.

When I get older, I want to be a world traveler, explorer, or reporter. I want to get out there and see all that I can. I put a picture of the world on my cape to represent that I am curious about new places and new things.

I also put a lot of words on my cape that describe me. I was in a play at school and I loved it and it felt good, so I put the words creative and dramatic on my cape. I also like to do crafts by myself and with others. I do well in school and I like to solve problems, so I put the word smart on my cape. I have a good sense of humor and am a good friend to others, so I put the words funny and a good friend at the top of my cape.

The things on my cape represent who I am and who helps me to be the best hero I can be.

Section E
Life Story Integration

25

Trauma Memory Integration Tools

Additional Story Pages For Chapter 10 of the Real Life Heroes Life Storybook

RESOURCE CHECKLIST

SERVICE PROVIDERS

☐ Recognize and respect family strengths, caring for children, and ethnic heritage, as well as the impact of any violence, abuse, neglect, losses, or hardships.

☐ Demystify children's behaviors, including predictable reactions to the difficult work of overcoming trauma, the need to grieve losses, and the pulls and pressures to repeat traumatic experiences.

☐ Engage and contract wherever possible to work with parents, extended family, caregivers, children, and other therapists to change trauma cycles for the good of all, utilizing psycho-education on trauma to replace any shaming and pathologizing with positive steps toward creating safety, building strengths, and fostering enduring positive attachments.

☐ Practice *and* test strength and viability of safety plans for children, caring adults, and for themselves.

☐ Develop back-up plans for rebuilding attachments if primary caregivers become unable or unwilling to raise children in placement.

CARING ADULTS: PARENTS, GUARDIANS, OR PRIMARY CAREGIVERS

☐ Understand impact of trauma on children's neurophysiological development and behavior, as well as how caring adults can help children rebuild trust and learn new behavioral patterns.

☐ Demonstrate and encourage use of creative arts and words to express feelings, beliefs, and memories.

☐ Modulate own anxiety, anger, and impulses well enough to protect children from becoming overwhelmed or feeling they must 'parent' adults or protect adults from facing traumas.

☐ Develop, implement, and practice safety plans for self and children.

☐ Accept and acknowledge validity of children's experiences.

Resource Checklist—*continued*

CHILDREN

☐ Understand at age-appropriate level how traumas, including neglect and family violence, lead to natural reactions, including hyper-arousal, agitation, startle responses, hyper-vigilance, avoidance, and re-experiencing past sensory experiences (auditory, smell, tactile, visual, motor) in the present as flashbacks.

☐ Understand how reminders of past traumas 'trigger' repetitions of trauma reactions, the 'ABCs of Trauma.'

☐ Demonstrate age-appropriate skills to:

  ☐ Identify and express basic feelings.

  ☐ Self-monitor how feeling states change (*Knots* and *Self-Control Power* thermometers) without immediate fear/flight/fight responses.

  ☐ Differentiate internal reactions (e.g., hyper-arousal) from outside precipitating events.

  ☐ Associate words with feelings and think about what is happening.

  ☐ Utilize calming messages, imagery, and movement to reduce stress (e.g., 'SOS' and slow breathing).

  ☐ Remind self of goals and use self-talk to guide behavior.

  ☐ Reduce blaming and shaming of self and others.

  ☐ Focus on one step at a time when working on an activity.

  ☐ Reinforce themselves for small achievements.

  ☐ Recognize 'triggers' and alarm signals in their bodies and work to calm self without dangerous re-enactments of trauma cycles.

  ☐ Manage frustrations and modulate anger and fear sufficiently to avoid harm to themselves or others.

THROUGH THE TOUGH TIMES

"This is a story of how I got through another 'tough time' in my life. I am going to draw this story with five pictures that, together, make a story that begins before the 'tough time' and ends at a time when the 'tough time' was over and I felt safer and better."

(Please make your story the same way you did for your first 'Five-Chapter' Story in Chapter 10 of the *Real Life Heroes Life Storybook*. Remember to start two pages ahead with Chapter 2 of your story. After you draw pictures for Chapters 2, 3, and 4, then draw on the next page what happened before the 'tough time.' Complete directions can be found in Chapter 10 of the *Real Life Heroes Life Storybook*.)

CHAPTER 1

What Happened Before the 'Tough Time'

Draw what happened in the box below.

CHAPTER 2

The 'Tough Time'

Next, show what you and other people did that helped you get through the 'tough time.'

CHAPTER 3

What Helped Make things Better

Next, draw a time when things were better, when you felt safer, and the 'tough time' was over. This can be right after the 'tough time,' or months or years later.

CHAPTER 4

A Better Time

Go back four pages to draw Chapter 1 of your story, then come back to this page and think about how you are now older, stronger, and smarter. Draw below what you and people who care about you could do to make things better if the 'tough time' started to happen again.

CHAPTER 5

What I and People Who Care about Me Would Do if the 'Tough Time' Happened Again

---

Congratulations! You've just made another 'Five-Chapter' Story, a hero's story about 'moving through' a 'tough time.' Imagine you are the director for a movie of your story. Movies have music and rhythm.

Go back and use drum beats to tell the story from Chapter 1 through Chapter 5 with rythm.

Next, use a musical instrument like a xylophone, a keyboard, or a guitar to share feelings with music as you go through each chapter of your story from Chapter 1 through Chapter 5. Start with Chapter 1 and make a strong ending in Chapters 4 and 5 using your musical instrument. Now, show action from Chapters 1 to 5 with looks on your face, the loudness and tone of your voice, your posture, movement of your arms or legs, or show what happened with puppets or a dance. The more details you add, the richer your movie will be. It's time to add some words and feelings for your movie. Start by answering the questions below. You can come back later and add more details to make your movie stronger.

I was ___ years old. This is what happened in Chapter 1, 'Before the Tough Time':

_____

_____

_____

_____

This was how I was feeling before the 'tough time' on Thermometers:.

My Thermometers

Knots (Stress)	Self-control Power	Mad	Sad	Glad	Feel safe

10 HIGH   10   10   10   10   10   10

1 LOW   1   1   1   1   1   1

This is what happened in Chapter 2, 'The Tough Time':

_____

_____

_____

_____

The worst part of the 'tough time' was when:

_____

_____

_____

_____

And this was how I was feeling in the worst part of the 'tough time':

My Thermometers

Knots (Stress)   **Self-control Power**   **Mad**   **Sad**   **Glad**   **Feel safe**

10 HIGH   10   10   10   10   10   10

1 LOW   1   1   1   1   1   1

Draw how you felt in your body during the worst part using different colors for each feeling.

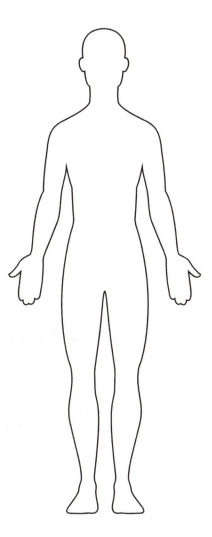

What helped me get through this 'tough time' was that:

_____
_____
_____
_____
_____
_____
_____
_____

And, in Chapter 4, when things got better, this is what was happening:

_____

_____

_____

_____

_____

_____

_____

_____

_____

_____

This is how I was feeling when things got better:

My Thermometers

Knots (Stress)	Self-control Power	Mad	Sad	Glad	Feel safe

10 HIGH

1 LOW

Acknowledgments

The second edition of the *RLH Toolkit* builds on lessons learned from research, training, and clinical testing over the last ten years and from the children and families I have been privileged to work with as a psychologist. The second edition includes contributions from colleagues in research and training and from practitioners who have shared what they have learned. I have been inspired by my colleagues in the National Child Traumatic Stress Network (NCTSN) and have tried to incorporate some of the wisdom, practical tips, and research findings I learned from 11 years of collaborative work in the NCTSN in workgroups addressing treatment in child welfare, Complex Trauma, and training of resource parents. I am grateful to NCTSN colleagues who co-led development of training programs with me and to co-authors of articles stemming from RLH research and NCTSN projects, including Margaret Blaustein, Julian Ford, Mandy Habib, Jim Henry, Margaret Richardson, Joseph Spinazzola, and Patricia van Horn. I am also grateful to Jerry Dunn and the staff of the Children's Advocacy Services of Greater St Louis, to Sue Green at the Institute on Trauma at SUNY-Buffalo, and to Mandy Habib, Victor Labruna, and Keri Schumacher at Adelphi University for their help and advice in shaping training materials.

The second edition was shaped in large part by lessons I learned from my training and research in the HEROES Project at Parsons Child and Family Center. I am especially grateful to Audrey Lafrenier, Chief Operating Officer, to Marylynne Brady-Johnson, Chief of Training, to Joanne Trinkle, my co-director, to Drs. Jim Henry and Margaret Richardson, Western Michigan University researchers, and to the therapists, supervisors, and directors of programs at Parsons Child and Family Center and the Albany County Children's Mental Health Clinic who worked with me to develop and test use of *Real Life Heroes®* in seven programs and to evaluate results with 119 children and families as part of the HEROES Project. I am grateful for the highly valued consultation and practice tips provided by our Project Implementation Specialist, Michael Clarkson-Hendrix, and our wonderful HEROES Program-Based Clinical Coaches, Gail Darrigo, Karin Haus,

Marianne Milks-Hines, Melissa Mace, Sydney Madden, Wenonah McLauchlin, and Susan Wuerslin. Special thanks also to Kelly Busch for adapting the *RLH Toolkit* for dissemination and use in the HEROES Project, and to the practitioners, program supervisors, and administrators who contributed their skills and insights to improve the training programs and help the children and families in the HEROES Project research. I am grateful to Emily Delorenzo and Megan Brophy, who coordinated data collection and data entry for the project, to Mike Conway, who provided comparison data analyses using Parsons agency measures, to data collectors, Jacqueline Pagnotta, Melissa Bynum, Tana James, and Ashley Degnan, to Kelly Busch, Project Administrative Assistant, to Lisa Richardson, who provided consultation on learning collaborative research, and to Parsons Directors and agency leaders, Damarise Alexander-Mann, Marylynne Brady-Johnson, David Cook, Tony Cortese, Claire Crawley, Lorraine DiRocco, Michael Donahue, Gillian Gecewicz, Dr. Virginia Khoury, Sharon Mahota, Mary Purdy, Dr. Ernesto Roldan, Diane Rosenbaum, Ray Schimmer, Pam Silkowski, Mark Snyder, Kacey Sornberger, Robin Sorriento, and Tammi Wrest. The second edition also benefited from art and music therapy enhancements by Anne Baker, Tom Templeton, and Jonathan Hubert. I am also grateful for the assistance I received at Parsons from Tammy Gollmer in preparing training materials.

The *RLH Toolkit* was originally developed as a practical treatment guide for treatment of traumatic stress in child and family services and children's mental health programs and for use with *Real Life Heroes: A Life Storybook for Children*, second edition (Routledge, 2007). The *RLH Toolkit* and *Life Storybook* were both adapted from *Rebuilding Attachments with Traumatized Children: Healing from Losses, Violence, Abuse and Neglect* (Routledge, 2004). *Real Life Heroes®* incorporates neuropsychological research (e.g., Schore, 2003a; Siegel, 1999; Siegel & Hartzell, 2003; van der Kolk, 2003), trauma therapies (e.g., Briere & Scott, 2014; Cohen, Deblinger & Mannarino, 2006; Figley, 1989; Ford & Russo, 2006;

Herman, 1992b; Pynoos & Nader, 1988; Shapiro, 2001; van der Kolk, 2003), cognitive behavioral interventions (e.g., Beck, 1976; Cohen et al., 2003; Lazarus, 1971), and life story and narrative therapies (e.g., Freedman & Combs, 1996; Jewett, 1978; Kliman, 1996; White & Epston, 1990). I am grateful to Robert Geffner, Ph.D., my original editor, for his support, inspiration, and assistance with the 2004 and 2007 editions of *Rebuilding Attachments for Traumatized Children*, the first two editions of the *RLH Life Storybook*, and the first edition of the *RLH Toolkit*. For the second edition, I am very grateful for the support of George Zimmar, Executive Editor for Routledge Press and step by step assistance from Meira Bienstock.

Adaptations of the original *RLH Toolkit* were based on consultations with therapists and researchers involved in studies of the *Real Life Heroes*® model, including the RLH Pilot Study conducted at Parsons Child and Family Center. The author is grateful to Joe Benamati, Carrie Blanchard, Julie Bouse, Melissa Brinkman, Cheryl Brown-Merrick, Amber Douglas, Laurie Gendron, Christi Hart, John Hornik, Susannah Kratz, Jennifer LeMay, Sandy Miles, Alaina Mormile, Sydney Mullin, Mary Purdy, Lynne Ross, Janice Slavik, Danielle Stokely, Peg Sutton, Marian Truax, and Heather Verkade for their recommendations and additions to early drafts of the *RLH Toolkit*. Caroline Peacock and Courtney Hawkins provided valuable tips on engaging adolescents. Recommendations concerning telling the 'trauma story' were enhanced by training and consultation in Trauma Focused-Cognitive Behavioral Therapy provided by Esther Deblinger through the National Child Traumatic Stress Network. Trauma psycho-education and skill-building activities incorporated adaptations of TARGET and FREEDOM developed by Julian Ford.

Dr. Amber Douglas drafted the initial outlines for dissemination and evaluation of the first four chapters of the first edition of the *RLH Toolkit*. Melanie Carbin and Elizabeth Power provided valuable editorial advice on shaping the *RLH Toolkit* and Marilyn Orenstein helped prepare preliminary versions. Judy Riopelle helped edit and prepare the research editions and Joann Sutton helped organize later versions for use by Parsons staff. Judy also developed the format and style for the *Bookmark*, added graphics to multiple sections, and helped make the *RLH Toolkit* much more readable. Amy Scheele prepared the Heroes Library list, as well as the original *Knots* (Sutton, 2004) and *Self-Control Power* thermometers (adapted from Ford et al., 2001; Walk, 1956). Kathy Tambasco provided graphic and word processing assistance and Dennis Chapko resolved computer problems. Rick Johnson and Amber Douglas provided editorial advice for revised editions. Amber also developed fidelity checklists and surveys for research studies. Listings for the Heroes Library included contributions from David Bullow, Amy Scheele, and research therapists listed above.

Research on the *Real Life Heroes*® model and development and testing of the *RLH Toolkit* were supported in part by grants from the Substance Abuse and Mental Health Services Administration (SAMHSA), U.S. Department of Health and Human Services (HHS). The views, policies, and opinions expressed are those of the author and do not necessarily reflect those of SAMHSA or HHS.

As with all my books, I know that this publication was inspired by the courage and heroism in my own family. I am truly privileged to have had the support of my parents, brothers and sisters, my mother and father-in-law, and my brother and sisters-in-law, my children, their spouses, and my grandchildren. I am grateful to my daughter, Michelle, for her 'improv' lessons. Most of all, I am grateful for the love and support of my wife, Dr. Laura Kagan, whose wisdom, suggestions, and tolerance of my working on these books have helped me every step of the way.

Glossary

RLH Terms and Tools

Action Cycles: Interactive behavior patterns of youths, caregivers, and other people that can become entrenched over time and often appear to repeat themes of past traumas. Action Cycles are modeled after concepts of repeating interaction patterns in family therapy (e.g. Minuchin & Fishman, 1981).

Centering Activities: Breathing, yoga, mindfulness, movement, 'improv,' and storytelling activities are listed in Part V of the *RLH Toolkit* as suggested activities linked to *RLH Life Storybook* chapters. Centering Activities are intended to be used at the beginning of sessions to promote development of self- and co-regulation, attunement, focusing skills, sharing, and trust. Centering Activities are also encouraged for 'homework' and 'teamwork' practice guided by caregivers, home-based support workers, residential counselors, and other service providers working as part of a trauma-informed treatment team. Use of Centering Activities can help transform conflict-ridden Action Cycles into supportive and stress-reducing activities that are fun and reinforce caring and safety for children and caregivers.

Changing the Story (the ABCs of Trauma): Chapter 8 of the *Life Storybook* invites youths and caregivers to change Action Cycles that start with **A**ction (what happened) and lead to **B**odily reactions, **C**atastrophic thinking, **D**istress, **E**mptiness, and **F**ailing to achieve your goals. Youths and caregivers are invited to transform these interactive patterns by visualizing themselves as directors of their own movies and rewriting the script with an understanding of how traumatic stress Action Cycles work and how they can use: **A**ction (what happened) and **B**odily reactions as signals and then change **C**atastrophic thinking into **C**ourageous thinking with use of *SOS for Stress*, accept and understand feelings of **D**istress to **D**efeat trauma, and change **E**mptiness and feeling alone into **E**xcellence based on building skills, helping others and feeling linked to family members, friends, and caring adults.

Chapter Checkpoints: This is a check-off list of key components for each chapter that is intended to function as a guide (cheat sheet) for practitioners, a fidelity measure, and as a tool for supervision to identify challenges and lead to development of strategies to overcome difficulties in application of the model with diverse children, families, and programs.

Circles of Caring: This is an adaptation of the hierarchical mapping technique (Antonucci, 1986) that engages youths to highlight the strength of relationships with important people in their lives and to identify people with whom they have felt safe enough to share the best and worst times in their lives. *Circles of Caring* is used along with *My Thermometers* to assess how children feel and their level of affect regulation in their primary relationships.

'Five-Chapter' Stories: In Chapter 10, children are asked to draw what happened in a 'tough time' (Chapter 2), and then to follow this with a drawing of what helped them get through the 'tough time' (Chapter 3), a time after the traumatic event when they felt safe and cared for (Chapter 4), what led up to the traumatic memory (Chapter 1), and what they and others who love them have learned to help them prevent or reduce the impact of future traumas (Chapter 5). This structure emphasizes 'moving through' traumas, highlighting what helped to get to a Safe Place and Safe Relationships, and what is different now that can help children and caregivers make things better in the future. 'Moving through' traumas is a component of many trauma treatments, and Chapter 5 was modeled after development of a 'healing theory' (Figley, 1989) and telling the trauma story including worst parts in TF-CBT (Cohen, Deblinger & Mannarino, 2006).

Glockenspiel: German word for xylophones or note bells used in sessions.

Knots: Level of stress felt in a particular situation rated on a thermometer scale from 0 to 10, with 10 being the greatest possible stress and 0 being perfectly calm. This is illustrated by a rope that is perfectly flexible with 0 *Knots* and totally stiff and tight with 10 or more *Knots*.[1]

HEROES Challenge: This is an acronym intended to inspire courage, beginning with **H**eroes using tough times in their lives to grow stronger, **E**motions and feelings are natural (use them to grow smarter), **R**elationships matter (heroes work together to make things better), **O**pen up your options, **E**xperiment (check out new solutions), **S**tronger and Stronger (discover your skills and make them stronger; remember who cared about you and find people who care enough to help you grow).

Life Story Integration: *Real Life Heroes®* activities help youths and caregivers to develop the security and courage stop avoiding traumatic memories and to use the self- and co-regulation skills and emotionally supportive relationships they develop to help them reduce the power of memories of 'tough times' and incorporate them into a resiliency-centered life story. In this way, youths and caregivers can come to see traumatic events as just parts of their lives. Youths and caregivers can grow stronger than traumatic memories and transform identities from seeing themselves as victims, as damaged goods, or as shamefully bad people into positive images of themselves using their experiences (good and bad) to grow stronger than the nightmares of the past, to help others, and to achieve their goals.

Looking Back: Chapter 9 of the *Life Storybook* provides an outline for youths and caregivers to organize memories of moves and relationships, including their beliefs about what happened that led to their needing to move. The format encourages expression of losses and can expose dysfunctional beliefs that may be contributing to feelings of shame and depression. These losses and beliefs can then be addressed in therapy, including work on trauma memory reintegration in Chapter 10, *Through the Tough Times*.

Message (to other children): After completing the *Life Storybook*, children are encouraged to share a brief (de-identified) message about what they learned that could help other children who are facing similar 'tough times.' This message continues the RLH maxim of heroes helping others, which, in turn, helps boost self-esteem.

Mind Power: Use of mindfulness and focusing skills to increase a child or caregiver's capacity to stay modulated in stressful situations. Mind Power is modeled after 'Mind Sight' (Siegel, 2006) and the 'concentration muscle' (Goleman, 2014).

My Life Story: Children and caregivers are invited to use Chapter 12 to develop a summary of important events in their lives, how these were experienced (bodily reactions, feelings, beliefs, actions), and what they have learned that has helped them make sense of what happened and how this has made them stronger and better able to face future stressors and accomplish their goals. This can be developed and shared as a narrative, a picture story, in music, or as a movie.

My Thermometers: Six self-rating scales for assessing feelings, including Stress (*Knots*), *Self-Control Power*, *Mad*, *Sad*, *Glad*, and *Feeling Safe*, using 0–10 levels, with 10 being the highest and 0 the lowest level possible.

The Pledge: The *Life Storybook* begins with a page for caregivers, therapists, and other caring adults to commit themselves to support youths sharing their thoughts and feelings and acknowledging that the *Life Storybook* belongs to youths.

Pocket Power Card: A fold-up 3 × 5 card that condenses a *Youth Power Plan* or *Caregiver Power Plan* into abbreviated Goals, Warning Signs, Triple S (Step by Step for Success), With Help from (Name/Phone #), and (how) Adults can help the youth. On the back of the card, youths and caregivers are asked to draw a picture or attach a photo of a time when they felt safe with someone who cared about them.

Power Plans: Resiliency-centered safety plans that incorporate triggers to stress reactions, what helps, what doesn't help, and multisensory strategies for presenting and reducing traumatic stress reactions.

REAL: This is an acronym for the core components of *Real Life Heroes®*: **R**elationships, **E**motional Self- and Co-Regulation, **A**ction Cycles, and **L**ife Story Integration.

Safety First Card: A brief guide to staying regulated using multisensory strategies and identifying people to go to to get help.

Self-Control Power: Level of ability to stay sufficiently modulated and do what the child (or caregiver) wants to do to achieve their goals. This is rated on 0–10 thermometer scales, with '0' representing feeling out of control and '10' feeling able to keep oneself in control.[2]

Shield: Children and caregivers are asked to create a shield that includes pictures of their skills, their families, and their heritage that give them strengths to face challenges. The RLH shield asks youths and caregivers to sketch what helps them feel brave enough to share their mistakes with people they trust and to strive to make things better.

SOS *Pocket Power Card*: A fold-up 3 × 5 card that includes a drawing of someone who helps children feel safer and stronger along with 'SOS for Stress.'

SOS for Stress: Three easy-to-remember steps (adapted from Ford & Russo, 2006) that can be used by children and caregivers to help keep them modulated in stressful situations. SOS is an easy-to-remember acronym to encourage the individual to: **S**low down with focused breathing and mindfulness, **O**pen your eyes and increase awareness of resources and relationships that can help, and **S**eek help and help others, a maxim from *Real Life Heroes*® accentuating the importance of getting help, learning from others, and giving back by helping others.

'Three-Chapter' Stories: Children are encouraged to take important pictures, especially drawings of themselves feeling safe in emotionally supportive relationships, and to add a picture of what happened after this first drawing and then a picture of what happened before. The three drawings and added narrative together make a 'Three-Chapter' Story with a beginning (Chapter 1), a middle (Chapter 2, the first drawing), and an end (Chapter 3). In *Real Life Heroes*®, end stories are intended to be times when the youth or caregiver felt safe and cared for, even if things changed later on. Writing 'Three-Chapter' Stories strengthens youths' and caregivers' sense that they can 'move through' memories of good times and bad times, including traumatic memories.

Tough Times: Adverse experiences, including traumas, hard times, and other challenges that generate stress for children and caregivers.

Notes

1. Adapted from Sutton (2004).
2. Adapted from Purdy (2004).

References

Abbuhl, J. (2006, February 15). Personal communication.

Achenbach, T., & Rescoria, L. (2000a). *Child Behavior Checklist 1½–5*. Burlington, VT: ASEBA, University of Vermont.

Achenbach, T., & Rescoria, L. (2000b). *Child Behavior Checklist 6–18*. Burlington, VT: ASEBA, University of Vermont.

Alexander, D. W. (1993a). *All my dreams*. Creative Healing Book Series. Plainview, NY: The Bureau for At-Risk Youth.

Alexander, D. W. (1993b). *It happened in autumn*. Creative Healing Book Series. Plainview, NY: The Bureau for At-Risk Youth.

Alexander, D. W. (1993c). *It's my life*. Creative Healing Book Series. Plainview, NY: The Bureau for At-Risk Youth.

Alexander, D. W. (1993d). *When I remember*. Creative Healing Book Series. Plainview, NY: The Bureau for At-Risk Youth.

Alexander, P. (2013). Relational trauma and disorganized attachment. In J. D. Ford & C. A. Courtois (Eds.), *Treating Complex Traumatic stress disorders in children and adolescents: Scientific foundations and therapeutic models* (pp. 39–61). New York, NY: Guilford Press.

American Psychiatric Association. (2013). *Diagnostic and statistical manual of mental disorders: DSM-5* (5th ed.). Washington, DC: American Psychiatric Association.

Antonucci, T. C. (1986). Hierarchical mapping technique. *Generations, 10*, 10–12.

ATTACh. (2008). *Therapeutic parenting: A handbook for parents of children who have disorders of attachment*. Lake Villa, IL: Association for the Treatment and Training in the Attachment of Children.

ATTACh. (2014). *Training resources for therapists*. Association for Treatment and Training in the Attachment of Children. Retrieved from www.attach.org/resources/training/.

Austin, D. (2002). The wounded healer: The voice of trauma—a wounded healer's perspective. In J. Sutton (Ed.), *Music, music therapy and trauma: International perspectives*. Philadelphia, PA: Jessica Kingsley.

Ayres, A. J. (1979). *Sensory integration and the child*. Torrance, CA: Western Psychological Services.

Ayres, A. J. (2004). *Sensory integration and the child* (2nd ed.). Los Angeles, CA: Western Psychological Services.

Baker, A. (2013). Personal communication.

Baker, A. J. L., Brown, E., Schneiderman, M., Sharma-Patel, K., & Berrill, L. M. (in press). *Mental health treatments for children and families in foster care*. New York, NY: New York Foundling.

Bal, S., De Bourdeaudhuij, I., Crombez, G., & Van Oost, P. (2005). Predictors of trauma symptomatology in sexually abused adolescents: A 6-month follow-up study. *Journal of Interpersonal Violence, 20*, 1390–1405.

Beck, A. T. (1976) *Cognitive therapy and the emotional disorders*. New York, NY: International Universities Press.

Beck, A. T. (2001). *Beck youth inventories*. San Antonio, TX: The Psychological Corporation.

Beck, P. (2010). *A zombie's guide to the human body: Tasty tidbits from head to toe*. New York, NY: Scholastic.

Becker-Weidman, A. (2002, May 17). *Understanding attachment disorder: The broken bond*. Workshop presentation. Albany, New York.

Becker-Weidman, A., Ehrmann, L., & LeBow, D. H. (2012). The attachment therapy companion: Key practices for treating children and families. New York, NY: Norton.

Benamati, J. (2004) *Systematic Training to Assist in the Recovery from Trauma (S.T.A.R.T.): A trauma informed curriculum for residential childcare workers*. Albany, NY: Parsons Child & Family Center.

Bennett, D. S., Sullivan, M. W., & Lewis, M. (2010). Neglected children, shame-proneness, and depressive symptoms. *Child Maltreat, 15*(4): 305–314.

Benson, L. (2010). Personal communication.

Benson, L. (2011). Personal communication.

Berliner, L. (2005) Results of randomized clinical trials move the field forward. *Journal of Abuse and Neglect, 29*, 103–105.

Black, C. (1984). *The story game: A game of feelings*. Bainbridge Island, WA: MAC Publishing.

Blaustein, M., & Kinneburgh, C. (2010). *Treating traumatic stress in children and adolescents: How to foster resilience through attachment, self-regulation, and competency*. New York, NY: Guilford Press.

Bloom, S. (1997). *Creating sanctuary: Toward the evolution of sane societies*. New York, NY: Routledge.

Bloom, S., & Farragher, B. (2013). *Restoring sanctuary*. New York, NY: Oxford University Press.

Bolger, K. E., & Patterson, C. J. (2003). Sequelae of child maltreatment: Vulnerability and resilience. In S. Luthar (Ed.), *Resilience and vulnerability: Adaptation in the context of childhood adversities* (pp. 156–181). New York, NY: Cambridge University Press.

Briere, J. (1996). *Trauma Symptom Checklist for Children*. Lutz, FL: Psychological Assessment Resources.

Briere, J. (2002). Treating adult survivors of childhood abuse and neglect: Further development of an integrative model. In J. E. B. Meyers et al. (Eds.), *The APSAC manual on child maltreatment* (2nd ed., pp. 175–202). Newbury Park, CA: Sage.

Briere, J. (2014, October 28). *Keynote address*. Children's Institute International, Trauma-Informed Care Conference, Los Angeles, CA.

Briere, J., & Lanktree, C. (2013). *Integrative treatment of traumatic stress-A (ITCT-A) treatment guide* (2nd ed.). Los Angeles, CA: University of Southern California. Retrieved from http://keck.usc.edu/Education/Academic_Department_and_Divisions/Department_of_Psychiatry/Research_and_Training_Centers/USC_ATTC/~/media/KSOM/Education/Academic%20Department%20and%20Divisions/attc/ITCT-A-TreatmentGuide-2ndEdition-rev20131106.pdf.

Briere, J., & Scott, C. (2014). *Principles of trauma therapy*. Thousand Oaks, CA: Sage.

Brohl, K. (2007). *Working with traumatized children: A handbook for healing*. Washington, DC: CWLA Press.

Brom, D., Horenczyk, R., & Ford, J. D. (2009). *Treating traumatized children: Risk, resilience and recovery*. New York, NY: Routledge.

Brown, B. (2010). *Courage is a heart word (and a family affair) by Brené Brown*. PBS Parents Expert Q&A. Retrieved from www.pbs.org/parents/experts/archive/2010/11/courage-is-a-heart-word-and-a.html.

Brown, B. (2012). *Daring greatly*. New York, NY: Gotham.

Cain, B. (2001). *Double-dip feelings*. Washington, DC: Magination Press.

Campbell, J. (1968). *The hero with a thousand faces*. Princeton, NJ: Princeton University Press.

Casebeer Art Productions (1989). *Projective Storytelling Cards*. Reading, CA: Northwest Psychological Publishers.

Cave, C., & Maland, N. (2003). *You've got dragons*. Atlanta, GA: Peachtree.

CEBC (2014). *Information and resources for child welfare professionals*. California Evidence-Based Clearinghouse for Child Welfare. Retrieved from www.cebc4cw.org/.

Chadwick Trauma-Informed Systems Project. (2013). *Creating trauma-informed child welfare systems: A guide for administrators* (2nd ed.). San Diego, CA: Chadwick Center for Children and Families.

Child Welfare Collaborative Group, & National Child Traumatic Stress Network (2008). The essential elements of trauma-informed child welfare practice. *Child welfare trauma toolkit: The essential elements* (2nd ed.). Los Angeles, CA, & Durham, NC: National Center for Child Traumatic Stress.

Child Welfare Collaborative Group, National Child Traumatic Stress Network, & The California Social Work Education Center. (2013) *Child welfare trauma training toolkit* (2nd ed.). Los Angeles, CA, & Durham, NC: National Center for Child Traumatic Stress.

Cicchetti, D., & Lynch, M. (1995). Failures in the expectable environment and their impact on individual development: The case of child maltreatment. In D. Cicchetti & D. J. Cohen (Eds.), *Developmental psychopathology, volume 2: Risk, disorder, and adaptation* (pp. 32–71). New York, NY: John Wiley & Sons.

Cicchetti, D., Ackerman, B. P., & Izard, C. E. (1995). Emotions and emotion regulation in developmental psychopathology. *Development and Psychopathology*, 7(1), 1–10.

Clarkson-Hendrix, M. (2011). Personal communication.

Cloitre, M., Courtois, C. A., Charuvastra, A., Carapezza, R., Stolbach, B. C., & Green, B. L. (2011). Treatment of Complex PTSD: Results of the ISTSS expert clinician survey on best practices. *Journal of Traumatic Stress*, 24(6), 615–627.

Cloitre, M. Koenen, K., Cohen, L., & Han, H. (2002). Skill training in affective and interpersonal regulation followed by exposure: A phase-based treatment for PTSD related to childhood abuse. *Journal of Consulting Clinical Psychology*, 70(5), 1067–1074.

Cohen, J. A., Deblinger, E., & Mannarino, A. P. (2006). *Treating trauma and traumatic grief in children and adolescents*. New York, NY: Guilford Press.

Cohen, J. A., Greenberg, T., Padlo, S., Shipley, C., Mannarino, A. P., Deblinger, E., & Stubenbort, K. (2001). *Cognitive behavioral therapy for traumatic bereavement in children treatment manual*. Pittsburgh, PA: Allegheny General Hospital.

Cohen, J. A., Mannarino, A. P., & Deblinger, E. (2003). *Child and parent trauma-focused cognitive behavioral therapy treatment manual*. Unpublished Manuscript. Pittsburgh, PA: Allegheny General Hospital.

Cohen, J. D., Mannarino, A. P., Murray, L. K., & Igelman R. (2006). Psychosocial interventions for maltreated and violence-exposed children. *Journal of Social Issues*, 62, 737–766.

Conners (1997). *Conners Parent Rating Scales—Revised (Long Version)*. North Tonawanda, NY: Multi-Health Systems.

Cook, A., Blaustein, M., Spinazzola, J., & van der Kolk, B. (Eds.) (2003). *Complex trauma in children and adolescents*. White Paper. Retrieved from www.nctsnet.org/products/complex-trauma-children-and-adolescents-2003.

Cook, A., Spinazzola, J., Ford, J., Lanktree, C., Blaustein, M., Cloitre, M., . . . Mallah, K. (2005). Complex trauma. *Psychiatric Annals*, 35(5).

Cook, D. (2005). Self-control communication.

Cousineau, P. (Ed.) (1990). *The hero's journey: Joseph Campbell on his life and work*. San Francisco, CA: Harper & Row.

Cunningham, C. (1992). *All Kinds of Separation*. Indianapolis, IN: Kidsrights.

Curtis, N. M., Ronan, K. R., & Bourdin, C. M. (2004). Multisystemic treatment: A metaanalysis of outcome studies. *Journal of Family Psychology*, 18, 411–419.

DeBellis, M. D., Baum, A. S., Birmaher, B., Keshavan, M. S., Eccard, C. H., Boring, A. M., . . . & Ryan, N. D. (1999). Developmental traumatology part I: Biological stress systems. *Biological Psychiatry*, 45(10), 1259–1270.

Deblinger, E. (2005). Self-control communication. TF-CBT consultations (2/9/05).

Deblinger, E., & Heflin, A. H. (1996). *Treating sexually abused children and their non-offending parents: A cognitive behavioral approach*. Thousand Oaks, CA: Sage.

DeRosa, R., Habib, M. Pelcovitz, D., Rathus, J., Sonnenklar, J., Ford, J., Sunday, S., Layne, C., Saltzman, W., & Turnbull, A. (2008). *Structured psychotherapy for adolescents responding to chronic stress*. Manhasset, NY: Northshore Hospital-Long Island Jewish Health System.

Doidge, N. (2007). *That brain that changes itself*. New York, NY: Viking.

Dolan, Y. (1991). *Resolving sexual abuse*. New York, NY: Norton.

Egeland, B., & Sroufe, L. A. (1981). Attachment and early maltreatment. *Child Development, 52*, 44–52.

Eggert, L. L. (1994). *Anger management for youth: Stemming aggression and violence*. Bloomington, IN: National Educational Service.

Evans, M. D. (1986). *This is me and my two families*. New York, NY: Magination Press.

Fahlberg, V. (1991). *A Child's Journey through Placement*. Indianapolis, IN: Perspectives Press.

Farber, E. A., & Egeland, B. (1987). Invulnerability among abused and neglected children. In E. J. Anthony & B. J. Choler (Eds.), *The invulnerable child* (pp. 253–288). New York, NY: Guilford Press.

Felitti, V. J., Anda, R. F., Nordenberg, D., Williamson, D. F., Spitz, A. M., Edwards, V., et al. (1998). Relationship of childhood abuse and household dysfunction to many of the leading causes of death in adults: The adverse childhood experiences (ACE) study. *American Journal of Preventive Medicine, 14*(4), 245–258.

Fey, T. (2011). *Bossypants*. New York, NY: Little Brown & Company.

Figley, C. (1989). *Helping traumatized families*. San Francisco, CA: Jossey-Bass.

Flynn, L. (2013). *Yoga for children: 200+ yoga poses, breathing exercises, and meditations for healthier, happier, more resilient children*. Avon, MA: Adams Media.

Foa, E. B., Johnson, K. M., Feeny, N. C., & Treadwell, K. R. H. (2001). The child PTSD symptom scale (CPSS): A preliminary examination of its psychometric properties. *Journal of Clinical Child Psychology, 30*, 376–384. Child PTSD Symptom Scale (CPSS). Retrieved from www.med.upenn.edu/ctsa.

Ford, J. D. (2005). Trauma treatment implications of altered affect regulation and information processing following child maltreatment. *Psychiatric Annals, 35*(5), 410–419.

Ford, J. D., & Cloitre, M. (2009). Best practices in psychotherapy for children and adolescents. In C. A. Courtois & J. D. Ford (Eds.), *Treating complex traumatic stress disorders: An evidence-based guide* (pp. 59–81). New York, NY: Guilford Press.

Ford, J. D., & Courtois, C. (Eds.) (2013). *Treating Complex Traumatic stress disorders in children and adolescents: Research and therapeutic models*. New York, NY: Guilford Press.

Ford, J. D., & Russo, E. (2006). A trauma-focused, present-centered, emotional self-regulation approach to integrated treatment for post-traumatic stress and addiction: Trauma adaptive recovery group education and therapy (TARGET). *American Journal of Psychotherapy, 60*(5): 335–355.

Ford, J. D., & St. Juste, M. C. (2006). *TARGET-A: Trauma affect regulation: Guide for education and therapy*. Farmington, CT: University of Connecticut.

Ford, J. D., Cruz St. Juste, M., & Mahoney, K. (2005). *TARGET-A: Trauma Adaptive Recovery Group Education and Therapy (10+ Session Adolescent Version) Facilitator Guide*. Farmington, CT: University of Connecticut Health Center.

Ford, J., Mahoney, K., & Russo, E. (2001). *TARGET and FREEDOM (for children)*. Farmington, CT: University of Connecticut Health Center.

Ford, J. D., Mahoney, K., & Russo, E. (2003). *TARGET trauma adaptive recovery group education and therapy (9 session version) leader guide and participant handouts*. Farmington, CT:

University of Connecticut Health Center. (*Note*: Includes current handouts from TARGET-AR/AT Trauma Adaptive Recovery Group Education and Therapy; Parent Education: Understanding how trauma affects parents and children.)

Foster-Green, J. (2014). Personal communication.

Freedman, J., & Combs, G. (1996). *Narrative therapy: The social construction of preferred realities*. New York, NY: Norton.

Freeman, L. (1988). *It's my body*. Seattle, WA: Parenting Press.

Gardner, R. (1975). *Psychotherapeutic approaches to the resistant child*. New York, NY: Jason Aronson.

Ghosh-Ippen, C. (2006). Master's Session, International Society of Traumatic Stress Studies, Los Angeles, CA.

Gil, E. (1991). *The healing power of play*. New York, NY: Guilford Press.

Gilbert, P. (2009). *The compassionate mind: A new approach to life's challenges*. Oakland, CA: New Harbinger.

Goleman, D. (2014). *What makes a leader: Why emotional intelligence matters*. Florence, MA: More Than Sound.

Gordon, J. (2014, October 20). A breathing antidote for stress responses. *Psychotherapy Networker Daily Posts*. Retrieved from http://daily.psychotherapynetworker.org/daily/mind-body/a-breathing-antidote-for-stress-responses/?mqsc=E3781019&utm_source=WhatCountsEmail&utm_medium=Psychotherapy%20Networker%20PN%20Daily&utm_campaign=102014%20MindBody%20Gordon.

Graham, S., Doubleday, C., & Guarino, P. A. (1984). The development of relations between perceived controllability and the emotions of pity, anger, and guilt. *Child Development, 55*(2), 561–565.

Greenwald, R. (1999). *Eye movement desensitization and reprocessing (EMDR) in child and adolescent psychotherapy*. Northvale, NJ: Jason Aronson.

Greenwald, R. (2008). Progressive counting: A new trauma resolution method. *Journal of Child and Adolescent Trauma, 1*, 249–262.

Greenwald, R. (2013). *Progressive counting within a phase model of trauma-informed treatment*. New York, NY: Routledge.

Greenwald, R., & Rubin, A. (1999a). Brief assessment of children's post-traumatic symptoms: Development and preliminary validation of parent and child scales. *Research on Social Work Practice, 9*, 61–75.

Greenwald, R., & Rubin, A. (1999b). *Child report of post-traumatic symptoms/Parent report of post-traumatic symptoms (CROPS/PROPS)*. Baltimore, MD: Sidran Institute.

Greenwald, R., McClintock, S. D., Bailey, T. D., & Seubert, A. (2013). *Treating early trauma memories reduces the distress of later related memories*. Forthcoming.

Greeson, J. K. P., Briggs, E. C., Kisiel, C. L., Layne, C. M., Ake, G. S., Ko, S. J., Gerrity, E. T., Steinberg, A. M., Howard, M. L., Pynoos, R. S., & Fairbank, J. A. (2011) Complex trauma and mental health in children and adolescents placed in foster care: Findings form the National Child Traumatic Stress Network. *Child Welfare, 90*(6), 91–108.

Griffin, G., McClelland, G., Holzberg, M., Stolbach, B., Maj, N., & Kisiel, C. (2011). Addressing the impact of trauma before diagnosing mental illness in child welfare. *Child Welfare, 90*(6), 69–90.

Griffin, J. L., Cohen, J., Kliethermes, M., & Mannarino, A. (2014, March 3). *The application of trauma-focused cognitive-behavioral therapy (TF-CBT) for youth with Complex Trauma*. Annual Meeting, National Child Traumatic Stress Network, Falls Church, Virginia.

Grillo, C. A., Lott, D. A., & Foster Care Subcommittee of the Child Welfare Committee. (2010). *Caring for children who have experienced trauma: A workshop for resource parents*. Los Angeles, CA, & Durham, NC: National Center for Traumatic Stress.

Guber, T., & Kalish, L. (2005). *Yoga pretzels*. Oxford, UK: Barefoot Books. Retrieved from www.yogaed.com.

Gunnar, M. R., & Donzella, B. (2002). Social regulation of the cortisol levels in early human development. *Psychioneuroendocrinoogy, 27*(1–2), 199–220. Special Issue: Stress and Drug Abuse.

Habib, M., & Labruna, V. (2006). *The Trauma History Checklist and Interview*. Unpublished measure.

Haine, R. A., Ayers, T. S., Sandler, I. N., Wolchik, S. A., & Weyer, J. L. (2003). Locus of control and self-esteem as stress-moderators or stress-mediators in parentally bereaved children. *Death Studies, 27*(7), 619–640.

Harper, J. C. (2013). *Little flower yoga for kids: A yoga and mindfulness program to help your child improve attention and emotional balance*. Oakland, CA: New Harbinger.

Hazzard, A., Celano, M., Gould, J., Lawry, S., & Webb, C. (1995). Predicting symptomatology and self-blame among child sex abuse victims. *Child Abuse Negl., 19*(6), 707–714.

Hebb, D. (1949). *The organization of behavior*. New York, NY: Wiley & Sons.

Herman, J. (1992a). *Trauma and recovery*. New York, NY: Basic Books.

Herman, J. (1992b). Complex PTSD: A syndrome in survivors of prolonged and repeated trauma. *Journal of Traumatic Stress, 5*(3), 377–391.

Herman, J. (2011). *Throwing off the burden of shame: Social bonds and recovery from the traumas of gender-based violence*. International Society of Traumatic Stress, 27th Annual Meeting, Baltimore, Maryland.

Herman, J. (2014, October 2014). *PTSD as a shame disorder*. ISTSS online trauma training webinars. Retrieved from www.istss.org/source/ContinuingEd/webinar_details.cfm?mtg=WEB1014&utm_source=ISTSS%2DInformz&utm_medium=email&utm_campaign=default.

Horner-Johnson, W., & Drum, C. E. (2006). Prevalence of maltreatment of people with intellectual disabilities: A review of recently published research. *Mental Retardation and Developmental Disabilities Research Reviews, 12*, 57–69.

Hubert, J. (2013). Personal communication.

Hughes, B. M. & Koomar, J. (2010) cited in Warner, E., Cook, A., Wescott, A., & Koomar, J. (2011). SMART; Sensory motor arousal regulation treatment. Cambridge, MA: The Trauma Center at JRI.

Hughes, D. (1998). *Building the bonds of attachment: Awakening love in deeply troubled children*. Northvale, NJ: Jason Aronson.

Hughes, D. A. (1997). *Facilitating developmental attachment*. Northvale, NJ: Jason Aronson.

Hughes, D. A. (2007). *Attachment-focused family therapy*. New York, NY: Norton.

Hughes, D. A. (2009). *Attachment-focused parenting: Effective strategies to care for children*. New York, NY: W. W. Norton.

Hughes, D. A. (2011). *Attachment-focused family therapy: Workbook*. New York, NY: Norton.

Hughes, D. A., & Baylin, J. (2012). *Brain-based parenting*. New York, NY: Norton.

James, B. (1989). *Treating traumatized children*. Lexington, MA: Lexington Books.

James, B. (1994). *Handbook for treatment of attachment-trauma problems in children*. New York, NY: Lexington.

Jessie (1991). *Please tell*. Center City, MN: Hazeldon Foundation.

Jewett, C. (1978). *Adopting the older child*. Cambridge, MA: The Harvard Common Press.

Johnston, C. (1999). Personal communication.

Kagan, L. (2005). Self-control communication.

Kagan, M. (2010). Personal communication.

Kagan, R. (1996). *Turmoil to turning points: Building hope for children in crisis placements*. New York, NY: Norton.

Kagan, R. (2003). *Wounded angels: Lessons of courage from children in crisis*. Washington, DC: Children's Press, Child Welfare League of America.

Kagan, R. (2004). *Rebuilding attachments with traumatized children: Healing from losses, violence, abuse and neglect*. New York, NY: Routledge.

Kagan, R. (2007a). *Real life heroes: A life storybook for children* (2nd ed.). New York, NY: Routledge.

Kagan, R. (2007b). *Real life heroes practitioner's manual*. New York, NY: Routledge.

Kagan, R. (2016a). *Real life heroes life storybook* (3rd ed.). New York, NY: Routledge.

Kagan, R. (2016b). *Wounded angels: Inspiration from children in crisis* (2nd ed.). New York, NY: Routledge.

Kagan, R., Douglas, A., Hornik, J., & Kratz, S. (2008). Real Life Heroes pilot study: Evaluation of a treatment model for children with traumatic stress. *Journal of Child and Adolescent Trauma, 1*(1), 5–22.

Kagan, R., & Schlosberg, S. (1989). *Families in perpetual crisis*. New York, NY: Norton.

Kagan, R., Henry, J., Richardson, M., Trinkle, J., & LaFrenier, A. (2014a). Evaluation of *Real Life Heroes* Treatment for Children with Complex PTSD. *Psychological Trauma: Theory, Research, Practice, and Policy, 6*(5), 588–596.

Kagan, R., Henry, J., Richardson, M., Trinkle, J., & LaFrenier, A. (2014b). *HEROES Project Final Report*. Albany, NY: Parsons Child and Family Center.

Kaminsky, M. (2004, February). *Who Is a Hero?* Columbus, OH: Highlights for Children.

Kerns, K., Klepac, L., & Cole, A. (1996). Peer relationships and preadolescents' perceptions of security in the child-mother relationship. *Developmental Psychology, 32*, 457–466.

Kim, J., & Cicchetti, D. (2010). Longitudinal pathways linking child maltreatment, emotion regulation, peer relations, and psychopathology. *Journal of Child Psychology and Psychiatry, 51*(6), 706–716.

Kinneburgh, K. (2013). Personal communication.

Kisiel, C., Fehrenbach, T., Small, L., & Lyons, J. (2009). Assessment of Complex Trauma exposure, responses and service needs among children and adolescents in child welfare. *Journal of Child and Adolescent Trauma, 2*, 143–160.

Kliman, G. W. (1996). *The self-control life history book method: A manual for preventive psychotherapy with foster children*. San Francisco, CA: The Children's Psychological Trauma Center.

Kolko, D., & Swenson, C. C. (2002). *Assessing and treating physically abused children and their families.* Thousand Oaks, CA: Sage.

Kushner, M. G., Riggs, D. S., Foa, E. B., & Miller, S. M. (1993). Perceived controllability and the development of posttraumatic stress disorder (PTSD) in crime victims. *Behaviour Research and Therapy, 31*(1), 105–110.

Lanktree, C., & Briere, J. (2008). *Integrative treatment of complex trauma for adolescents (ITCT-A): A guide for the treatment of multiply traumatized youth.* Los Angeles, CA: UCLA.

Lanktree, C. B., & Briere, J. (2016) *Treating Complex Trauma in children and their families: An integrative approach.* Thousand Oaks, CA: Sage.

Lansky, V. (1991). *101 ways to make your child feel special.* Chicago, IL: Contemporary Books.

Layne, C. M., Saltzman, W. S., Savjak, N., & Pynoos, R. S. (1999). *Trauma/grief-focused group psychotherapy manual.* Sarajevo, Bosnia: UNICEF Bosnia & Herzegovina.

Lazarus, A. (1971). *Behavior therapy and beyond.* New York, NY: McGraw-Hill Book Company.

Lee, S. (1963). *The Amazing Spider-Man.* New York, NY: Marvel Enterprises.

Lieberman, A. (2011, March 3). *Developing the trauma narrative: two evidence-based models.* NCTSN All_Network Conference, Baltimore, Maryland.

Lieberman, A. F., & Amaya-Jackson, L. (2005). Reciprocal influences of attachment and trauma: Using a dual lens in the assessment and treatment of infants, toddlers, and preschoolers. In L. J. Berlin, Y. Ziv, L. Amaya-Jackson, & M T. Greenberg (Eds.), *Enhancing early attachments theory, research, intervention, and policy.* New York, NY: Guilford Press.

Lieberman, A. F., & Van Horn, P. (2005). *"Don't hit my mommy!" A manual for child-parent psychotherapy with young witnesses of family violence.* Washington, DC: Zero to Three Press.

Lieberman, A., & Van Horn, P. (2011). *Psychotherapy with infants and young children: Repairing the effects of stress and trauma on early attachment.* New York, NY: Guilford Press.

Linehan, M. M. (1993). *Cognitive-behavioral treatment of borderline personality disorder.* New York, NY: Guilford Press.

McDonough, Y. Z. (2002). *Who was Harriet Tubman?* New York, NY: Grosset & Dunlap.

MacLean, K. L. (2009). *Moody cow meditates.* Somerville, MA: Wisdom Publications.

Macy, R. D., Barry, S., & Gil, N. G. (2003). *Youth facing threat and terror: Supporting preparedness and resilience.* San Francisco, CA: Jossey-Bass.

Mannarino, T., Griffen, J., Cohen, J., & Kliethermes, M. (2014, March 3). *The application of TF-CTB for youth with Complex Trauma.* All-Network Conference Pre-Meeting Institute. Lecture conducted from NCTSN, Falls Church, VA.

Marcal, S. (2015). Personal communication.

Markowitz, J. (2005). Personal communication.

Marra, T. (2004). *Depressed and anxious: The dialectical behavior therapy workbook for overcoming depression and anxiety.* Oakland, CA: New Harbinger.

Miller, A. L., Rathus, J. H., & Linehan, M. M. (in press). *Dialectical behavior therapy for suicidal adolescents.* New York, NY: Guilford Press.

Miller, W. I. (2002). *The mystery of courage.* Cambridge, MA: Harvard University Press.

Minuchin, S., & Fishman, H. C. (1981). *Family therapy techniques.* Cambridge, MA: Harvard University Press.

Mitlin, M. (2008). *Emotional bingo for children.* Torrance, CA: Creative Therapy Store.

Mormile, A. (2005). Self-control communication.

Mullin, S. (2004). Personal communication.

Munson, L., & Riskin, K. (1995). *In their own words: A sexual abuse workbook for teenage girls.* Washington, DC: Child Welfare League of America.

Nadeau, K. G., & Dixon, E. B. (1997). *Learning to slow down and pay attention: A book for kids about ADD.* Washington, DC: Magination Press.

NCTSN (2008). *Child trauma toolkit for educators.* National Child Traumatic Stress Network. Retrieved from http://nctsn.org/resources/audiences/school-personnel/trauma-toolkit.

NCTSN (2012a). *Creating trauma informed systems.* National Child Traumatic Stress Network. Retrieved from www.nctsn.org/resources/topics/creating-trauma-informed-systems.

NCTSN (2012b). *Empirically supported treatments and promising practices.* National Child Traumatic Stress Network. Retrieved from www.nctsn.org/resources/topics/treatments-that-work/promising-practices.

NCTSN (2012c). *Resources for parents and caregivers.* National Child Trauma Stress Network. Retrieved from www.nctsn.org/resources/audiences/parents-caregivers.

NCTSN (2012d). *Think trauma training: A training for staff in juvenile justice residential settings.* National Child Trauma Stress Network. Retrieved from www.nctsnet.org/products/think-trauma-training-staff-juvenile-justice-residential-settings.

Nooner, K. B., Linares, L. O., Batinjane, J., Kramer, R. A., Silva, R., & Cloitre, M. (2012). Factors related to posttraumatic stress disorder in adolescence. *Trauma, Violence, & Abuse, 13*(3), 153–166.

Obama, B. (2010). *Of thee I sing: A letter to my daughters.* New York, NY: Random House.

O'Conner, J. J. (1983). Color your life techniques. In C. E. Schaefer & J. J. O'Connor (Eds.), *Handbook of play therapy.* New York, NY: Wiley.

Ogden, P., & Fisher, J. A. (2015). *Sensorimotor psychotherapy: Interventions for trauma and attachment.* New York, NY: orton.

Ogden, P., Minton, K., & Pain, C. (2006). *Trauma and the body: The theory and practice of sensorimotor psychotherapy.* New York, NY: W. W. Norton.

Parnell, L. (1999). *EMDR in the treatment of adults abused as children.* New York, NY: Norton.

Peacock, C., & Hawkins, C. (2004). Self-control communication.

Pearson Clinical, & Embury, S. (2007). *Resiliency scales for children and adolescents: A profile of personal strengths.* San Antonio, TX: Harcourt Assessment.

Perry, B. D. (2014, January 29). *The impact of trauma and neglect on young children.* Webinar. New York University, Clinic Technical Assistance Center.

Perry, B. D., & Szalavitz, M. (2006). *The boy who was raised as a dog and other stories from a child psychiatrist's notebook.* New York, NY: Basic Books.

Pitman, R. K., Altman, B., Greenwald, E., Longpre, R. E. et al. (1991). Psychiatric complications during flooding therapy for posttraumatic stress disorder. *Journal of Clinical Psychiatry, 52,* 17–20.

Pratt, K. (2004). Personal communication.

Purdy, M. (2003). Personal communication.

Purdy, M. (2004). Personal communication.

Pynoos, R. S., & Nader, K. (1988). Psychological first aid and treatment approach to children exposed to community violence. *Journal of Traumatic Stress, 1,* 445–471.

Pynoos, R., Rodriguez, N., Steinberg, A., Stuber, M., & Frederick, C. (1998). *UCLA PTSD Index for DSM IV.* Los Angeles, CA: UCLA Trauma Psychiatry Service.

Rappaport, S. (2006). Personal communication.

Richardson, M., Coryn, C., Henry, J., Black-Pond, C., & Unrau, Y. (2012). Development and evaluation of the trauma-informed system change instrument: Factorial validity and implications for use. *Child and Adolescent Social Work Journal, 29*(2), 151–166.

Richardson, M., Henry, J., Black-Pond, C., & Sloane, M. (2008). Multiple types of maltreatment: Behavioral and developmental impact on children in the child welfare system. *Journal of Child & Adolescent Trauma, 1,* 317–330.

Roberts, G. E. (1986). *Roberts' apperception test for children.* Los Angeles, CA: Western Psychological Services.

Rodriguez, N., Steinberg, A. S., Saltzman, W. S., & Pynoos, R. S. (2001). *PTSD index: Psychometric analyses of the adolescent version.* Symposium conducted at the Annual Meeting of the International Society for Traumatic Stress Studies, New Orleans, Louisiana.

Rojano, R. (1998, October 9). *Community family therapy.* Workshop presented at the Sidney Albert Institute Fall Institute, Albany, New York.

Ross, L. A., Streider, F., & Vrabel, C. (2012). Organization Organizational Impact and Intervention of STS. NCTSN Secondary Traumatic Stress Speaker Series. Retrieved from www.nctsn.org.

Rothbaum, B., & Schwartz, A. (2002). Exposure therapy for posttraumatic stress disorder. *American Journal of Psychotherapy, 56*(1): 59–75.

Rowling, J. (1999). *Harry Potter and the prisoner of Azkaban.* New York, NY: Arthur A. Levine Books.

Rubenstein, L. (2014). *Visiting feelings.* Washington, DC: Magination Press.

Saltzman, W. R., Layne, C. M., & Pynoos, R. S. (2003). *Trauma/grief-focused group psychotherapy: Supplementary materials.* Unpublished treatment manual, University of California, Los Angeles.

Saxe, G. N., Ellis, B. H., & Kaplow, J. B. (2007). *Collaborative treatment of traumatized children and teens: The trauma systems therapy approach.* New York, NY: Guilford Press.

Scheele, A. (2005). Self-control communication.

Schiraldi, G. R. (1999). *The post-traumatic stress disorder sourcebook: A guide to healing, recovery, and growth.* Los Angeles, CA: Lowell House.

Schore, A. N. (2003a). Early relational trauma, disorganized attachment, and the development of a predisposition to violence. In M. F. Solomon & D. J. Siegel (Eds.), *Healing trauma: Attachment, mind, body, and brain.* New York, NY: Norton.

Schore, A. N. (2003b, May 31). *Regulation of the right brain: A fundamental mechanism of attachment, trauma, dissociation, and psychotherapy.* Presentation, Psychological Trauma: Maturational Processes and Therapeutic Interventions, Boston, MA.

Scott, S. L., Carper, T., Middleton, M., White, R., Renk, K., & Grills-Taquechel, A. (2010). Relationships among locus of control, coping behaviors, and levels of worry following exposure to hurricanes. *Journal of Loss and Trauma, 15*(2), 123–137.

Seuss, Dr. (1990). *Oh, the places you will go.* New York, NY: Random House.

Seuss, Dr. (1996). *My many colored days.* New York, NY: Random House.

Shapiro, F. (2001). *Eye movement desensitization and reprocessing: Basic principles, protocols, and procedures* (2nd ed.). New York, NY: Guilford Press.

Shipman, K., Edwards, A., Brown, A., Swisher, L., & Jennings, E. (2005). Managing emotion in a maltreating context: A pilot study examining child neglect. *Child Abuse & Neglect, 29*(9), 1015–1029.

Shonkoff, J. P. (2010). Building a new biodevelopmental framework to guide the future of early childhood policy. *Child Development, 81,* 357–367.

Siegel, D. J. (1999). *The developing mind.* New York, NY: Guilford Press.

Siegel, D. J. (2006). *The mindful brain: Reflection and attunement in the cultivation of well-being.* New York, NY: Norton.

Siegel, D. J. (2011). *Mindsight: The new science of personal transformation.* New York, NY: Bantam.

Siegel, D. J. (2014) *Brainstorm: The power and the purpose of the teenage brain.* New York, NY: Penguin.

Siegel, D. J., & Bryson, T. P. (2012). *The whole-brain child: 12 revolutionary strategies to nurture your child's developing mind.* New York, NY: Random House.

Siegel, D. J., & Bryson, T. P. (2014). *No-drama discipline: The whole-brain way to calm the chaos and nurture your child's developing mind.* New York, NY: Bantam.

Siegel, D. J., & Hartzell, M. (2003). *Parenting from the inside out: How a deeper self-understanding can help you raise children who thrive.* New York, NY: J. P. Tarcher/Putnam.

Siegel, R. D. (2010). *The mindfulness solution: Everyday practices for everyday problems.* New York, NY: Guilford Press.

Snel, E. (2013). *Sitting still like a frog: Mindfulness exercises for kids.* Boston, MA: Shambhala.

Spaulding Center for Children (2014). *Training curricula.* The Spaulding Institute for Children. Retrieved from http://spaulding.org/institute/training/curricula/.

Sroufe, L. (1995). *Emotional development.* Cambridge, UK: Cambridge University Press.

Stambaugh, L. F., Ringeisen, H., Casanueva, C. C., Tueller, S., Smith, K. E., & Dolan, M. (2013). *Adverse childhood experiences in NSCAW.* OPRE Report #2013-26. Washington, DC: Office of Planning, Research and Evaluation, Administration for Children and Families, U.S. Department of Health and Human Services. Available at: National Data Archive on Child Abuse and Neglect (NDACAN), Cornell University, ndacan@cornell.edu.

Stamm, B. H. (2009). *Professional Quality of Life: Compassion Satisfaction and Fatigue Version 5 (ProQOL).* Retrieved from www.isu.edu/~bhstamm.

Stanchfield, J. (2007). *Tips and tools: The art of experiential group facilitation*. Oklahoma City, OK: Wood 'n' Barnes.

Stauffer, L., & Deblinger, E. (2003). *Let's talk about taking care of you*. Hatfield, PA: Hope for Families.

Strand, V., Hansen, S., & Layne, C. (2012). *NCTSN core curriculum on child trauma: Report on results of coding project to identify common intervention objectives and practice elements across 26 trauma-focused intervention manuals*. Los Angeles, CA: National Child Traumatic Stress Network.

Strauss, M. (2013). *Day by day: Making a difference in the lives of traumatized and suicidal children and adolescents*. Workshop presented for Parsons Child Family Center, Albany, New York.

Sutton, P. (2003). Personal communication.

Sutton, P. (2004). Self-control communication.

Tinker, R. H., & Wilson, S. A. (1999). *Through the eyes of a child: EMDR with children*. New York, NY: Norton.

van der Kolk, B. (1996). The complexity of adaptation to trauma: Self-regulation, stimulus discrimination, and characterological development. In B. van der Kolk, A. McFarlane, & L. Weisaelth (Eds.), *Traumatic stress: The effects of overwhelming experience on mind body, and society* (pp 182–213). New York, NY: Guilford Press.

van der Kolk, B. (2003). Posttraumatic stress disorder and the nature of trauma. In M. F. Solomon & D. J. Siegel (Eds.), *Healing trauma: Attachment, mind, body, and brain*. New York, NY: Norton.

van der Kolk, B. (2005). Developmental trauma disorder: Towards a rational diagnosis for children with Complex Trauma histories. *Psychiatric Annals, 35*(5), 401–408.

van der Kolk, B. (2014). *The body keeps the score: Brain, mind and body in the healing of trauma*. New York, NY: Viking.

van Gulden, H., & Bartels-Rabb, L. M. (1995). *Real parents, real children: Parenting the adopted child*. New York, NY: Crossroads.

Verdick, E., & Lisovskis, M. (2003). *How to take the grrrr out of anger*. Minneapolis, MN: Free Spirit.

Viorst, J. (1972). *Alexander and the horrible, no good, very bad day*. New York, NY: Simon & Schuster.

Viorst, J. (1987). *Alexander and the terrible, horrible, no good, very bad day*. New York, NY: Athenum.

Vogler, C. (1998). *The writer's journey: Mythic structure for writers*. Studio City, CA: Michael Weise Productions.

Walk, R. D. (1956). Self-ratings of fear in a fear-involving situation. *Journal of Abnormal and Social Psychology, 52*, 171–178.

Warner, E., Cook, A., Westcott, A., Koomar, J. (2014) *SMART: Sensory motor arousal regulation treatment manual*. Brookline, MA: The Trauma Center.

Warner, E., Koomar, J., Lary, B., & Cook, A. (2013). Can the body change the score? Application of sensory modulation principles in the treatment of traumatized adolescents in residential settings, *Journal of Family Violence, 28*(8), 729–738.

Wehrenberg, M. (2008). *The 10 best-ever anxiety management techniques*. New York, NY: Norton.

Wesselman, D., & Shapiro, F. (2013). Eye movement desensitization and reprocessing in D. Ford & C. A. Courtois (Eds.), *Treating Complex Traumatic stress disorders in children and adolescents* (pp. 203–224). New York, NY: Guilford Press.

Wheeler, C. (1978). *Where am I going? Making a child's life storybook*. Juneau, AK: The Winking Owl Press.

White, M., & Epston, D. (1990). *Narrative means to therapeutic ends*. New York, NY: Norton.

Whitehouse, E., & Pudney, W. (1996). *A volcano in my tummy*. Gabriola Island, BC: New Society.

Wilgocki, J., & Wright, M. K. (2002). *Maybe days*. Washington, DC: Magination Press.

Williams, M. L. (2005). *Cool cats, calm kids: Relaxation and stress management for young people*. Atascadero, CA: Impact.

Wolfelt, A. (1991). Children. *Bereavement Magazine, 5*(1): 38–39.

Wolmer, L., Hamiel, D., Barchas, J. D., Slone, M., & Laor, N. (2011). Teacher-delivered resilience-focused intervention in schools with traumatized children following the second Lebanon war. *Journal of Traumatic Stress, 24*(3), 309–316.

Zahn-Waxler, C., & Van Hulle, C. (2012). Empathy, guilt, and depression: When caring for others becomes costly to children. In B. Oakley, A. Knafo, G. Madhavan, & D. S. Wilson (Eds.), *Pathological altruism* (pp. 321–344). New York, NY: Oxford University Press.

Made in the USA
Columbia, SC
10 August 2019